NOLO *Your Legal Companion*

"In Nolo you can trust." —THE NEW YORK TIMES

Whether you have a simple question or a complex problem, turn to us at:

NOLO.COM
Your all-in-one legal resource

Need quick information about wills, patents, adoptions, starting a business—or anything else that's affected by the law? **Nolo.com** is packed with free articles, legal updates, resources and a complete catalog of our books and software.

NOLO NOW
Make your legal documents online

Creating a legal document has never been easier or more cost-effective! Featuring Nolo's Online Will, as well as online forms for LLC formation, incorporation, divorce, name change—and many more! Check it out at **http://nolonow.nolo.com**.

NOLO'S LAWYER DIRECTORY
Meet your new attorney

If you want advice from a qualified attorney, turn to Nolo's Lawyer Directory—the only directory that lets you see hundreds of in-depth attorney profiles so you can pick the one that's right for you. Find it at **http://lawyers.nolo.com**.

ALWAYS UP TO DATE

Sign up for NOLO'S LEGAL UPDATER

Old law is bad law. We'll email you when we publish an updated edition of this book—sign up for this free service at nolo.com/legalupdater.

Find the latest updates at NOLO.COM

Recognizing that the law can change even before you use this book, we post legal updates during the life of this edition at **nolo.com/updates**.

Is this edition the newest? ASK US!

To make sure that this is the most recent edition available, just give us a call at **800-728-3555**.

(Please note that we cannot offer legal advice.)

7th edition

Working for Yourself

Law & Taxes for Independent Contractors, Freelancers & Consultants

By Attorney Stephen Fishman

SEVENTH EDITION	FEBRUARY 2008
Editor	ALAYNA SCHROEDER
Cover Design	SUSAN PUTNEY
Production	MARGARET LIVINGSTON
Proofreader	EMILY K. WOLMAN
Index	ELLEN SHERRON
Printing	CONSOLIDATED PRINTERS, INC.

Fishman, Stephen.

  Working for yourself : law & taxes for independent contractors, freelancers & consultants / by Stephen Fishman. -- 7th ed.

    p. cm.

  ISBN-13: 978-1-4133-0752-8 (pbk.)

  ISBN-10 1-4133-0752-3 (pbk.)

  1. Independent contractors--Legal status, laws, etc.--United States--Popular works. 2. Independent contractors--Taxation--United States--Popular works. 3. Self-employed--Taxation--Law and legislation--United States--Popular works. I. Title.

KF390.I54F57 2008

343.7305'26--dc22

2007035517

Quantity sales: For information on bulk purchases or corporate premium sales, please contact the Special Sales Department. For academic sales or textbook adoptions, ask for Academic Sales. Call 800-955-4775 or write to Nolo, 950 Parker Street, Berkeley, CA 94710.

Acknowledgments

Many thanks to:

Barbara Kate Repa, Janet Portman, Amy DelPo, Lisa Guerin, Stephanie Bornstein, and Alayna Schroeder for their superb editing.

Malcolm Roberts, CPA, for reviewing the tax materials.

Gary Gerard for sharing his experiences as an independent contractor.

The many independent contractors throughout the country who permitted me to interview them.

Ellen Sherron for the helpful index.

Emily K. Wolman for thorough proofreading.

Margaret Livingston for diligent production work.

Table of Contents

Appendixes

Index

Your Legal Companion for Working for Yourself

Working for yourself gives you freedom employees rarely get to experience in their professional careers. Whether you label yourself "self-employed," an "independent contractor," a "freelancer," a "consultant," or even a "business owner," you have a unique opportunity to choose how you'll do business, where you'll do business, and how the operation will run.

Of course, with that freedom comes a lot of responsibility, too. You'll generate your own work, choose and set up the right business entity, follow legal and tax rules, and maybe even manage other employees. The good news is, this book will help you do it.

This book is a guide to law and taxes for people who either work for themselves or would like to. It covers all the legal and tax basics self-employed people need to know including:

- the benefits and drawbacks of working for yourself
- the different types of business entities, and which one is right for you
- whether to work at home or rent an office
- how to insure your business
- how to price services, write client agreements, and get paid
- how to handle your taxes and use your self-employed status to reduce them, and
- how to manage employees and record-keeping.

This book is intended only for those self-employed people who provide personal services, such as writers, consultants, artists, photographers, lawyers, and doctors. If your business involves selling goods (rather than services) to the public, this book is not for you. Instead, you should refer to *Legal Guide for Starting & Running a Small Business*, by Fred Steingold (Nolo).

As you will discover reading this book—if you haven't found out already—being self-employed can be both a dream and a nightmare. There are a lot of rewards and a lot of risks. The goal of this book is to help you navigate the risks so that they do not detract from the rewards, which we hope will be rich and plentiful. ●

Working for Yourself:
The Good, the Bad, and the Ugly

Working for yourself can be both financially and spiritually satisfying. But the lot of the self-employed is not always an easy one. You have to make the often difficult transition from having an employer take care of you to handling everything on your own. For example, you won't have a company payroll department to withhold and pay your taxes for you.

Many self-employed people (including those with plenty of clients) get into trouble because they don't run their operations in a businesslike manner. Spending a few hours now to learn the nuts and bolts of self-employment law and taxes can save you countless headaches—not to mention substantial time and money—later on. You don't have to start wearing a green visor and bow tie, but you do need to learn a few rudiments of business and tax law.

Before you delve into the details of the following chapters, read this chapter for an overview of the pros and cons of being self-employed as compared to being an employee. It may help you make an informed decision if you're thinking about striking out on your own—or help confirm that you made the right decision if you're already working for yourself.

Working for Yourself: The Good

Being self-employed can give you more freedom and privacy than working for an employer. It can also result in substantial tax benefits.

Independence

When you're self-employed, you are your own boss—with all the risks and rewards that entails. Most self-employed people bask in the freedom that comes from being in business for themselves. They would doubtless agree with the following sentiment expressed by one self-employed person:

"I can choose how, when, and where to work, for as much or as little time as I want. In short, I enjoy working for myself."

The self-employed are masters of their own economic fates. The amount of money they make is directly related to the quantity and quality of their work, which is not necessarily the case for employees. The self-employed don't have to ask their bosses for a raise; they go out and find more work.

Likewise, if you're self-employed, you're normally not dependent upon a single company for your livelihood, so the hiring or firing decisions of any one company won't have the same impact on you as on that company's employees. One self-employed person explains: "I was laid off six years ago and chose to start my own company rather than sign on for another ride on someone else's roller coaster. It's scary at first, but I'm now no longer at someone else's mercy."

Higher Earnings

You can often earn more when you're self-employed than as an employee for someone else's business. For example, an employee in a public relations firm decided to go out on her own when she learned that the firm billed her time out to clients at $125 per hour while paying her only $17 per hour. She now charges $75 per hour and makes a far better living than she ever did as an employee.

According to the *Wall Street Journal*, self-employed people who provide services are usually paid at least 20% to 40% more per hour than employees performing the same work. This is because firms that hire self-employed workers (referred to throughout this book as "hiring firms") don't have to pay half of the self-employed worker's Social Security taxes, or pay for unemployment compensation taxes, workers' compensation coverage, or employee benefits like health insurance and sick leave for workers who are not their employees. Of course, how much you're paid is a matter for negotiation between you and your clients. Self-employed people whose skills are in great demand may receive far more than employees doing similar work.

Tax Benefits

Self-employment also provides many tax benefits that employees lack. For example, no federal or state taxes are withheld from your paychecks by an employer as they must be for employees. Instead, the self-employed normally pay estimated taxes themselves directly to the IRS four times a year. This means you can hold on to your hard-earned money longer. It's up to you to decide how much estimated tax to pay (although there are penalties if you underpay). The lack of withholding combined with control over estimated tax payments can result in improved cash flow for the self-employed.

More important, you can take advantage of many tax deductions that are limited or unavailable for employees. When you're self-employed, you can deduct any necessary expenses related to your business from your taxable income as long as they are a reasonable amount and ordinarily incurred by businesses of your type. This may include, for example, office expenses (including those for home offices), travel expenses, entertainment and meal expenses, equipment costs, and insurance payments. These will be covered in greater detail in Chapter 4.

In contrast to the numerous deductions available to the self-employed, an employee's work-related deductions are severely limited. Some deductions available to the self-employed may not be taken by employees—for example, an employee may not deduct the cost of commuting to and from work, but a self-employed person traveling from his or her office to that of a client may ordinarily deduct this expense. And, even those expenses that are deductible for employees may be deducted only to the extent they add up to more than 2% of the employee's adjusted gross income. This means

that most of an employee's expenses related to employment cannot be deducted fully.

In addition, the self-employed can establish retirement plans, such as SEP-IRAs and Keogh Plans, that have tax advantages. These plans also allow them to shelter a substantial amount of their incomes until they retire.

Because of these tax benefits, the self-employed often ultimately pay less in taxes than employees who earn similar incomes.

More Privacy

If you're seeking to shield yourself from the prying eyes of the government, you'll have far more success if you're self-employed than if you work for an employer. The government uses employers to keep track of employees for a variety of purposes. For example, there is a federal law that requires all employers to report the name, address, and Social Security number of each newly hired employee to the Department of Health and Human Services. This information is then placed in a huge database that is supposedly used solely to aid in the collection of overdue child support.

Many states have similar requirements. Some mandate that employers provide them with even more information, such as telephone numbers, dates of birth, and details of insurance coverage provided to new employees.

When you're self-employed, however, such laws don't apply to you, making it far more difficult for the government to keep tabs on you through your work.

Working for Yourself: The Bad

Despite its advantages, being self-employed is no bed of roses. Here are some of the major drawbacks.

No Job Security

As discussed above, one of the best things about being self-employed is that you're on your own. On the other hand, this can be one of the worst things about it too.

When you're an employee, you must be paid as long as you have your job, even if your employer's business is slow. This is not the case when you're self-employed. If you don't have business, you don't make money. As one self-employed person says: "If I fail, I don't eat. I don't have the comfort of punching a timeclock and knowing the check will be there on payday."

No Free Benefits

Although not always required by law, employers often provide their employees with health insurance, paid vacations, and paid sick leave. More generous employers may also provide retirement benefits, bonuses, and even employee profit sharing.

When you're self-employed, you get no such benefits. You must pay for your own health insurance, often at higher rates than employers pay. Time lost due to vacations and illness comes directly out of your bottom line. And you must fund your own retirement. If you don't earn enough money to purchase or create these benefits for yourself, you will have to forgo some or all of them.

No Unemployment Insurance

The self-employed also don't have the safety net provided by unemployment insurance. Because hiring firms (companies that hire self-employed people) do not pay unemployment compensation taxes for the self-employed, self-employed people cannot collect unemployment benefits when their work for a firm ends.

No Workers' Compensation

Employers must generally provide workers' compensation coverage for their employees. Employees are entitled to collect workers' compensation benefits for injuries that occur on the job even if the injury was their own fault.

Hiring firms usually do not provide workers' compensation coverage for the self-employed people they hire. If a work-related injury is a self-employed person's fault, he or she has no recourse against the hiring firm. (See Chapter 6.) And even if it's the hiring firm's responsibility, the self-employed person will have to deal with the expense and hassle of a lawsuit.

No Free Office Space or Equipment

Employers normally provide their employees with an office or space in which to work and the equipment they need to do the job. This is not usually the case when a company hires a self-employed person, who must normally provide his or her own workplace and equipment.

Few or No Labor Law Protections

A wide array of federal and state laws protect employees from unfair exploitation by employers. Among other things, these laws:

- impose a minimum wage
- require many employees to be paid time and a half for overtime
- prohibit discrimination and harassment
- require employers to provide family and medical leave, leave for military service, or time off to vote or serve on a jury, and
- protect employees who wish to unionize.

Few such legal protections apply to the self-employed.

Complete Business Responsibility

When you're self-employed, you must run your own business. This means, for example, that you'll need to have at least a rudimentary recordkeeping system or hire someone to keep your records for you. (See Chapter 14.) You'll also likely have to file a far more complex tax return than you did when you were an employee. (See Chapter 8.)

Others May Discriminate

Because you don't have a guaranteed annual income as employees do, insurers, lenders, and others businesses may refuse to provide you with services or may charge you more than employees for similar services. It can be particularly difficult, for example, for a self-employed person to obtain disability insurance, particularly if he or she works at home. Health insurance may be easier to get, but the premium payments could cost you an arm and a leg without the benefit of an employer's group rate.

Also, it may be more difficult to buy a house because lenders are often wary of self-employed borrowers. To prove you can afford a loan, you'll likely have to provide a prospective lender with copies of your recent tax returns and a profit-and-loss statement for your business.

Working for Yourself: The Ugly

Unfortunately, the bad aspects of self-employment discussed above do not end the litany of potential woes. Being self-employed can, in some respects, get downright ugly.

Double Social Security Tax

For many, the ugliest and most unfair thing about being self-employed is that they must pay twice as much Social Security and Medicare taxes as employees. Employees pay a 7.65% tax on their salaries, up to a salary amount capped by the Social Security tax limit ($97,500 in 2007). Employers pay a matching amount. In contrast, self-employed people must pay the entire tax themselves—a whopping 15.3% on their income up to the amount capped by the Social Security tax limit. This is in addition to federal and state income taxes. In practice, the Social Security tax is a little less than 15.3% because of certain deductions, but it still takes a big bite out of what you earn from self-employment. (See Chapter 10.)

Personal Liability for Debts

Employees are not liable for the debts incurred by their employers. An employee may lose his or her job if the employer's business fails but will owe nothing to the employer's creditors.

This is not necessarily the case when you're self-employed. If you're a sole proprietor or partner in a partnership, you are personally liable for your business debts. You could lose much of what you own if your business fails. However, there are ways to decrease your personal exposure, such as obtaining insurance. (See Chapter 6.)

Deadbeat Clients

Ugliest of all, you could do lots of business and still fail to earn a living. Many self-employed people have great difficulty getting their clients to pay them on time or at all. When you're self-employed, you bear the risk of loss from deadbeat clients. Neither the government nor anyone else is going to help you collect on your clients' unpaid bills.

Clients who pay late or don't pay at all have driven many self-employed people back to the ranks of those working for the boss. However, there are many strategies you can use to help alleviate payment problems. (See Chapter 7.)

How to Use This Book

This book will help you make what's good about self-employment even better, make the bad aspects less daunting, and—hopefully—make the ugly aspects a little more attractive.

Exactly which portions of the book you'll need to read depends on whether you're already self-employed or are just starting out.

Starting Up Your Business

If you're just starting out, there are a number of tasks you'll need to complete before or soon after you start doing business. These include:

- choosing the legal form for your business (see Chapter 2)

- choosing a name for your business (see Chapter 3)

- deciding where to set up your office (see Chapter 4)

- obtaining business licenses and permits and a federal taxpayer ID number (see Chapter 5)

- obtaining insurance for your business and yourself (see Chapter 6), and

- setting up at least a rudimentary bookkeeping system (see Chapter 14).

You should read the chapters discussing these tasks first.

Ongoing Legal and Tax Issues

Once your business is up and running, there are a number of ongoing legal and tax issues you may have to tackle. These include:

- deciding how to price your services and taking steps to ensure you get paid (see Chapter 7)

- understanding basic tax rules (see Chapter 8)

- paying estimated taxes (see Chapter 11)

- keeping track of your tax-deductible business expenses (see Chapters 9 and 14)

- dealing with taxes for any employees or independent contractors you hire (see Chapter 13)

- taking steps to ensure that the IRS doesn't view you as an employee if you're audited (see Chapter 15)

- deciding how to fund your retirement (see Chapter 16)

- using written client agreements (see Chapters 18, 19, and 20), and

- dealing with ownership of the copyrights, patents, and trade secrets you create (see Chapter 17).

You can read the appropriate chapters when a problem arises or read them in advance to help you avoid problems from the outset. ●

Choosing the Legal Form
for Your Business

As a self-employed person, one of the most important decisions you have to make is what legal form your business will take. There are several alternatives—and the form you choose will have a big impact on how you're taxed, whether you'll be liable for your business's debts, and how the IRS and state auditors will treat you.

There are four main business forms that we'll discuss in this chapter:

- sole proprietorship
- corporation
- partnership, and
- limited liability company.

If you own your business alone, you need not be concerned about partnerships; this business form requires two or more owners. If, like most self-employed workers, you're running a one-person business, your choice is between a sole proprietorship, a corporation, or limited liability company.

Don't worry too much about making the wrong decision. Your initial choice about how to organize your business is not set in stone. You can always switch to another legal form later. It's common, for example, for self-employed people to start out as sole proprietors, then incorporate later when they become better established and make substantial income.

Sole Proprietorships

A sole proprietorship is a one-owner business. It is by far the cheapest and easiest legal form for organizing your business. You don't have to get permission from the government or pay any fees to be a sole proprietor, except perhaps for a fictitious business name statement or business license. (See Chapter 5.) You just start doing business; if you don't incorporate or have a partner, you are automatically a sole proprietor. If you're already running a one-person business and haven't incorporated, you're a sole proprietor.

The majority of self-employed people are sole proprietors. Most sole proprietors run small operations, but a sole proprietor can hire employees and nonemployees, too. Indeed, some one-owner businesses are large operations with many employees.

Tax Concerns

When you're a sole proprietor, you and your business are one and the same for tax purposes. You don't pay taxes or file tax returns separately for your sole proprietorship. Instead, you must report the income you earn or losses you incur on your own personal tax return, IRS Form 1040. If you earn a profit, you add the money to any other income you have—for example, interest income or your spouse's income if you're married and file a joint tax return. That becomes the total that is taxed. If you incur a loss, you can use it to offset income from other sources.

Although you are taxed on your total income regardless of its source, the IRS also wants to know about the profitability of your business. To show whether you have a profit or loss from your sole proprietorship, you must file IRS Schedule C, *Profit or Loss From Business*, with your tax return. On this form you list all your business income and deductible expenses. (See Chapter 9.) If you have more than one business, you must file a separate Schedule C for each.

Sole proprietors are not employees of their proprietorships; they are business owners. Their businesses don't pay payroll taxes on a sole proprietor's income or withhold income tax. However, sole proprietors do have to pay self-employment taxes —that is, Social Security and Medicare taxes—on their net self-employment income. These taxes must be paid four times a year (along with income taxes) in the form of estimated taxes. Chapters 10 and 11 will cover this in more detail.

Ways to Organize Your Business		
Type of Organization	**Main Advantages**	**Main Disadvantages**
Sole Proprietorship	• Simple and inexpensive to create and operate. • Owner reports profit or loss on personal tax return.	• Owner personally liable for business debts. • Not a separate legal entity.
C Corporation	• Clients have less risk from government audits. • Owners have limited personal liability for business debts. • Owners can deduct fringe benefits as business expense. • Owners can split corporate profit among owners and corporation, paying lower overall tax rate.	• More expensive to create and operate than sole proprietorship or partnership. • Double taxation threat because the corporation is a separate taxable entity. • No beneficial employment tax treatment.
S Corporation	• Clients have less risk from government audits. • Owners have limited personal liability for business debts. • Owners can save on employment taxes by taking distributions insteasd of salary.	• More expensive to create and operate than sole proprietorship. • Fringe benefits for shareholders are limited.
Partnership	• Simple and inexpensive to create and operate. • Owners report profit or loss on personal tax returns.	• Owners personally liable for business debts. • Two or more owners required. • No beneficial employment tax treatment.
Limited Liability Company	• Owners have limited liability for business debts if they participate in management. • Profit and loss can be allocated differently than ownership interests.	• No beneficial employment tax treatment.
Adapted from *Legal Guide for Starting & Running a Small Business*, by Fred S. Steingold (Nolo).		

Hiring firms don't withhold any taxes from a sole proprietor's compensation, but any firm that pays a sole proprietor $600 or more in a year must file Form 1099-MISC to report the payment to the IRS.

EXAMPLE:

Annie operates a computer consulting business as a sole proprietor. She must report all the income she receives from her clients on her individual tax return, IRS Form 1040, and file Schedule C. She need not file a separate tax return for her business. In one recent year, she earned $50,000 from consulting and had $15,000 in business expenses, leaving a net business income of $35,000. She reports her gross profits from consulting and her business expenses on Schedule C. She must add her $35,000 profit to any other income she has and report the total on her Form 1040. She must pay both income and self-employment taxes on this profit.

Businesses Owned and Operated by Spouses

Many businesses are co-owned by a husband and wife. These businesses can be organized in a variety of ways—as an S or C corporation, a limited liability company (LLC), or a formal partnership.

If you and your spouse don't take any steps to choose a business form, the IRS will treat your business as a partnership. This results in a complex tax return. You must file IRS Form 1065 (*U.S. Return of Partnership Income*) to report your partnership's income and expenses. Your partnership income and expenses are split between you and your spouse. The partnership must give each spouse a Schedule K-1 showing the spouse's share of these items. All the amounts from both spouses' Schedules K-1s are then recombined and included on their joint Form 1040.

As of 2007, however, it's possible for married couples to avoid this hassle. Instead of filing a partnership return, married couples who jointly own a business can elect to be taxed as a sole proprietorship, eliminating Form 1065 and the Schedule K-1s. Instead, each spouse reports his or her share of the business income or loss on a separate IRS Schedule C. In addition, each spouse files his or her own Schedule SE showing that spouse's contribution to Social Security and Medicare. This way, both spouse's get credit for paying Social Security and Medicare taxes.

To do this, however, the husband and wife can be the only owners of the business. In addition, both spouses must materially participate in the business.

Prior to 2007, married taxpayers in the nine community property states (Arizona, California, Idaho, Louisiana, New Mexico, Nevada, Texas, Washington, and Wisconsin) were permitted to treat their business as a sole proprietorship, but taxpayers in the other 41 states were not. Now, all married taxpayers have this option.

Liability Concerns

One concern many business owners have is liability—that is, whether and to what extent they are legally responsible for paying their business' debts or judgments entered against their businesses in a lawsuit.

Business Debts

When you're a sole proprietor, you are personally liable for all the debts of your business. This means that a business creditor—a person or company to whom you owe money for items you use in your business—can go after all your assets, both business and personal. This may include, for example, your personal bank accounts, your car, and even your house. Similarly, a personal creditor—a person or company to whom you owe money for personal items—can go after your business assets, such as business bank accounts and equipment.

EXAMPLE:

Arnie, a sole proprietor consultant, fails to pay $5,000 to an office equipment supplier. The supplier sues him in small claims court and wins a $5,000 judgment. As a sole proprietor, Arnie is personally liable for this judgment. This means that the supplier can tap not only Arnie's business bank account, but his personal savings accounts as well. The supplier can also go after Arnie's personal assets, such as his car and home.

Lawsuits

If you're a sole proprietor, you'll also be personally liable for business-related lawsuits. Such lawsuits could result in many kinds of liability, including the following:

- **Premises liability:** Responsibility for injuries or damages that occur at your office, workshop, lab, or other place of business.

IRS Audit Rates Are Higher for Sole Proprietors

Does your business structure affect your chances of being audited by the IRS? The short answer is yes. The following chart shows the most recently reported IRS audit rates for all types of businesses.

IRS Audit Rates

	2005 Audit Rate	2006 Audit Rate
Sole Proprietors		
Income under $25,000	3.68%	3.78%
$25,000 to $100,000	2.21%	2.09%
$100,000 and over	3.65%	3.90%
Partnerships (includes most LLCs)	0.33%	0.40%
C Corporations		
Assets under $250,000	0.74%	0.70%
$250,000 to $1 million	0.96%	1.00%
$1 million to $5 million	1.02%	1.20%
$5 million to $10 million	2.67%	3.40%

As you can see, sole proprietors have a much greater chance of being audited by the IRS than businesses operated as partnerships or corporations. In 2006, 3.90% of sole proprietors earning more than $100,000 from their business were audited. In contrast, only 0.40% of S corporations and 0.74% of C corporations with less than $250,000 in assets were audited. Thus, sole proprietors earning over $100,000 were five times more likely to be audited than most corporations!

These statistics undoubtedly reflect the IRS's belief that sole proprietors habitually underreport their income, take deductions to which they are not entitled, or otherwise cheat on their taxes. Also, the IRS believes sole proprietors have greater opportunity to cheat on tax returns because they are often self-prepared. In contrast, tax returns for corporations, partnerships, and LLCs are usually prepared by tax professionals.

However, the IRS promises that audits for corporations and partnerships will increase in the next few years. Moreover, audit rates for all types of businesses are relatively low, so this factor alone probably shouldn't dictate your choice of business entity.

- **Infringement liability:** When someone claims that you have infringed on a patent, copyright, trademark, or trade secret.

- **Employer liability:** Liability for injuries or damages caused by an employee while he or she was working for you.

- **Product liability:** Responsibility for injuries or damages caused by a product that you manufacture or sell to the public.

- **Negligence liability:** When someone claims that you failed to use "reasonable care" in your actions, resulting in injuries or damages.

Fortunately, you can obtain insurance to protect yourself against these types of risks. This will be covered in Chapter 6.

Audit Concerns

If you are a self-employed person who does work for a client, you are generally considered an independent contractor of the client that hired you. In some cases, however, a self-employed person's relationship to a client will have qualities that make it look more like an employer-employee relationship. When this happens, the government

Bankruptcy For the Self-Employed

What happens if your debts get out of control? The final resort for people and businesses who find themselves in overwhelming debt is bankruptcy. There are several different types, as described below.

Chapter 7 bankruptcy is the familiar personal bankruptcy used by individuals who can't pay their personal debts, such as credit card debt and other consumer debts. However, personal debts are not limited to consumer debt. If you're a sole proprietor, your business debts are legally your personal debts.

If you successfully complete Chapter 7 bankruptcy, your unsecured debts are discharged—that is, you are no longer legally obligated to pay them. To obtain such a bankruptcy discharge you must surrender many of your assets to the Bankruptcy Court—for example, cash in the bank and some of your real and personal property. The court then uses the assets to pay your creditors.

However, you don't have to surrender all your assets. Some assets are exempt from bankruptcy, which means that you can keep them. For example, depending on how much they are worth, creditors may not be allowed to take your car, business tools, home, or home furnishings. Retirement accounts are also exempt. The amount of property that is exempt varies from state to state—some states are much more generous to debtors than others.

Chapter 13 bankruptcy is a reorganization bankruptcy in which you agree to a plan to repay your debts over five years. All your disposable income must go to your debtors. If you finish your repayment plan, any remaining unpaid balance on your unsecured debts is wiped out. In theory, you get to keep your assets in a Chapter 13 bankruptcy. In practice, however, many people end up spending down their assets, including exempt ones, because the definition of disposable income is so restrictive that it doesn't leave them enough to live on.

Chapter 11 bankruptcy is similar to Chapter 13, except it is used by businesses and individuals with very large debts.

Under the federal bankruptcy law that went into effect on October 16, 2005, it is much more difficult for individuals to obtain a discharge of their debts through Chapter 7 bankruptcy. Among other things, the law may prevent you from filing for Chapter 7 bankruptcy if your debts are primarily consumer debts and your income is above the median for your state. For a family of four, that's $59,000 in Texas; $73,000 in California; and $74,500 in New York. Instead, you'll be required to repay your debts through Chapter 13 bankruptcy, which has also been made more onerous for debtors.

The law also places new limits on the "homestead exemption"—the amount of home equity that you are allowed to keep when you file for bankruptcy. This will make it more difficult for debtors to keep their homes when they go bankrupt.

Some legal experts fear that these changes to the bankruptcy laws will have a chilling effect on entrepreneurs—that is, people will be less willing to take financial risks because it is now much harder to wipe out debts through bankruptcy. Certainly, this is something you should consider before you incur any debts for your business.

RESOURCE

For a complete discussion of bankruptcy and the types and amounts of property your creditors can't reach, see:

- *The New Bankruptcy: Will It Work for You?*, by Stephen Elias
- *How to File for Chapter 7 Bankruptcy*, by Stephen Elias, Albin Renauer, and Robin Leonard, and
- *Chapter 13 Bankruptcy: Repay Your Debts*, by Robin Leonard.

(All are published by Nolo.)

will call you an employee of the client—whether or not you and the client view the relationship that way. This employee label can have serious tax consequences for both you and your client.

Because of these major consequences—which include heavy fines and back taxes—most companies will hire only self-employed people whom they are certain will be viewed by the government as independent contractors and not as employees. One thing the hiring firm will look at is what sort of business entity you are.

A disadvantage of the sole proprietorship business form is that it won't help you establish that you're self-employed in the eyes of the IRS or state auditors. Sole proprietors who provide services can look a lot like employees—especially if they work on their own without assistants and deposit their compensation in a personal bank account. After all, this is exactly what employees do. For this reason, some hiring firms prefer to hire self-employed people who have incorporated their businesses.

Corporations

The word "corporation" usually conjures up images of huge businesses such as General Motors or IBM. However, a business doesn't have to be large to be a corporation. Virtually any business can be a corporation, even if it has only one owner. Indeed, most corporations have only a few owners; such small corporations are often called "closely held" corporations.

Relatively few self-employed people are incorporated—but don't let this stop you from considering this form for your business. Incorporating your business can result in tax savings, limit your liability for business debts, and even help you get clients.

What Is a Corporation?

A corporation is a legal form you can use to organize and conduct a business. Unlike a sole proprietorship, it has a legal existence distinct from its owners and is considered its own legal "person." That means it can hold title to property, sue and be sued, have bank accounts, borrow money, hire employees, and do anything else in the business world that a human being can do.

In theory, every corporation consists of three groups of people:

- those who direct the overall business, called "directors"
- those who run the day-to-day business affairs, called "officers," and
- those who just invest in the business, called "shareholders."

However, in the case of a small business corporation, these three groups often boil down to the same person—that is, a single person can direct and run the corporation and own all the corporate stock. So, if you want to incorporate your one-person business, you don't have to go out and recruit a board of directors or officers.

Your Employment Status

When you incorporate your business, if you continue to work in the business, you automatically become an employee of your corporation, whether full or part time. This is so even if you're the only shareholder and are not subject to the direction and control of anybody else. In effect, you wear two hats: You're both an owner and an employee of the corporation.

EXAMPLE:

Ellen, an independent truck driver, forms a one-person trucking corporation, Ellen's Trucking, Inc. She owns all the stock and runs the business. The corporation hires her as an employee with the title of president.

When you have incorporated your business, clients hire your corporation, not you personally. You sign any written agreement on behalf of your corporation. When you're paid, the client should issue the check to the corporation and you should deposit it in the corporate bank account, not your personal account. You can then pay the money to yourself in the form of salary, bonus, or dividends. The method you choose to pay yourself can have important tax consequences, discussed below.

You must withhold Social Security and Medicare taxes from any employee salary your corporation pays you, and you must pay this money to the IRS just as an employer would for any employee. However, your total Social Security and Medicare taxes will be about the same as if you were a sole proprietor. They're just paid from two different accounts: Half are paid by your corporation and half are withheld from your salary. Because all the money is yours, there is no real difference here from being a sole proprietor. Some additional state payroll taxes will be due, however—mostly state unemployment taxes.

You can also have your corporation provide you with employee fringe benefits such as health insurance and pension benefits.

Self-Employed by Any Other Name

Strictly speaking, when you incorporate your business, you are no longer self-employed; you are an employee of your corporation. Legally speaking, your corporation is neither self-employed nor an employee of the clients or customers for whom it provides services. Only individual human beings can be self-employed or employees.

However, people who own single-shareholder corporations and sell services to clients still often refer to themselves as self-employed when they communicate with clients and customers and other self-employed people. This is understandable because their employee status is mainly a legal technicality.

Audit Risks

Many potential clients are fearful of hiring self-employed people because they are afraid they could get in trouble if the IRS audits them and claims that the self-employed workers should have been treated as employees. For years, tax experts have believed that firms that hire corporations have a much smaller chance of having worker classification problems with the IRS than firms that hire sole proprietors to do the same work. This is because taking the time and trouble to incorporate is strong evidence that a worker is operating as an independent business.

The IRS confirmed this view in a manual issued in 1996 to train IRS auditors on how to determine the status of workers. The manual provides that an incorporated worker will usually not be treated as an employee of the hiring firm but instead as an employee of the worker's corporation.

Because of this clear direction from the IRS, some hiring firms try to avoid hiring sole proprietors or partnerships and deal with incorporated businesses only. Others give preference to a corporation if they have a choice between hiring a sole proprietor and a corporation. The ability to get more business may alone justify the time and expense involved in incorporating.

Incorporating may be particularly helpful if you're a computer programmer, systems analyst, engineer, or drafter, or if you perform similar technical services. Because special IRS rules make it harder for firms that hire such workers to win IRS worker-classification audits, hiring firms generally classify them as employees. But they may make an exception if you're incorporated and they are able to hire your corporation instead of hiring you personally.

However, don't get the idea that you and your clients need not worry about the IRS at all if you incorporate. The IRS also directs that an incorporated worker may be reclassified as an employee of the hiring firm if the worker does not follow corporate formalities or otherwise abuses the corporate form. IRS auditors may disregard your corporate status and find that you're a hiring firm's employee if you act like one—for example, if you:

- deposit your earnings directly into your personal bank account instead of putting them into a separate corporate account
- fail to file tax returns for your corporation
- don't issue yourself stock, or
- fail to follow other corporate formalities, such as holding an annual meeting or keeping corporate records.

IRS Docks Doc, but Not M.D., Inc.

A case from 1995 shows why many clients prefer to hire corporations rather than sole proprietors. An outpatient surgery center hired two doctors to work as administrators. They both performed the same services. However, one of the doctors had formed a medical corporation of which he was an employee. The surgery center signed a written contract with the corporation, not the doctor. It also paid the corporation, not the doctor. The other doctor was a sole proprietor and had no written contract with the center.

The court concluded that the incorporated doctor was not an employee of the surgery center, but the unincorporated doctor was an employee. As a result, the center had to pay substantial back taxes and penalties for the unincorporated doctor, but not for the doctor who was incorporated. (*Idaho Ambucare Center v. U.S.*, 57 F.3d 752 (9th Cir. 1995).)

Liability Concerns

In theory, forming a corporation provides its owners (the shareholders) with "limited liability." This means that the shareholders are not personally liable for corporate debts or lawsuits. The main reason most small business owners go to the trouble of forming corporations is to obtain such limited liability. However, while incorporating your business can insulate you from liability to a certain extent, the protection is not nearly as great as most people think.

Business Debts

Corporations were created to enable people to invest in businesses without risking their personal assets if the business failed or became unable to pay its debts. In theory, corporation owners are not personally liable for corporate debts or lawsuits. That is, they can lose what they invested in the corporation, but corporate creditors can't go after their personal assets such as their personal bank accounts or homes.

This theory holds true where large corporations are concerned. If you buy stock in IBM, for example, you don't have to worry about IBM's creditors suing you. But it often doesn't work that way for small corporations. Major creditors (like banks) are probably not going to let you shield your personal assets by incorporating. Instead, they will likely demand that you personally guarantee business loans or extensions of credit—that is, sign a legally enforceable document pledging your personal assets to pay the debt if your business assets fall short. This means that you will be personally liable for the debt, just as if you were a sole proprietor.

EXAMPLE:
Lisa forms a corporation to run her part-time home business. She applies for a business credit card from her bank. She reads the application carefully and finds that it contains a clause stating that she will be personally liable for the credit card balance—even though the credit card will be in the corporation's name, not Lisa's own name. Lisa asks the bank to remove the clause. It refuses, stating that its policy is to require

personal guarantees from all small, incorporated businesses such as Lisa's. Lisa goes ahead and signs the application. Now, if Lisa's corporation fails to pay off the credit card, the bank can sue her personally and collect against her personal assets, such as her personal bank account.

Not only banks and lenders require personal guarantees—other creditors may as well. For example, you may be required to personally guarantee payment of your office lease or leases for expensive equipment, like a photocopier or truck. Standard forms used by suppliers often contain personal guarantee provisions that make you personally liable when your company buys office equipment or similar items.

You can avoid having to make a personal guarantee for some business debts. These will most likely be routine and small debts. It's not likely, for example, that your office supply store will make you personally guarantee that your corporation will pay for its purchases. But, of course, if it gets wise to the fact that your business is not paying its bills, it won't extend you any more credit.

Lawsuits

If forming a corporation could shield you from personal liability for business-related lawsuits, incorporating would be clearly worthwhile. However, it's important to understand that the small business owner gets relatively little protection from most lawsuits by incorporating, as the following subsections explain.

Personal Liability Negligence

The people who own a corporation (the shareholders) are *personally liable* for any damages caused by their own "negligence" (carelessness) or intentional wrongdoing in carrying out corporation business. Lawyers are well aware of this rule and will take advantage of it if doing so serves their clients' interests. If you form a corporation that

lacks the money or insurance to pay for a legal claim brought against it, you can be certain that the lawyer for the person suing you will seek a way to sue you personally, to collect against your personal assets. Here are some examples of how you could be sued personally even though you've formed a corporation:

- A visitor slips and falls at your place of business and breaks a hip. The visitor's lawyer sues you personally for negligence, claiming you failed to keep your premises safe.
- An employee accidentally injures someone while running an errand for you. The injured person sues you personally for damages claiming you negligently hired, trained, or supervised the employee.
- A product you invented, designed, manufactured, or distributed injures several users. The injured people sue you personally for negligence.
- Someone sues you, claiming you've infringed upon a patent or copyright. Even if you've formed a corporation, you can be personally liable for such claims.

In all these cases, forming a corporation will prove useless to protect you from personal liability.

Piercing the Corporate Veil

Another way you can be personally liable even though you've formed a corporation is through a legal doctrine called "piercing the corporate veil." Under this legal rule, corporate owners risk being reached personally through their corporation's structure if they treat the corporation as their "alter ego," rather than as a separate legal entity— meaning they behave as if they and the corporation are one and the same, without following the formalities required for corporate status. For example, they fail to contribute money to the corporation or issue stock, they take corporate funds or assets for personal use, they commingle corporate and personal funds, or they don't observe corporate formalities such as keeping minutes and holding board meetings, a court might disregard the corporate form and hold the owners personally liable.

Inactive Shareholders Are Not Liable for Corporate Debts or Wrongs

As discussed above, shareholders who actively participate in the management of the company can be held personally liable, either for their own negligence or wrongdoings, or under the doctrine of piercing the corporate veil. However, shareholders who are not active in the business face no such personal liability unless they provide a personal guarantee. Because they aren't active, they don't commit any personal wrongs for which they could be sued. This is why, for example, the ordinary shareholders in the disgraced Enron Corporation are not personally liable for its debts or wrongdoing. But shareholders who were active in the company—for example, its president and chief financial officer—can be held personally (and even criminally) liable for their actions.

The Role of Insurance

If incorporating won't relieve you of personal liability, how can you protect yourself from business-related lawsuits? There's a very simple answer: Get insurance. An insurer will defend you in such lawsuits and pay any settlements or damage awards up to a certain amount, as defined by the insurance policy you choose. All wise business owners—whether sole proprietors, partners, LLC members, or corporation owners—get their businesses insured. Liability insurance and many other forms of business insurance are available to protect you from the types of lawsuits described above. Chapter 6 will provide details on obtaining liability insurance.

Note carefully, however, that insurance won't protect you from liability for business debts—for example, if you fail to repay a loan or default on a lease. This is where bankruptcy comes in.

Corporate Taxation Basics

There are two different types of corporations, for which federal income tax rules differ greatly:

- C corporations, sometimes called regular corporations, and
- S corporations, also called small business corporations.

Basically, C corporations pay taxes as corporate entities while S corporations don't—individual shareholders split up the S corporation's tax burden. You can choose to form either type of corporation. Each has its benefits and its drawbacks. Generally, S corporations are best for small businesses that either make little income or suffer losses. C corporations can be better for successful businesses with substantial profits. You can start out as an S corporation and switch to a C corporation later, or vice versa.

As explained in the next two sections, you can save money on taxes by incorporating. You can also gain some less tangible benefits—for example, small corporations are audited less often than sole proprietorships. And, even when small corporations are audited, the IRS takes a less rigorous look at their tax deductions than it does for those of sole proprietors.

RESOURCE

For additional information on corporate taxation, see:

- *Tax Savvy for Small Business,* by Frederick W. Daily (Nolo), and
- IRS Publication 542, *Corporations.* You can obtain this IRS publication free by calling the IRS at 800-TAX-FORM, visiting your local IRS office, or downloading them from the IRS website at www.irs.gov.

SEE AN EXPERT

If, after reading this chapter, you're not sure whether a C or S corporation is best for you, consult an accountant or other tax professional for help. (See Chapter 21.)

Taxes for C Corporations

When you form a corporation, it automatically becomes a C corporation for federal tax purposes. C corporations are treated as separate entities from their owners for tax purposes. C corporations must pay income taxes on their net income and file their own tax returns with the IRS using either Form 1120 or Form 1120-A. They also have their own income tax rates, which are lower than individual rates at some income levels. C corporations can take the same deductions as sole proprietorships to determine their net profits, plus some additional deductions as well. This separate tax identity is a unique attribute of C corporations—an attribute that can lead to tax savings.

Income Splitting

When you form a C corporation, you create two separate taxpayers: your corporation and yourself. You don't pay personal income tax on income your incorporated business earns until it is distributed to you (as individual income) in the form of salary, bonuses, or dividends. This allows you to split the income your business earns with your corporation. It also lets you save on income tax because the corporate tax rate may be lower than your personal tax rate. A C corporation pays less income tax than an individual on the first $75,000 of taxable income. (See the chart "2007 Individual and Corporate Tax Rates," below.)

In addition, you can keep up to $250,000 of your business earnings in your corporate bank account without penalty. You can use this money to expand your business, buy equipment, or pay yourself

employee benefits, such as health insurance and pension benefits. However, if you keep more than $250,000, you'll become subject to an extra 15% tax called the "accumulated earnings tax." This tax is intended to discourage you from sheltering too much of your corporation's earnings.

There is another substantial tax benefit to income splitting: You don't have to pay Social Security and Medicare taxes, also called employment taxes, on the profits you retain in your corporation. This is a 15.3% tax on salaries paid to employees, including yourself (up to a ceiling amount—$97,500 in 2007). For example, if you retain $10,000 in your corporation rather than paying it to yourself as salary, you'll save $1,530 in taxes.

EXAMPLE:

Betty owns and operates an incorporated construction contracting business. In one year, the corporation makes a net profit of $20,000, after paying Betty a salary of $50,000. Rather than pay herself the $20,000 in additional salary or bonuses, Betty decides to leave the money in her corporation. She uses the money to buy equipment. The corporation pays only a 15% corporate income tax on these retained earnings. Had Betty taken the $20,000 as salary, she would have had to pay a 28% personal income tax on her earnings.

Of course, income splitting is a viable option only if your business earns enough money for you to leave some in your corporate bank account, rather than distributing it all to yourself in the form of salary, bonuses, and benefits. Many self-employed people don't make enough money to even consider income splitting—particularly when they're starting out.

Personal Service Corporations

Special tax rules apply to self-employed people engaged in occupations involving professional services. The IRS calls corporations formed by such people "personal service corporations," or PSCs. These corporations are required to pay corporate tax at a flat rate of 35%.

C corporations formed by self-employed consultants are PSCs if all of the corporation's stock is owned by consultants who are corporate employees. Consulting means getting paid to give a client your advice or counsel. You're not a consultant if you get paid only if the client buys something from you or from someone else through you. Unfortunately for their wallets, huge numbers of self-employed people qualify as consultants and are taxed at this high flat rate.

EXAMPLE:

Acme Corporation hires Data Analysis, Inc., a C corporation solely owned by Tony, a data analyst, to determine its data-processing needs. Tony, who is an employee of his corporation, studies Acme's business and recommends the type of data and information its employees need. Tony doesn't provide Acme with computer hardware or software; he just makes recommendations about how Acme's data-processing system should be designed.

Tony is a consultant and his corporation is a personal service corporation because all the stock is owned by consultant-employees—that is, by Tony. Therefore, the corporation will be subject to a flat tax rate of 35%.

A C corporation will also qualify as a personal service corporation if all the stock is owned by corporate employees performing the following activities or professions:

- accounting (including bookkeeping and tax return preparation; *Rainbow Tax Service v. Comm'r*, 128 T.C. 5 (2007))
- health services—including doctors, nurses, dentists, or other health care professionals
- engineering

- law
- performing arts, or
- actuarial science.

Because the 35% flat tax on personal service corporations is so high, income splitting is not nearly as attractive for these corporations as it is for corporations that are not PSCs. But because earnings retained in the PSC are not subject to the 15.3% Social Security and Medicare tax, there are modest tax benefits to keeping money in a PSC. For example, if a PSC owner who is in the 25% income tax bracket has his PSC pay him $10,000 in salary, he would have to pay a 25% income tax on the $10,000 plus a 15.3% Social Security and Medicare tax on the amount—40.3% in taxes. But if he left the $10,000 in his PSC, the corporation would have to pay only the 35% flat tax.

However, Social Security taxes are subject to an annual income ceiling ($97,500 in 2007), so the advantage of not having to pay these taxes on funds left in a PSC disappears at higher income levels. For example, if a PSC pays its owner a $125,000 annual salary, he would be in the 28% income tax bracket and have to pay a 2.9% Medicare tax on the entire $125,000 and a 12.9% Social Security tax on the first $97,500; his earnings over $97,500 would not be subject to the 12.9% Social Security tax. So, if the PSC pays him another $10,000 in salary, the amount would be subject to a total tax of 31.9% (28% plus 2.9%). If he left the $10,000 in his PSC, it would have to pay a 35% income tax.

Comparison of Tax Rates

The chart below offers a comparison of the tax rates for individuals, corporations, and personal service corporations.

The individual income tax brackets shown are adjusted annually for inflation. This table shows the 2007 brackets. For later brackets, see IRS Publication 505, *Tax Withholding and Estimated*

		2007 Individual and Corporate Tax Rates		
Taxable Income	**Individual Rate (Single)**	**Individual Rate (Married filing jointly)**	**Corporate Rate (Other than personal service corporations)**	**Personal Service Corporation Rate**
Up to $7,825	10%	10%	15%	35%
$7,826-$15,650	15%	10%	15%	35%
$15,561-$31,850	15%	15%	15%	35%
$31,851-$50,000	25%	15%	15%	35%
$50,001-$63,700	25%	15%	25%	35%
$63,701-$75,000	25%	25%	25%	35%
$75,001-$77,000	25%	25%	34%	35%
$77,001-$100,000	28%	25%	34%	35%
$100,001-$128,500	28%	25%	39%	35%
$128,501-$169,850	28%	28%	39%	35%
$169,851-$195,850	33%	28%	39%	35%
$195,851-$335,000	33%	33%	39%	35%
$335,001-$349,700	33%	33%	34%	35%
$349,701-$10,000,000	35%	35%	34%	35%

Tax. You can obtain a free copy by calling the IRS at 800-TAX-FORM, visiting your local IRS office, or downloading it from the IRS website at www.irs.gov.

Fringe Benefits

The other significant tax benefit of forming a C corporation is that your corporation can provide you—its employee—with fringe benefits, which it can then deduct from the corporation's income as a business expense. No other form of business entity can do this.

Possible employee fringe benefits include:

• health insurance for you and your family

• disability insurance

• reimbursement of medical expenses not covered by insurance

• deferred compensation plans

• group term life insurance

• retirement plans, and

• death benefit payments up to $5,000.

You do not have to include the value of premiums or other payments your corporation makes for your benefits in your personal income for income tax purposes. With health insurance costs skyrocketing, the ability to fully deduct these expenses is one of the best reasons to form a C corporation.

EXAMPLE:

Marilyn incorporates her marketing business, of which she is the only employee. Marilyn's corporation provides her with health insurance for her and her family at a cost of $6,000 per year. The entire cost can be deducted from the corporation's income for corporate income tax purposes, but is not included as income on Marilyn's personal tax return.

Sole proprietors, S corporation owners, and partners in partnerships may deduct all of their health insurance premiums from their personal income tax, including their own health insurance premiums and those for their spouses and dependents. But this is a special personal deduction, not a business deduction. Thus, it doesn't reduce their income for Social Security and Medicare tax purposes.

These business owners get no other tax-advantaged fringe benefits. If the entity provides the owner with another type of fringe benefit, the owner must include its value—and pay income tax on it—on the owner's personal tax return. For example, if an entity taxed as a partnership provides an owner with disability insurance, the owner must include the value of the insurance in his or her taxable income for the year. But there is one way around this: The business owner can hire his or her spouse as an employee and provide the spouse with benefits. (See Chapter 6.)

However, C corporations retain another important advantage in the area of health care costs: A C corporation can establish a medical reimbursement plan that reimburses employees for medical expenses not covered by insurance. A C corporation can deduct these costs fully as a business expense. In contrast, if an unincorporated self-employed person or S corporation owner pays for uninsured health expenses out of his or her own pocket, the personal income tax deduction he or she may take is limited to only those amounts exceeding 7.5% of adjusted gross income.

Interest-Free Loans

Yet another benefit of forming a C corporation is that the shareholders can borrow up to $10,000 from the corporation free of interest. If you borrow any more than that, however, you must either pay interest or pay tax on the amount of interest you should have paid. The interest rate is determined by IRS tables. No other form of business entity offers this benefit.

Borrowing money from your corporation is a very attractive option because the loan is not taxable income to you. However, shareholder loans must be true loans. As proof of the loan's veracity, you should sign a promissory note obligating you to repay it on a specific date or in regular installments. The loan should also be secured by your personal property, such as your house or car.

Taxes for S Corporations

When you incorporate, you can elect to form an S corporation instead of a C corporation. An S corporation is taxed like a sole proprietorship. Unlike a C corporation, it is not a separate taxpaying entity. Instead, the corporate income and losses are passed directly to the shareholders—that is, you and anyone else who owns your business along with you. The shareholders must split the taxable profit according to their shares of stock ownership and report that income on their individual tax returns.

An S corporation normally pays no taxes but must file an information return with the IRS on Form 1120-S, indicating how much the business earned or lost and each shareholder's portion of the corporate income or loss.

EXAMPLE:

Alice owns ABC Programming, Inc., an S corporation, and is its sole shareholder and sole employee. In one year, ABC earned $100,000 in gross income and had $90,000 in deductions, including an $80,000 salary for Alice. The corporation's $10,000 net profit is passed through directly to Alice, who must report it as income on her personal tax return. The S corporation files an information return with the IRS on Form 1120-S but pays no income taxes itself.

S corporations have been very popular with small business owners. Owning an S corporation can give you the best of both worlds. You're taxed as a sole proprietor, which is simpler than being taxed as a C corporation and is particularly helpful when you're starting out with little business income (or perhaps even losses). At the same time, you still have the limited liability of a corporation owner. And there's another benefit: You can save on self-employment taxes by setting up an S corporation.

Deducting Business Losses

You must report income or loss from an S corporation on your individual tax return. This means that if your business has a loss, you can deduct it from income from other sources, including your spouse's income if you're married and file a joint return. You can't do this with a C corporation because it's a separate taxpaying entity; its losses must be subtracted from its income and can't be passed on to you. The ability to deduct business losses on your personal tax return may be particularly helpful when you're starting out, if you have incurred business losses you can use to reduce your total taxable income.

EXAMPLE:
Jack and Johanna are a married couple who file a joint income tax return. Johanna earns $80,000 a year from her job. Jack quits his job as an employee-salesperson and becomes self-employed. He forms an S corporation with himself as the sole shareholder and only employee. In his first year in business, his

company earns $20,000 and has $40,000 in expenses. Jack and Johanna report this $20,000 loss on their joint tax return and subtract it from their total taxable income. Because Johanna's $80,000 salary puts them in the 25% income tax bracket (see the "2007 Individual and Corporate Tax Rates" chart, above), they've saved $5,000 in income tax (25% x $20,000).

No Income Splitting

When you operate an S corporation, you can't split your income between two separate taxpaying entities as you can with a C corporation. If your business does well, income splitting can reduce your federal income taxes because C corporations may pay less tax than individuals at certain income levels. (Whether C corporations actually pay less tax or not depends on their exact income—for example, they pay more than married taxpayers on amounts up to $15,561, but less than single taxpayers on amounts from $31,851 to $50,000; see the "2007 Individual and Corporate Tax Rates" chart, above, for more details.) Of course, income splitting is only beneficial anyway if your business earns enough that you can afford to leave some of the cash in it, rather than distributing it to yourself as salary, bonus, or benefits.

Self-Employment Tax

An important tax benefit of forming an S corporation is that it can save you Social Security and Medicare tax. This is a flat 15.3% tax on your first $97,500 in income in 2007; the taxable income ceiling is adjusted annually for inflation. If you earn more than that amount, you also pay a 2.9% Medicare tax on the excess.

If you're a sole proprietor, partner in a partnership, or limited liability company member, all the income you receive from your business is subject to these taxes, called self-employment taxes. (See Chapter 10.) If you incorporate your business and

Beware of Double Taxation

When you're a sole proprietor and you want to take money out of your business for personal use, you can simply write yourself a check. Such a transfer has no tax impact because all of your sole proprietorship profits are taxed to you personally. It makes no difference whether you leave the money in the business or put it in your personal bank account.

Things are very different when you form a C corporation. Any direct payment of your corporation's profits to you will be considered a dividend by the IRS and taxed twice. First, the corporation will pay corporate income tax on the profit and then you'll pay personal income tax on what you receive from the corporation. This is referred to as "double taxation."

Income from dividends (payments of profits from corporations to their shareholders) used to be taxed at ordinary income tax rates, which currently range from 10% to 35%. Under tax changes that took effect in 2003, however, qualified dividends are taxed at a maximum of 15% for the years 2003 through 2010. Unless Congress acts again, the tax on dividends will rise to a maximum of 38.6% in 2011 and 39.6% in 2012. (In 2008, for those in the 10% or 15% tax bracket, the tax rate on qualified dividends is zero, but will go up to 10% in 2009.)

In real life, however, this problem rarely arises for small corporations. Ordinarily, you'll be an employee of your corporation, and the salary, benefits, and bonuses you receive will be deductible expenses for corporate income tax purposes. If you handle things right, your employee compensation will eat up all the corporate profits so there's no taxable income left on which your corporation will have to pay income tax. You'll pay income tax only once—personal income tax on your employee compensation.

EXAMPLE: Al has incorporated his consulting business. He owns all the stock and is the company's president and sole employee. In one recent year, the corporation earned $100,000 in profits. During that year, Al's corporation paid him an $80,000 salary and a $20,000 Christmas bonus. The salary and bonus are tax-deductible corporate business expenses, leaving the corporation with a net profit of zero. As a result, Al's corporation pays no income taxes. Al simply pays personal income tax on the income he received from the corporation, just as any other employee would.

The only time you might have a problem with double taxation is when your business profits are so great that you can't reasonably pay them all to yourself in the form of employee compensation. The IRS allows corporate owner-employees to pay themselves only a reasonable salary for work they actually perform. Any amounts that are deemed unreasonable are treated as disguised dividends by the IRS and are subject to double taxation. One way to avoid this is to leave the excess profits in your corporation and distribute them to yourself as salary, bonus, or benefits in future years.

you are an employee of your corporation, the same 15.3% tax must be paid. You pay half out of your employee compensation, and your corporation pays the other half.

Whether you are a sole proprietor, partner in a partnership, limited liability company member, or employee of your C corporation, you must pay Social Security and Medicare taxes on all the income you take home.

Only S corporations offer you a way to take home some money without paying these taxes. You report your corporation's earnings on your personal tax return, and you must pay Social Security and Medicare taxes on any employee salary your S corporation pays you. You do not, however, have to pay such tax on distributions from your S corporation—that is, on the net profits that pass through the corporation to you personally. The larger your distribution, the less Social Security and Medicare tax you'll pay.

EXAMPLE:

Mel, a consultant, has formed an S corporation of which he's the sole shareholder and only employee. In one year, his corporation had a net income of $50,000. If Mel pays this entire amount to himself as employee salary, he and his corporation will have to pay a 15.3% Social Security and Medicare tax on all $50,000—a total tax of $7,650.

Instead, Mel decides to pay himself only a $30,000 salary. The remaining $20,000 is passed through the S corporation and reported as an S corporation distribution on Mel's personal income tax return, not as employee salary. Because it is not viewed as employee earnings, Mel does not have to pay Social Security or Medicare tax on this amount. Mel pays only $4,590 in Social Security and Medicare taxes instead of $7,650—a tax saving of $3,060.

Theoretically, if you took no salary at all, you would not owe any Social Security and Medicare taxes. As you might expect, however, this is not allowed. The IRS requires S corporation shareholder-employees to pay themselves a reasonable salary—at least what other businesses pay for similar services.

S corporation owners may also avoid Social Security and Medicare taxes by keeping their business earnings in their corporation. The owners would still have to pay personal income tax on the amounts so retained, but they would not be subject to Social Security or Medicare tax.

When you reduce the Social Security tax you pay in this way, you might receive smaller Social Security benefits when you retire, because benefits are based on your contributions. However, you can more than offset this loss by putting the money you save now into a tax-advantaged retirement plan such as an IRA, SEP-IRA, 401(k), or Keogh Plan. You'll probably earn more money from your contributions to such plans than you'd collect from making a similar contribution to Social Security. In addition, your contributions to such plans are usually tax deductible, and you can start taking the money out when you reach age 59½. In contrast, you can't collect Social Security until you're at least 62. (For more on retirement plans, see Chapter 16.)

S Corporation Rules

The IRS has rules on who can establish an S corporation and how these corporations must operate. For example:

- an S corporation cannot have more than 100 shareholders
- none of an S corporation's shareholders can be nonresident aliens—that is, noncitizens who don't live in the United States
- an S corporation can have only one class of stock—for example, you can't create preferred stock giving some shareholders special rights, and

- S corporation shareholders can only be individuals, estates, or certain trusts—a corporation can't be an S corporation shareholder.

If you're running a one-person business, are a U.S. citizen or live in the United States, and will be the only shareholder, these restrictions will not affect the operations of your S corporation.

How to Elect S Corporation Status

To establish an S corporation, you must first form a regular C corporation under your state law. (See "Forming a Corporation," below.) Then, you must file Form 2553 with the IRS. If you want your corporation to start off as an S corporation, you must file the form within 75 days of the start of the tax year for your business.

State Tax Rules

Check with the appropriate state agency, usually the Secretary of State, to find out how an S corporation files and pays state taxes. Typically, states impose a minimum annual corporate tax or franchise fee. You may also face a state corporation tax on S corporation income—for example, California imposes a 1.5% tax on S corporation profits in addition to a minimum annual franchise tax of $800. However, you can deduct any state and local taxes from your federal income taxes as business expenses.

Disadvantages of the Corporate Form

Although there are many advantages to incorporating, there are also some disadvantages. You'll have to maintain minimal corporate formalities that will take some time and effort. And you'll have to pay some taxes and fees that other business entities don't pay.

Corporate Formalities

The IRS and state corporation laws require corporations to hold annual shareholder meetings and document important decisions with corporate minutes, resolutions, or written consents signed by directors or shareholders. Fortunately, this is not a substantial burden for small businesses with only one or a few shareholders and directors. Such corporations usually dispense with holding real annual meetings. Instead, the secretary of the corporation prepares minutes for a meeting that takes place on paper only. There are also standard minute and consent forms you can use to ratify important corporate decisions.

If you're audited and the IRS discovers that you have failed to comply with corporate formalities, you may face drastic consequences. For example, if you fail to document important tax decisions and tax elections with corporate minutes or signed consents, you may lose crucial tax benefits and risk substantial penalties. Even worse, if you neglect these basic formalities, the IRS or a court may conclude that your corporation is a sham—and you may lose the limited liability afforded by your corporate status. This could leave you personally liable for corporate debts.

In addition, certain institutions—such as banks, trusts, escrow and title companies, and landlords—often insist on a board or shareholder resolution that approves a corporate transaction with the institution—for example, borrowing money or renting property.

RESOURCE

For information on handling corporate formalities in a streamlined manner, see *The Corporate Records Handbook: Meetings, Minutes & Resolutions*, by Anthony Mancuso (Nolo).

More Complex Bookkeeping

It is absolutely necessary that you maintain a separate corporate bank account if you incorporate. You'll need to keep a more complex set of books than you would as a sole proprietor. You'll also need to file a somewhat more complex tax return, or file two returns if you form a C corporation. And because you'll be an employee of your corporation, you'll need to pay yourself a salary and file employment tax returns. (See Chapter 8.) All of this takes time and costs money.

SEE AN EXPERT

You'll probably want to use the services of an accountant or bookkeeper, at least when you are starting out. A seasoned pro may be able to set up a bookkeeping system, make employment tax payments, provide guidance about tax deductions, and prepare tax returns for you.

RESOURCE

If you have a computer, you can also use accounting software packages for small businesses, such as *QuickBooks, Mind Your Own Business, Peachtree Accounting*, and many others.

Some Increased Taxes and Fees

Finally, there are some fees and taxes you'll have to pay if you incorporate that are not required if you're a sole proprietor. For example, because you'll be an employee of your corporation, your corporation will have to contribute to a fund that provides unemployment compensation for you. The cost varies from state to state but is at least several hundred dollars per year.

You'll also have to pay a fee to your state to form your corporation, and you may have to pay additional fees throughout its existence. In most states, the fees are between $100 and $300. California corporations also have to pay a minimum $800 franchise tax to the state every year after their first year in business, even if the corporation has no profits. Fortunately, you can deduct any state and local fees and taxes from your federal income taxes as business expenses.

Forming a Corporation

You create a corporation by filing the necessary forms with and paying the required fees to your appropriate state agency—usually the office of the secretary of state or corporations commissioner. Each state specifies the forms to use and the filing cost.

You'll also need to choose a name for your corporation (see Chapter 3), adopt corporate bylaws, issue stock, and set up your corporate records. This all sounds complicated, but it really isn't that difficult to do yourself. You can obtain preprinted articles, bylaws, and stock certificates and simply fill in the blanks.

There's No Place Like Home for Incorporating

People who live in high-tax states such as California and New York often hear that they can save money by incorporating in low-tax states such as Nevada or Delaware.

This is a myth. You won't save a dime by incorporating outside your own state. If you form an out-of-state corporation, you will have to qualify to do business in your home state anyway. This process is similar to incorporating in your state and costs the same amount. And you will have to pay any state corporate income taxes levied by your home state for income you earn there. Even if another state has more modern or flexible corporation laws, these mostly favor large, publicly held corporations, not the small, closely held corporations that self-employed people form.

RESOURCE

For detailed guidance on forming a corporation in any of the 50 states, see *Incorporate Your Business: A Legal Guide to Forming a Corporation in Your State* (Nolo). If you want to incorporate in California, see *How to Form Your Own California Corporation* (Nolo). Both are written by Anthony Mancuso.

Professional Corporations

As explained above, you may be required to form a special kind of corporation called a "professional" corporation if you're involved in certain types of professions. The list of professionals who must form professional corporations varies from state to state but usually includes:

- accountants
- engineers
- lawyers
- psychologists
- social workers
- veterinarians, and
- health care professionals such as doctors, dentists, nurses, physical therapists, optometrists, opticians, and speech pathologists.

Call your state's corporate filing office—usually the office of the secretary of state or corporations commissioner—to see who is covered in your state.

Ownership Requirements

Typically, a professional corporation must be organized for the sole purpose of performing professional services, and all shareholders must be licensed to render that service. For example, in a medical corporation, all the shareholders must be licensed physicians.

Formation Requirements

You must use special forms and procedures to establish a professional corporation—for example,

you might be required to obtain a certificate of registration from the government agency that regulates your profession, such as the state bar association. Also, you must include special language in your articles of incorporation.

Limits on Limited Liability

In most states, you cannot use a professional corporation to avoid personal liability for your own malpractice or negligence—that is, your failure to exercise a reasonable amount of care while carrying out your professional responsibilities.

EXAMPLE:

Janet, a civil engineer, forms a professional corporation of which she is the sole shareholder. She designs a bridge that collapses, killing dozens of commuters. Even though Janet is incorporated, she could be held personally liable (along with her corporation) for any damages caused by her negligence in designing the bridge. Both Janet's personal assets and those of her corporation are at risk.

You can usually obtain additional business insurance to protect you against these types of risks, but it can be expensive. (See Chapter 6.)

However, if you're a professional involved in a group practice with other professionals, incorporating will shield you from personal liability for malpractice committed by other members of the group.

EXAMPLE:

Marcus is a doctor involved in an incorporated medical practice with Susan, Florence, and Louis. One of Louis's patients claims he committed malpractice and sues him personally and the group. Though both the group and Louis can be held liable, Marcus, Susan, and Florence cannot be held personally liable for

Louis's malpractice. This means that their personal assets are not at risk.

Tax Rates

As explained previously, personal service corporations are subject to a flat tax rate of 35% as opposed to other corporations, which are taxed at 15%–39% based on income.

Partnerships

If you are not the sole owner of your business, you cannot organize as a sole proprietorship. Instead, you automatically become a partner in a partnership unless you incorporate or form a limited liability company.

A partnership is much the same as a sole proprietorship except that there are two or more owners. Like a sole proprietorship, a partnership is legally inseparable from the owners (the partners). Ordinarily, a partnership does not pay taxes as an entity, although it files an annual tax form. Instead, partnership income and losses are passed through the partnership to the partners and reported on the partners' individual federal tax returns. Partners must file IRS Schedule E with their returns, showing their partnership income and deductions. However, partnerships have the option of being taxed as a regular C corporation or S corporation. This is done by filing IRS Form 2553, *Election by a Small Business Corporation*. See the more detailed discussion of this option in "Limited Liability Companies (LLCs)," below.

Like sole proprietors, partners are neither employees nor independent contractors of their partnership; they are self-employed business owners. A partnership does not pay payroll taxes on the partners' income or withhold income tax. Like sole proprietors, partners must pay income taxes (see Chapter 9) and self-employment taxes (see Chapter 10) on their partnership income.

RESOURCE

For a detailed discussion of partnerships, including how to write partnership agreements, see *Form a Partnership: The Complete Legal Guide,* by Ralph Warner and Denis Clifford (Nolo).

Ownership

The main difference between a partnership and a sole proprietorship is that one or more people own the business along with you. This means that, among other things, you have to decide:

- how each partner will share in the partnership profits or losses
- how partnership decisions will be made
- what the duties of each partner are
- what happens if a partner leaves or dies, and
- how disputes will be resolved.

Although not required by law, you should create a written partnership agreement answering these and other questions.

Personal Liability

Partners are personally liable for all partnership debts and lawsuits, just like sole proprietors. This means that you'll be personally liable for business debts your partners incur, whether or not you know about them.

Limited Partnerships

A limited partnership is a special kind of partnership with two types of partners. One or more "general partners" run the partnership business. The other "limited partners" invest in the partnership but don't help run it. The limited partners are a lot like corporate shareholders in that they aren't personally liable for the partnership's debts. The general partners are treated just like partners in normal partnerships and are liable for all partnership debts and lawsuits.

Limited partnerships are most commonly used to set up real estate and similar investments. Self-employed people rarely form them. If there are people who want to invest in your business but don't want to work in it or have any personal liability, you'd probably be better off forming a corporation and selling them shares. That way, you'll have the limited liability afforded by corporate status.

Registered Limited Liability Partnerships

In all states, professionals may set up a special type of partnership called a "registered limited liability partnership" (RLLP). In some states, including California, certain types of professionals are not allowed to form limited liability companies (LLCs, discussed in the next section), so RLLPs were established as an alternative.

RLLPs give their partner-owners the same type of limited liability as owners of professional corporations: The partners remain personally liable for their own malpractice but have limited liability for malpractice by other partners in the firm. In addition, in most states the RLLP partners receive personal liability protection from business debts and other lawsuits, such as slip-and-fall suits.

RLLPs are limited to professionals in certain occupations—typically people who work in the medical, legal, and accounting fields, and a few other professions in which a professional-client relationship exists. The list of professionals who may form an RLLP in a particular state is normally the same as the list of those eligible to form a professional corporation.

You need at least two partners to form an RLLP, and the partners must usually be licensed in the same or related professions. RLLPs are taxed like any other partnership—that is, they are pass-through tax entities. The owners are taxed on all profits on their individual income tax returns at their individual tax rates. The RLLP itself is not taxed on profits.

RESOURCE

For more information on RLLPs, look up your state RLLP law. You can find it online through Nolo's website at www.nolo.com/statute/state.cfm. Click on your state and then search in your state's codes to find the RLLP act. You can also try calling your secretary of state or LLC filing office for further information.

Limited Liability Companies (LLCs)

The limited liability company, or LLC, is the newest type of business form in the United States. An LLC is taxed like a sole proprietorship or partnership but provides its owners with the same limited liability as a corporation. LLCs have become extremely popular with self-employed people because they are simpler and easier to run than corporations.

RESOURCE

For a complete discussion of limited liability companies, see *Form Your Own Limited Liability Company*, by Anthony Mancuso (Nolo).

LLC Owners

When LLCs first began in the mid-1990s, most states required that they have two or more owners (or "members"), which made life difficult for people running one-person businesses. This is no longer the case. Every state now allows one-person LLCs.

Generally speaking, you are considered a business owner, not an employee, when you form an LLC. If, however, you receive a guaranteed salary or pay from the LLC (instead of or in addition to a share in the LLC's profits), you will be considered an employee of the LLC. For example, if an LLC owner is guaranteed $10,000 per year regardless of the LLC's profits, the owner is treated as an employee of the LLC, which means the $10,000 is subject to income tax withholding and employment taxes.

In some states, people involved in certain professions are not allowed to form regular LLCs. Instead, they must form "professional" LLCs and comply with special rules. Typically, these rules provide that only licensed professionals may own a membership interest in the professional LLC and require each member to carry a specified amount of malpractice insurance. These restrictions usually apply to doctors and other licensed health care professionals, lawyers, accountants, and, in some states, engineers. In a few states, however, such professionals are not allowed to form LLCs at all. Instead, they must form limited liability partnerships, as discussed in the previous section. These states include California and Rhode Island.

Even if you are allowed to form an LLC, doing so may not be advantageous if you are a professional and practice with others, rather than by yourself. This is because LLC laws in most states do not protect an LLC owner from personal liability for the malpractice of another professional in the practice. Thus, if you form an LLC, you could end up being personally liable for the malpractice of your co-owners. You'd be better off forming a professional corporation or RLLP, both of which will shield you from personal liability for the malpractice of your co-owners.

Tax Treatment

IRS rules permit LLC owners to decide for themselves how they want their LLC to be taxed. An LLC can be taxed as a pass-through entity or as a regular C corporation.

Pass-Through Entity

Ordinarily, LLCs are pass-through entities. This means that they pay no taxes themselves.

Instead, all profits or losses are passed through the LLC to be reported on the LLC members' individual tax returns. This is the same as for a sole proprietorship, S corporation, or partnership.

If the LLC has only one member, the IRS treats it as a sole proprietorship for tax purposes. The members' profits, losses, and deductions are reported on his or her Schedule C, the same as for any sole proprietor. If the LLC has two or more members, each year it must prepare and file the same tax form used by a partnership—IRS Form 1065, *U.S. Return of Partnership Income*— showing the allocation of profits, losses, credits, and deductions passed through to the members. The LLC must also prepare and distribute to each member a Schedule K-1 form showing the member's allocations.

Changing Your Tax Treatment

Owners of LLCs have the option of being taxed as a C or an S corporation by making an "election" to receive corporation tax treatment with the IRS. Most businesses don't make this election. However, you might choose to be taxed as an S corporation if you want to save on employment taxes. Or, you might want to be taxed as a C corporation because you want maximum deductions for fringe benefits.

If you want to make an election to change your tax treatment, you simply check the appropriate box on IRS Form 8832, *Entity Classification Election*, and file it with the IRS. The election can be made at any time. Once you file the form, your LLC will be treated exactly like a C corporation by the IRS (most states also recognize the election for state tax purposes). You'll have to file corporate tax returns and will have all the benefits and burdens of C corporation tax treatment described above.

If you want your LLC partnership to be taxed as an S corporation, you may do so by filing an S corporation election with the IRS, IRS Form 2553, *Election by a Small Business Corporation*. But you must meet all the conditions for S corporation

Choosing a Form of Business

There is no one best business form—and choosing the one that will work best for you can be difficult. It all depends on your goals and preferences. The following chart may help you analyze which business form best furthers your own personal goals.

Goal	Sole Proprietorship	Partnership	LLC	S Corporation	C Corporation
Easiest and cheapest to form and operate	✓	✓			
Simplest tax returns	✓	✓			
Avoid state and federal unemployment taxes	✓	✓	✓		
Deduct losses from your personal taxes	✓	✓	✓	✓	
Distribute high profits	✓	✓	✓	✓	
Limit your personal liability			✓	✓	✓
Added credibility for your business				✓	✓
Save on Social Security taxes				✓	
Retain earnings in business (split income)					✓
Provide tax-deductible benefits to employees, including yourself					✓
Benefit from lower corporate tax rates					✓

status to be treated as one. Your business will still be an LLC for all other nontax purposes. If it turns out you don't like your corporation tax treatment, you can change back to partnership tax treatment by making another election, but ordinarily you must wait five years to do so. (Treas. Reg. § 301.7701-3(c)(1)(iv).)

Choosing to be taxed as a corporation has significant tax consequences, so it's wise to consult a tax pro before making the change. (Partnerships also have the option of choosing corporation tax treatment, as described above.)

Liability Concerns

LLC owners (members) enjoy the same limited liability from business debts and lawsuits as corporation owners.

Pros and Cons of an LLC

LLCs appear to be a clear favorite over partnerships because they offer the same tax benefits but also provide limited liability. They are also a serious alternative to corporations, because they are simpler but offer the same limited liability as corporations and have some tax advantages.

Advantages of LLCs

LLCs provide the same limited liability as corporations. However, as discussed previously, such "limited liability" can be more mythical than real.

Setting up an LLC takes about the same amount of time and money as setting up a corporation, but an LLC is simpler and easier to run thereafter. With a corporation, you must hold and record regular and special shareholder meetings to transact important corporate business. Even if you're the only corporate owner, you need to document your decisions. This isn't required for an LLC.

LLCs also allow more flexibility to allocate profits and losses among the business's owners than corporations do. The owners of an S corporation must pay taxes on profits or get the benefits of losses in proportion to their stock ownership. For example, if there are two shareholders and each owns 50% of the stock, they must each pay tax on 50% of the corporation's profits or get the benefits of 50% of the losses. In contrast, if you form an LLC, you have near total flexibility on how to allocate profits and losses among the owners—for example, one owner could get 75% of the profits and the other 25%. Of course, this will be useful only if two or more people own your business.

Unlike an LLC, a C corporation cannot allocate profits and losses to shareholders at all. Shareholders get a financial return from the corporation by receiving corporate dividends or a share of the corporate assets when it is sold or liquidated.

LLCs don't have to comply with the rules limiting who can form and own an S corporation.

And finally, LLC members are not employees of the LLC, so the LLC doesn't have to pay federal and state unemployment taxes for them. When you form a corporation, you are an employee of the corporation and such taxes must be paid.

Disadvantages of LLCs

Perhaps the biggest drawback of LLCs is that they don't offer the opportunity to save on self-employment taxes, as an S corporation does. LLC members who actively manage the business must pay self-employment tax on all the income they receive from the LLC—whether in the form of salary or distributions. In contrast, you can save on self-employment taxes by forming an S corporation because S corporation distributions—as opposed to salaries—are not subject to self-employment tax.

Moreover, money you retain in an S corporation or C corporation is not subject to self-employment taxes. This is not the case with an LLC that is treated as a pass-through entity. Whether you distribute your LLC profits to yourself or leave them in your company, you must pay self-employment taxes on your entire share of LLC profits.

In addition, firms that hire LLCs and pay them more than $600 per year must file Form 1099-MISC with the IRS to report the amount of the payment. (This requirement doesn't apply if the LLC has opted to be taxed as a corporation.) Generally speaking, hiring firms do not have to file Form 1099-MISC when they hire a corporation. For this reason, some businesses prefer to hire corporations instead of LLCs because they can avoid filing the 1099-MISC form altogether. Firms don't like filing the forms because they often lead to audits.

Forming an LLC

To form an LLC, you must file articles of organization with the appropriate state agency, usually the secretary of state. Your company's name will have to include the words "limited liability company" or "LLC" or a similar phrase as set forth in your state law. You should also create a written operating agreement, which is similar to a partnership agreement.

RESOURCE

For a complete explanation of how to form limited liability companies, see *Form Your Own Limited Liability Company,* by Anthony Mancuso (Nolo).

Choosing and Protecting Your Business Name

This chapter will help you choose a name for your business, which you should do shortly after you decide on the legal form. You'll need to have a business name before you can establish bank accounts, print stationery, and market your business to others.

Naming your business can be confusing because you have the option of using different names in different contexts:

- **Legal name:** This is the official name of your business. It is the name you must always use when you sign legal documents (for example, contracts), file tax returns, sign leases, apply for bank loans, or file lawsuits.

- **Trade name:** This is the name you use to identify your business to the public—for example, on your business stationery, in advertising, on business cards, in websites, in marketing literature, and so on. Your legal name and your trade name can be, but are not required to be, the same.

Choosing a Legal Name

The legal name you choose will depend in part on what legal form your chose for your business. If, like the vast majority of self-employed people, you're a sole proprietor, your legal name will be simply your personal name.

EXAMPLE:

Joe Dokes forms his one-person business as a sole proprietorship. Therefore, his business's legal name is "Joe Dokes." This is the name he'll use to sign contracts, file tax returns, and so on.

Things become slightly more complicated if you form a general partnership. In this case, you can use either the last names of all the partners or a name you create as your legal name. If you want to use something other than your last names, you must draft and sign a written partnership

agreement that includes your partnership's legal name. Before you do this, read "Avoiding Conflicts With Other Trade Names," below. In addition, you must register your partnership's legal name, as described in "Registering a Fictitious Business Name," below.

EXAMPLE:

Charles Smith and Mary Jones enter into a partnership to invent and market a new type of can opener. They can call their partnership "Smith and Jones" or "The Smith and Jones Partnership," or they can choose a different name by drafting and signing a written partnership agreement. They decide to do the latter, naming their partnership "The Open Sesame Group."

If you create a corporation or limited liability company (LLC), you must choose its legal name. Like racehorses, corporations must have unique names. Once you decide upon a name, you must get permission to use it by registering the name with the appropriate agency in your state, usually the secretary of state's office.

Choosing a Trade Name

Your trade name is your public name—the moniker customers, clients, and other businesses will use when contacting you. Once you have picked a legal name, you must decide whether you also want to use it as your trade name.

Using Your Legal Name as Your Trade Name

The simplest thing to do is to use your legal name as your trade name. If, like most self-employed people, you're a sole proprietor, this means you'll use your personal name as your trade name. If you're a partnership, LLC, or corporation, you'll use the name you've chosen as your legal name (or the last names of the partners).

If you use your legal name as your trade name, you may add words at the end of it to make it clear that you are in business—for example, a sole proprietor consultant named Joe Dokes could use the name "Joe Dokes Consulting." There is no requirement that you do this, but you might find it helpful for marketing or identification purposes.

Depending on the state you live in, you may have to register your name if you add a word to the end. No matter where you live, however, you will always have to register your name if the additional words imply that your sole proprietorship has more than one owner—for example "Joe Dokes and Company."

Using a Made-Up Name as Your Trade Name

Instead of using your legal name as your trade name, you have the option of making up a new name that differs from your legal name.

EXAMPLE:

Roseanne Zeiss quits her job with a public relations firm and sets up her own public relations business as a sole proprietor. The legal name of Roseanne's sole proprietorship is "Roseanne Zeiss." Instead of using this as her trade name, she decides to call her business "AAA Publicity" so she'll come first in her local business telephone directory.

For marketing purposes, self-employed people often prefer to make up names for their businesses rather than use their personal names. A made-up name can sound catchier, help identify what your business does, or make you seem more businesslike. But there is an additional benefit to making up a business name: It can help establish your legal status as an independent contractor. Employees, obviously, don't use business names. We'll discuss why this is so important in Chapter 15.

You can obtain bank accounts in your new name (provided you file a fictitious business name statement, discussed below). To help avoid confusion, if you use a made-up trade name, you'll usually need to provide it along with your legal name when you file lawsuits, apply for loans, and conduct most business transactions.

Avoiding Conflicts With Other Trade Names

Your trade name—regardless of whether it is the same as your legal name—should not be substantially similar to that of another business in your field. If your name is so similar to a name already being used that it may confuse the public, you could be sued under state and federal unfair competition laws. If you lose such a lawsuit, you may be required to change your business's name and even pay money damages.

Before selecting your trade name, conduct a name search. If you find the same or a similar name for a company involved in a field that is the same as or related to yours, it's probably best to choose a different name to avoid potential headaches later on. Similar names used by companies in fields entirely unrelated to yours probably won't pose a problem, unless the name is a famous trademark like McDonald's. For example, even if your name is Joe McDonald, don't name your business "McDonald's Consulting." Companies with famous names are usually fanatical about protecting them.

Here's how to do a quick and free name search:

- Type in your proposed name or names in an Internet search engine such as Google (www.google.com) to see if other people or companies are using similar names.

- Check telephone books and business directories for the cities in which you plan to do business, as well as surrounding areas.

- Find out if there is a similar federally registered trademark by using the U.S. Patent and Trademark Office's website at www.uspto.gov. Click "Trademarks" on the home page and then "Search TM database."

- Find out if there is a similar unregistered trademark at the Thomas Register, a comprehensive listing of companies, brand names, products, and services (www.thomasnet.com).

- See if there is a similar Internet domain name by doing a search at any domain name registration website—for example, Register. com (www.register.com) or Network Solutions (www.networksolutions.com).

Registering a Fictitious Business Name

In most states, a person or entity doing business in the state under a name other than their own "true name" must register that business name with the county clerk or secretary of state's office as a "fictitious business name" or a "doing business as" (DBA) name. For a sole proprietorship or partnership, a business name is generally considered "fictitious" unless it contains the full name (first and last names) of the owner or all the general partners and does not suggest the existence of additional owners. Generally, using a name that includes words like "company," "associates," "brothers," or "sons" suggests additional owners and will make it necessary for a business to register.

If you fail to register, you open yourself up to many problems. For example, you may not be able to open a bank account in your business name. You also may be barred from suing on a contract you signed using the business name. There is usually a time limit within which you must register your name—often within a month or two after you start doing business.

To register, you usually file a certificate with the county clerk (most likely at your county courthouse) that states who is doing business under the name. In many states, you must publish the statement in a local newspaper to help creditors identify the people behind an assumed business name. This makes it easier to track down those who change their business names to confuse and avoid creditors. Some communities have newspapers that specialize in publishing such legal notices. Some states require, instead of or in addition to publication, that you file the statement with the state department of revenue or some other state agency.

Contact your county clerk and ask about the registration requirements in your locale. You'll have to fill out a simple form and pay a fee—usually between $15 and $50. In most counties, you can check to see if anyone is using a similar name in your county before you attempt to register—either by searching the county clerk's records at its office, calling the clerk, mailing in a request, or using the clerk's website.

Naming a Corporation or Limited Liability Company

If you form a corporation or limited liability company (LLC), you must get permission to use your corporate name by registering it with your state's secretary of state or similar official.

Registering a Corporate Name

To register a corporate name, you must follow these three steps:

- **Step 1: Select a permissible name.** All but three states—Maine, Nevada, and Wyoming—require you to include a word or its abbreviation that indicates corporate status, such as "Corporation," "Incorporated," "Company," or "Limited" (or "Corp.," "Inc.," Co.," or "Ltd."). Several states also require that the name be in English or Roman characters.

- **Step 2: Clear your name.** Next, you must make sure that your corporate name is distinguishable from any corporate name already registered in your state. Your state won't register a corporate name that too closely mimics a name already on file. The secretary of state or other corporate filing agency will do a search for you prior to authorizing the use of your name. In most states, you can check on the availability of names by using the secretary of state's website or calling its office.

- **Step 3: Reserve your corporate name.** A corporation can usually reserve a name before incorporating if the name qualifies for registration otherwise. This freezes out other would-be registrants from claiming that or a similar name during the period of reservation, usually 120 days. Most states permit you to extend the reservation for one or more additional 120-day periods for an additional fee.

The reservation process involves sending an application for reservation to the secretary of state, or the designated office, with a fee. Some states even permit you to reserve a corporate name over the telephone. You can find out about your state's procedures by calling the office of the secretary of state or corporate commissioner.

Registering a Limited Liability Company Name

Registering a name for a limited liability company (LLC) is very similar to registering a corporate name. You must choose a name that conforms with your state's LLC requirements. Most states require you to use the words "Limited Liability Company," "Limited Company," or their abbreviations ("LLC" or "LC") in your name.

You then call the appropriate state office and ask if the name or names you've chosen are available. Most states allow you to reserve LLC names for 30 to 120 days by paying a small fee, usually no more than $50.

RESOURCE

For a detailed discussion of LLC name requirements, see *Form Your Own Limited Liability Company*, by Anthony Mancuso (Nolo).

Legal Effect of Registering a Name

People often think that once they have complied with all the registration requirements for their trade name, they have the right to use that name for all purposes. This isn't so.

Registering a corporate or LLC name or registering a trade name by filing a fictitious business name or "doing business as" statement does not make your name a trademark. Though registering a name allows you to do business under that name, it does not give you any ownership right in the name—meaning it does not allow you to prevent others from using it. If someone else uses your name to identify a product or service to the public before you do, it doesn't make any difference that you registered the name as a legal, trade, corporate, or LLC name. Because they were the first to use the name publicly in the marketplace, they will have the exclusive right to use that name in the marketplace.

Simply put, if the name you have registered was already in use or federally registered as a trademark or service mark, you will have to limit your use of the name to your checkbook and bank account. The minute you try to use the name in connection with marketing your goods or services, you risk infringing the existing trademark or service mark.

If you plan to use your business name in your future marketing plans, in addition to complying with name registration requirements, you must make sure that no one else is using the name as a trademark. If you plan to market your goods or services on the Internet, you'll also want to check to see whether someone else has already taken your proposed name as his or her domain name. If so, at the very least you'll have to use a slightly modified name to do business in cyberspace.

Choosing a Trademark

A trademark is a distinctive word, phrase, logo, or other graphic symbol that's used to distinguish one product from another—for example, Ford cars and trucks, Kellogg's cornflakes, IBM computers, and Microsoft software.

A service mark is similar to a trademark, except that trademarks promote products while service marks promote services. Some familiar service marks include: McDonald's (fast-food service), Kinko's (photocopying service), Blockbuster (video rental service), CBS's stylized eye in a circle (television network service), and the Olympic Games' multicolored interlocking circles (international sporting event).

The word "trademark" is also a generic term used to describe the entire body of state and federal law that covers how businesses distinguish their products and services from the competition. Each state has its own set of laws establishing when and how trademarks can be protected. There is also a federal trademark law called the Lanham Act (15 U.S.C. § 1050 and following), which applies in all 50 states.

If, like many self-employed people, you operate within a single state, you'll be covered primarily by your state trademark law should you claim or become subject to a claim of trademark infringement. But if you do business in more than one state, you may be covered by both federal and state law. The various trademark laws don't differ greatly except that some state laws allow trademark owners to collect greater damages from infringers than federal law.

RESOURCE

For a detailed discussion of trademarks, see *Trademark: Legal Care for Your Business & Product Name*, by Stephen Elias (Nolo).

Trade Names Are Not Trademarks

Your trade name is neither a trademark nor a service mark and is not entitled to trademark protection unless you use it to identify a particular product or service that you produce and sell to the public. Businesses often use shortened versions of their trade names as trademarks—for example, Apple Computer Corporation uses the name "Apple" as a trademark on its line of computer products.

A trade name acts like a trademark when it is used in such a way that it creates a separate commercial impression—in other words, when it acts to identify a product or service. This can be hard to figure out, especially when comparing trade names and service marks, because both often appear in similar places—on letterheads, advertising copy, signs, and displays. But some general principles apply:

- If the full name, address, and phone are used, it's probably a trade name.
- If a shortened version of the trade name is used, especially with a design or logo beside or incorporating it, the trade name becomes a trademark.

EXAMPLE:

Joe, a self-employed computer programmer, calls his unincorporated business "Acme Software Development." He files a fictitious business name statement with his county clerk. When he uses the name "Acme Software Development" along with his office address on his stationery, it is just a trade name, not a trademark. However, Joe develops a software utility program that he calls "Acme Tools" and markets it over the Internet. "Acme Tools" is a trademark.

Selecting a Trademark

Not all trademarks are treated equally by the law. The best trademarks are "distinctive"—that is, they stand out in a customer's mind because they are inherently memorable. The more distinctive or "strong" a trademark is, the more legal protection it will receive. Less distinctive or "weak" marks may be entitled to little or no legal protection. Obviously, it is much better to have a strong trademark than a weak one.

Good examples of distinctive marks are arbitrary, fanciful, or coined names such as "Kodak" and "Xerox." Examples of poorly chosen marks include the following:

- Personal names, including nicknames, first names, surnames, and initials.

- Marks that describe the attributes of the product or service or its geographic location. For example, marks such as "Quick Printing" or "Oregon Marketing Research" are initially weak and subject to few legal protections until they have been in use long enough to be easily recognized by customers.

- Names with bad translations, unfortunate homonyms (sound-alikes), or unintended connotations. For example, a French soft drink called "Pschitt" had to be renamed for the U.S. market.

Generally, selecting a mark begins with brainstorming for general ideas. After you have selected several possible marks, your next step may be to use formal or informal market research techniques to see how the potential marks will be accepted by consumers. Then, you have to conduct a trademark search, to find out whether the same or similar marks are already being used.

Registering a Trademark

If you use all or part of your business name or any other name as a trademark or service mark, consider registering it as such (in addition to your state trade or corporate name registration). Trademark registration is not mandatory, but it's a good idea: It makes it easier for you to protect your mark against would-be copiers and puts others on notice that the mark is already taken.

If you do business only in one state, register your mark with your state trademark office. Most local service businesses that don't do business across state lines or sell to interstate travelers fall into this category. If you do business in more than one state, register with the U.S. Patent and Trademark Office (USPTO) in Washington, DC. To register, you must fill out an application and pay a fee. Be prepared to work with your state or federal trademark officials to get your registration approved.

The USPTO has a useful website at www.uspto .gov that contains information about trademarks and trademark registration. You can register your trademark online using the Trademark Electronic Application System (TEAS). TEAS allows you to fill out a trademark registration form and check it for completeness over the Internet. You then submit the form directly to the USPTO over the Internet, making an official filing online. If you don't want to use the Internet, you can call the USPTO at 800-786-9199 to order a trademark registration form, as well as a number of useful publications about trademark registration.

"Intent to Use" Registration

If you intend to use a trademark on a product or for a service sold in more than one state in the near future, you can reserve the right to use the mark by filing an "intent to use" registration with the U.S. Patent and Trademark Office (USPTO).

If the mark is approved, you have six months to actually use the mark on a product sold to the public and file papers with the USPTO describing the use, accompanied by a $100 fee. If necessary, you may extend this period by five additional six-month periods if you have a good explanation for each extension. The ownership becomes effective when you put the mark in use and complete the application process, but ownership will be deemed to have begun on the date you filed the application.

You should file an intent to use registration as soon as you have decided on a trademark for a forthcoming product. Don't delay: Your competitors are trying to come up with good trademarks too and may be considering using a mark like the one you want to use.

Court Clamps Down on Copycats

A Sandusky, Ohio, insurance agent invented the term "securance"—a contraction of the words "security" and "insurance." He used the word as a service mark to market his insurance services on stationery, billboards, newspaper advertisements, and giveaway items such as calendars and pencils. He registered the mark with the State of Ohio and the USPTO. Four years later, the Nationwide Mutual Insurance Company began using the word as its own service mark in its national advertising.

The agent sued the company for trademark infringement and won. The court held that the agent had the exclusive right to use the word "securance" to identify insurance services in the geographic areas in which he did business, because he had been the first to use it. The court ordered the insurer to stop using the word in its advertising in the entire state of Ohio. (*Younker v. Nationwide Mut. Ins. Co.,* 191 N.E.2d 145 (1963).)

RESOURCE

For step-by-step guidance on how to register a trademark, see *Trademark: Legal Care for Your Business & Product Name,* by Stephen Elias (Nolo).

Using a Trademark Notice

The owner of a trademark that has been registered with the U.S. Patent and Trademark Office (USPTO) is entitled to use a special symbol along with the trademark. This symbol notifies the world of the registration. Use of trademark notices is not mandatory but makes it much easier for the trademark owner to collect damages in case of infringement. It also deters others from using the mark.

The most commonly used notice for trademarks registered with the USPTO is an "R" in a circle, or ®, but "Reg. U.S. Pat. & T.M. Off." may also be used. The "TM" superscript, or ™, may be used to denote marks that have been registered on a state basis only or marks that are in use but have not yet been officially registered by the USPTO. Do not use the copyright symbol, or ©, as it has nothing to do with trademarks.

Enforcing Trademark Rights

Depending on the strength of the mark and whether and where it has been registered, a trademark owner may be able to bring a court action to prevent others from using the same or similar marks on competing or related products.

Trademark infringement occurs when an alleged infringer uses a mark that is likely to cause consumers to confuse the infringer's products with the trademark owner's products. A mark need not be identical to one already in use to infringe upon the owner's rights. If the proposed mark is similar enough to the earlier mark to risk confusing the average consumer, its use will likely be infringement.

Choosing an Internet Domain Name

There are millions of business-related sites on the Web. Most businesses have a website, regardless of their size of geographic reach. Many self-employed people have websites as well.

If you want to create a website, you'll have to choose an Internet "domain name"—the site's address on the Web.

What Is a Domain Name?

Every business on the Web has a domain name— a unique address in cyberspace at which a website is located. If you enter a particular domain name in a Web browser, your computer will go to the website at the domain name you entered. Most Web business addresses consist of two main sections: a beginning section containing the letters "www" and a section containing the domain name itself. For example, the domain name for Nolo's website is www.nolo.com.

Clearing a Domain Name

Because each domain name must be unique so that all the computers attached to the Internet can find it, no two different businesses can have the same domain name. If somebody is already using a name you want, you probably won't be able to use it.

It's easy to find out if someone is already using a domain name you want to use. Go to the website www.networksolutions.com and type in the name

you want to use. Then click on "Search." The website will tell you if the name is available or if it is already taken, in which case it will suggest alternatives. To find out who owns the name you want, go to www.networksolutions.com/whois/index.jhtml. Type the domain name in the search field and you can see the registration records for the domain name, including the name and contact information for the name owner. If you have your heart set on a particular domain name that is already taken, you can try to purchase the name from the person or company that owns it.

Registering a Domain Name

If you register your domain name, no one else can use it for the same purpose on the Internet.

Registering a domain name is very easy. There are several private companies that will register a name for you for a small fee. You just go to one of their websites, type in the name you want, and provide your contact information and a credit card number. Two of the best known registration services are Network Solutions, Inc. at www.networksolutions.com and Register.com at www.register.com.

The registration fees these services charge vary, so you might want to check several to see which will give you the best deal.

Conducting a Name Search

Before choosing a trademark or domain name, conduct a name search to see if someone in a related business is already using the same or a similar name. If the name you want is already in use, choose a different name. Obviously, you don't want to spend money on marketing and advertising a name or mark only to discover that it infringes another name or mark and you must change it.

You can hire a search firm to do a trademark search for you, or you can do one yourself.

Hiring a Search Firm

Traditionally, most trademark searches were conducted by specialized trademark search firms at the behest of trademark attorneys who were handling the trademark registration process. Even today, some of the largest trademark search firms refuse to conduct searches for anyone but a lawyer. But most search firms aren't so choosy. They'll conduct a search for anyone willing to pay them.

The services provided by various trademark search firms, and the fees they charge for different types of searches, vary considerably. For this reason, it pays to shop around and compare services and prices.

You can find a trademark search firm by:

- looking in the Yellow Pages under "trademark consultants" or "information brokers"
- consulting legal journals or magazines, which usually contain ads for search firms, or
- doing an Internet search.

Doing a Search on Your Own

As with searching for conflicts with your trade name, many resources are available to help you do all or part of a trademark search yourself, including:

- The U.S. Patent and Trademark Office (USPTO) online trademark database, which may be accessed for free from the USPTO website at www.uspto.gov.
- Numerous private trademark search companies, which will do a search for you for a fee. You can find a list of these on the Yahoo Internet

The Role of Attorneys in Trademark Searches

If you decide to hire a trademark attorney to advise you on choosing and registering a trademark or service mark, the attorney will arrange for the trademark search. Some attorneys do it themselves, but most farm the search out to a search firm.

Once the report comes back from the search firm, the attorney will interpret it for you and advise you on whether to go ahead with your proposed mark. While hiring an attorney means someone else does all the work for you, you will have to pay for this privilege.

directory. Go to www.yahoo.com, click on "Directory" (above the search box), and then enter "trademark services" in the search box and search.

- Patent and Trademark Depository Libraries (PTDLs) located throughout the country. Using a PTDL to do your own federal trademark search may cost you the least money, but it will cost you in time and transportation expenses unless you live or work near one. A list of such libraries can be found at www.uspto .gov/go/ptdl/ptdlib_1.html.

RESOURCE

For more on trademark searches, see *Trademark: Legal Care for Your Business & Product Name*, by Stephen Elias (Nolo). ●

Home Alone or Outside Office?

When you're self-employed, you have the option of working from home or from an outside office. This chapter covers the pros and cons of working from home, paying special attention to zoning and other restrictions and the home office tax deduction. It also covers the benefits and practicalities of renting an outside office.

Pros and Cons of Working at Home

Legally, it makes little difference where you do your work. The basic legal issues discussed in this book (such as deciding on a legal form and name for your business and collecting from clients) are the same whether you run your business from your garage or from the top floor of a high-rise office building. Your choice may, however, affect whether you can deduct your office expenses; otherwise, your taxes will be the same regardless of where you work.

For the most part, the issues to consider when deciding whether to work at home are more practical than legal: whether you can afford to pay office rent, whether a home office is more convenient (such as for child care or to avoid a commute), whether working at home will disrupt your home or neighborhood, and so on.

Benefits of Working at Home

Working at home is popular among the self-employed because it can save time and money and improve productivity.

No Office Rent Expenses

For many self-employed people, the greatest benefit of working at home is that you don't have to pay rent for an office. Office rents vary enormously depending upon the area, but you'll likely have to pay several hundred dollars per month for even a small office. In large cities, you may have to spend much more. Look at the commercial real estate advertising section in your Sunday newspaper to get an idea of going rates.

If you work at home, you can use the money you save in office rent to expand your business or pay your living expenses. And while you can deduct your office rent as a business expense, you may also be able to deduct home office expenses.

One way to reduce the cost of office space is to obtain it from a client that hires you. Many hiring firms are willing to provide independent contractors with desk space. This is particularly likely if having you around will make life easier for them. Some firms may even offer to provide you with office space at no cost to you. However, to safeguard your self-employed status, it's best that you pay something for the space. It doesn't have to be much, and you can charge the client slightly more for your services to cover the cost. Your client shouldn't mind arranging things this way, because it will help the client if the IRS conducts an audit and questions your status.

No Commuting Time or Expenses

Working at home means you don't have to commute to an outside office every day. The American Automobile Association estimated that it cost 62¢ per mile to drive a car in 2007. Using this figure, if working at home allows you to drive 6,000 fewer miles per year (500 miles per month), you'd save $3,720 per year.

Not having to commute also saves you time. If you commute just 30 minutes each day, you're spending 120 hours each year behind the wheel of your car. That's three full 40-hour weeks that you could use earning money in your home office.

You Can Deduct Some Commuting Costs

When you have an outside office, you can't deduct your commuting expenses—that is, what it costs to get from your home to your office and back again. However, if your main office is at home, you may deduct the cost of driving from home to meet clients or to other locations to conduct business.

You Can Deduct Home Office Expenses

If you arrange things correctly, you can deduct your home office expenses—including a portion of your home rent or mortgage payment, utilities, and other expenses. The home office deduction is covered in detail later in this chapter.

The home office deduction is particularly valuable if you rent your home. It enables you to deduct a portion of what is likely your largest single expense (your rent), an item that is not ordinarily deductible from your personal income tax.

Benefits Other Than Money

Of course, the benefits of working at home are not just monetary. For many self-employed people, other factors are equally valuable, such as the increased flexibility they have over their daily schedule. You can, if you wish, work in the evenings or late at night in your pajamas—something that can be difficult to do if you're renting an office!

When you work at home, it's also easier to deal with child-care issues and household chores and errands. You may also have more contact with your family.

Drawbacks of Working at Home

There are, however, potential drawbacks to working from home. Fortunately, there are usually things you can do to avoid or ameliorate the problems.

Clients Don't Take You Seriously

The major problem many self-employed people who work at home say they have is that clients don't take them seriously. Some clients may be reluctant to deal with a home-based business-person. This can make it harder for you to get your business established.

There are many things you can do to help create and maintain a professional image. For example:

- Obtain a separate telephone line for your business and use it only for business calls.
- Use an answering service to answer your business phone when you're not home.
- Obtain and use professional-looking business cards, envelopes, and stationery.
- Hold meetings at clients' offices instead of at your home.
- Rent a mailbox to receive your business mail instead of using your home address.
- Use an assumed name for your business rather than your own name (see Chapter 3).
- Consider incorporating or forming a limited liability company so that clients will be hiring a business, not you personally (see Chapter 2).

Restrictions on Home-Based Businesses

Another major problem for the home-based self-employed is restrictions on home businesses imposed by cities, condominium associations, and deed restrictions. It may actually be illegal for you to work at home. These restrictions are explained later in this chapter.

Obtaining Services Can Be Difficult

Businesses that provide services to other businesses sometimes discriminate against those who work at home. For example, UPS charges more for deliveries to a home business than to an outside business office. And many temporary agencies won't deal with a home-based business because they're afraid they won't get paid.

Lack of Security

Your home is likely not as secure as an office building that is filled with people, has burglar alarms, employs security guards, or has security cameras. If you're handling large amounts of cash or other valuable items, you may prefer to work in a more secure environment than your home.

However, there are many commonsense precautions you can take to make your home office more secure. For example:

- Rent a post office box to receive your mail instead of having it delivered to your home.
- Refuse to let equipment servicers or vendors visit without an appointment.
- Obtain good locks and use them.
- Exercise caution when communicating about your absence (for example, if you have a separate business phone line, don't leave an outgoing telephone message like, "I will be on vacation for a week").

Isolation, Interruptions, and Other Factors

Finally, some people have trouble adapting to working at home because of the isolation. They miss the social interaction of a formal office setting. However, renting an outside office where you'll be all by yourself won't necessarily end the isolation problem.

In contrast, other self-employed people find it difficult to get any work done at home because of a lack of privacy or interruptions from children and other family members. Others gain weight because the refrigerator is always nearby or end up watching television instead of working.

Most of the millions of self-employed people who work at home, however, are not fazed by these problems.

Businesses Well Suited to Home Offices

Home offices can work well for any business that is normally done in a simple office setting. This includes a multitude of service businesses—for example:

- desktop publishing
- accounting or bookkeeping
- computer programming
- consulting
- writing or editing
- telemarketing
- graphic artwork, and
- financial planning.

A home office is also an ideal choice for businesses that do work primarily at clients' offices or other outside locations—for example:

- building contracting
- traveling sales
- house and carpet cleaning
- home repair work
- courier or limousine service
- piano tuning
- pool cleaning
- hazardous waste inspection, and
- catering.

Businesses Poorly Suited to Home Offices

Any business that will disrupt your household or neighborhood is not well suited for the home. These include businesses that generate substantial amounts of noise, pollution, or waste.

A home office is not your best choice if substantial numbers of clients or customers must visit you in your office. This could create traffic and parking problems in your neighborhood and cause neighbors to complain. One possible solution to this problem is to rent an office part time or by the hour just to meet clients. Such rentals are available in many cities and will be cheaper than renting a full-time office. Look in your Yellow Pages under "office rentals" or "business identity programs."

You may also have problems if your business requires you to store a substantial amount of inventory. However, you can still spend most of your time at home by renting a separate storage space for your inventory.

Finally, a home office may not work well if you need to have several employees working with you. This could cause parking problems in your neighborhood and space problems in your home. Moreover, many local zoning laws prevent home businesses from having more than one or two employees. One way around this problem is to allow your employees to work from their own homes, too.

Restrictions on Home-Based Businesses

If you decide to work at home, you may have issues with local zoning laws, land use restrictions in your lease, or condominium rules. You should investigate these potential problems before you open your home office. Even if your community is unfriendly to home offices, there are many things you can do to avoid problems before they arise.

Zoning Restrictions

Municipalities have the legal right to establish rules on the types of activities you can conduct in their different geographical areas. For example, they often establish commercial zones for stores and offices, industrial zones for factories, and residential zones for houses and apartments.

Though some communities have no zoning restrictions at all (for example, Houston), most do. These restrictions often include laws that limit the kinds of business you can conduct in a residential zone. The purpose of these restrictions is to help maintain the peace and quiet of residential neighborhoods.

Fortunately, while some communities remain hostile to home businesses, the growing trend across the country is to permit them. Many cities—Los Angeles and Phoenix, for example—have updated their zoning laws to permit many home businesses.

Research Your Local Zoning Ordinance

Your first step to determine whether you might have a problem working at home is to read your local zoning ordinance carefully. Get a copy from your city's or county's website, your city or county clerk's office, or your public library.

Zoning ordinances that limit businesses in residential areas are worded in many different ways. Some are extremely vague, allowing "customary home-based occupations." Others allow homeowners to use their houses for a wide but unspecific array of business purposes—for example, "professions and domestic occupations, crafts, and services." Still others contain a detailed list of approved occupations, such as "law, dentistry, medicine, music lessons, photography, [and] cabinetmaking."

Ordinances permitting home-based businesses typically include detailed regulations on how to carry out business activities. These regulations vary widely, but the most common ones limit your use of on-street signs, car and truck traffic, and the number of employees who can work at your house on a regular basis (some prohibit employees altogether). Some ordinances also limit the percentage of your home's floorspace that you can devote to your business. Study your ordinance carefully to see how these rules apply to you. If you still aren't sure whether your business is allowed, you may be tempted to discuss the matter with zoning or planning officials. However, until you figure out the rules and politics of your locality, gather information without identifying or calling attention to yourself. For example, have a friend who lives nearby make general inquiries.

Hard Lobbying Can Pay Off

If your town has an unduly restrictive zoning ordinance, you can try to get it changed. For example, a self-employed person in the town of Melbourne, Florida, was surprised to discover that his local zoning ordinance barred home-based businesses. He decided to try to change the law.

He sent letters to his local public officials but got no response. He then reviewed the zoning ordinances favoring home offices from nearby communities and drafted an ordinance that he presented to the city council. He enlisted support from a local home business association and got a major story about his battle printed in the local newspaper. After several hearings, the city council voted unanimously to amend the zoning ordinance to allow home offices.

Determine The Attitude Toward Enforcement

Even if your locality has restrictive zoning laws, you won't necessarily have problems with your home business. In most communities, such laws are rarely enforced unless one of your neighbors complains to local officials. Neighbors usually complain because you make a lot of noise or have large numbers of clients, employees, or delivery people coming and going, causing parking or traffic problems. If you're unobtrusive—for example, you work quietly in your home office all day and rarely receive business visitors—it's unlikely that your neighbors will complain (or even notice).

Unfortunately, some communities are extremely hostile toward home businesses and actively try to prevent them. This is most likely to be the case if you live in an upscale, purely residential community. Even if you're unobtrusive, these communities may bar you from working at home if they discover what you're up to. If you live in such a community, you'll need to factor this into the decision of whether to work from home:

You'll really need to keep your head down to avoid discovery.

To determine your community's enforcement style, talk to your local chamber of commerce and other self-employed people in your town. Friends or neighbors who are actively involved with your local government may also be good resources.

Keeping Your Home Business Unobtrusive

There are many ways to keep your home business unobtrusive so as to ward off neighbor complaints. If you get a lot of deliveries, arrange for mail and packages to be received by a private mailbox service such as Mail Boxes, Etc. Don't put your home address on your stationery and business cards. Also, try to visit your clients in their offices instead of having them come to your home office.

A husband and wife team of psychiatrists who ran a 24-hour group therapy practice in a quiet neighborhood of Victorian homes provide a perfect example of how to get neighbors to complain about a home office: They paved every inch of their yard for parking and installed huge lights to illuminate the entire property.

Inform Your Neighbors

Good neighbor relations are the key to avoiding zoning problems. You may want to tell your neighbors about your plans to start a home business so they'll know what to expect and will have the chance to air their concerns to you directly. Explain that there are advantages for them to you working at home—for example, having someone home during the day could improve security for the neighborhood. You might even offer to meet a neighbor's repairperson or accept his or her packages. If any of your neighbors stay home during the day, try to be particularly helpful to them because they are more likely to complain about a home office than neighbors who spend their days at work.

On the other hand, if your relations with your neighbors are already shaky or you happen to be surrounded by unreasonable people, you may be better off not telling them you work at home. If you're inconspicuous and do not cause problems, they may never know what you're doing.

If Your Neighbors Complain

If your neighbors complain about your home office, you'll probably have to deal with your local zoning bureaucracy. If local zoning officials decide you should close your home business, they'll first send you a letter ordering you to do so. If you ignore this and any subsequent letters, they may file a civil lawsuit against you seeking an injunction—that is, a court order that enjoins (stops) you from operating your home business in violation of the zoning ordinance. If you violate such an injunction, a judge can fine you or even put you in jail.

Immediately after receiving the first letter from zoning officials, talk with the person at city hall who administers the zoning law, usually someone in the zoning or planning department. City officials may drop the matter if you'll agree to make your home business less obtrusive.

If this doesn't work, apply to your planning or zoning board for a "variance": an exception that lets you violate the zoning ordinance. To obtain a variance, you'll need to show that your business does no harm to your neighborhood and that relocation would deprive you of your livelihood. Be prepared to answer the objections of unhappy neighbors who may loudly oppose the proposed variance at the planning commission meeting.

You can also try to get your city council or zoning board to change the local zoning ordinance. To do this, you'll probably have to lobby some city council members or planning commissioners. It will be useful to enlist the support of the local

Home-Based Entrepreneur Fights City Hall—and Wins

Many self-employed people have successfully fought rulings that their home businesses violate local zoning laws. For example, Judy ran a theatrical costume business from her home in Los Angeles for several years. She never received any complaints from her neighbors about her business, but someone with a grudge against her alerted the Los Angeles Building Department that Judy was operating a home business in violation of the Los Angeles zoning ordinance.

The Building Department sent an inspector to look at her property. He handed her an order on the spot that required her to stop doing business at home. Judy decided to fight. She applied for a zoning variance from the Los Angeles Planning Commission but was turned down after a hearing.

Refusing to take no for an answer, Judy appealed to the Los Angeles Zoning Appeals Board. She was prepared for the appeal and enlisted the support of her neighbors. She was head of the Neighborhood Watch—a group of volunteers dedicated to keeping the locale safe—so she already knew most of them. Nearly 140 neighbors signed a petition urging the board to permit her home office; several also wrote letters to the board.

Judy drew a map of her property and took pictures to show that her home business did not disrupt the neighborhood. She also conducted a neighborhood traffic survey, which showed that her business did not increase traffic substantially in the neighborhood.

The appeals board was so impressed by her evidence that it granted her one of the first variances ever for a home office in Los Angeles.

chamber of commerce and other business groups. Try to get your neighbors to help as well—for example, have as many of them as possible sign a petition favoring the zoning change. Many people with home offices are organizing on local, state, and national levels to lobby for new zoning laws that permit home offices.

Finally, you can take the matter to court, claiming that the local zoning ordinance is invalid or that the city has misinterpreted it. You'll probably need the help of a lawyer familiar with zoning matters to do this.

RESOURCE

For detailed guidance on how to handle neighbor disputes, including disputes over home-based businesses, see *Neighbor Law: Fences, Trees, Boundaries & Noise*, by Cora Jordan (Nolo).

Private Land Use Restrictions

The government uses zoning laws to restrict how you can use your property. However, there may also be private restrictions on how you can use your home. Restrictions are commonly found in:

- property deeds
- homeowner association rules, or
- leases.

Property Deed Restrictions

Property deeds often contain restrictions, called "restrictive covenants," limiting how you can use your property. Restrictive covenants often bar or limit the use of home-based business offices.

You can find out if your property is subject to such restrictions by reading your title insurance policy or deed. If your neighbors believe you're violating these restrictions, they can take action in court to stop you. Such restrictions are usually enforced by the courts unless they are unreasonable or the character of the neighborhood has changed so much since they were written that it makes no sense to enforce them.

Restrictions Strictly Enforced

Sheldon and Raye Isenberg, both psychiatrists, purchased a home in an Illinois subdivision. Their deed contained a restrictive covenant providing that "no lot shall be used except for single residential purposes."

Sheldon and Raye together saw about 30 patients per week at their home. However, there seemed to be little or no disruption of the neighborhood. The patients never came late at night or on the weekends, and they parked in the Isenbergs' driveway, not on the street. No one who had a criminal or drug use record or who might endanger others was permitted to come to the Isenbergs' home.

The only problem that ever occurred was when two patients mistook a neighbor's house for the Isenbergs' and the neighbor spotted them in his yard. Nevertheless, several of the Isenbergs' neighbors took them to court, claiming they violated the express words of the restrictive covenant. The judge found that the restrictive covenant was valid and ordered the Isenbergs to stop using their home as an office. (*Wier v. Isenberg*, 420 N.E.2d 790 (Ill. App. 1981).)

Homeowners' Association Rules

One in six Americans lives in a planned community that has a homeowners' association. When you buy property in such a development, you automatically become a member of the homeowners' association—and you become subject to its rules, which are usually set forth in a lengthy document called "Covenants, Conditions, and Restrictions" (CC&Rs). CC&Rs often regulate, in minute detail, what you can do on, in, and to your property. The homeowners' association is in charge of modifying and enforcing these rules.

The CC&Rs for many developments specifically bar home-based business offices. The homeowners' association may be able to impose fines and other penalties against you if your home business violates the rules. It could also sue you in court to get money damages or other penalties. Some homeowners' associations are very strict about enforcing their rules against home businesses while others are less so.

Carefully study the CC&Rs before you buy into a condominium, planned development, or cooperative to see if home-based business offices are prohibited. If so, you may want to buy somewhere else.

If you're already in a development that bars home-based business offices, you may be able to avoid problems if you're unobtrusive and your neighbors are unaware that you have a home office. However, the best course may be to seek to change the CC&Rs. Most homeowner associations rule through a board of directors whose members are elected by all the members of the association. Lobby members of the board about changing the rules to permit home offices. If that fails, you and like-minded neighbors could try to get seats on the board and gain a voice in the association's policymaking.

Lease Restrictions

If you're a renter, check your lease before you start your home business. Many standard lease forms prohibit tenants from conducting a business on the premises—or prohibit certain types of businesses. Your landlord could evict you if you violate such a lease provision.

Most landlords don't want to evict their tenants. Many don't care what you do on your premises as long as it doesn't disturb your neighbors or cause damage. Keep up good neighbor relations to prevent complaints.

However, if you have business visitors, your landlord may require you to obtain liability insurance in case a visitor has an accident such as a trip or fall on the premises. (See Chapter 6.)

Deducting Your Home Office Expenses

If you elect to work from home, the federal government allows you to deduct your home office expenses from your income taxes. This is so whether you own or rent your home. Although this tax deduction is commonly called the "home office deduction," it is not limited to home offices. You can also take it if, for example, you have a workshop or studio at home.

Even if you've heard stories about how difficult it is to qualify for the home office deduction, don't dismiss it immediately. Changes in the tax law that took effect in 1999 made it much easier for many self-employed people to qualify for the deduction. Even if you haven't qualified for the deduction in the past, you may be entitled to it now.

Because some people claim that the home office deduction is an audit flag for the IRS, many self-employed people who may qualify for it are afraid to take it. Although taking the home office deduction might increase your chance of being audited, the chances are still relatively small. Also, you have nothing to fear from an audit if you're entitled to the deduction.

However, if you intend to take the deduction, you should also make the effort to understand the requirements and set up your home office so as to satisfy them. Before you start moving your furniture around, read on.

Sideline Business May Qualify for Home Office Deduction

You don't have to work full time in a business to qualify for the home office deduction. If you satisfy the requirements, you can take the deduction for a sideline business you run from a home office. However, the total amount you deduct cannot exceed your income from the business.

EXAMPLE: Barbara works full time as an editor for a publishing company. An avid bowler, she also spends about 15 hours a week writing and publishing a bowling newsletter. She does all the work on the newsletter from an office in her apartment. Barbara may take the home office deduction. But she can't deduct more than she earns as income from the newsletter.

Regular and Exclusive Business Use

You can't take the home office deduction unless you *regularly* use part of your home *exclusively* for a trade or business.

Unfortunately, the IRS doesn't offer a clear definition of "regular use." The only guidance the agency offers is that you must use a portion of your home for business on a continuing basis—not just for occasional or incidental business. You'll likely satisfy this test if you use your home office a few hours each day.

"Exclusive use" means that you use a portion of your home *only* for business. If you use part of your home as your business office and also use that part for personal purposes, you cannot meet the test of exclusive use and cannot take the home office deduction.

EXAMPLE:

Johnny, an accountant, has a den at home furnished with a desk, chair, bookshelf, filing cabinet, and sofa. He uses the desk and chair for both business and personal reasons. The bookshelf contains both personal and business books, and the filing cabinet contains both personal and business files. He does both business and personal reading on the sofa. Johnny cannot claim a business deduction for the den because it is not used exclusively for business purposes.

You needn't devote an entire separate room in your home to your business. But some part of the room must be used exclusively for business.

EXAMPLE:

Paul, an accountant, keeps his desk, chair, bookshelf, and filing cabinet in one part of his den and uses them exclusively for business. He uses the remainder of the room—one-third of the space—to store a bed for house guests. Paul can take a home office deduction for the two-thirds of the room used exclusively as an office.

As a practical matter, the IRS isn't going to make a surprise inspection of your home to see whether you're complying with these requirements. However, complying with the rules from the beginning avoids having to lie to the IRS if you are audited.

This means, simply, that you'll have to arrange your furniture and belongings so as to devote a portion of your home exclusively to your home office. The more space you use exclusively for business, the more your home office deduction will be worth.

Although not explicitly required by law, it's a good idea to physically separate the space you use for business from the rest of the room. For example, if you use part of your living room as an office, separate it from the rest of the room with room dividers or bookcases.

Qualifying for the Deduction

Unfortunately, satisfying the requirement of using your home office regularly and exclusively for business is only half the battle.

You must also meet one of these three requirements:

- your home office must be your principal place of business
- you must meet clients or customers at home, or
- you must use a separate structure on your property exclusively for business purposes.

Ways to Solidify Home Office Deduction

Here are some ways to convince the IRS that you qualify for the home office deduction:

- Take a picture of your home office and draw up a diagram showing your home office as a portion of your home.
- Have all your business mail sent to your home office.
- Use your home office address on all your business cards, stationery, and advertising.
- Obtain a separate phone line for your business and keep that phone in your home office. You can deduct the monthly fee for a second phone line in your home (including a cell phone) if you use it for business. You can't deduct the monthly fee for a single phone line, even if you use it partly for business, although you can deduct the cost of business calls you place from that line.
- Encourage clients or customers to regularly visit your home office and keep a log of their visits.
- To make the most of the time you spend in your home office, communicate with clients by phone, fax, or email instead of going to their offices. Use a mail or messenger service to deliver your work to customers.
- Keep a log of the time you spend working in your home office. This doesn't have to be fancy: Notes on your calendar will do.

Home as Principal Place of Business

The most common way to qualify for the home office deduction is to use your home as your principal place of business. Indeed, most self-employed people will be able to qualify for the home office deduction on this basis.

If You Do Most of Your Work at Home

If, like many self-employed people, you do all or most of your work in your home office, your home is your principal place of business. You should have no trouble qualifying for the home office deduction. This would be the case, for example, for a writer who does most of his or her writing at home or a salesperson who sells by phone and makes most of his or her sales calls from home.

If You Do Only Administrative Work at Home

Of course, many people who work for themselves spend the bulk of their time working away from home. This is the case, for example, for:

- building contractors who work primarily on building sites
- travelling salespeople who visit clients at their places of business, and
- house painters, gardeners, and home repair people who work primarily in their customers' homes.

Fortunately, even if you work primarily outside your home, your home office will qualify as your principal place of business if:

- you use the office to conduct administrative or management activities for your business, and
- there is no other fixed location where you conduct such activities.

What this means is that to qualify for the home office deduction, your home office does not need to be the place where you generate most of your business income. It's sufficient that you use it regularly to administer or manage your business—for example, to keep your books, schedule appointments, do research, and order supplies. As long as you have no other fixed location where you regularly do such things (an outside office), you can take the deduction.

EXAMPLE:

Sally, a handyperson, performs home repair work for clients in their homes. She also has a home office that she uses regularly and exclusively to keep her books, arrange appointments, and order supplies. Sally is entitled to a home office deduction.

You don't have to personally perform at home all the administrative or management activities your business requires to qualify for the home office deduction. Your home office can qualify for the deduction even if:

- you have others conduct your administrative or management activities at locations other than your home—for example, another company does your billing from its place of business

- you conduct administrative or management activities at places that are not fixed locations for your business, such as in a car or a hotel room, or

- you occasionally conduct minimal administrative or management activities at a fixed location outside your home, such as your outside office.

Meeting Clients or Customers at Home

Even if your home office is not your principal place of business, you may deduct your expenses for the part of your home used exclusively to meet with clients, customers, or patients. You must physically meet with others at home; phoning them from home is not sufficient. And the meetings must be a regular part of your business—occasional meetings don't qualify.

There is no numerical standard for how often you must meet clients at home for those meetings to be considered regular. However, the IRS has indicated that meeting clients one or two days a week is sufficient. Again, exclusive use means that you use the space where you meet clients only for business. You are free to use the space for business purposes other than meeting clients—for example, doing your business bookkeeping or other paperwork. But you cannot use the space for personal purposes such as watching television.

EXAMPLE:

June, an attorney, works three days a week in her city office and two days in her home office, which she uses only for business. She meets clients at her home office at least once a week. Because she regularly meets clients at her home office, it qualifies for the home office deduction, even though her city office is her principal place of business.

If you want to qualify for this deduction, encourage clients or customers to visit you at home. Keep a log or appointment book showing all their visits.

Using a Garage or Other Separate Structure for Business

You can also deduct expenses for a separate freestanding structure, such as a studio, garage, or barn, if you use it exclusively and regularly for your business. The structure does not have to be your principal place of business or a place where you meet patients, clients, or customers.

As always, when the home office deduction is involved, exclusive use means you use the structure only for business—for example, you can't use it to store gardening equipment or as a guest house. Regular use is not precisely defined but it's probably sufficient for you to use the structure ten or 15 hours a week.

EXAMPLE:

Deborah is a freelance graphic designer. She has her main office in an industrial park but also works every weekend in a small studio in her backyard. Because she uses the studio regularly and exclusively for her design work, it qualifies for the home office deduction.

Storing Inventory or Product Samples at Home

You can take the home office deduction if you're in the business of selling retail or wholesale products and you store inventory or product samples at home. To qualify, you can't have an office or other business location outside your home. And you must store your inventory at a particular place in your home—for example, a garage, closet, or bedroom. You can't move your inventory from one room to another. You don't have to use the storage space exclusively to store your inventory to take the deduction. It's sufficient that you regularly use it for that purpose.

EXAMPLE: Janet sells costume jewelry door to door. She rents a home and regularly uses half of her attached garage to store her jewelry inventory. She also uses it to park her Harley Davidson motorcycle. Janet can deduct the expenses for the storage space even though she does not use her garage exclusively to store inventory. Her garage accounts for 20% of the total floor space of her house. Because she uses only half of the garage for storing inventory, she may deduct one half of this, or 10%, of her rent and certain other expenses.

Amount of Deduction

To figure out the amount of the home office deduction, you need to determine what percentage of your home you use for business. To do this, divide the square footage of your home office by the total square footage of your home. For example, if your home is 1,600 square feet and you use 400 square feet for your home office, you use 25% of the total area for business.

Or if all the rooms in your home are about the same size, figure the business portion by dividing the number of rooms used for business by the number of rooms in the home. For example, if you use one room in a five-room house for business, you use 20% of the area for business. Claiming 20% to 25% of your home as a home office is perfectly acceptable. However, claiming anything over 40% will likely raise questions with the IRS (unless you store inventory at home).

The home office deduction is not one deduction, but many. First, you are entitled to deduct from your gross income the percentage you use for you home office of:

- your rent if you rent your home, or
- depreciation, mortgage interest, and property taxes if you own your home.

In addition, you may deduct this same percentage of other expenses for keeping up and running an entire home. The IRS calls these indirect expenses. They include:

- utility expenses for electricity, gas, heat, and trash removal
- homeowner's or renter's insurance
- home maintenance expenses that benefit your entire home, including your home office—for example, roof and furnace repairs or exterior painting
- condominium association fees
- snow-removal expenses

- casualty losses if your home is damaged—for example, in a storm, and

- security system costs.

You may also deduct the entire cost of expenses solely for your home office. The IRS calls these direct expenses. They include, for example, painting your home office or paying someone to clean it. If you pay a housekeeper to clean your entire house, you may deduct your business use percentage of the expense.

EXAMPLE:

Jean rents a 1,600-square-foot apartment and uses a 400-square-foot room as a home office for her consulting business. Her percentage of business use is 25% (400 ÷ 1,600). She pays $12,000 in annual rent and has a $1,200 utility bill for the year. She also spent $200 to paint her home office. She is entitled to deduct 25% of her rent and utilities ($3,300) plus the entire cost of painting her office, for a total home office deduction of $3,500.

Be sure to keep copies of all your bills and receipts for home office expenses, including:

- IRS Form 1098 sent by whoever holds your mortgage, showing the interest you paid on your mortgage for the year

- property tax bills and your canceled payment checks

- utility bills, insurance bills, and receipts for repairs to your office area and your canceled payments checks, and

- your lease and your canceled rent checks, if you're a renter.

The home office deduction can be very valuable if you're a renter because you get to deduct part of your rent—a substantial expense that is not ordinarily deductible.

If you own your home, the home office deduction is worth less because you're already allowed to

deduct your mortgage interest and property taxes from your income tax. But taking the home office deduction will allow you to deduct these items from your self-employment taxes. You'll save $153 in self-employment taxes for every $1,000 in mortgage interest and property taxes you deduct. You'll also be able to deduct a portion of repairs, utility bills, cleaning and maintenance costs, and depreciation.

Depreciating Office Furniture and Other Personal Property

Whether or not you qualify for or take the home office deduction, you can depreciate or expense (under Section 179) the cost of office furniture, computers, copiers, fax machines, and other personal property you use for your business in your home office. You deduct these costs directly on your Schedule C, *Profit or Loss From Business*. You do not have to list them on the special tax form used for the home office deduction.

If you use the property for both business and personal reasons, the IRS requires you to keep records showing when the item was used for business and when for personal reasons—for example, a diary or log with the dates, times, and reason the item was used. (See Chapter 14.)

Profit Limit for Deductions

There is an important limitation on taking the home office deduction: It may not exceed the net profit you earn from your home office in that year. If you run a successful business out of your home office, this limitation isn't a problem, because your profits will exceed your deductions. But if your business earns very little money or even loses money, this could prevent you from deducting part or all of your home office expenses in a given year.

If your deductions exceed your profits in a particular year, you can, however, deduct this excess in the following year and in each succeeding year until you deduct the entire amount. There is no limit on how far into the future you can deduct these expenses: You can claim them even if you are no longer living in the home where they were incurred.

So, whether or not your business is making money, you should keep track of your home office expenses and claim the deduction on your tax return. You do this by filing IRS Form 8829. When you plug in the numbers for your business income and home office expenses and complete the form, it will show you how much you can deduct in the current year and how much you must carry over to the next year.

This limitation applies to the home office deduction only; it does not apply to business expenses that you can deduct under other provisions of the tax code. Your "net profit" for calculating your home business deduction limit is the gross income you earn from your business minus your business deductions other than your home office deduction. You must also subtract the home office portion of any mortgage interest, real estate taxes, and casualty losses you incurred.

Tax preparation software can calculate your net profit for home office deduction purposes, but it's a good idea to understand how it works. First, start with your gross income from your business. If you sell goods, this is the total sales of your business minus the cost of goods sold; if you sell services, it's all the money you earn. List this amount on line 7 of your Schedule C.

Next, figure out how much money you earned from your home office. If you do all of your work at home, this will be 100% of your gross business income. But if you work in several locations, you must determine what portion of your gross income came from working in your home office. To do this, consider how much time you spend working in your home office and the type of work you do there.

Once you have determined the amount of gross profit you earned from your home office, you must subtract from this amount business expenses for which you will take other deductions on your tax return, including:

- the home office percentage of your mortgage interest and real estate taxes (if you own your home), plus any casualty losses, and
- all of your business expenses that are not part of the home office deduction, even if you incurred them while doing business at home—meaning all the deductions you listed in Part II of your Schedule C (car expenses, business travel, insurance, depreciation of business equipment, business phone, supplies, salaries, and so on).

The remainder is your net profit—the most you can deduct for using your home office.

EXAMPLE:

Sam runs a part-time consulting business out of his home office, which occupies 20% of his home. In one year, his gross income from the business was $4,000, and he had $1,000 in expenses separate from his home office deduction. He paid $10,000 in mortgage interest and real estate taxes for the year. His home office deduction for the year is limited to $1,000. He calculates this as follows:

Gross income from business:	$4,000
Minus business portion of mortgage interest and taxes ($10,000 x 20%)	– $2,000
Balance:	$2,000
Minus direct business expenses:	–$1,000
Home office deduction limitation:	$1,000

Sam's total home office expenses for the year amount to $4,000, including $2,000 in mortgage interest and real estate taxes, plus $2,000 in other expenses, such as utilities and depreciation of his home. Sam first deducts those home office expenses that are not deductible as personal itemized deductions—everything other than mortgage interest, real estate taxes, and casualty losses. These expenses were $2,000. He may deduct only $1,000 of this amount because his home office deduction profit limit is $1,000. Because he has reached his profit limit, Sam can't deduct as a home office deduction any portion of his $2,000 mortgage interest and real estate tax expenses. However, he may deduct the entire amounts of these ($10,000 that includes the home business portion) as personal itemized deductions on Schedule A. Sam may deduct the $1,000 in unused home office expenses the following year, if he has sufficient income from his business.

Special Concerns for Homeowners

In the past, homeowners who took the home office deduction were subject to a special tax trap: If they took a home office deduction for more than three of the five years before they sold their home, they had to pay capital gains taxes on the home office portion of the profit they made from the sale. For example, if you made a $50,000 profit on the sale of your house, but your home office took up 20% of the space, you would have had to pay this tax on $10,000 of your profit (20% x $50,000 = $10,000).

Fortunately, IRS rules no longer require this. As long as you live in your home for at least two of the five years before you sell it, the profit you make on the sale—up to $250,000 for single taxpayers and $500,000 for married taxpayers filing jointly—is not taxable. However, you will have to pay a capital gains tax on the depreciation deductions you took after May 6, 1997, for your home office. This is taxed at a 25% rate (unless your income tax bracket is lower than 25%).

EXAMPLE:

In 2004, Sally bought a home for $200,000 and used one of the rooms as her home office. She sells her home in 2008 for $300,000, realizing a $100,000 gain (profit). The depreciation deductions she had taken for her home office between 2004 and 2008 amounted to $2,000. She must pay a tax of 25% of $2,000, or $500.

IRS Reporting Requirements

All unincorporated taxpayers who take the home office deduction must file IRS Form 8829 with their tax returns. Renters who take the deduction must also file Form 1099-MISC.

IRS Form 8829

If you qualify for the home office deduction and are a sole proprietor or partner in a partnership, you must file IRS Form 8829, *Expenses for Business Use of Your Home*, along with your personal tax return. The form alerts the IRS that you're taking the deduction and shows how you calculated it. You should file this form even if you're not allowed to deduct your home office expenses (because your business had little or no profits). By filing, you can apply the deduction to a future year in which you earn a profit.

If you organize your business as an S corporation instead of a sole proprietorship or partnership, you don't have to file Form 8829. This is one of the major advantages of forming an S corporation. Filing Form 8829 calls your home office deduction to the attention of the IRS. If you can avoid filing it, you are less likely to face an audit.

RESOURCE

For additional information, see IRS Publication 587, *Business Use of Your Home.* You can obtain this and all other IRS publications by calling the IRS at 800-TAX-FORM, visiting your local IRS office, or downloading the publications from the IRS website at www.irs.gov.

Filing Requirement for Renters

If you're a renter and take the home office deduction, you should file an IRS Form 1099-MISC each year, reporting the amount of your rental payments attributable to your home office.

EXAMPLE:

Bill rents a house and takes the home office deduction. He spends $12,000 per year on rent and uses 25% of his house as a home office. He should file Form 1099 reporting $3,000 of his rental payments.

You should file three copies of Form 1099:

- File one copy with the IRS by February 28.
- Give one copy to your landlord by January 31.
- File one copy with your state tax department, if your state has income taxes. (See Chapter 9.)

Your landlord may not appreciate receiving a Form 1099 from you, but it is helpful if you're audited by the IRS and your home office deduction is questioned, because it shows you were really conducting a business out of your home.

Form 1099 is not required if your landlord is a corporation. (Form 1099 need not be filed for payments to corporations.) Form 1099 is also not required in the unlikely event that your rental payments for your home office total less than $600 for the year.

Pros and Cons of an Outside Office

While there are obviously benefits to having a home office, there are benefits to having an outside office, too. It can help establish your credibility and provide a more professional setting for meeting clients or customers than a home office. And it can help you keep your home and work lives separate and may enable you to work more efficiently. Renting an outside office will also help establish that you are self-employed if you're audited by the IRS or your state tax department. (See Chapter 15.)

The drawbacks of having an outside office are the flipside of the benefits of having a home office. You must pay rent for your office and drive to and from it every day. You won't be entitled to a home office deduction, although you can deduct your outside office rent, utilities, commuting costs, and other expenses. You also lose much of the flexibility afforded by a home office.

Leasing a Workplace

If you decide against working at home, you'll most likely have to rent an outside office or workspace. If you rent a space for your business activities, you'll be renting commercial property, not residential property, and you'll be signing a commercial lease. Renting commercial space is not like renting an apartment or house; it's a business transaction. As a businessperson, you are presumed to be an adult who can protect yourself. For this reason, few of the consumer protection laws that protect residential tenants—for example, caps on security deposits—apply to commercial leases.

Despite what a prospective commercial landlord might say, there are no "standard" commercial lease forms. This means that you can negotiate virtually every term in the lease to suit your needs. This section provides an overview of the key elements you will need to negotiate with the landlord before you sign a commercial lease. However, for a detailed, step-by-step explanation of everything you should know, refer to *Negotiate the Best Lease for Your Business*, by Janet Portman and Fred Steingold (Nolo).

Rent

Probably foremost in your mind is the amount you will have to pay for your workspace. Depending on the commercial rental market in your area, your rent may be highly negotiable. Commercial rent is typically charged by the square foot—for example, $10 per square foot. When negotiating your rental term, find out how the square footage for which you will be charged is determined—for example, does it include common areas such as hallways, elevators, and restrooms?

In addition to negotiating the amount of rent and square footage, you should understand exactly what your rent will cover. There are two basic types of commercial leases: a net lease and a gross lease. In a net lease, your rent pays for your right to occupy the space only; you must pay for maintenance, insurance, and property taxes separately. In a gross lease, your payment to the landlord covers all of these things—rent, maintenance, insurance, and taxes.

Often a commercial lease includes a formula for increases to your rent—for example, an increase of a set amount each year or an increase tied to the Consumer Price Index (CPI).

Term

You can also negotiate the "term," or how long the lease will last, usually anywhere from 30 days to many years. A short-term lease of no more than six months to one year is probably best when you're starting out. If you think you might want to stay longer but want to play it safe, you can include an option to renew if you choose to stay after the term expires. That way, the landlord can't evict you merely because you reached the end of your lease term.

Security Deposit

Just as you would for an apartment, you will have to provide a security deposit for your commercial space. You should negotiate the amount of the deposit and when it will be returned to you. Try to get the landlord to agree to a lease provision that returns a portion of the deposit to you if you pay rent on time for one year.

Permitted Uses

Commercial leases typically include a clause that provides how you may use the property. Again, like the other clauses discussed in this section, you can negotiate this clause so that the permitted uses suit your needs.

A permitted-uses clause is written in one of two ways: Either it lists everything you're forbidden to do, which means you're free to do anything not on the list, or it lists all the ways you are permitted to use the property, which means your intended use must be specifically mentioned in the lease.

If you're going to be storing waste products or your work may create a good deal of noise, odors, vibrations, or other types of environmental pollution, make sure the landlord is aware of this and specifically permits it in the lease.

Improvements

Is the space you want to lease going to be improved or modified in any way and, if so, by whom? Will new fixtures be installed? If so, make sure the lease states who will pay for such changes and who will own any new fixtures when the lease ends. Usually, the landlord ends up owning improvements.

Maintenance

The lease should also specify who will maintain and repair the leased space. Some leases state that the landlord will provide basic maintenance services. Others make the tenant pay for everything—including cleaning, building security, heating, and maintenance of the air-conditioning system.

Insurance

If you're signing a net lease, you'll be required to help the landlord pay for property and liability insurance on the premises. (In a gross lease, insurance costs are figured into your rent amount.) If there are multiple tenants, the landlord will often obtain the insurance and require you to contribute to the cost. Your contribution should be based on how much space you use—for example, if you're renting 10% of the building, you should pay only 10% of the insurance costs. If you are the only tenant, you may have to obtain and pay for the insurance yourself.

If the landlord gets the insurance for the premises, make sure you are listed on the policy as an additional insured. This will make it easier for you to deal with the insurance company if you make a claim or share in a payout.

CROSS REFERENCE

See Chapter 6 for a detailed discussion of insurance for the self-employed.

Termination Clause

Make sure the lease includes a clause that details what happens if you end the lease early. In some leases, you have no right to terminate before the lease term ends, so you will be on the hook for the rent until the end of the rental term. In others, you can terminate the lease early, but only if you pay a penalty to the landlord. It's always in your interest to be able to get out of a lease as easily, quickly, and cheaply as possible.

Sublease Clause

If you may want to rent part or all of the space you lease to someone else, you will want to include a "sublease clause." Having the right to sublease benefits you in the event that you no longer need all the space you've rented or if you want, but are not allowed, to terminate your lease early. Most leases allow you to sublease only if you get prior permission from the landlord. Some leases permit the landlord to withhold permission for any reason. If the lease allows the landlord to deny you permission to sublease, make sure the landlord may do so only if he or she has a "reasonable basis."

Dispute Resolution

Finally, you should negotiate how you and the landlord will resolve any disputes that may arise. Some leases require the parties to submit to mediation or arbitration instead of allowing them to file a lawsuit, while others don't. (See Chapter 21 for a detailed discussion of this issue.)

Deducting Your Outside Office Expenses

Virtually all the expenses you incur for an outside office or other workplace that you rent for your business are deductible, including:

- rent
- utilities
- insurance
- repairs
- improvements
- real estate broker fees and commissions to obtain the lease
- fees for option rights, such as an option to renew the lease
- burglar alarm expenses
- trash and waste removal
- security expenses
- parking expenses
- maintenance and janitorial expenses
- lease cancellation fees, and
- attorneys' fees to draft a lease.

If you sign a net lease, you'll have to pay part (or all) of the landlord's maintenance expenses, property taxes, insurance, and maybe even mortgage payments. For tax purposes, these payments are treated the same as rent.

A rental deposit is not deductible in the year it is made if it is to be returned at the end of the lease. However, if the landlord applies the deposit to pay rent you owe, make repairs, or because you've breached the lease, you may deduct the amount in that year.

None of the rules applicable to the home office deduction apply to outside offices. Thus, there is no profit limit on deductions for outside rental expenses—you get your entire deduction even if it exceeds the profits from your business. You report rental expenses for an outside office just like any other business expense. You don't have to file IRS Form 8829, which is required when sole proprietors take the home office deduction.

Timing of Deductions

Because you will ordinarily be in your office for more than one year, some of the expenses you pay may benefit your business for more than a single tax year. In this event, you may have to deduct the expense over more than one year instead of currently deducting it all in a single year. (This discussion assumes that you are a cash basis taxpayer and use the calendar year as your tax year. For more information on the cash basis method of accounting, see Chapter 14.)

Current Versus Multiyear Deductions

You may currently deduct any expense you pay for use of your office during the current tax year.

EXAMPLE:
In 2008, Leona paid $800 rent each month for the outside office she uses for her psychotherapy practice. The $9,600 Leona paid in 2008 is fully deductible on her 2008 taxes. The rental payments were a current expense because they benefited Leona only for a single tax year—2008.

But if an expense you pay applies beyond the current tax year, the general rule is that you can deduct only the amount that applies to your use of the rented property during the current tax year. You can deduct the rest of your payment only during the future tax year to which it applies.

EXAMPLE:
Last January, Steve leased an outside office for three years for $6,000 a year. He paid the full lease amount up front: $18,000 (3 x $6,000). Each year, Steve can deduct only $6,000—the part of the rent that applies to that tax year.

Subject to the exceptions noted below, these rules also apply to office expenses, not just to rent you pay in advance. For example, they apply to all expenses you pay to get a lease.

EXAMPLE:
Maxine pays $2,000 in attorneys' fees to draft her office lease. The lease has a five-year term, so the payment was for a benefit that lasts beyond the end of the following tax year. Thus, Maxine may not currently deduct the entire $2,000 in one year. Instead, she must deduct the $2,000 in equal amounts over five years (60 months). This comes to $33.33 per month. Her lease began on March 1, 2008, so she can deduct $333.33 for 2008 (10 months x $33.33 = $333.33).

12-Month Rule

There is an important exception to this general rule. Under the "12-month rule," cash basis taxpayers may currently deduct any expense in the current year so long as it is for a right or benefit that extends no longer than the earlier of:

• 12 months, or
• until the end of the tax year after the tax year in which you made the payment.

EXAMPLE 1:

Stephanie leased an office for five years beginning July 1, 2008. Her rent is $12,000 per year. She paid the first year's rent ($12,000) on June 30. Under the general rule discussed above, Stephanie may deduct in 2008 only the part of her rent payment that applies to 2008. Her lease started July 1, 2008 (which is 50% of 2008), so she may deduct 50% of the $12,000, or $6,000. However, if Stephanie uses the 12-month rule, her entire $12,000 payment is deductible in 2008. The fact that 50% of her payment was for 2009 doesn't matter because the benefit she obtained—the use of her office—lasted for only 12 months: from July 1, 2008, to July 1, 2009.

EXAMPLE 2:

Steve paid three years of rent in advance. He may not use the 12-month rule because the benefit he obtained from his payment lasted for three years, which is both more than 12 months and beyond the end of the tax year after the tax year in which he made the payment.

EXAMPLE 3:

Assume that Maxine (from the example in the previous section) paid $2,000 in attorneys' fees to draft a lease that lasts for one year, starting March 1, 2008. She may currently deduct the whole amount under the 12-month rule.

To use the 12-month rule, you must apply it when you first start using the cash method for your business. You must get IRS approval if you haven't been using the rule and want to start doing so. Such IRS approval is granted automatically. (See Chapter 19.)

Determining Your Lease Term

How long a lease lasts is important because it can determine whether you can currently deduct an expense or must deduct it over the entire lease term. If you must deduct an expense over the entire lease term, the length of the lease will determine the amount of your deduction each year. It might seem simple to calculate how long a lease lasts just by looking at the lease term in the lease agreement. However, things are not so simple if your lease includes an option to renew.

The IRS says that the term of the lease for rental expense deductions includes all renewal options plus any other period for which you and the lessor reasonably expect the lease to be renewed. For example, a one-year lease with an option to renew for five years would be a six-year lease for deduction purposes.

However, this rule applies only if less than 75% of the cost of getting the lease is for the term remaining on the purchase date (not including any period for which you may choose to renew or extend the lease). Sound confusing? It is.

EXAMPLE 1:

You paid $10,000 to get a lease with 20 years remaining on it and two options to renew for 5 years each. Of this cost, you paid $7,000 for the original lease and $3,000 for the renewal options. Was 75% of the cost of the lease paid for the initial 20-year lease term? No. $7,000 is less than 75% of the total $10,000 cost of the lease. Thus, the IRS rule discussed above applies. The lease term for deduction purposes is the remaining life of your present lease plus the renewal periods—30 years in all. The $10,000 will have to be amortized (deducted in equal amounts) over 30 years.

EXAMPLE 2:

Assume the same facts as in Example 1, except that you paid $8,000 for the original lease and $2,000 for the renewal options. The $8,000 cost of getting the original lease was 80% of the total cost of the lease, not less than 75%. Thus, the IRS rule doesn't apply and you can amortize the entire $10,000 over the 20-year remaining life of the original lease.

The crucial question is how you figure out how much of the cost of the lease was for the original lease term and how much was for the renewal term or terms. The IRS says only that the lease costs should be allocated between the original and renewal terms based on the facts and circumstances. The IRS also says that in some cases it may be appropriate to make the allocation using a present value computation. In such a computation, a present value—a value in today's dollars—is assigned to an amount of money in the future, based on an estimated rate of return over the long term. You'll probably want an accountant to do this for you.

Improvements and Repairs

Landlords often give commercial tenants an allowance to make improvements before they move in. You get no deduction for these improvements— the landlord gets to depreciate improvements it paid for, not you. However, if you pay for improvements with your own money, you may deduct the cost as a business expense.

Improvements may be depreciated over several years as described in Chapter 9. They are depreciated over their recovery periods assigned by the IRS, not over the whole term of the lease. For example, the cost of installing new carpet would be depreciated over five years, even if the lease term is ten years.

If you treat your expenses for improvements as rent, you deduct the cost the same as any other rent. Rent is deductible in a single year unless it is prepaid in advance. This means you'll get your deduction much more quickly than if you depreciated the improvements over several years. However, if the cost of the improvement is substantial, part of the cost may have to be treated as prepaid rent and deducted over the whole lease term as described above. Whether an improvement must be depreciated or treated as rent depends on what you and your landlord intended. Your intent should be written into your lease agreement.

Unlike for improvements, the cost of repairs may be deducted in a single year. How do you tell the difference between a repair and an improvement? A repair keeps property in good operating condition, but it does not:

- materially add to the value of your property
- substantially prolong its useful life, or
- make it more useful. (Treas. Reg. § 1.162-4.)

In contrast, an improvement adds to the value of property, prolongs its life, or adapts it to new uses. For example, mending a tear in an office carpet is a repair, but installing a brand new carpet is an improvement. ●

Obtaining Licenses, Permits, and Identification Numbers

Once you've decided how to organize and name your business, you'll need to obtain any necessary licenses, permits, and identification numbers. You may have to fill out paperwork and pay some fees, but it's well worth the effort. You can face fines and other penalties if you don't satisfy government requirements for your business.

Also, having all required business licenses helps you look like an independent businessperson instead of an employee. Potential clients may even ask you for copies of your licenses, permits, or numbers before agreeing to hire you because this information will help them if they're audited.

Business Licenses

The type of business licenses and permits that you need (if any) depends on the kind of work you do and where you do it. You may be required to get licenses or permits from federal, state, and local governments. Professional organizations, other self-employed people, and your local chamber of commerce may all be able to give you information on licensing requirements for your business.

Federal Licenses and Permits

The federal government doesn't require licenses or permits for most small businesses. One notable exception, however, is the trucking industry. Trucking companies must be licensed by the Federal Motor Carrier Safety Administration (www.fmcsa.dot.gov). License requirements are also imposed on investment advisors by the Securities and Exchange Commission (www.sec.gov).

State Requirements

A few states require all businesses to obtain state business licenses (in addition to any local licenses required).

Most states don't issue or require general business licenses. However, all states require special licenses for people who work in certain occupations. Doctors, lawyers, architects, nurses, and engineers must be licensed in every state. Most states require licenses for other occupations that require extensive training or that expose consumers to potential hazards or fraud. For example, most states license barbers, bill collectors, building contractors, tax preparers, insurance agents, cosmetologists, real estate agents or brokers, and auto mechanics. Your state may require licenses for other occupations, too.

Procedures for obtaining a license vary from state to state and occupation to occupation. You may have to meet specific educational requirements or have training or experience in the field. You may even have to pass a written examination. Of course, you'll have to pay a license fee. Some states may also require that you have liability insurance before you can be issued a license. (See Chapter 6.)

If your state government discovers that you're doing business without a required license, a variety of bad things can happen to you. You'll undoubtedly be ordered to stop doing business. You may also be fined. And depending on your occupation, failure to obtain a license may be a crime—a misdemeanor or even a felony.

Many states have agencies designated to help businesses get started. This is the first place you should call to obtain information on your state's license requirements. These agencies often have free or inexpensive publications that discuss licensing rules. You can find your state's agency at the IRS website at www.irs.gov. Select the "Business" tab, then "Small Business/Self-Employed." On the left side of the page, you can choose "State Links," and select your state.

Also, most state agencies have websites that may contain information about licensing requirements. A good place to start an Internet search for such information is at www.statelocalgov.net/index.cfm.

Also, the Library of Congress maintains a list of state government websites at www.loc.gov/rr/news/stategov/stategov.html.

Local Requirements

Many cities, counties, and municipalities require business licenses or permits for all businesses—even one-person, home-based operations. Usually, you just have to pay a fee to get such licenses; they are simply a tax in disguise. Other cities have no license requirements at all or exempt very small businesses.

If you're doing business within a city's limits, you'll need to contact your city government to find out about licensing requirements. If you're in an unincorporated area, you'll need to contact your county government. If you're doing business in more than one city or county, you may have to get a license for each one.

To find out what to do, call the appropriate local official in charge of business licensing. This is often the city or county clerk, planning or zoning department, city tax office, building and safety department, or public works department. You may need more than one local license, so you may have to deal with more than one local agency. Your local chamber of commerce may be able to direct you to the appropriate agency or contact person.

To obtain a license, you'll be required to fill out an application and pay a fee. Fees vary by locality, ranging from as little as $15 to several hundred dollars. Fees are often based on your projected gross revenues—for example, 10 cents per $1,000 of revenue projected. Periodically, you'll be required to renew your license and pay an additional fee, usually every year. You also may be required to post your license at your place of business.

Many self-employed people, particularly those who work at home, never bother to get a local business license. If your local government discovers you're running an unlicensed business, it may fine you and bar you from doing business until you obtain a license.

> **CAUTION**
>
> **Watch out for zoning restrictions.** If you work at home, be careful about applying for a local business license. You'll have to provide your business address to obtain one. Before granting a license, many cities first check to see whether the area in which your business is located is zoned for business. If your local zoning ordinance bars home-based business offices in your neighborhood, you could be in for trouble. (See Chapter 4.)

Employer Identification Numbers (EINs)

A federal employer identification number, or EIN, is a nine-digit number the IRS assigns to businesses for tax filing and reporting purposes. The IRS uses the EIN to identify the taxpayer.

When an EIN Is Required

Use your EIN on all business tax returns, checks, and other documents you send to the IRS. Your state tax authority may also require your EIN on state tax forms.

Sole Proprietors

If you're a sole proprietor, you must have an EIN to:

- hire employees
- have a Keogh or solo 401(k) retirement plan (see Chapter 16)
- buy or inherit an existing business that you operate as a sole proprietorship
- incorporate or form a partnership, or
- file for bankruptcy.

Also, some banks require you to have an EIN before they'll set up a bank account for your business.

If you're a sole proprietor and don't have any employees or a Keogh plan, you can't obtain an EIN; you use your Social Security number instead.

Corporations, Partnerships, and Limited Liability Companies

You must have an EIN if you form a corporation, partnership, or limited liability company, even if you were formerly a sole proprietor.

Obtaining an EIN

EINs are free and easy to obtain. You can get one by filing IRS Form SS-4, *Application for Employer Identification Number*, with the IRS. Filling out the form is simple—just follow its detailed instructions.

Note these possible trouble spots:

- **Space 1:** List your full legal name if you're a sole proprietor. If you've incorporated, list the corporation's name—the name on your articles of incorporation or similar document establishing your corporation.
- **Space 7:** Leave this space blank if you're a sole proprietor.
- **Space 12:** For most self-employed people, the closing month of the tax year is December, the last month of the calendar year.
- **Space 13:** If you don't plan to hire any employees, enter "N/A" in this space.

Applying Online

The fastest and easiest way to obtain an EIN is to apply directly through the IRS website by going to www.irs.gov/businesses/small and clicking "Employer ID Numbers (EINs)." You can fill out an online interactive form and submit it electronically to the IRS. As long as you pass the system's automatic validity checks, you will immediately be issued an EIN. If your application doesn't pass the validity checks, you will have the opportunity to review and correct it.

Otherwise, simply print out a copy of the confirmation notice for your records and begin using your new EIN immediately.

Applying by Mail

If you do not want to apply online, you can obtain your EIN by mailing a completed SS-4 to the appropriate IRS service center listed in the form's instructions. The IRS will mail the EIN to you in about a month.

Applying by Phone

You can also get an EIN over the phone by using the IRS's Tele-TIN program. Here's how:

- Fill out the SS-4 form.
- Call the IRS at 800-829-4933. An IRS representative will take the information off your SS-4 and assign you an EIN that you can start using immediately.
- Write your EIN in the upper right-hand corner of the SS-4 and sign and date the form.
- Mail or fax the signed SS-4 within 24 hours to the Tele-TIN unit at the IRS service center address for your state. The addresses are provided in the SS-4 instructions, or the IRS representative can give you the fax number.

Sales Tax Permits

Almost all states and many municipalities impose sales taxes of some kind. The only states without sales tax are Alaska, Delaware, Montana, New Hampshire, and Oregon. However, many cities, counties, and boroughs in Alaska have their own local sales taxes. In addition, the other four states impose sales-type taxes on certain types of business transactions.

In some states, sales tax is imposed on sellers, who then have the option of passing the tax along to their purchasers. In other states, the tax is imposed directly on the purchaser, and the seller is responsible for collecting the tax and remitting it to the state. In a few states, sellers and purchasers split the sales tax.

Form **SS-4**
(Rev. July 2007)
Department of the Treasury
Internal Revenue Service

Application for Employer Identification Number

(For use by employers, corporations, partnerships, trusts, estates, churches, government agencies, Indian tribal entities, certain individuals, and others.)

▶ See separate instructions for each line. ▶ Keep a copy for your records.

OMB No. 1545-0003

EIN

Type or print clearly.

1 Legal name of entity (or individual) for whom the EIN is being requested
Harry Flashman

2 Trade name of business (if different from name on line 1)

3 Executor, administrator, trustee, "care of" name

4a Mailing address (room, apt., suite no. and street, or P.O. box)
555 Main St.

5a Street address (if different) (Do not enter a P.O. box.)

4b City, state, and ZIP code (if foreign, see instructions)
Ann Arbor, MI 48104

5b City, state, and ZIP code (if foreign, see instructions)

6 County and state where principal business is located
Washtenaw

7a Name of principal officer, general partner, grantor, owner, or trustor

7b SSN, ITIN, or EIN

8a Is this application for a limited liability company (LLC) (or a foreign equivalent)? . . . . ☐ Yes ☐ No

8b If 8a is "Yes," enter the number of LLC members . . . . . ▶

8c If 8a is "Yes," was the LLC organized in the United States? . . . . ☐ Yes ☐ No

9a **Type of entity** (check only one box). **Caution.** If 8a is "Yes," see the instructions for the correct box to check.

☒ Sole proprietor (SSN) 123 | 45 | 6789
☐ Partnership
☐ Corporation (enter form number to be filed) ▶
☐ Personal service corporation
☐ Church or church-controlled organization
☐ Other nonprofit organization (specify) ▶
☐ Other (specify) ▶

☐ Estate (SSN of decedent)
☐ Plan administrator (TIN)
☐ Trust (TIN of grantor)
☐ National Guard ☐ State/local government
☐ Farmers' cooperative ☐ Federal government/military
☐ REMIC ☐ Indian tribal governments/enterprises
Group Exemption Number (GEN) if any ▶

9b If a corporation, name the state or foreign country (if applicable) where incorporated

State

Foreign country

10 **Reason for applying** (check only one box)
☐ Started new business (specify type) ▶
☒ Hired employees (Check the box and see line 13.)
☐ Compliance with IRS withholding regulations
☐ Other (specify) ▶

☐ Banking purpose (specify purpose) ▶
☐ Changed type of organization (specify new type) ▶
☐ Purchased going business
☐ Created a trust (specify type) ▶
☐ Created a pension plan (specify type) ▶

11 Date business started or acquired (month, day, year). See instructions.
Aug. 1, 2007

12 Closing month of accounting year December

13 Highest number of employees expected in the next 12 months (enter -0- if none).

Agricultural	Household	Other
	1	

14 Do you expect your employment tax liability to be $1,000 or less in a full calendar year? ☒ Yes ☐ No (If you expect to pay $4,000 or less in total wages in a full calendar year, you can mark "Yes.")

15 First date wages or annuities were paid (month, day, year). **Note.** If applicant is a withholding agent, enter date income will first be paid to nonresident alien (month, day, year) . . . . ▶ Sept. 1, 2007

16 Check **one** box that best describes the principal activity of your business.
☐ Construction ☐ Rental & leasing ☐ Transportation & warehousing
☐ Real estate ☐ Manufacturing ☐ Finance & insurance
☐ Health care & social assistance ☐ Wholesale-agent/broker
☐ Accommodation & food service ☐ Wholesale-other ☐ Retail
☒ Other (specify) Consulting

17 Indicate principal line of merchandise sold, specific construction work done, products produced, or services provided.

18 Has the applicant entity shown on line 1 ever applied for and received an EIN? ☐ Yes ☒ No
If "Yes," write previous EIN here ▶

Third Party Designee
Complete this section **only** if you want to authorize the named individual to receive the entity's EIN and answer questions about the completion of this form.

Designee's name

Designee's telephone number (include area code)
( )

Address and ZIP code

Designee's fax number (include area code)
( )

Under penalties of perjury, I declare that I have examined this application, and to the best of my knowledge and belief, it is true, correct, and complete.

Name and title (type or print clearly) ▶ Harry Flashman, Owner

Applicant's telephone number (include area code)
(315) 555-5555

Applicant's fax number (include area code)
(315) 554-5555

Signature ▶ *Harry Flashman*   Date ▶ *August 15, 2007*

For Privacy Act and Paperwork Reduction Act Notice, see separate instructions.   Cat. No. 16055N   Form **SS-4** (Rev. 7-2007)

Selling Products or Services

If you sell tangible personal property—things you can hold in your hand or physically touch—to the public, you'll most likely have to pay sales taxes. All states that have sales taxes impose them on sales of goods or products to the public.

On the other hand, if you only provide services to clients or customers—that is, you don't sell or transfer any type of personal property—you probably don't have to worry about sales taxes because most states either don't tax services at all or tax only certain services. Notable exceptions are Hawaii, New Mexico, and South Dakota, which impose sales taxes on all services, subject to certain exceptions.

Determining whether you're selling property or providing a service can be difficult because the two are often involved in the same transaction. For example, a piano tuner may have to replace some piano wire to tune a piano, or a dentist may provide a patient with a gold filling in the process of filling a tooth. In these instances, many state taxing authorities look at the true object of the transaction to determine if sales tax will be assessed. That is, they look at whether the main purpose of the transaction is to provide the consumer with a service or to sell property. It seems clear that the main purpose of hiring a piano tuner or dentist is to obtain a service—that is, the tuning of the piano or filling of the tooth. The property used to provide the service is incidental.

CAUTION

Contacting your state sales tax department. Each state's sales tax requirements are unique. A product or service taxable in one state may be tax-free in another. The only way to find out if the products or services you provide are subject to sales taxes is to contact your state sales tax department. You can find your state's tax agency at www.taxadmin.org/fta/link. If you don't understand the requirements, seek help from a tax professional. (See Chapter 21.)

Obtaining a State Sales Tax Permit

If the products or services you provide are subject to sales tax, you'll have to fill out an application to obtain a state sales tax permit. Complete and mail the application before you make a taxable sale. Many states impose penalties if you make a sale before you obtain a sales tax permit. Generally, you pay sales taxes four times a year, but you might have to pay them monthly if you make a lot of sales. Be sure to collect all the taxes due. If you fail to do so, you can be held personally liable for the full amount of uncollected tax.

CAUTION

Watch out for rule changes. States constantly change their sales tax laws, so be on the lookout for changes that affect how you do business. Professional organizations and your state chamber of commerce can be good sources of information on your state's sales tax rules.

CHAPTER

6

Insuring Your Business and Yourself

Many employees don't worry much about health, liability, or property insurance; their employers take care of their insurance needs. Unfortunately, this is not the case when you're self-employed. Self-employed people must purchase all their insurance themselves and usually need more coverage than employees. Insurance is the single greatest expense for many of the self-employed.

The best time to obtain insurance is when you first become self-employed or even before you quit your job to do so. Insurance is cheapest and easiest to obtain before you have a problem. Don't wait to buy insurance until you become ill, are being sued, or have business property damaged or stolen. By then it may be too late. And even if you're able to obtain insurance, it will likely not provide coverage for your preexisting condition or problem.

Health Insurance

Health insurance pays at least part of your doctor, hospital, and prescription expenses if you or a family member get sick. When you're self-employed, you have to obtain your own health insurance. Your clients or customers need not and will not provide it for you. Even if you're in perfect health, you should obtain health insurance. Medical costs for even relatively minor illnesses or injuries can be huge. And if you're uninsured, the reality is that you may have difficulty finding a doctor or hospital willing to treat you.

Although the laws of most states prevent an insurer from denying you coverage because of a preexisting medical problem, it can still be very difficult for self-employed people to obtain affordable health insurance if you or a family member have a chronic or serious illness. Some people who would like to quit their jobs and go into business for themselves refrain from doing so because they're afraid they won't be able to get health insurance.

Obtaining Health Coverage Through Your Spouse or Partner

If you are married and your spouse has a job that provides health insurance coverage, you likely can obtain coverage through your spouse's policy. Substantial numbers of self-employed people obtain their health insurance coverage this way: A 1999 survey sponsored by the Small Business Administration found that one-third of all home business owners obtained health insurance coverage through their spouses.

Unfortunately, this method won't work if your spouse does not have a job that provides health coverage or if you are not married. If you have a partner but are not married, however, some employers provide health care coverage for employees' domestic partners as well, so be sure to have your partner check his or her policy.

Be aware, though, that such benefits are taxable income when an employer provides them to an employee's unmarried domestic partner, whether of the same or opposite sex. This means that the fair market value of the coverage for the domestic partner must be included in the employee's wages for tax purposes. The only way domestic partner coverage can be a tax-free employee benefit is where the domestic partner qualifies as the employee's dependent. To do so:

- the domestic partner must be a member of the employee's household during the employee's entire taxable year
- the employee's home must be the domestic partner's principal place of abode, and
- the employee must provide over half of the domestic partner's support. (IRC Sec. 152.)

The third requirement frequently excludes domestic partners from qualifying as a dependent. Typically, both partners are working and therefore neither is providing more than one-half of the other's support.

The availability and cost of health insurance depends on many factors; some are within your control and others are not. Among the factors you have no control over are:

- your age and gender
- your health history, and
- where you live.

The most important factors over which you do have control are whether you obtain a group or an individual policy and the type of plan you purchase.

Group and Individual Policies

You can obtain health insurance either through a group or as an individual. Group policies insure all members of the group, who pay into a pool that covers medical costs. Insurers prefer to cover large groups because the risks and administrative costs are spread over many people.

Industry trade associations, professional groups, and other membership organizations sometimes obtain health insurance as groups, so you can often get the benefits of a group policy by joining one of theirs. There is a professional group or trade association for virtually every occupation. If you don't know of a group you can join, ask other self-employed people in your field. Most of these organizations have websites, so you may be able to find one using a search engine such as Google (www.google.com). You can also ask your local library if it has a book or database that lists professional associations in your area. For example, the electronic database "Business Organizations, Agencies, and Publications Directory" (Gale Research) lists thousands of membership organizations. You may also be able to obtain health insurance by joining your local chamber of commerce.

Additionally, there are national membership organizations for the self-employed that provide insurance, such as the National Association of the Self-Employed, which you can reach by phone at 800-232-6273 or on the Web at www.nase.org. Other organizations set up specifically to provide health and other insurance benefits to members include the Support Services Alliance (www.ssainfo.com) and the Small Business Service Bureau (www.sbsb.com).

In addition, several states have formed cooperatives that small business owners may join to obtain group health insurance coverage. These are called Cooperatives for Health Insurance Purchasing (or CHIPs, for short). To find out if your state offers a CHIP, call the Institute for Health Policy Solutions at 202-789-1491, or visit their website at www.ihps.org.

Individual coverage is often more expensive than group coverage, and individual coverage limits are usually lower than those offered under group coverage. For example, a group health insurance policy often does not impose any limit on the total benefits paid during your lifetime, while individual coverage often limits total lifetime benefits to one or two million dollars. With the skyrocketing costs of medical care, you can reach the limit surprisingly quickly if you have a chronic illness.

Types of Plans

Today, a bewildering array of health insurance plans are available, described by a bewildering amount of jargon in their policies. As a self-employed person, you will likely be able to choose between traditional and managed care plans.

The type of plan that will be best for you depends on how much money you can afford to spend for health insurance, your prior health history, which plans are available in your area and will accept you, and how important choice of doctors is to you. It's best to shop around and investigate as many different plans as possible, because costs and benefits vary widely.

Traditional Plans

The traditional form of health insurance is now becoming increasingly rare. In this type of fee-for-service plan, you're allowed to go to any doctor or hospital you choose. Either you or your doctor must submit a claim to the insurer for reimbursement of the cost. However, the plan will pay only for care that is medically necessary and covered by the plan.

These plans typically require you to pay a deductible—a portion of your medical bills—before your insurance kicks in to cover the rest. They also require a copayment—a small payment you make for each doctor's appointment or prescription the insurance covers.

The deductible can be anywhere from $100 to several thousand dollars per year. Ordinarily, the deductible accumulates throughout the calendar year. This means any medical bills you pay from January 1 to December 31 count toward your deductible for that year; on New Year's Day, you start again at zero. Once you have met your deductible, your insurer starts paying benefits.

The copayment is usually 20% of the cost of a given service or prescription, although 10% or 30% copayments are not uncommon.

The higher the deductible and copayment, the lower your premium—or basic payment for coverage—will be. However, if you get sick, you'll have to pay a substantial amount out of your own pocket. For example, if you have a policy with a $1,000 deductible and a 20% copayment, you'll have to pay the first $1,000 of your yearly medical expenses yourself; thereafter, the insurer will pay 80% of the cost and you'll have to pay the other 20%. If you incur $5,000 in medical expenses under such a plan, you'd have to pay $1,800 of the cost yourself.

If you have substantial medical bills, a 20% co-payment will be a real hardship. To avoid this, most insurance plans change your copayment percentage to 0% after you've incurred a certain amount of paid expenses for the year. This is called the "out-of-pocket maximum."

Managed Care

Managed care has become the norm in the United States. Under a managed care plan, instead of paying for each service you receive separately, your coverage is paid for in advance. Managed care is usually cheaper than a traditional plan, but you get a more limited choice of doctors and hospitals.

- **Health maintenance organizations (HMOs).**
  HMOs are prepaid health programs that require you to use doctors and hospitals that are part of the organization's network. Some HMOs employ their own doctors and run their own hospitals, while others are affiliated with private physicians. With an HMO, you get your medical care for a fixed price. Ordinarily, you don't pay a deductible, but you may be charged a copayment—$15 or $20—for certain services. However, you can't go to a doctor or hospital outside the plan except in a medical emergency.

  HMOs often offer the lowest premiums around, but these savings come at a price. When you're in an HMO, your primary care doctor is in complete control of your care. You can't visit a specialist without a referral from another doctor. HMOs often discourage referrals to expensive specialists; your primary doctor's compensation from the HMO may even be reduced if he or she refers you to someone else.

  Many HMOs also require you to get prior approval for any treatment you get. And they may have detailed guidelines governing your care. For example, HMO rules may not allow you to be given experimental treatments.

- **Preferred provider organization plans (PPOs).**
  PPOs are a cross between traditional fee-for-service plans and HMOs. PPOs establish networks of doctors and hospitals that agree

to provide care at a price that is usually lower than would be available outside the plan. You obtain full benefits only if you go to a doctor or hospital within the network. You can go to a doctor or hospital outside the network, but you'll usually be required to pay a deductible and copayment.

- **Point of service plans.** Point of service plans are similar to PPOs, except that you ordinarily have a primary care physician who is in charge of your medical care. PPOs generally don't require this.

Comparing Plans

When comparing health insurance plans, read the plan literature carefully. If you don't understand something, ask for an explanation.

First, compare the plans' coverage. No plan covers everything, though HMOs typically provide broader coverage than fee-for-service plans. Most plans don't cover eyeglasses, hearing aids, or cosmetic surgery. However, you may pay for such items with funds from a Health Savings Account, discussed in the next section. Look carefully to see what medical expenses are covered. Expenses to check include:

- inpatient hospital services
- outpatient surgery
- physician visits in the hospital
- office visits
- skilled nursing care
- medical tests and x-rays
- prescription drugs
- mental health care
- drug and alcohol abuse treatment
- home health care visits
- rehabilitation facility care
- physical therapy
- hospice care

- maternity care
- preventive care and checkups, and
- well-baby care.

See if the plan excludes preexisting conditions or specific illnesses.

Next, compare the amount of the premium and the deductible or copayment for each plan you consider. Just as important as the premium, however, is the maximum amount the plan will pay. You should seek a benefit limit of at least $1 million. Beware of plans that advertise a high benefit ceiling but have a much lower benefit limit per claim or a lower maximum benefit per year.

Finally, see what type of hoops the plan requires you to jump through to get treatment. You may be required to get advance authorization for treatment or obtain a second opinion before you're allowed to have surgery. To save money, more and more traditional plans are imposing these types of restrictions as well.

If you're looking for a new plan but want to continue with your current doctor, make sure he or she belongs to the plan you're considering. Ask for your doctor's opinion about the various plans before you sign up. Most doctors belong to several plans and can tell you which are easy to deal with and which are Byzantine bureaucracies.

Health Savings Accounts

On January 1, 2004, a new era in health insurance funding began with the inauguration of health savings accounts, or HSAs. HSAs are tax-exempt accounts that you can use to save money for future medical costs.

RESOURCE

You can get more information on HSAs from IRS Publication 969, *Health Savings Accounts and Other Tax-Favored Health Plans*, which you can obtain by calling 800-TAX-FORM, visiting your local IRS office, or downloading it from the IRS website at www.irs. gov. The United States Treasury Department also has a web site with useful information at www.treas.gov/offices/public-affairs/hsa. In addition, a useful private website with information on HSAs can be found at www.hsainsider.com.

What Are Health Savings Accounts?

The Health Savings Account concept is very simple: Instead of relying on health insurance to pay for small or routine medical expenses, you pay for them yourself. To help you do this, you establish an HSA with a health insurance company, bank, or other financial institution. Your contributions to the account are tax-deductible and you don't have to pay tax on the interest you earn on the money in your account. You can withdraw the money in your HSA to pay for almost any health-related expense without having to pay tax on the withdrawals.

In case you or a family member develops a serious health problem, you must also obtain a health insurance policy with a high deductible—for 2008, at least $1,100 for individuals and $2,200 for families. You can use the money in your HSA to pay this large deductible and any copayments you're required to make.

Using an HSA can save you money in two ways. First, you can take a tax deduction for the money you deposit in your account. Second, you can save money on your health insurance premiums with your high-deductible health insurance policy, which should cost less than a traditional comprehensive or HMO coverage policy.

To participate in the HSA program, you need two things:

- a high-deductible health plan that qualifies under the HSA rules, and
- an HSA account.

Obtaining an HSA-Qualified Health Plan

To set up an HSA, you must first obtain health care coverage from an "HSA-qualified" plan—a bare-bones health plan that meets HSA criteria, including:

- **The plan must have a high deductible.** Your plan must have a $1,100 minimum annual deductible if the plan is for yourself or a $2,200 minimum deductible if it is for you and your family.

- **The insurer must agree to participate and give a roster of its enrolled participants to the IRS.** If your insurer fails to report to the IRS that you are enrolled in an HSA-qualified insurance plan, the IRS will not permit you to deduct your HSA contributions.

- **The plan must have a cap on the annual out-of-pocket payments it can require you to make each year.** Out-of-pocket payments include deductibles, copayments, and other amounts (other than insurance premiums) you must pay for benefits covered by your health plan. As of 2008, the maximum annual out-of-pocket payments that your insurer can require are $5,600 for individuals and $11,200 for families.

In addition, if you set up an HSA for your family, your health insurance plan deductible must apply to the whole family, not to each family member separately. With such a per-family deductible, expenses incurred by each family member accumulate and are credited towards the family deductible. For example, a family of four would meet the $2,200 deductible if each family member paid $550 during the year (4 x $550 = $2,200). The family deductible is a unique feature of the HSA program.

Also, you can opt for a deductible that is larger than the minimum amount. However, keep in mind that there are limits on how much money you can contribute to your HSA account each year. To be on the safe side, you may wish to keep your deductible to these minimums. If you opt for a larger deductible, your account may not have enough money in it to cover the deductible if you become seriously ill—particularly if you develop a chronic illness that will require payments year after year. In 2008, the maximum annual contribution to an HSA is $2,900 for individuals and $5,800 for families. These amounts will be adjusted each year for inflation.

HSA Deductibles and Out-of-Pocket Caps in 2008		
Type of Coverage	Minimum Annual Deductible	Maximum Annual Out-of-Pocket Payments
Self only	$1,100	$5,600
Family	$2,200	$11,200

You may be able to obtain HSA-qualified health insurance coverage from many HMO, PPO, or traditional plans; such policies will be clearly labeled as HSA-qualified on the cover or declaration page of the policy. You might also be able to convert a high-deductible health insurance policy you already have to an HSA-qualified health insurance policy, or your present health insurer may offer a different, HSA-qualified plan. Ask your health insurer for details.

If you need or want a new health insurance plan, you can obtain an HSA-qualified health plan from any health insurer that decides to participate in the program. One way to find participating health insurers is to enter the search terms "Health Savings Account" or "HSA" into an Internet search engine such as Google (www.google.com). Several websites provide detailed information about HSAs—for example, www.hsainsider.com.

You cannot establish an HSA if you're covered by health insurance other than a high-deductible HSA plan—for example, if your spouse has family coverage for you from his or her job. You may have to change your existing coverage if you decide you want to establish an HSA. In addition, people eligible to receive Medicare may not participate in the HSA program.

Opening an HSA Account

Once you are covered by an HSA-qualified health insurance policy, you may open your HSA account. You must establish your HSA with a "trustee" who keeps track of your deposits and withdrawals, produces annual statements, and reports your HSA deposits to the IRS. Any person, insurance company, bank, or financial institution already approved by the IRS to be a trustee or custodian of an IRA is automatically approved to serve as an HSA trustee. Others may apply for approval under IRS procedures for HSAs.

Typically, health insurers administer both the health insurance plan and the HSA. However, you don't have to have your HSA administered by your insurer; your trustee can administer your account instead. Whoever administers your account will usually give you a checkbook or debit card to use to withdraw funds from the account. You can also make withdrawals by mail or in person.

Before deciding on a trustee for your HSA account, look at the plans offered by several companies to see which provides the best deal. Compare the fees charged to set up the account, as well as any other charges—for example, some companies may charge an annual service fee. Ask about special promotions and discounts, and find out how the trustee invests the money in its HSA accounts.

Making Contributions to Your HSA

Once you set up your HSA-qualified health plan and HSA account, you can start making contributions to your account. There is no minimum amount you are required to contribute each year; you may contribute nothing if you wish. But there are maximum limits on how much you may contribute (and thus deduct from your federal income taxes) each year:

- If you have individual coverage, the maximum you may contribute to your HSA each year is $2,900.

- If you have family coverage, the maximum you may contribute to your HSA each year is $5,800.

These maximums will be adjusted for inflation each year.

Taxpayers who have HSAs may make a one-time tax-free rollover of funds from their Individual Retirement Accounts (IRAs) to their HAS. The rollover amount is limited to the maximum HSA contribution for the year (minus any HSA contributions you've already made for the year).

Individuals who are 55 to 65 years old have the option of making additional tax-free catch-up contributions to their HSA accounts, gradually increasing to $1,000 by 2009 (see chart below). This rule is intended to compensate for the fact that older folks won't have as many years to fund their accounts as younger taxpayers. If you're in this age group, it's wise to make these contributions if you can afford them, so your HSA account will have enough money to pay for future health expenses.

Maximum Annual Catch-Up Contribution	
2007	$600
2008	$700
2009 and later	$1,000

Deducting HSA Contributions

The amount you contribute each year to your HSA account, up to the annual limit, is deductible from your federal income taxes. This is a personal deduction you take on the first page of your IRS Form 1040. You deduct it from your gross income, just like a business deduction. This means that you get the full amount of the deduction, whether or not you itemize your personal deductions.

EXAMPLE:

Martin, a self-employed contractor, establishes an HSA for himself and his family with a $2,200 deductible. Every year, he contributes the maximum amount to his HSA account— $2,900 in 2008. He can then reduce his taxable income by this amount and, because he is in the 25% federal income tax bracket, save $525 in federal income tax each year.

Where to Invest Your HSA Contributions

The contributions you make to your HSA account may be invested just like contributions you would make to an IRA. You can invest your HSA account savings in almost anything—money market accounts, bank certificates of deposit, stocks, bonds, mutual funds, Treasury bills, and notes. However, you can't invest in collectibles such as art, antiques, postage stamps, or other personal property. Most HSA funds are invested in money market accounts and certificates of deposit.

Every year, you may roll over up to $500 of unused funds in your HSA into an IRA, without paying any tax on the money.

Withdrawing HSA Funds

If you or a family member needs health care, you can withdraw money from your HSA to pay your deductible or any other medical expenses. You pay no federal tax on HSA withdrawals used to pay qualified medical expenses. Qualified medical expenses are broadly defined to include many types of expenses ordinarily not covered by health insurance—for example, acupuncture, chiropractors, eyeglasses and contact lenses, dental care, fertility treatment, laser eye surgery, and treatment for learning disabilities. This is one of the great advantages of the HSA program over traditional health insurance. (You can find a complete list of qualified medical expenses in IRS Publication 502, *Medical and Dental Expenses,* available by calling 800-TAX-FORM or online at www.irs.gov.)

HSA participants do not have to obtain advance approval from their HSA trustee or insurer before withdrawing funds from their accounts. HSA participants themselves determine whether an expense is a qualified medical expense. You should keep records of your medical expenses to show that your withdrawals were for qualified medical expenses and are therefore excludable from your gross income.

Note, however, that you may not use HSA funds to purchase nonprescription medications. The only way to deduct these is to hire your spouse and establish a medical reimbursement plan.

EXAMPLE:

Jane, a self-employed consultant and single mother, obtains family health insurance coverage with a $2,500 deductible. She sets up an HSA at her bank and deposits $2,500 every year for three years. She deducts each contribution from her gross income for the year for income tax purposes. Jane pays no taxes on the interest she earns on the money in her account, which is invested in a money market fund. By the end of three years, Jane has accumulated $7,500 in the account. Jane becomes ill after the third year and is hospitalized. She withdraws $2,000 from her HSA to pay her deductible. She also withdraws $3,000 to pay for speech therapy for her son, which is not covered by her health insurance. She pays no federal tax on these withdrawals.

Tax-Free Withdrawals

Generally, if you withdraw funds from your HSA to use for something other than qualified medical expenses, you must pay regular income tax on the withdrawal plus a 10% penalty. For example, if you were in the 25% federal income tax bracket, you'd have to pay a 35% tax on your nonqualified withdrawals.

Once you reach the age of 65 or become disabled, however, you can withdraw your HSA funds for any reason without penalty. If you use the money for nonmedical expenses, you will have to pay regular income tax on the withdrawals. When you die, the money in your HSA account is transferred to the beneficiary you've named for the account. The transfer is tax-free if the beneficiary is your surviving spouse. Other transfers are taxable.

If you elect to leave the HSA program, you can keep your HSA account and withdraw money from it tax-free for health care expenses. However, you won't be able to make any additional contributions to the account.

Uses for HSA Funds

Ordinarily, you may not use HSA funds to purchase health insurance or pay for health insurance premiums—only to cover the deductible and other out-of-pocket costs required by a plan you purchase with other funds. However, there are three exceptions to this general rule. You can use HSA funds to pay for:

- a health plan during any period of continuation coverage required under any federal law—for example, when you are laid off from your job and purchase continuing health insurance coverage from your employer's health insurer pursuant to COBRA

- long-term health care insurance, or

- health insurance premiums you pay while you are receiving unemployment compensation.

Are HSAs a Good Deal?

Should you get an HSA? It depends.

HSAs are a good deal if you're young or in good health and you don't go to the doctor often or take many expensive medications. You can purchase a health plan with a high deductible, pay substantially lower premiums, and have the security of knowing you can dip into your HSA if you get sick and have to pay the deductible or other uncovered medical expenses. You also get the benefit of deducting your HSA contributions from your income taxes. And you can use your HSA funds to pay for many health-related expenses that aren't covered by traditional health insurance.

If you don't tap into the money you put in your HSA, it will keep accumulating free of taxes. If you enjoy good health while you have your HSA, you may end up with a substantial amount in your account that you can withdraw without penalty for any purpose once you turn 65. Unlike all other existing tax-advantaged savings or retirement accounts, HSAs provide a tax break when funds are deposited and when they are withdrawn. No other account provides both a "front end" and "back end" tax break. With IRAs, for example, you must pay tax either when you deposit or when you withdraw your money. This feature can make your HSA an extremely lucrative tax shelter—a kind of super IRA.

On the other hand, HSAs are not for everybody. You could be better off with traditional comprehensive health insurance if you or a member of your family has substantial medical expenses. When you're in this situation, you'll likely end up spending all or most of your HSA contributions each year and earn little or no interest on your account (but you'll still get a deduction for your contributions). Of course, whether traditional health insurance is better than an HSA depends on its cost, including the deductibles and copayments you must make.

In addition, depending on your medical history and where you live, the cost of an HSA-qualified health insurance plan may be too great to make the program cost-effective for you. However, if your choice is an HSA or nothing, get an HSA.

HSAs for Employees

Employers may provide HSAs to their employees. Any business, no matter how small, may participate in the HSA program. The employer purchases an HSA-qualified health plan for its employees, who establish their own individual HSA accounts. The employer may pay all or part of its employees' insurance premiums and make contributions to their HSA accounts. Employees may also make their own contributions to their individual accounts. The combined annual contributions of the employer and employee may not exceed the limits described in "Making Contributions to Your HSA," above.

HSAs are portable when an employee changes employers—meaning an employee can keep the HSA and move it with him or her to the next employer. Contributions and earnings belong to the account holder, not the employer. Employers are required to report amounts contributed to an HSA on the employee's Form W-2.

Health insurance payments and HSA contributions made by a business on behalf of its employees are currently deductible business expenses. The employees do not have to report employer contributions to their HSA accounts as income.

Tax Reporting for HSAs

You'll need to report to the IRS how much you deposit into and withdraw from your HSA each year. You can do this by filing IRS Form 8889, *Health Savings Accounts*. You'll also have to keep a record of the name and address of each person or company you pay with funds from your HSA.

Insurance From a Former Job

If your employer provides you with group health insurance coverage and you're laid off or quit, you may be able to keep your old health insurance coverage for a limited period of time. A federal

Comparing Health Costs for a Typical Family

The Joneses are a family of three whose health care costs are equal to the national average. They pay $650 per month for traditional health insurance. Their policy has a $500 per person deductible and an out-of-pocket expense cap of $1,500. They incur $1,200 in uninsured medical and dental expenses each year.

Compare their annual health expenses if they switch to an HSA-qualified insurance plan with a $4,500 family deductible. Assume their high-deductible policy costs $400 per month and they put the $250 they save on insurance premiums each month into their HSA account. They use the money in their HSA account to pay their annual $1,200 in uninsured health expenses. Assume also that the breadwinner in this family is self-employed and qualifies for the self-employed health insurance deduction and that the family is in the 25% federal income tax bracket.

	Traditional Health Plan	HSA Health Plan
Annual health insurance premiums	$7,800	$4,800
Annual HSA contribution	0	$3,000
Annual amount spent on uninsured health costs	$1,200	$1,200
Total annual premiums	$9,000	$9,000
HSA account balance on December 31	0	$1,800
Tax savings from HSA contribution	0	$750 (25% x $3,000)
Tax savings from self-employed health insurance deduction	$1,950 (25% x $7,800)	$1,200 (25% x $4,800)
Net cost	$7,050 ($9,000 – $1,950)	$5,250 ($9,000 – $1,800 – $750 – $1,200)

workplace law called COBRA—short for the Consolidated Omnibus Budget Reconciliation Act—requires your former employer to offer you and your spouse and dependents continuing insurance coverage if you lose your job (unless you're fired or forced to resign because of gross misconduct).

The law applies to all employers with 20 or more employees. Your employer's health plan administrator is supposed to inform you within 14 days after you leave your job that you can continue your coverage. Coverage must be offered regardless of any preexisting medical conditions you have. You have 60 days after receiving the notice to decide whether to obtain the continuing coverage.

If you elect to obtain this coverage, it's retroactive to the date you left your job.

You usually have to pay for this coverage yourself. Your employer may charge you up to 102% of what it pays for the coverage; the extra 2% is for administrative costs. However, some employees who are laid off are able to negotiate free coverage for a time as part of a severance package.

Your coverage can last for anywhere from 18 to 36 months, depending on the reason you left your job. At the end of that time, you have the right to convert to an individual policy. However, such a policy will likely be much more expensive than your employer's group policy.

Employers and health insurance plan administrators who violate COBRA can be fined. Unfortunately, the law generally cannot be enforced by any means other than a complex and expensive lawsuit. Such lawsuits are usually brought only by large groups of former employees who can afford to share the legal fees involved. If you run into problems claiming COBRA benefits, you can try calling your state labor department or IRS office—both agencies administer COBRA.

Many states have laws similar to COBRA that are easier to enforce and, more importantly, usually provide broader benefits and apply to smaller employers than does COBRA. These laws vary greatly from state to state. Contact your state insurance department for more information.

Disability Insurance

Disability insurance is designed to replace the income you lose if you become so sick or injured that you're unable to work for a period of time or never able to work again.

How Important Is Disability Insurance?

Disability insurers have compiled some very scary statistics in an attempt to show that disability insurance is absolutely essential. But is it really? If you work in a physically demanding occupation such as homebuilding or roofing, you may have a good chance of injuring yourself some time during your working life. But if you do office work, your chances of being disabled to such an extent that you are unable to work at all for an appreciable period of time are much lower—particularly if you work at home and don't commute to work. Only you can decide whether to get disability insurance. But many self-employed people do just fine without it.

Disability insurance pays you a regular benefit during the time you're unable to work. The cost of disability insurance depends on many factors:

- **The amount of coverage you obtain.** The maximum benefit you can obtain is usually two-thirds of your income. You can also obtain a smaller benefit and pay a smaller premium. At a minimum, try to obtain a benefit large enough to pay your monthly mortgage costs or rent and other fixed expenses.

- **The term of your coverage.** Some disability insurance plans offer only short-term benefits; the periods range from 13 weeks to five years. More expensive long-term plans pay you until you turn 65 or pay indefinitely. If you can afford it, a long-term policy is best.

- **The elimination period.** Most policies require you to wait a while after you become disabled before you start getting benefits. These elimination periods range from 30 to 730 days. A 90-day period is most common.

- **The nature of your work.** The amount of your premiums will also depend on the nature of your work. People in hazardous occupations—construction, for example—pay more than people with relatively safe jobs.

- **How your policy defines "disability."** More expensive plans pay you full benefits if you can't work in your particular occupation, even if you may be able to do other types of work. Less expensive plans pay you only if you are unable to work in any occupation for which you're suited.

- **Your health.** Your current health is also an important factor. Usually, some type of physical exam will be required. If you smoke or suffer from a preexisting medical condition, be prepared to pay more and search harder for coverage.

Unfortunately, it can be difficult for self-employed people to obtain disability insurance. Many disability insurers don't like to issue policies to the self-employed because their incomes often fluctuate dramatically and they may not be able to pay their premiums. Also, because the self-employed don't have employers to supervise them and verify they're disabled, it can be difficult for an insurer to know for sure whether they're really unable to work. This is a particular problem if you work at home. Some insurers won't issue a disability policy to anyone who works more than half time at home.

Also, many insurers will not issue you a policy until you've been self-employed for at least six months. They want to see how much money you've earned during this period so they'll know whether you can afford the cost of their premiums.

You'll have an easier time obtaining disability coverage if you can show an insurer that you're operating a successful, established business—for example, if you have:

- employees
- long-term contracts with clients
- a detailed financial forecast statement showing how much money you expect your business to earn in future years, and
- good credit references.

If you're still employed, try to obtain an individual disability policy before you quit your job and become self-employed.

If you're already self-employed, try to obtain group coverage though a professional organization or trade group. If this doesn't work, you'll have to obtain an individual policy.

There are five main disability insurers: Chubb Group of Insurance Companies, Northwestern Mutual Life Insurance Company, Paul Revere Life Insurance Company, Provident Life & Accident Insurance Company, and UNUM Life Insurance Company of America. Try to get quotes from them all. You can likely find them listed in your local Yellow Pages under insurance. If not, check out their websites or find local insurance agents who represent them.

Business Property Insurance

Business property insurance helps compensate for loss to your business assets: computers, office furniture, equipment, and supplies. If, for example, your office burns down or is burglarized and all your business equipment is lost, your business property insurance will pay you a sum of money. Three main factors determine the cost of such insurance: policy limits, value of coverage, and scope of coverage.

Policy Limits

All policies have a maximum limit on how much you will be paid, no matter how great your loss. The greater your policy limit, the more expensive the insurance will be.

Value of Coverage

Property insurance can pay you the cost of replacing your property or its actual present cash value. A "replacement cost" policy will replace your property at current prices regardless of what you paid for it. An "actual cash value" policy will pay you only what your property was worth when it was lost or destroyed. If the item has depreciated in value, you may obtain far less than the amount needed to replace it. A replacement cost policy is always preferable, but it costs more than a cash value policy.

Scope of Coverage

Business property insurance comes in one of two forms: "named peril" or "special form." Named peril policies cover you only for the types of harm listed in the policy. For example, the cheapest type of named peril policy covers only losses caused by fire, lightning, explosion, windstorm, hail, smoke, aircraft, vehicles, riot, vandalism, sprinkler leaks, sinkholes, and volcanoes. In contrast, a special form policy will cover you for anything except for certain perils that are specifically excluded—for example, earthquakes. Special form policies cost somewhat more.

Before you purchase business property insurance, take an inventory of all your business property and estimate how much it would cost you to replace it if it was lost, destroyed, damaged, or stolen. Obtain replacement value business property coverage with a policy limit equal to this amount. If you can't afford that much coverage, consider a policy with a higher deductible. This is usually much wiser than obtaining coverage with a lower policy limit. If you insure your property for less than its full value, you won't be covered if you suffer a total loss.

Losses from earthquakes and floods aren't normally covered by business property policies. You can obtain earthquake insurance through a separate policy or as an "endorsement" (or enhancement) to your business property coverage. Flood insurance is usually handled through a separate policy called "difference in conditions." Unfortunately, if you live in a part of the country where these hazards are common, such insurance can be expensive.

Cheap Insurance for Your Computer

If the only valuable business equipment you have is a computer, you may need only computer insurance. A company called Safeware will insure your computer equipment against any type of loss except theft of computer equipment left in an unattended car. The rates are based on the replacement cost of your computer—not its present cash value—and are quite reasonable. You can contact Safeware by telephone at 800-800-1492 or online at www.safeware.com.

If You Work at Home

If you work at home, there are several ways to obtain insurance coverage for your business property.

- **Homeowner's policies.** Your homeowner's insurance policy may provide you with a limited amount of insurance for business property—usually no more than $2,500 for property damaged or lost in your home and $250 away from your home. If you have very little business property, this might be enough coverage for you. But note that computer equipment may not be covered at all.

- **Homeowner's insurance endorsements.** You can double the amount of business property covered by your homeowner's policy by purchasing an endorsement—for example, increasing your coverage from $2,500 to $5,000. The cost is usually only about $20 per year. However, these endorsements are usually available only for businesses that generate $5,000 or less in annual income. If business visitors occasionally come to your home, you can obtain a "rider" (or add-on) to your home-owner's policy that covers your liability should a visitor be injured while there—for example, a slip and fall. The cost is very modest, usually around $50 per year.

- **In-home policies.** The insurance industry has created a special policy for people who work at home. These in-home business policies insure your business property at a single location for up to $10,000. The cost is usually around $200 per year. For an additional premium, the policy includes liability coverage ranging from $300,000 to one million dollars. Liability premium costs are based on how much coverage you buy. There's also coverage available to protect against lost valuable papers, records, accounts receivable, off-site business property, and equipment.

- **BOP policies.** "Business owner's packaged" policies (BOPs) are for businesses not based at home or for larger home-based businesses. Such policies combine both property and liability coverage in a single policy. BOPs are more expensive than in-home policies but provide the most comprehensive coverage available for small businesses.

- **Business property policies.** Some policies just cover your business property. This might be a good idea if you have extremely valuable business equipment.

If You Rent an Office

If you rent an office outside your home, read your lease carefully to see if it requires you to carry insurance. Many commercial landlords require their tenants to carry insurance to cover any damage the tenant does to the premises or injuries suffered by clients or visitors.

The lease may specify how much insurance you must carry. Your best bet is probably to get a BOP policy providing both property and liability coverage. Your landlord may require you to submit proof that you have insurance—for example, a photocopy of the first page of your policy.

Liability Insurance

Liability insurance protects you when you're sued for something you did (or failed to do) that injures another person or damages property. It pays the legal fees for defending yourself against a lawsuit as well as any settlement or judgment against you up to the policy limit. Liability insurance also pays an injured person's medical bills. In our lawsuit-happy society, such insurance is often a must.

There are two different types of liability insurance:

- general liability insurance, and

- professional liability insurance.

You may need both types of coverage.

Incorporating Provides Some Lawsuit Protection

Incorporating your business gives you some protection from lawsuits, but not as much as you may think. For example, incorporating may protect your personal assets from lawsuits by people who are injured on your premises, but it won't protect you from personal liability if someone is injured or damaged because of your malpractice or negligence—that is, your failure to exercise your professional responsibilities with a reasonable amount of care.

Also, unless you have a decent insurance policy, all the assets of your incorporated business—which will probably amount to a large portion of your net worth—can be taken to satisfy a court judgment an injured person obtains against you. (See Chapter 2.)

General Liability Insurance

General liability insurance provides coverage for the types of lawsuits any business owner could face. For example, this type of insurance protects you if a client visiting your home office slips on the newly washed floor and breaks an arm, or if you knock over and shatter an heirloom vase while visiting a client at his or her home.

You definitely need this coverage if clients or customers visit your office. If you already have a homeowners' or renters' insurance policy, don't assume you're covered for these types of claims. Such policies ordinarily don't provide coverage for injuries to business visitors unless you obtain and pay for a special endorsement.

You also need general liability insurance if you do any part of your work away from your office—for example, in clients' offices or homes. You could injure someone or damage property while working there.

On the other hand, if you have little or no contact with the public, you may not need such insurance. For example, a freelance writer who works at home and never receives business visitors probably wouldn't need general liability coverage.

However, whether you want it or not, some clients may require you to carry liability insurance as a condition of doing business with you. Many clients are afraid that if you injure someone while working for them and you don't have insurance, the injured person will sue them instead. This fear is well founded: Lawyers tend to go after the person with the most money or insurance to pay a judgment. You might think this means you'd be better off with no insurance at all because people won't sue you, but this is not necessarily the case. If you have any money or property, there's a good chance you'll get sued. Liability insurance will protect you from losing everything you own.

Luckily, general liability insurance is not terribly expensive. You can usually obtain it for a few hundred dollars per year. You can purchase coverage:

- as part of a package policy such as a "business owner's package" (BOP) policy, or
- by obtaining a separate general liability insurance policy known as a "commercial general liability" (CGL) policy, which may cost the most but will give you more coverage.

If you work at home, you may also be able to add an endorsement to your homeowner's policy to cover injuries to business visitors.

Professional Liability Insurance

General liability insurance does not cover professional negligence—that is, claims for damages caused by a mistake you made or something you failed to do when performing professional services. You need a separate professional liability insurance policy, also known as "errors and omissions" or E&O coverage. Some types of workers—doctors and lawyers, for example—are required by state law to obtain such insurance.

EXAMPLE:

Susan, an architect, designs a factory building that collapses, costing her client a fortune in damages and lost business. The client claims that Susan's design for the building was faulty and sues her for the economic losses it suffered. Susan's general liability policy won't cover such a claim. She needs a special E&O policy for architects.

Professional liability insurance policies commonly cover the following types of workers:

- accountants
- architects
- attorneys
- doctors
- engineers
- insurance agents and brokers
- pension plan fiduciaries, and
- stockbrokers.

You can obtain E&O coverage for many other occupations as well if you're willing to pay the price. Because of the growing number of professional negligence suits and the huge costs of litigation, such insurance tends to be expensive, ranging from several hundred to several thousand dollars per year. The premiums you'll have to pay depend on many factors, including the following:

- The claims history for your type of business. Insurance costs more for businesses that generate lots of lawsuits.
- The size of your business. The more work you do, the more opportunity there is for you to make a mistake resulting in a lawsuit.
- Your knowledge and experience in your field. Less experienced self-employed people are more likely to make mistakes.

Home-Based Architect Gets Liability Insurance

Mel, an architect, recently left a job with a large architectural firm in San Francisco to set up his own architecture business, designing homes and small commercial offices. He works out of an office in a detached studio in his backyard. Mel needs liability insurance.

First, Mel needs general liability insurance because clients, delivery people, and other business visitors come and go from his home office every week. Mel could be subject to a huge lawsuit if, for example, a client was injured after slipping on a roller skate left by Mel's son. Mel calls his homeowners' insurer and obtains an endorsement to his existing homeowners' policy that covers injuries to business visitors and insures up to $25,000 worth of his business equipment. He has to pay an additional $150 annual premium for $500,000 in liability coverage.

Mel also needs E & O insurance because he could be subject to a lawsuit for professional negligence if a problem occurs with one of his buildings. He shops around and decides to purchase coverage through the American Institute of Architects in Washington, DC—a leading membership organization for architects. Mel obtains a $1 million architect liability policy for $3,300 per year.

- The size of your clients' businesses. Mistakes involving large businesses will likely result in larger lawsuits than those involving small businesses.

If you need E & O insurance, the first place to look is a professional association. Many of them arrange for special deals with insurers offering lower rates, and those that don't can at least direct you to a good insurer.

Umbrella Coverage

Another type of liability insurance policy is called "umbrella coverage." An umbrella policy is designed to supplement regular liability insurance. It protects you if you suffer a major liability loss that exceeds the limits of your regular liability policy. For example, if you have a general liability insurance policy with a limit of $1 million dollars and are sued for $2 million and lose, an umbrella policy will pay the $1 million not covered by your regular liability policy.

Umbrella coverage is relatively inexpensive because it merely supplements your regular insurance. You must have a regular liability policy before you can obtain umbrella coverage. There are no standard umbrella policies. Ideally, you want a policy that pays for all defense costs over your regular policy's limits, with no cap. Your regular liability coverage and umbrella coverage should run concurrently—that is, they should cover the same time periods. This avoids unintended coverage gaps.

Car Insurance

If, like most self-employed people, you use your automobile for business as well as personal use—for example, visiting clients or transporting supplies—you need to be certain that your automobile insurance will protect you from accidents that may occur while on business. The personal automobile policy you already have may cover your business use of your car. On the other hand, it may specifically exclude coverage if you use your car for business.

Review your policy and discuss the matter with your insurance agent or auto insurer. You may need to purchase a separate business auto insurance policy or obtain a special endorsement covering your business use. Whatever you do, make sure your insurer knows that you use your car for business purposes (in addition to personal use and driving to and from your office). If you do not inform your insurer about this, it may cancel your coverage if a claim occurs that reflects a business use—for example, if you get into an accident while on a business trip.

If you keep one or more cars strictly for business use, you will definitely need a separate business automobile policy. You may be able to purchase such a policy from your personal auto insurer.

Workers' Compensation Insurance

Each state has its own workers' compensation system that is designed to provide replacement income and cover medical expenses for employees who suffer work-related injuries or illnesses. Employers are required to pay for workers' compensation insurance for their employees, through either a state fund or a private insurance company.

Before the first workers' compensation laws were adopted about 80 years ago, an employee injured on the job had only one recourse: to sue the employer in court for negligence—a difficult, time-consuming, and expensive process. The workers' compensation laws changed all this by establishing a no-fault system. Injured employees gave up their rights to sue in court. In return, employees became entitled to receive compensation without having to prove that the employer caused the injury. In exchange for paying for workers' compensation insurance, employers were spared from having to defend themselves against lawsuits by injured employees (and the resulting money damages).

Restricted to Employees

Workers' compensation is for employees, not self-employed people or independent contractors. If you are determined to be an independent contractor under your state's workers' compensation insurance law, your clients or customers need not provide you with workers' compensation coverage.

Each state has its own test to determine if a worker qualifies as an employee or independent contractor for workers' compensation purposes.

RESOURCE

For detailed information on how states classify workers for workers' compensation purposes, see *Working With Independent Contractors*, by Stephen Fishman (Nolo).

You should meet your state's definition for an independent contractor if you act to preserve your status as an independent contractor. (See Chapter 15.) However, whether you're an independent contractor or employee for workers' compensation purposes is the hiring firm's determination to make, not yours.

Your Worker Status

Not having to provide you with workers' compensation coverage saves your clients a lot of money but also presents them with a problem: If you're injured while working on a client's behalf, you could file a workers' compensation claim and allege that you're really the client's employee. If you prevail on your claim, you can collect workers' compensation benefits even if your injuries were completely your own fault. The state workers' compensation agency can also impose fines and penalties against your client if it determines that the client misclassified you as an independent contractor.

Many hiring firms respond to these fears by requiring you to obtain your own workers' compensation coverage, even if you choose not to. They're afraid that if you don't have your own coverage, you'll file a workers' compensation claim against them if you're injured on the job. Also, many workers' compensation insurers require hiring firms to pay additional premiums for any independent contractors they hire that don't have their own workers' compensation coverage.

If You Have Employees

Even if your clients don't require you to have it, you must obtain workers' compensation coverage if you have employees, depending on the state you live in and the number of employees you have. The workers' compensation laws of about one-third of the states exclude many small employers. (See the chart below.)

State Employee Minimum for Workers' Compensation		
Workers' comp not required if you have:		
Two or fewer employees	Three or fewer employees	Four or fewer employees
Arkansas	Florida	Alabama
Georgia	South Carolina	Mississippi
New Mexico		Missouri
North Carolina		Tennessee
Virginia		
Wisconsin		

Many knowledgeable clients will want to see proof that you have workers' compensation insurance for your employees before they hire you because your state law will probably require your client to provide the insurance if you don't. The purpose of these laws is to prevent employers from avoiding paying for workers' compensation insurance by subcontracting work out to independent contractors who don't insure their employees.

Obtaining Coverage

Most small businesses buy insurance through a state fund or from a private insurance carrier.

Some states require that you purchase coverage from the state fund, including North Dakota, Ohio, Washington, and West Virginia.

In other states, you have a choice of buying coverage from either the state or a private insurance company. These states include Arizona, California, Colorado, Hawaii, Idaho, Kentucky, Louisiana, Maine, Maryland, Minnesota, Montana, New Mexico, New York, Oklahoma, Oregon, Pennsylvania, Rhode Island, Texas, and Utah.

If private insurance is an option in your state, you may be able to save money on premiums by coordinating your workers' compensation insurance with your property damage and liability insurance.

Cost of Coverage

The cost of workers' compensation varies from state to state. What you will have to pay depends upon a number of factors, including:

- the size of your payroll
- the nature of your work, and
- how many claims your employees have filed in the past.

As you might expect, it costs far more to insure employees in hazardous occupations, such as construction, than to insure those who work in relatively safe jobs, such as clerical work. It might cost $200 to $300 a year to insure a clerical worker but perhaps ten times as much to insure a construction worker or roofer.

Other Types of Insurance

There are several other types of insurance policies that may be useful for self-employed people:

- business interruption insurance, to replace the income you lose if your business property is damaged or destroyed due to fire or other disasters and you're forced to close, relocate, or reduce your business while you recover and rebuild
- electronic data processing (EDP) insurance, to compensate you for the cost of reconstructing the data you lose when your computer equipment is damaged or destroyed, and

---

After An Injury: Suing a Client for Negligence

Even if you have your own workers' compensation insurance, you can still sue a hiring firm for damages if its negligence caused or contributed to a work-related injury. Because you're not the hiring firm's employee, the workers' compensation provisions barring lawsuits by injured employees won't apply to you. The damages available through a lawsuit may far exceed the modest workers' compensation benefits to which you may be entitled.

EXAMPLE: Trish, a self-employed trucker, contracts to haul produce for the Acme Produce Co. Trish is self-employed and Acme does not provide her with workers' compensation insurance. At Acme's insistence, however, Trish obtains her own workers' compensation coverage. Trish loses her little finger when an Acme employee negligently drops a load of asparagus on her hand. Because Trish is self-employed, she can sue Acme in court for negligence even though she has workers' compensation insurance. If she can prove Acme's negligence, Trish can collect damages for her lost wages, medical expenses, and pain and suffering. These damages could far exceed the modest workers' compensation benefits Trish may be entitled to for losing her finger.

However, if you receive workers' compensation benefits and also obtain damages from the person that caused the injury, you may have to reimburse your workers' compensation insurer for any amounts it paid for your medical care. Your insurer might also be able to bring its own lawsuit against the firm that hired you.

- product liability insurance, which covers liability for injuries caused by products you design, manufacture, or sell.

If you're interested in any such coverage, talk to several agents who have experience dealing with self-employed people in your field. Professional and trade organizations may also be able to offer help.

Ways to Find and Save on Insurance

There are a number of things you can do to make it easier to find and pay for insurance.

Seek Out Group Plans

For many self-employed people, the cheapest and easiest way to obtain insurance is through a professional organization, trade association, or similar membership organization. There are hundreds of such organizations representing every conceivable occupation—for example, the American Society of Home Inspectors, the Association of Independent Video and Filmmakers, and the Graphic Artists Guild.

There are also national membership organizations that allow all types of self-employed people to join—for example, the National Association of the Self Employed. Many of these organizations give their members access to group health and business insurance. Because these organizations have many members, they can often negotiate cheaper rates with insurers than you can individually. Your local chamber of commerce or your alumni association may also offer insurance benefits.

If you don't know the name and address of an organization you may be eligible to join, ask other self-employed people or conduct a web search.

Buy From an Insurance Company

If you're unable to arrange coverage through a group, try to purchase insurance from one of the growing number of companies that sell policies directly to the public rather than using insurance agents or brokers. These companies can usually offer you lower rates because they don't have to pay commissions to insurance agents. Other self-employed people may be able to recommend a company to you, or you can find them listed in the Yellow Pages under "insurance."

Be Wary of Insurance Agents

Insurance agents or brokers can be a useful source of information. The terms "agent" and "broker" mean different things in different parts of the country, however. In some states, an agent is a person who represents a specific insurance company, and a broker is a person who is free to sell insurance offered by various companies. Elsewhere, the term "insurance agent" is used more broadly to cover both types of representatives. If you want to use an agent, find one who is familiar with businesses such as yours and who represents more than one insurer.

However, be wary about what any agent tells you. Insurance agents are salespeople who earn their livings by selling insurance policies to the public, for which they are paid commissions by insurance companies. The more insurance they sell you, the more money they make. Agents often recommend insurance from companies that pay them the highest commissions, whether or not it's the cheapest or best policy for you. If you use an agent, try to get quotes from more than one and compare them with the coverage you can obtain through a professional organization or by dealing directly with an insurer.

Comparison Shop

Insurance costs vary widely from company to company. You may be able to save a lot by shopping around. Also, review your coverage and rates periodically as insurance costs go up and down. If you're shopping for insurance during a

Check on an Insurer's Financial Health

Several insurance companies have gone broke in recent years. If this happens and you have a loss covered by a policy, you may receive only a small part of the coverage you paid for—or none at all. The best way to avoid this is to obtain coverage from an insurer that is in good financial health.

You can check out insurers' financial status in these standard reference works, which rate insurance companies for financial solvency:

- *Best's Insurance Reports* (Property-Casualty Insurance Section)
- *Moody's Bank and Financial Manual* (Volume 2)
- *Duff & Phelps* (Insurance Company Claims-Paying Ability Rating Guide), and
- *Standard & Poor's*.

An insurance agent should be able to give you the latest rating from these publications. They may also be available in your public library.

time when prices are low, try locking in a low rate by signing up for a contract for three or more years.

Increase Your Deductibles

Your premiums will be lower if you obtain policies with high deductibles. For example, the difference between obtaining a policy with a $250 or a $500 deductible may be 10% in premium costs, and the difference between a $500 and $1,000 deductible may save you an additional 3% to 5%.

Find a Comprehensive Package

It's often cheaper to purchase a comprehensive insurance package that contains many types of coverage than to buy coverage piecemeal from several companies. Many insurers offer special policies or packages for small business owners that combine liability coverage for injuries to clients or their property while on your premises with fire, theft, and business interruption insurance.

Use the Internet

You can obtain a great deal of information about insurance online. Insurance companies, agents, and organizations all have their own websites. Some good places to start are:

- **America's Health Insurance Plans.** This is a nationwide trade association of over 250 health insurers. Its website contains useful articles on all aspects of health insurance. You can find it at www.ahip.org.

- **Quicken.com.** The massive Quicken.com website provides a lot of information about insurance, as well as insurance price quotes. You can find it at www.quicken.com/insurance.

- **Insure.com.** This website contains a good deal of basic information on all forms of insurance. It also provides links to other websites from which you can obtain insurance quotes and apply for insurance online. You can find it at www.insure.com.

- **Yahoo! Insurance Center.** This website also provides information on insurance and online quotes. It can also help you locate insurance agents and brokers. You can find it at http://insurance.yahoo.com.

Deduct Your Business Insurance Costs

You can deduct the premiums for any type of insurance you obtain for your business from your income taxes. This includes business property insurance, liability insurance, insurance for business vehicles, and workers' compensation insurance. Car insurance and homeowners' or renters' insurance premiums are deductible to the extent you use your car or home for business. (See Chapter 9.)

The premiums for health insurance you obtain for yourself are deductible if you're a sole proprietor, partner in a partnership, or S corporation owner. They are also deductible if you form a C corporation that provides insurance for you as its employee. (See Chapter 2.)

You may not deduct premiums for life or disability insurance for yourself. But if you become disabled, the disability insurance benefits you receive are not taxable. ●

Pricing Your Services and Getting Paid

Two difficult problems self-employed workers face are deciding how much to charge clients and making sure they get paid for their services. This chapter will help you figure out how to set your fees and give you ideas about what to do when clients or customers don't pay what they owe you.

Pricing Your Services

New and experienced self-employed people alike are often perplexed about how much to charge. No book can tell you how much your services are worth, but this section gives you some factors to consider in making this determination.

How the Self-Employed Are Paid

There are no legal rules controlling how (or how much) you are paid. It is entirely a matter for negotiation between you and your clients. Some clients insist on paying all self-employed people they hire a particular way—for example, paying a fixed fee. Others are more flexible. Many self-employed people also have strong preferences for particular payment methods—for example, some insist on being paid by the hour.

When you're first starting out, you may wish to try several different payment methods with different clients to see which works best for you. However, if the customary practices in your field dictate a particular payment method, you may have no choice in the matter. Other self-employed workers and professional organizations can give you information on the practices in your particular field.

This section provides an overview of the most common payment methods for the self-employed. However, these are by no means the only ways you can be paid. Certain fields may use other methods—for example, freelance writers are often paid a fixed amount for each word they write.

RESOURCE

For more information on payment methods and setting fees, see:

- *Selling Your Services: Proven Strategies for Getting Clients to Hire You (or Your Firm)*, by Robert Bly (Holt Paperbacks), and
- *The Contract and Fee Setting Guide for Consultants and Professionals*, by Howard Shenson (Wiley).

Fixed Fee

In a fixed-fee agreement, you charge a set amount for an entire project. Your fixed fee can include all your expenses—for example, materials costs, travel expenses, phone and fax expenses, and photocopying charges—or you can bill them separately to the client.

Most clients like fixed-fee agreements because they know exactly what they'll have to pay for your services. However, fixed fees can be risky for you. If you underestimate the time and expense required to complete the project, you could earn much less than your work was worth or even lose money. Many self-employed people refuse to use fixed fee agreements for this reason. For example, one self-employed technical writer always charges by the hour because she says she's never had a project that didn't last longer than both she and the client anticipated.

EXAMPLE:

Ellen, a graphic artist, agrees to design a series of book covers for the Scrivener & Sons Publishing Co. Her fixed-price contract provides that she'll be paid $5,000 for all the covers. Ellen estimates that the project will take 75 hours at most, so she would earn at least $66 per hour, more than her normal hourly rate of $50 per hour.

However, due to the publisher's exacting standards and demands for revisions, the project ends up taking Ellen 125 hours. As a result, she earns only $40 per hour for the project—far less than what she would have charged had she billed by the hour.

Although fixed-fee agreements can be risky, they can also be very rewarding if you work efficiently and accurately estimate how much time and money a project will take. Surveys of the self-employed have consistently found that fixed-fee agreements are more profitable than other types of contracts. For example, a study conducted by the hosts of America Online's consultants' forum found that self-employed people who charged fixed fees earned on average 150% more than those who charged by the hour for the same services. A similar survey conducted by a trade journal called *The Professional Consultant* found that self-employed people charging fixed fees earned 95% more than their colleagues who charged by the hour or day.

Reducing the Risks of Fixed Fees

There are several ways to reduce the risks involved in charging a fixed fee.

- First, carefully define the scope of the project in writing before determining your fee. If this will take a substantial amount of time, you may wish to charge the client a flat fee or hourly rate to compensate you for the work involved in this assessment process.
- Leave some room for error or surprises when you calculate your fee—that is, charge the client as if the project will take a bit longer than you think it will.
- Consider placing a cap on the total number of hours you'll work on the project. Once the cap is reached, you and the client must negotiate new payment terms. For example, the client might increase your fixed fee or agree to pay you by the hour until the project is finished.
- Make sure your agreement with the client contains a provision allowing you to renegotiate your price if the client makes changes or the project takes longer than you estimated. (See Chapter 19.)

Unit of Time

It's safer for you to be paid for your time—that is, by the number of hours or days you spend on a project—rather than a fixed fee. This is especially true if you are unsure how long or difficult the project will be or if the client is likely to demand substantial changes midstream. Many self-employed people refuse to work any other way. This method of payment is customary in many fields, including law and accounting.

However, clients are often nervous about paying by the hour, afraid you'll spread out the project for as long as possible to earn more money. Clients will often seek to place a limit on the total number of hours you can spend on the project to limit the total amount they'll have to spend. Others will require you to provide a time estimate. If you do this, be sure to call the client before spending more time on the project than you estimated.

As with fixed fees, it's a good idea to leave some margin for error when you provide a time estimate. One self-employed person says she determines how many hours a job will take by first deciding how long it should take, doubling that number and then adding 25%. You may not need to go to this extreme, but it's wise to be conservative when estimating the time any project will require.

Fixed and Hourly Fee Combinations

You can also combine a fixed fee with an hourly payment to reduce the risk that you'll be underpaid. If you can't accurately estimate how much time or effort some part of the project might take, charge by the hour for the indeterminable portion and charge a fixed fee for the rest of the project. For example, if your work involves some tasks that are essentially mechanical and others that are highly creative, you can probably accurately estimate how long the mechanical work will take but may have great difficulty estimating how much time the creative work will require. You can reduce the risk of underpayment by charging a fixed fee for the mechanical work and billing by the hour for the creative work.

EXAMPLE:

Bruno, a freelance graphic artist, is hired by Scrivener & Sons Publishing Co. to produce the cover for its new detective thriller, *And Then You Die*. Bruno has absolutely no idea how long it will take him to come up with an acceptable design for the cover. He charges Scrivener $75 per hour for this design work. Once a design is accepted, however, Bruno knows exactly how long it will take him to produce a camera-ready version. He charges Scrivener a fixed fee of $1,000 for this routine production work.

Retainer Agreements

With a retainer agreement, you receive a fixed fee up front in return for promising to be available to work a certain number of hours for the client each month or to perform a specified task. Often, the client pays a lump sum retainer fee at the outset of the agreement. Or, you can be paid on a regular schedule—for example, monthly, quarterly, or annually.

EXAMPLE:

Jean, an accountant, agrees to perform up to 20 hours of accounting services for Acme Co. every month, for which Acme pays her $1,500 per month.

Many self-employed people like retainer agreements because they provide a guaranteed source of income. But in return for this security, you usually have to charge somewhat less than you do when paid on a per-project basis. Also, retainer agreements can contradict your work status. If you spend most of your time working for a single client, the IRS may view you as that client's employee. (See Chapter 15.)

Performance Billing

Perhaps the riskiest form of billing is performance billing, also known as charging a contingency fee. Basically, this means you get paid according to the value of the results you achieve for a client. If you get poor results, you may receive little or nothing. Clients generally favor this type of arrangement because they don't have to pay you if your services don't benefit them. Using this type of fee arrangement can help you get business if a client is skeptical that you'll perform as promised or if you're providing a new service with benefits that are not generally understood.

This type of fee arrangement is used most often for sales or marketing projects in which the fee is based on a percentage of the increased business.

EXAMPLE:

Alice, a marketing consultant, contracts to perform marketing services for Acme Co. to help increase its sales. Acme agrees to pay her 25% of the total increase in gross sales over the next 12 months. If sales don't go up, Alice gets nothing.

Some self-employed people reduce the risks involved in performance billing by requiring their clients to pay them a minimum amount regardless of the results they achieve. For example, a contract might provide that a sales trainer would receive $5,000 for providing training services plus 10% of the increase in the client's sales for a specified number of months after the training program.

If you use a performance contract, don't tie your compensation to the client's profits. Clients can easily manipulate their profits—and therefore reduce your compensation—through accounting gimmicks. Use a standard that is easier to measure and harder to manipulate, such as the client's gross sales or some measurable cost saving.

Commissions

Self-employed people who sell products or services are often paid by commission—that is, a set amount for each sale they make. Many independent sales representatives, brokers, distributors, and agents are paid on a commission basis.

EXAMPLE:

Mark is a self-employed salesperson who sells industrial filters. He receives a commission from the filter manufacturer for each filter he sells. The commission is equal to 20% of the price of the filter.

If you're a good salesperson, you can earn far more on commission than with any other payment method. But if business is poor, your earnings will suffer.

Determining Your Hourly Rate

However you're paid, you need to determine how much to charge per hour. This is so even if you're paid a fixed fee for an entire project. To determine the fixed fee you should charge, you must estimate how many hours the job will take, multiply the total by your hourly rate, then add the amount of your expenses. Knowing how much you should earn per hour will also help you know whether using a retainer agreement or performance billing is cost-effective or whether a sales commission is fair.

If you're experienced in your field, you probably already know what to charge because you are familiar with market conditions—how much demand for and supply of your services exists and how much others in your field charge. However, if you're just starting out, you may have no idea what you can or should charge. If you're in this boat, try using a two-step approach to determine your hourly rate:

- calculate what your rate should be, based on your expenses, then
- investigate the marketplace to see if you should adjust your rate up or down.

Hourly Rate Based on Expenses

A standard formula for determining an hourly rate requires you to add together your labor and overhead costs, add the profit you want to earn, then divide the total by your hours worked. This is the absolute minimum you must charge to pay your expenses, pay yourself a salary, and earn a profit. Depending on market conditions, you may be able to charge more for your services or you might have to charge less.

To determine how much your labor is worth, pick a figure for your annual salary. This can be what you earned for doing similar work when you were an employee, what other employees earn for similar work, or how much you'd like to earn.

Next, compute your annual overhead. Overhead includes all the costs you incur to do business—for example:

- rent and utilities
- business insurance
- stationery and supplies
- postage and delivery costs
- office equipment and furniture
- clerical help
- travel expenses
- professional association memberships
- legal and accounting fees
- telephone expenses
- business-related meals and entertainment
- advertising and marketing costs—for example, the cost of a Yellow Pages ad or a brochure, and
- the cost of your fringe benefits, such as medical insurance, disability insurance, your retirement fund contribution, and your income and self-employment taxes.

If you're just starting out, you'll have to estimate these expenses or ask other self-employed people to give you some idea of their overhead costs.

You're also entitled to earn a profit over and above your labor and overhead expenses. Your salary is part of your costs—it does not include profit. Profit is the reward you get for taking the risks of being in business for yourself. It also provides money you can use to expand and develop your business. Profit is usually expressed as a percentage of total costs. There is no standard profit percentage, but a 10% to 20% profit is common.

Finally, you must determine how many hours you'll work during the year. Assume you'll work a 40-hour week for purposes of this calculation, although you may choose to work less or end up working more. If you want to take a two-week vacation, you'll have a maximum of 2,000 billable hours (50 weeks x 40 hours). If you want more time off, you'll have fewer billable hours.

However, you'll probably spend at least 25% to 35% of your time on tasks such as bookkeeping and billing, marketing your services, upgrading your skills, and doing other things you can't bill to clients. Assuming a 40-hour workweek and two weeks of vacation away from work, this means you'll likely have at most 1,300 to 1,500 hours for which you can get paid each year.

EXAMPLE:

Sam, a self-employed computer programmer, earned a $50,000 salary as an employee and wants to receive at least the same salary. He estimates that his annual overhead amounts to $20,000 per year. He wants to earn a 10% profit and estimates he'll have 1,500 billable hours each year. To determine his hourly rate, Sam must:

- add his salary and overhead together ($50,000 + $20,000 = $70,000)

- multiply this total by his 10% profit margin and add the amount to his salary and overhead ($70,000 x 10% = $7,000; $70,000 + $7,000 = $77,000), and

- divide the total by his annual billable hours ($77,000 ÷ 1,500 = $51.33).

Sam determines that his hourly rate should be $51.33. He rounds this off to $50. However, depending on market conditions, Sam might end up charging more or less.

Hourly Rate Worksheet

You can use the worksheet below to calculate your hourly rate.

A Calculating Shortcut

An easier but less accurate way to calculate your hourly rate is to find out what hourly salary you'd likely receive if you were to provide your services as an employee in someone else's business and multiply this by 2.5 or 3. This is a much more crude way that business management experts have developed to calculate how much money you must earn to pay your expenses and salary plus earn a profit.

EXAMPLE: Betty, a freelance word processor, knows that employees performing the same work receive $15 per hour. She should charge $37.50 to $45 per hour.

If you don't know what employees receive for doing work similar to yours, try calling several employment agencies in your area and ask what you'd earn per hour as an employee.

You can also obtain salary information for virtually every conceivable occupation from *The Occupational Outlook Handbook,* published by the U.S. Department of Labor and available on the Internet at www.bls.gov/oco. You should also be able to find it in your public library.

Hourly Rate Worksheet

Annual salary you want to earn _____

Desired profit % _____

Billable hours per year _____

Yearly Expenses

- Marketing _____

- Travel _____

- Legal and accounting costs _____

- Insurance _____

- Supplies _____

- Rent _____

- Utilities _____

- Telephone _____

- Professional association memberships _____

- Business meals and entertainment _____

- Benefits _____

- Taxes _____

- Other _____

Total Expenses _____

Calculation:

- Step 1: Salary + Expenses = X _____

- Step 2: X x Profit % = Y _____

- Step 3: X + Y = Z _____

- Step 4: Z ÷ Billable Hours = Hourly Rate _____

Investigate the Marketplace

It's not enough to calculate how much you'd like to earn per hour. You also have to determine whether this figure is realistic. This requires you to do a little sleuthing to find out what other self-employed people are charging for similar services and what the clients you'd like to work for are willing to pay. There are many ways to gather this information, such as the following:

- Contact a professional organization or trade association for your field. It may be able to tell you what other self-employed people are charging in your area.

- Some professional organizations even publish pricing guides. For example, the National Writers Union publishes *Freelance Rates and Standard Practice: National Writers Union Guide to Freelance Rates & Standard Practice* (Writer's Digest Books), which lists rates for all types of freelance writing assignments. The Graphic Artists Guild puts out a *Handbook of Pricing & Ethical Guidelines* for freelance graphic artists.

- Ask other self-employed people what they charge. You can communicate about pricing with other self-employed people on the Web.

- Talk with potential clients and customers—for example, attend trade shows and business conventions.

Experimenting With Charging

Pricing is an art, not an exact science. There are no magic formulas, and sayings such as "Charge whatever the market will bear" are not very helpful. The best way—indeed, the only way—to discover how to charge and how much to charge is to experiment. Try out different payment methods and fee structures with different clients and see which work best for you.

You may discover that you may not be able to get your ideal hourly rate because other self-employed people are charging less in your area. However,

if you're highly skilled and performing work of unusually high quality, don't be afraid to ask for more than other self-employed people with lesser skills charge. Lowballing your fees won't necessarily get you business. Many potential clients believe they get what they pay for and are willing to pay more for quality work.

One approach is to start out charging a fee that is at the lower end of the spectrum for self-employed people performing similar services, then gradually increase it until you start meeting price resistance. Over time, you should be able to find a payment method and fee structure that enables you to get enough work and that adequately compensates for your services.

The Self-Employed Should Be Paid More Than Employees

Don't be afraid to ask for more per hour than employees earn for doing similar work. Self-employed people should be paid more than employees. Unlike for employees, hiring firms do not provide the self-employed with employee benefits such as health insurance, vacations, sick leave, or retirement plans. Nor do hiring firms have to pay payroll taxes for them. This saves a hiring firm a bundle—employee benefits and payroll taxes add at least 20% to 40% to employers' payroll costs. Hiring firms often hire independent contractors because they cost less than employees.

In addition, in our economic system, people in business for themselves are supposed to earn more than employees because they take much greater risks. They have many business expenses employees don't have, such as office rent, supplies, and marketing costs. Unlike most employees, self-employed workers don't get paid if business is bad. It's only fair, then, that they should be paid more than employees when business is good.

Getting Paid

Hiring firms normally pay their employees like clockwork. Employers know that if they don't pay on time, their employees can get the state labor department to investigate and fine them. Also, employers usually depend upon their employees for the daily operation of their businesses, so they need to keep the workforce as content as possible.

Unfortunately, no similar incentives encourage hiring firms to pay the self-employed. Many self-employed people have trouble getting paid by their clients. Some hiring firms feel free to pay outside workers late; some never pay at all. Sometimes this is because of cash-flow problems, but often it's because hiring firms know that the self-employed don't always have the time, money, or will to force them to pay on time. One computer consultant complains that delaying payment is an almost automatic response for a lot of companies. They seem to figure that if you don't nag, you don't really want to get paid.

As an independent businessperson, it's entirely up to you to take whatever steps are appropriate and necessary to get paid. No government agency will help you. Here are some strategies you can use to get clients to pay on time—or at least eventually.

Avoid Payment Problems

Taking a healthy dose of preventive medicine before you sign on with a client can help you eliminate, or at least reduce, payment problems.

Use Written Agreements

If you have only an oral agreement with a client who fails to pay you, it can be very hard to collect what you're owed. Without a writing, the client can claim you didn't perform as agreed or can easily dispute the amount due. Unless you have witnesses to support your version of the oral agreement, it will be your word against the client's. At the very least, you should have something in writing that

describes the services you agree to perform, the deadline for performance, and the payment terms. (See Chapter 19.)

Find Out If a Purchase Order Is Required

A purchase order is a document a client uses to authorize you to be paid for your services. (See "Client Purchase Orders" in Chapter 20.) Some clients will not pay you unless you have a signed purchase order, even if you already have a signed contract. Find out whether your client uses purchase orders and obtain one before you start work to avoid payment problems later on.

Ask for a Down Payment

If you're dealing with a new client or one who has money problems, ask for a down payment before you begin work. Some self-employed people refer to such a payment as a "retainer." This will show that the client is serious about paying you. And even if the client doesn't pay you in full, you'll at least have obtained something. Some self-employed people ask for as much as one-third to one-half of their fees in advance.

Use Periodic Payment Schedules

For projects lasting more than a couple of months, try using payment schedules that require the client to pay you in stages—for example, one-third when you begin work, one-third when you complete half your work, and one-third when you finish the entire project. Complex projects can be divided into phases or milestones with a payment due when you complete each phase.

If a client misses a payment, you can stop work. If you're never paid in full, you'll at least have obtained partial payment, so the entire project won't be a loss. A staged payment schedule will also improve your cash flow.

Check Clients' Credit

The most effective way to avoid payment problems is to not deal with clients who have bad credit histories. A company that habitually fails to pay other creditors will likely give you payment problems as well. If you're dealing with a well-established company or government agency that is clearly solvent, you may forgo a credit check. But if you've never heard of the company, a credit check is prudent.

The most effective way to check a client's credit is to obtain a credit report from a credit reporting agency. Dun & Bradstreet, the premier credit reporting agency for businesses, maintains a data-base containing credit information on millions of companies. You can obtain a credit report on any company in Dun & Bradstreet's database by calling 800-234-3867. The report will be faxed to you the same day or mailed. You can also obtain reports online from Dun & Bradstreet's website at www.dnb.com.

A basic Dun & Bradstreet credit report contains information on the company's payment history and financial condition. It will also tell you whether the company has had any lawsuits, judgments, or liens filed against it and whether it has ever filed for bankruptcy. Dun & Bradstreet also assigns a credit rating to help you predict which companies will pay slowly or not at all.

A cheaper but more time-consuming way to check a potential client's credit is to ask the client to provide you with credit information and references. This is better than nothing but may not give you an accurate picture—potential clients may try to avoid tipping you off about their financial problems by giving you the names of references who have not had problems with them.

Credit checks are routine these days, so your request for credit credentials is not likely to drive away business. Be wary of any potential client that refuses to give you credit information. Provide the client with a request for credit information such as the sample form, below.

Call the accounting department of the credit references listed and ask if the company has experienced any payment problems with the client. Accounting departments are typically asked for this information and will usually provide it freely.

If a credit report or your own investigation reveals that a potential client has a bad credit history or is in financial trouble, you may prefer not to do business with that client. However, you may not be able to afford to work only for clients with perfect credit records. If you want to go ahead and do the work, obtain as much money up front as possible and be on the lookout for payment problems. If the client is a corporation or limited liability company, you may seek to have its owners sign a personal guarantee, discussed below.

Checking Form of Ownership

Your investigation of a potential client should include determining how its business is organized legally. This could have a big impact on your ability to collect a judgment against the client if it fails to pay you.

If you win a lawsuit against a client that fails to pay you, the court will order the client to pay you a specified sum of money. This is known as a court judgment. Unfortunately, if the client fails or refuses to pay the judgment, the court will not help you collect it. You've got to do it yourself or hire someone to help you. However, there are many legal tools you can use to collect a court judgment. For example, you can file liens on the client's property that make it impossible for the client to sell the property without paying you, get hold of the client's bank accounts, and even have business or personal property such as the client's car seized by local law enforcement and sold.

Your ability to collect a court judgment may be helped—or severely hindered—by the way the client's business is organized legally.

Request for Credit Information

Andre Bocuse Consulting Services

123 4th Street, Marred Vista, CA 90000
ph: 999-555-1234, fax: 999-555-1222
www.andrebocuse.com, consulting@andrebocuse.com

Please provide the following information so we can extend you credit for our services. All responses will be held in confidence. Please mail this form to the address shown above or fax it to 999-555-1222. Thank you.

1. Company name _____

   Address _____

   _____

2. Contact person _____

3. Federal tax ID no. _____

4. Type of business _____

5. Number of employees _____

6. Date business established _____

7. Check one of the following forms of business:

☐ **Corporation**   **State of incorporation** _____

Names, titles, and addresses of your three chief corporate officers:

Name/Title: _____

Address: _____

_____

_____

Name/Title: _____

Address: _____

_____

_____

Name/Title: _____

Address: _____

_____

_____

☐ **Partnership**

Names and addresses of the partners:

Name: _____

Address: _____

_____

_____

Name: _____

Address: _____

_____

_____

Request for Credit Information (continued)

Name: _____

Address: _____

_____

_____

Name: _____

Address: _____

_____

_____

Name: _____

Address: _____

_____

_____

☐ **Limited Liability Company**

Names and addresses of the owners:

Name: _____

Address: _____

_____

_____

Name: _____

Address: _____

_____

_____

Name: _____

Address: _____

_____

_____

Name: _____

Address: _____

_____

_____

Name: _____

Address: _____

_____

_____

☐ **Sole Proprietorship**

8. Purchase order required? Yes ☐ No ☐

Request for Credit Information (continued)

9. Bank References:

Bank #1: _____

Account # _____ Phone: _____

Contact Person: _____

Address: _____

_____

Bank #2: _____

Account # _____ Phone: _____

Contact Person: _____

Address: _____

_____

10. Please provide the following information for three vendors you use regularly:

Reference #1

Name: _____

Address: _____

_____

Phone: _____

Reference #2

Name: _____

Address: _____

_____

Phone: _____

Reference #3

Name: _____

Address: _____

_____

Phone: _____

My company and I authorize the disclosure and release of any credit-related information based on this document to Andre Bocuse Consulting.

Authorized Signature: _____

Printed Name: _____

Title: _____

Date: _____

What's in a Name? A Lot

Often, you can tell how a potential client's business is organized legally just by looking at its name. If it's a corporation, its name will normally be followed by the word "Incorporated," "Corporation," "Company," or "Limited," or the abbreviation "Inc.," "Corp.," "Co.," or "Ltd." Partnerships often have the word "Partnership" or "Partners" in their name, but not always. A limited liability company will usually have the words "Limited Liability Company," "Limited Company," or the abbreviation "L.C.," "LLC," or "Ltd. Co." in its name. Sole proprietors often use their own names, but they don't have to do so. They may use fictitious business names or DBAs that are completely different from their own names.

- If the client is a sole proprietorship—that is, owns the business individually—he or she is personally liable for any debts the business owes you. This means that both the proprietor's business assets and his or her own personal assets are available to satisfy the debt. For example, both the proprietor's business and personal bank accounts may be tapped to pay you.
- If the client is a partner in a partnership, you can go after the personal assets of all the general partners. Be sure to get all their names before you start work. If the partnership is a limited partnership, you can't touch the assets of the limited partners, so don't worry about getting their names.
- If the client is a corporation, you could have big problems collecting a judgment. Normally, you can't go after the personal assets of a corporation's owners, such as the personal bank accounts of the shareholders and officers. Instead, you're limited to collecting from the corporation's assets. If the corporation is

insolvent or goes out of business, there may be no assets to collect.

- If the client is a limited liability company (LLC), normally its owners will not be personally liable for any debts the business incurred, just as if it were a corporation.

Obtain a Personal Guarantee

If you're worried about the creditworthiness of a new or small incorporated client or limited liability company, you may ask its owners to sign a personal guarantee. A person who signs a personal guarantee, known as a "guarantor," promises to pay someone else's debt. This is the same as cosigning a loan. A guarantor who doesn't pay can be sued for the amount of the debt by the person to whom the money is owed.

You can ask for a personal guarantee from the officers or owners of a company you're afraid will not pay you. The guarantee legally obligates them to pay your fee if the company does not. This means that if the client fails to pay you, you can sue not only the client but the guarantors as well—and you can go after their personal assets if you obtain a court judgment.

EXAMPLE:

Albert, a self-employed consultant, contracts to perform services for Melt, Inc., a company involved in the ice cream business. Melt is a corporation owned primarily by Barbara, a multimillionaire. Albert's contract contains a personal guarantee requiring Barbara to pay him if the corporation doesn't.

Melt goes broke when botulism is discovered in its ice cream, and the company fails to pay Albert. Albert files a lawsuit against Barbara and easily obtains a judgment on the basis of the personal guarantee. When Barbara refuses to pay, Albert gets a court order enabling him to tap into one of her hefty personal bank accounts and is paid in full.

Having a personal guarantee will not only help you collect a judgment, it will also help prevent payment problems. The guarantors will have a strong incentive to make sure you're paid in full and on time. By doing so, they safeguard their personal assets.

Not many self-employed people ever think about asking for personal guarantees, so some clients may be taken aback if you do so. Explain that you need the added protection so you can extend the credit the client seeks. Also, note that signing a guarantee presents no risk at all to the business's owners as long as you're paid on time. You might also give the client a choice: The business's owners can either provide you with a personal guarantee or give you a substantial down payment up front.

A personal guarantee can be a separate document, but the easiest way to create one is to include a guarantee clause at the end of your contract with the client.

EXAMPLE:

Andre Bocuse, a self-employed consultant, agrees to perform consulting services for Acme Corp., a one-person corporation owned by Joe Jones. Because Andre has never worked for Acme before and is worried about being paid, he asks Joe Jones to sign a personal guarantee. This way he knows he can go after Jones's personal assets if Acme doesn't pay up. He adds the following clause to the end of his contract with Acme and has Jones sign it:

In consideration of Andre Bocuse entering into this Agreement with Acme Corporation, I personally guarantee the performance of all of the contractual obligations undertaken by Acme Corporation, including complete and timely payment of all sums due Andre Bocuse under the Agreement.

_____

Joe Jones

Send Invoices to Your Clients

Send invoices to your clients as soon as you complete work. You don't have to wait until the end of the month. Create a standard invoice to use with all your clients. Accounting or invoice computer software programs can create invoices for you. You can also choose to have your own invoices printed.

Your invoice should contain:

- your company name, address, and phone number
- the client's name
- an invoice number
- the date
- the client's purchase order number or contract number, if any
- the terms of payment
- the time period covered by the invoice
- a brief description of the services you performed (if you're billing by the hour, list the number of hours expended and the hourly rate)
- if you're billing separately for expenses or materials, the amounts of these items
- the total amount due, and
- your signature.

Include a self-addressed return envelope with your invoice. This tiny investment can help speed up payment.

Make at least two copies of each invoice: one for the client and one for your records. You may also want to make a third copy to keep in an unpaid invoices folder so you can keep track of when payments are overdue.

An example of a self-employed worker's invoice is provided below. An invoice you can use is provided as a tear-out form in Appendix A.

Terms of Payment

The terms of payment is one of the most important items in your invoice. It sets the ultimate deadline by which the client must pay you. This varies from industry to industry and will also vary from client to client. Thirty days is common, but some clients will want longer—45, 60, or even 90 days.

Obviously, the shorter the payment period, the better off you'll be. This is something you should discuss with the client before you agree to take a job. Some self-employed people ask for payment within 15 days or immediately after the services are completed. However, some clients' accounting departments aren't set up to meet such short deadlines. If you have a written client agreement, it should indicate how long the client has to pay you.

The standard way to indicate the payment terms in your invoice is to use the word "Net" followed by the number of days the client has to pay after receipt of the invoice. For example, "Net 30" means you want full payment in 30 days.

Some self-employed people offer discounts to clients or customers that pay quickly. A common discount is 2% for payment within ten days after the invoice is received. If such a discount can get a slow-paying client to pay you quickly, it's worth it. You're always better off getting 98% of what you're owed right away than having to wait months for payment in full.

If you decide to offer a discount, indicate on your invoice the percentage followed by the number of days the client has to pay to receive the discount—for example, "2% 10" means that the client can deduct 2% of the total due if it pays you within ten days. State your discount before the normal payment terms—for example, "2% 10 Net 30" means the client gets a 2% discount if it pays within ten days, but the full amount must be paid within 30 days.

Charge Late Fees

One way to get clients to pay on time is to charge late fees for overdue payments. One consultant was experiencing major problems with late-paying clients—40% of his clients were over 30 days late in paying him. After he began charging a late fee, the number dropped to 5%.

However, late fees don't always work; some clients simply refuse to pay them. Not paying a late fee when required in your invoice is a breach of contract by the client, but it's usually not worth the trouble to go to court to collect a late fee.

If you wish to charge a late fee, make sure it's mentioned in your agreement. You should also clearly state the amount of your late fee on all your invoices. For example, your invoices should include the phrase: "Accounts not paid within terms are subject to a _____% monthly finance charge."

The late fee is normally expressed as a monthly interest or finance charge.

CAUTION

Some states restrict late fees. Your state might have restrictions on how much you can charge as a late fee. You'll have to investigate your state laws to find out. Check the index to the annotated statutes for your state—sometimes called a "Code"—available online or in any law library. Look under the terms "interest," "usury," or "finance charges." Your professional or trade organization may also have helpful information on this issue.

No matter what state you live in, you can safely charge a late fee of the interest rate at which banks charge businesses to borrow money. Find out the current bank interest rate by calling your bank or looking in the business section of your local newspaper.

Invoice

JOHN SMITH

1000 GRUB STREET

MARRED VISTA, CA 90000

999-555-5555

Date: 4/30/20xx

Invoice Number: 103

Your Order Number: A62034

Terms: Net 30

Time period of: 4/1/20xx-4/30/20xx

To: Susan Elroy

    Accounting Department

    Acme Widget Company

    10400 Long Highway

    Marred Vista, CA 90000

Services:

Consulting services of John Smith on thermal analysis of Zotz 650 control unit. 50 hours @ $100.00 per hour.

Subtotal: $5,000

Material Costs: None

Expenses: 0

TOTAL AMOUNT OF THIS INVOICE: $5,000

Signed by: *John Smith*

The math has two steps. First, divide the annual interest rate by 12 to determine your monthly interest rate.

EXAMPLE:

Sam, a self-employed consultant, decides to start charging clients a late fee for overdue payments. He knows banks are charging 12% interest per year on borrowed money and decides to charge the same. He divides this rate by 12 to determine his monthly interest rate: 1%.

Then, multiply the monthly rate by the amount due to determine the amount of the monthly late fee.

EXAMPLE:

Acme Corp. is 30 days late paying Sam a $10,000 fee. Sam multiples this amount by his 1% finance charge to determine his late fee: $100 (0.01 x $10,000). He adds this amount to Acme's account balance. He does this every month the payment is late.

Collecting Overdue Accounts

If your invoice isn't paid on time, act quickly to collect. Clients who consistently pay late or do not pay at all can put you out of business. Moreover, often the longer a client fails to pay, the less likely it is that you'll ever be paid.

When an Account Is Overdue

Money that your clients or customers owe you is called an "account receivable." Keep track of the age of your accounts receivable so you know when a client's payment is late and how late it is. Many computer accounting programs can keep track of the age of your accounts receivable.

However, there is a simple way to do this without a computer. Make an extra copy of each of your invoices and keep them in a folder or notebook marked "Unpaid Invoices." When a client pays you, discard the extra copy of the applicable invoice. By looking in this notebook, you can tell exactly which clients haven't paid and how late their payments are.

Consider a client late if it fails to pay you within ten days after the due date on your invoice. At this point, you should contact the client and find out why you haven't been paid.

CAUTION

Find out where clients bank. When a client pays you by check, make a note of the name and address of the bank and the account number and place it in your client file. This information will come in handy if you ever have to collect a judgment against the client.

Contact the Client

Don't rely on collection letters. A phone call will have far more impact. Unfortunately, it can often be hard to get clients to return your collection calls. To reduce the time you spend playing phone tag, ask what time the client will be in and call back then. If you leave a phone message, state the time of day you receive return calls—for example, every afternoon from 1 p.m. to 5 p.m. If you can't reach the client by phone, try sending faxes. One self-employed worker even reports success from sending telegrams to nonpaying clients.

Your First Collection Call

During your first collection call, you want to either solve a problem that has arisen or handle a stalled payment. Write down who said what during this and each subsequent phone call.

Prepare before you make your call. You should know exactly how much the client owes you and have a copy of your invoice and any purchase order in front of you when you dial the number. Also, make sure you speak with the appropriate person. In large companies, this may be someone in the accounts payable or purchasing departments; in small companies, it could be the owner.

Politely inform the client that the payment is past due. About 80% of the time, late payments are caused by problems with invoices—for example, your client didn't receive an invoice or misplaced or didn't understand it. You may simply have to send another invoice or provide a brief explanation of why you charged as you did.

On the other hand, some clients may refuse to pay you because they are dissatisfied with your services or charges. In this event, schedule a meeting with the client as soon as possible to work out the problem. If the client is dissatisfied with only part of your work, ask for partial payment immediately.

Other clients may be satisfied with your services but not have the money to pay you. They may want an extension of time to pay or ask to work out a payment plan with you—for example, pay a certain amount every two weeks until the balance is paid. If such a client seems sincere about paying you, try to work out a reasonable payment plan. You are likely to get paid eventually this way—and you may also get repeat business from the client. If you agree to any new payment terms, set them forth in a confirming letter and send it to the client. The letter should state how much you'll be paid and by when. Keep a copy in your files.

Sample Confirming Letter #1

April 15, 20xx

Sue Jones, President
Acme Corporation
123 Main Street
Marred Vista, CA 90000

Re: Your contract # 1234
    Invoice # 102

Dear Sue:

Thank you for your offer to submit $500 per month to pay off your company's outstanding balance on the above account.

As agreed, I am willing to accept $500 monthly payments for four months until this debt is satisfied. The payments are due on the first of each month, beginning May 1, 20xx, and continuing monthly through August 1, 20xx.

As long as the payments are made on time, I will withhold all further action.

Thank you for your cooperation.

Very truly yours,

Andre Bocuse

Some clients may offer to pay a part of what they owe if you'll accept it as full payment. Although it may be galling to agree to this, it may make more economic sense than fighting with the client for full payment. If you agree to this orally, send the client a confirming letter setting forth the new payment terms. Keep a copy for yourself.

Beware of "Payment in Full" Checks

Be careful about accepting and depositing checks that have the words "Payment in Full" or something similar written on them. Where there's a dispute about how much the client owes you, depositing a full payment check usually means that you accept the check in complete satisfaction of the debt. Crossing out the words "Payment in Full" generally won't help you. You'll still be prevented from suing for the balance once you deposit the check.

However, in some states, you can cash a full-payment check and still preserve your right to sue for the balance by writing the words "Under Protest" or "Without Prejudice" on your endorsement.

Californians may cross out the full payment language, cash the check, and sue for the balance. However, the client may be able to get around this by sending a written notice that cashing the check means it was accepted as payment in full. (Calif. Civil Code § 1526.) Luckily, few clients are aware of this rule, so crossing out the full payment language usually works just fine.

Sample Confirming Letter #2

August 1, 20xx
John Anderson
200 Grub Street
Albany, NY 10000

Re: My Invoice # 102

Dear John:

As we agreed orally over the telephone, I'm willing to accept $4,500 as a full and complete settlement of your account.

This sum must be paid by September 1, 20xx, or this offer will become void.

Thank you for your cooperation, and I look forward to receiving payment.

Very truly yours,

Yolanda Allende

Subsequent Collection Efforts

If you haven't received payment after more than a month despite a first reminder, send the client another invoice marked "Second Notice." Call the client and send invoices monthly. If you've been dealing with someone other than the owner of the company, don't hesitate to call the owner. Explain that cashflow is important to your company and that you can't afford to carry this receivable any longer.

Be persistent. When it comes to collecting debts, the squeaky wheel usually gets the money. A client with a faltering business and many creditors who has the money to pay just one debt will likely pay the creditor who has made the most fuss.

At this point, you should feel free to stop all work for the client and not hand over any work you've completed but not yet delivered. You'll go broke fast if you keep working for people who don't pay you.

Don't Harass Deadbeat Clients

No matter how angry you are at a client who fails to pay you, don't harass him or her. Harassment includes:

- threatening or using physical force if the client doesn't pay
- using obscene or profane language
- threatening to sue the client when you don't really intend to do so
- threatening to have the client arrested
- phoning the client early in the morning or late at night
- causing a phone to ring repeatedly or continuously to annoy the client, or
- communicating with the client unreasonably often.

Many states have laws prohibiting these types of collection practices. And even in states that don't have specific laws against it, court decisions often penalize businesses that harass debtors. A client could sue you for engaging in this kind of activity. Use your common sense and deal with the client in a businesslike manner, regardless of how much he or she owes you—and however agitated that debt makes you feel.

If a Client Won't Pay

If a client refuses to pay or keeps breaking promises to pay, you must decide whether to write off the debt or take further action. If the client has gone out of business or is unable to pay you anything, either now or in the future, your best option may be to write off the debt. There's no point in spending time and money trying to get blood from a turnip.

But if the client is solvent, you should seriously consider:

- taking legal action against the client yourself
- hiring an attorney to take legal action against the client, or
- hiring a collection agency.

Sending a Final Demand Letter

Before you start any type of legal action against a client, send a final demand letter to the client stating that you will sue if you don't receive payment by a certain date. Many clients will pay you voluntarily after receiving such a letter—they don't want to be dragged into court and have their credit ratings damaged if you obtain a judgment against them.

In your letter, state how much the client owes you and inform the client that you'll take court action if full payment isn't received by a specific date. Here is an example of such a letter.

Sample Final Demand Letter

April 24, 20xx
Dick Denius
123 Grub Street
Anytown, AK 12345

Re: Your account number: 678

Dear Mr. Denius:

Your outstanding balance of $6,000 is over 120 days old.

If you do not make full payment by 5/15/20xx, a lawsuit will be filed against you. A recorded judgment will be a lien against your property and can have an adverse effect on your credit rating.

I hope to hear from you immediately so that this matter can be resolved without filing a lawsuit.

Very truly yours,

Natalie Kalmus

Suing in Small Claims Court

All states have a wonderful mechanism that helps businesses collect small debts: small claims court. Small claims courts are set up to resolve disputes involving relatively modest amounts of money. The limit is normally between $2,000 and $15,000, depending on the state in which you file your lawsuit. If you're owed more than the limit, you can still sue in small claims court for the limit and waive your right to collect the rest.

Small claims court is particularly well suited to collecting small debts because it's inexpensive and usually fairly quick. In fact, debt collection cases are by far the most common type of cases heard in small claims court.

You don't need a lawyer to go to small claims court. Indeed, a few states—including California, New York, and Michigan—bar you from bringing a lawyer to small claims court.

RESOURCE

For detailed advice about how to handle a small claims court suit, see *Everybody's Guide to Small Claims Court* (National and California editions), by Ralph Warner (Nolo).

You begin a small claims lawsuit by filing a document called a "complaint" or "statement of claim." These forms are available from your local small claims court clerk and are easy to fill out. You may also be asked to attach a copy of your written agreement, if you have one. You then notify the client, now known as the "defendant," of your lawsuit. Depending on your state, the notice can be delivered by certified mail or by a process server. Many clients pay up when they receive a complaint because they don't want to go to court.

A hearing date is then set. If the client doesn't show up in court, you'll win by default. A substantial percentage of clients don't contest claims for unpaid fees in court because they know they owe the money and can't win. If your client attends the court session, you present your case to a judge or court commissioner under rules that encourage a minimum of legal and procedural formality. Be sure to bring all your documentation to court, including your invoices, client agreement, and correspondence with the client.

Unfortunately, getting a small claims judgment against a client doesn't guarantee you'll be paid. Many clients will automatically pay a judgment you obtain against them, but others will refuse to pay. The court will not collect your judgment for you. You've got to do it yourself or hire someone to help you.

Big Fee, Small Claim

Gary, a freelance translator, recently contracted with the San Francisco office of a national brokerage firm to perform translating services on a rush basis. He completed the work on time and faxed it to the company with his invoice. The client failed to pay the invoice within 30 days.

Over the next three months, Gary sent the company a stream of collection letters demanding payment, but never heard a word. He finally got sick of waiting and decided to sue the client. He was owed $3,000 (well within the $7,500 California small claims court limit), so he filed his suit in the San Francisco small claims court.

He then had the San Francisco County Sheriff's Department serve his complaint on the client at its office. The next day he received a fax from the company's legal department at its New York headquarters apologizing for the delay in payment and promising to pay at once. He received a check within a few days.

Suing in Other Courts

If the client owes you substantially more than the small claims court limit for your state, you may wish to sue in a formal state trial court, usually

called the "superior court" or "municipal court." Debt collection cases are usually very simple, so you can often handle them yourself or hire a lawyer for the very limited purpose of giving you advice on legal points or helping with strategy. In truth, few collection cases ever go to trial. Usually, the defendant either reaches a settlement with you before trial or fails to show up in court and loses by default.

RESOURCE

For detailed guidance on how to represent yourself in courts other than small claims courts, see *Represent Yourself in Court: How to Prepare & Try a Winning Case*, by Paul Bergman and Sara J. Berman-Barrett (Nolo). This book explains how to handle a civil case yourself, without a lawyer, from start to finish.

Arbitration

Before you think about suing the client in court, look at your contract to see whether it contains an arbitration clause. If your contract has such a clause, you'll be barred from suing the client in small claims or any other court. This is not necessarily a bad thing. Arbitration is similar to small claims court in that it's intended to be speedy, inexpensive, and informal. The main difference is that a private decision maker paid for by the two parties, called an "arbitrator," not a judge, rules on the case. An arbitrator's judgment can be entered with a court and enforced just like a regular court judgment.

Hire an Attorney

Hiring an attorney to sue a client for an unpaid bill is usually not worth the expense involved unless the debt is very large and you know the client can pay. However, it can be effective to have a lawyer send a letter to a client. Some clients take communications from lawyers more seriously than they take a letter you write on your own. Some lawyers are willing to do this for a nominal charge.

Hire a Collection Agency

Collection agencies specialize in collecting debts. You don't pay them anything. Instead, they take a slice of the money they collect. This can range from 15% to 50% depending on the size, age, and type of debts involved. Collection agencies can be particularly good at tracking down "skips"—people who hide from their creditors.

Siccing a collection agency on a client will likely alienate the client and mean that you will not get any repeat business from him or her. Use this alternative only if you don't want to work for a particular client again.

You may have trouble finding an agency to deal with you if you have only a few debts, particularly if they're small. Try to get a referral to a good collection agency from colleagues or a professional organization or trade group. Ask for references before hiring any agency and call them to make sure the agency checks out. It's also advisable to get a fee agreement in writing.

Deducting Bad Debts From Income Taxes

In a few situations, you can deduct the value of an unpaid debt from your income taxes. This is called a "bad debt deduction." Unfortunately, if you're like the vast majority of self-employed people—a cash-basis taxpayer who sells services to your clients—you can't claim a bad debt deduction if a client fails to pay you. Because you don't report income until it is actually received, you aren't considered to have an economic loss when a client fails to pay. This rule seems absurd—you've lost the value of your time and energy when a client fails to pay you for your services—but it's strictly enforced by the IRS.

EXAMPLE:

Bill, a self-employed consultant, works 50 hours for a client and bills $2,500. The client never pays. Bill cannot deduct the $2,500 loss from his income taxes. Because Bill is a cash-basis taxpayer, he never reported the $2,500 as income because he never received it. As far as the IRS is concerned, this means Bill has no economic loss.

The only time a business can deduct a bad debt is if it actually lost cash on the account or it previously reported income from sale of the item. Few self-employed people give out cash, and only businesses using the accrual method of accounting report income from a sale for which no payment is received. There's no point in trying to switch to the accrual method to deduct bad debts. You won't reduce your taxes because the bad debt deduction merely wipes out a sale you previously reported as income. ●

Taxes and the Self-Employed

Employees don't need to worry much about taxes: All or most of their taxes are withheld from their paychecks by their employers and paid directly to the IRS and state tax department. The employer calculates how much to withhold. The employee's only responsibility is to file a tax return with the IRS and state tax department each year.

But when you become self-employed, your tax life changes dramatically. You have no employer to pay your taxes for you; you must pay them directly to the IRS and your state. This requires periodic tax filings you probably never made before—and it will be up to you to calculate how much you owe. To make these filings, you'll need to keep accurate records of your business income and expenses. And the tax return you must file each year will likely be more complicated than the ones you filed when you were an employee.

This chapter provides an overview of the new world of taxation you enter as a self-employed worker and explains some ways to navigate it.

Tax Basics for the Self-Employed

All levels of government—federal, state, and local—impose taxes. You need to be familiar with the requirements for each.

Federal Taxes

The federal government takes the biggest tax bite our of your earnings. When you're in business for yourself, the federal government may impose a number of taxes on you, including:

- income taxes
- self-employment taxes
- estimated taxes, and
- employment taxes.

Income Taxes

Everyone who earns more than a minimum amount must pay income taxes. Unless you're one of the few self-employed people who have formed a C corporation, you'll have to pay personal income tax on the profits your business earns. Fortunately, you may be able to take advantage of a number of business-related deductions to reduce your taxable income when you're self-employed. (See Chapter 9.)

By April 15 of each year, you'll have to file an annual income tax return with the IRS showing your income and deductions for the previous year and how much estimated tax you've paid. You must file IRS Form 1040 and include a special tax form in which you list all your business income and deductible expenses. Most self-employed people use IRS Schedule C, *Profit or Loss From Business*.

Tax matters are more complicated if you incorporate your business. If you form a C corporation, it will have to file its own tax return and pay taxes on its profits. Then, as an employee of your corporation, you'll have to file a personal tax return and pay income tax on the salary your corporation paid you.

Self-Employment Taxes

Self-employed people are entitled to Social Security and Medicare benefits when they retire, just like employees. And just like employees, they have to pay Social Security and Medicare taxes to help fund these programs. These taxes are called "self-employment taxes," or SE taxes. You must pay SE taxes if your net yearly earnings from self-employment are $400 or more. When you file your annual tax return, you must include IRS Form SE, showing how much SE tax you were required to pay.

Estimated Taxes

Federal income and self-employment taxes are pay-as-you-go taxes: You must pay these taxes as you earn or receive income during the year. Unlike employees, who usually have their income and Social Security and Medicare tax withheld from their pay by their employers, self-employed people normally pay their income and Social Security and Medicare taxes directly to the IRS. These tax payments, called "estimated taxes," are usually made four times every year on IRS Form 1040-ES—on April 15, June 15, September 15, and January 15. You have to figure out how much to pay; the IRS won't do it for you.

Employment Taxes

Finally, if you hire employees to help you in your business, you'll have to pay federal employment taxes for your employees. These consist of half your employees' Social Security and Medicare taxes and all of their federal unemployment tax. You must also withhold from earnings half your employees' Social Security and Medicare taxes and all their income taxes from their paychecks. You must pay these taxes monthly, by making federal tax deposits at specified banks. You may also deposit them directly with the IRS electronically. You'll have to keep records and file quarterly and annual employment tax returns with the IRS.

When you hire other self-employed people, however, you don't have to pay any employment taxes. You need only report payments over $600 for business-related services to the IRS and to your state tax department if your state has income taxes.

State Taxes

To complicate things further, you must pay state taxes in addition to federal taxes.

Income Taxes

All states except Alaska, Florida, Nevada, South Dakota, Texas, Washington, and Wyoming impose their own income taxes on the self-employed. New Hampshire and Tennessee impose income taxes on dividend and interest income only. Most states charge a percentage of the income shown on your federal income return. Depending on the state in which you live, these percentages range anywhere from 3% to 12%. If you're incorporated, your corporation will likely have to pay state income taxes and file its own state income tax return, too.

In most states, you have to pay your state income taxes during the year in the form of estimated taxes. These are usually paid at the same time you pay your federal estimated taxes. You'll also have to file an annual state income tax return with your state tax department. In all but five states—Delaware, Hawaii, Iowa, Louisiana, and Virginia—the return must be filed by April 15, the same deadline as your federal tax return.

Each state has its own income tax forms and procedures. Contact your state tax department to learn about your state's requirements and obtain the necessary forms. You can find your state's tax agency at www.taxadmin.org/fta/link.

Employment Taxes

If you live in a state with income taxes and have employees, you'll likely have to withhold state income taxes from their paychecks and pay this to your state tax department. You'll also have to provide your employees with unemployment compensation insurance by paying taxes to your state unemployment compensation agency.

Sales Taxes

Almost all states and many municipalities impose sales taxes of some kind. The only states without sales tax are Alaska, Delaware, Montana, New Hampshire, and Oregon.

All states that have sales taxes impose them on sales of goods or products to the public. If you only provide services to clients or customers, you probably don't have to worry about sales taxes, because most states either don't tax services at all or tax only certain specified services. Notable exceptions are Hawaii, New Mexico, and South Dakota—all of which impose sales taxes on all services, subject to certain exceptions.

If the products or services you provide are subject to sales tax, you'll have to fill out an application to obtain a state sales tax permit, discussed in Chapter 5. Many states impose penalties if you make a sale before you obtain this permit. Generally, you pay sales taxes four times a year, but you might have to pay monthly if you make a lot of sales.

Other State Taxes

Various states impose a hodgepodge of other taxes on businesses, too numerous and diverse to explain here. For example:

- Nevada imposes a Business Privilege Tax of $100 per year per employee.
- Hawaii imposes a general excise tax on businesses ranging from 0.15% to 4.5% of the gross receipts businesses earn.
- Washington state has a business and occupation tax on most businesses with a gross annual income over $12,000.

Contact your state tax department for information on these and other similar taxes your state might impose.

Local Taxes

You might have to pay local business taxes in addition to federal and state taxes. For example, many municipalities have their own sales taxes that you may have to pay to a local tax agency.

Some cities and counties also impose property taxes on business equipment or furniture. You

may be required to file a list of such property with local tax officials, along with cost and depreciation information. Some cities also have a tax on business inventory. This is why many retail businesses have inventory sales: They want to reduce their stock on hand before the inventory tax date.

A few large cities—for example, New York City—impose their own income taxes. Some also charge annual business registration fees or business taxes. Your local chamber of commerce should be able to give you good information on your local taxes. You can also contact your local tax department.

Calendar of Important Tax Dates

The calendar below shows you important tax dates during the year. If you're one of the few self-employed people who uses a fiscal year instead of a calendar year as your tax year, these dates will be different. If you have employees, you must make additional tax filings during the year.

The dates listed below represent the last day you have to take the action described. If any of the dates fall on a holiday or weekend, you have until the next business day to take the action.

Handling Your Taxes

Self-employed people commonly take care of their taxes in one of three ways. Your approach will depend on how complex your tax affairs are and whether you have the time, energy, and desire to do some or all of the work yourself.

First, self-employed people whose tax affairs are relatively simple can do their tax work themselves, particularly if they're comfortable using accounting and tax preparation computer programs.

EXAMPLE 1:

Steve, a freelance writer, does all of his taxes himself. He is a sole proprietor who works alone—he does not hire employees or

Tax Calendar	
Date	**Action**
January 15	Your last estimated tax payment for the previous year is due.
January 31	• If you file your tax return by now, you don't have to make the January 15 estimated tax payment. (See Chapter 11.) • If you hired independent contractors last year, you must provide them with Form 1099-MISC.
February 28	If you hired independent contractors last year, you must file all your 1099s with the IRS.
March 15	Corporations must file federal income tax returns.
April 15	• You must file your individual tax return with the IRS and pay any tax due. Or, you can pay the tax due and file for an extension of time to file your return. • You must make your first estimated tax payment for the year. • Partnerships must file information tax return. • Individual income tax returns due in all states except Delaware, Hawaii, Iowa, Louisiana, and Virginia.
April 20	Individual income tax returns due in Hawaii.
April 30	Individual income tax returns due in Delaware and Iowa.
May 1	Individual income tax returns due in Virginia.
May 15	Individual income tax returns due in Louisiana.
June 15	Make your second estimated tax payment for the year.
September 15	Make your third estimated tax payment for the year.

independent contractors. As a writer, he works at home and doesn't need much in the way of equipment or supplies. He has few business expenses other than his home office expenses.

Steve keeps track of his income and expenses using a simple computer accounting program. He also uses a computer tax preparation program to prepare his tax returns. He estimates that it takes him no more than one hour per month to do his bookkeeping and five hours to prepare his annual tax return.

Second, self-employed people with larger businesses often hire tax pros to do all the work for them. This may be a particularly good idea if you incorporate your business or have employees.

EXAMPLE 2:

Carol, a software tester, has formed a C corporation and has two employees. Her tax affairs are much more complicated than Steve's. She must file tax returns both for herself and her corporation. She must also withhold employment taxes from her own pay and her employees' pay and file quarterly and annual employment tax returns with the IRS and state of California. Her bookkeeping requirements are more complex than those of a sole proprietor like Steve.

Carol does none of her tax work herself. She hires an accountant to do her bookkeeping and prepare her tax returns and uses a payroll service to calculate and pay employment taxes for herself and her employees.

Third, self-employed people combine doing their taxes themselves with getting professional tax help. Even if you have a fairly complex tax return and want a tax pro to prepare it for you, you can still save money by doing some work, such as routine bookkeeping, yourself.

EXAMPLE 3:

Gary, a self-employed translator, is a sole proprietor like Steve. However, unlike Steve, he hires independent contractor translators to work for him. He has to keep track of his payments to the independent contractors and report them to the IRS and his state tax department. He also rents an outside office and must track this and other business expenses. A trained engineer with a mathematical bent, he does all his bookkeeping himself using a manual system. However, he hires an accountant to prepare his annual tax return that includes some rather complex business deductions like depreciating his business equipment.

Doing the Work Yourself

The more tax work you do yourself, the less you'll have to pay a tax pro such as an enrolled agent or certified public accountant (CPA) to help you. This will not only save you cash but will also give you more personal control over your financial life. This section describes the variety of tasks that you can do some or all of yourself.

Bookkeeping

Even if you hire a tax pro to prepare your tax returns, you'll save money if you keep good records. Tax pros have many horror stories about clients who come in with plastic bags or shoe boxes filled with a jumble of receipts and canceled checks. As you might expect, these people end up requiring more of the tax pro's time and paying much more than those who have a complete and accurate set of income and expense records. It is not difficult to set up and maintain a bookkeeping system for your business. You should do so when you first start business. (Chapter 14 describes a simple bookkeeping system adequate for most self-employed people, while Chapter 9 provides an overview of the business tax deductions you'll need to track.)

Paying Estimated Taxes

If your business makes money, you'll need to pay estimated taxes throughout the year. It's usually not too difficult to calculate what you owe and send in your money. You may have to make estimated tax payments soon after you start doing business, so don't delay this task. (See Chapter 11.)

If you live in one of the 43 states with income taxes—that is, all states but Alaska, Florida, Nevada, South Dakota, Texas, Washington, and Wyoming—call your state tax department to find out whether you must make estimated tax payments. (You can find your state's tax agency at www.taxadmin.org/fta/link.)

Paying State and Local Taxes

If you have to pay various state and local taxes, such as a gross receipts tax, sales tax, or personal property tax, seeking guidance from a tax pro can be very helpful, particularly if the expert is familiar with businesses similar to yours. Otherwise, you'll need to contact your state tax department and local tax office for information. However, once you learn about the requirements and obtain the proper forms, it's usually not difficult to compute these taxes on your own.

Filing Your Annual Tax Returns

The most difficult and time-consuming tax-related task you'll face is filing your annual tax return. This involves figuring out and calculating all your deductible expenses for the year and subtracting them from your gross income to determine your taxable income.

As you probably know, your federal tax return is due by April 15. If you live in a state that has income taxes, you'll have to file a state income tax return as well. These are also due by April 15 except in the states that have later dates. (See "Tax Calendar," above.)

One way to make your life easier is to hire a tax pro to prepare your returns the first year you're in business. You can then use those returns as a guide to do your own returns in future years.

Taxes at the Touch of a Button

Many self-employed people do their tax returns themselves. If your business is small, it's usually not that difficult. This task is made much easier by the availability of many excellent publications and computer programs.

Several tax preparation programs are available that contain all the necessary forms. The programs automatically put the information and numbers you type into the proper blanks on the forms. When you're done, the program prints out your completed tax forms. Most tax packages also have additional programs you can purchase for your state taxes.

These programs not only do all your tax calculations for you but they also contain online tax help and questionnaires that help you figure out what forms to use. Two of the most highly regarded tax preparation programs are *TurboTax* and *TaxCut*. There are versions of *TurboTax* specially designed for small business owners.

There are also several tax preparation guides that are published each year that provide much better guidance than the IRS instructions that come with your tax forms. These include *The Ernst and Young Tax Guide 2007* (CDS Books) and J.K. Lasser's *Your Income Tax* (Wiley).

Paying Employment Taxes

If you have employees, your tax life will be much more complicated than if you work alone or hire independent contractors. You'll need to file both annual and quarterly employment tax returns. You're also required to withhold part of your employees' pay and send it to the IRS along with a contribution of your own.

This is an area in which many business owners seek outside help, because calculating tax withholdings can be complex. Many use an accountant or payroll tax service to perform these tasks. However, if you have a computer, accounting programs such as *QuickBooks* and *PeachTree Accounting* can calculate your employee withholdings and prepare employment tax returns.

RESOURCE
If you handle your taxes yourself, you'll likely want to obtain a more detailed book on taxes specifically. Many excellent books are available, including:
- *Deduct It! Lower Your Small Business Taxes*, by Stephen Fishman (Nolo)
- *Home Business Tax Deductions*, by Stephen Fishman (Nolo), and
- *Tax Deductions for Professionals*, by Stephen Fishman (Nolo).

The IRS also has publications on every conceivable tax topic. These are free, but are sometimes difficult to understand. IRS Publication 910, *Guide to Free Tax Services*, contains a list of these publications; many of the most useful ones are cited in this book. One publication you should get is Publication 334, *Tax Guide for Small Business*. You can obtain these and all other IRS publications by calling the IRS at 800-TAX-FORM or by downloading them from the IRS's website at www.irs.gov.

Hiring a Tax Pro

Instead of doing it yourself, you can hire a tax professional to perform some or all of the work for you. A tax pro can also provide guidance to help you make key tax decisions, such as choosing the best setup for your business and helping you deal with the IRS if you get into tax trouble.

Big Changes in How Tax Preparers Handle Returns

Starting in 2007, the IRS imposes stiffer penalties on tax preparers who sign off on client tax returns that contain questionable or aggressive tax items that aren't disclosed to the IRS. Such a disclosure, typically filed on IRS Form 8275, may serve as an audit flag to the IRS. While clients may not want to make these disclosures, preparers may refuse to sign a client's return unless such a disclosure is included, or the aggressive or questionable items are removed—resulting in more taxes due for the client. These penalties do not apply to taxpayers who file their own returns.

Types of Tax Pros

There are several different types of tax pros, each differing widely in training, experience, and cost.

Tax preparers. As the name implies, tax preparers prepare tax returns. The largest tax preparation firm is H&R Block, but many smaller operations open for business in storefront offices during tax time. In most states, anybody can be a tax preparer; no license is required. Most tax preparers focus on individuals and lack the training or experience to handle taxes for businesses, so a tax preparer is probably not a wise choice.

Enrolled agents. Enrolled agents, or EAs, are tax advisors and preparers who are licensed by the IRS. They must have at least five years of experience and pass a difficult test. EAs are often the best choice for self-employed workers. They usually can do as good a job as a certified public accountant, but charge less. Many also offer bookkeeping and accounting assistance.

Certified public accountants. Certified public accountants, or CPAs, are licensed and regulated by each state. They undergo lengthy training and must pass a comprehensive exam. CPAs represent the high end of the tax pro spectrum. In addition to preparing tax returns, they perform sophisticated accounting and tax work. Large businesses routinely hire CPAs for tax help. However, if you're running a one-person business, you may not require a CPA's expertise—you might do just as well with a less expensive EA.

Tax attorneys. Tax attorneys are lawyers who specialize in tax matters. The only time you'll ever need a tax attorney is if you get into serious trouble with the IRS or state tax agency and need legal representation. Some tax attorneys also give tax advice, but they are usually too expensive for small businesses. You're probably better off hiring a CPA if you need specialized tax help.

Finding a Tax Pro

The best way to find a tax pro is to obtain referrals from business associates, friends, or professional associations. If none of these sources can give you a suitable lead, try contacting the National Association of Enrolled Agents at 202-822-NAEA (6232) or one of its state affiliates. You can find a listing of affiliates at the NAEA website at www.naea.org. Local CPA societies can give you referrals to local CPAs. You can also find tax pros in the Yellow Pages under "Accountants, Tax Return."

Your relationship with your tax pro will be one of your most important business relationships, so be selective about the person you choose. Talk with at least three tax pros before hiring one. You want a tax pro who takes the time to listen to you, answers your questions fully and in plain English, is knowledgeable, has experience with small businesses, and makes you feel comfortable. It can also be helpful if the tax pro already has clients in businesses similar to yours. A tax pro familiar with the tax problems posed by your type of business can often give you the best advice for the least amount of money.

Tax Pros' Fees

Ask about a tax pro's fees before hiring him or her and, to avoid misunderstandings, obtain a written fee agreement before he or she begins work.

Most tax pros charge by the hour. Hourly rates vary widely depending on where you live and on the type of tax pro you hire. Enrolled agents often charge $25 to $50 per hour. CPAs typically charge about $100 per hour. Some tax pros charge a flat fee for specific services—for example, preparing a tax return.

These fees are rarely set in stone, so you can usually negotiate. You'll be able to get the best possible deal if you hire a tax pro after the tax season when he or she is less busy—that is, during the summer or fall.

IRS Audits

You can report any income and claim any deductions you want to take on your tax return—after all, you (or your tax preparer) fill it out, not the government. However, the income and deductions listed on your tax return are subject to review by the IRS. This review is called a tax "audit." If an IRS auditor determines that you didn't pay enough tax, you'll have to pay the amount due plus interest and penalties.

The IRS: Clear and Present Danger or Phantom Menace?

A generation ago, the three letters in the alphabet Americans feared most were I-R-S. There was a simple reason for this: The IRS, the nation's tax police, enforced the tax laws relentlessly. In 1963,

an incredible 5.6% of all Americans had their tax returns audited. Everybody knew someone who had been audited. Jokes about IRS audits were a staple of nightclub comedians and cartoonists.

In 2006, only 0.80% of all Americans were audited, and an IRS audit was a relatively rare event. This lowering trend has persisted. There are several reasons for the change:

- **A decline in the IRS workforce.** Between 1997 and 2006, the IRS workforce declined by 14%.

- **An increase in workload.** At the same time the IRS workforce was declining, its workload was increasing, growing 12% between 1996 and 2004.

- **A new emphasis on service to taxpayers instead of enforcement.** Starting in the mid-1990s, the IRS began to change its emphasis from enforcement to providing taxpayer service. Staff duties were shifted from conducting audits to performing service functions like answering taxpayer questions.

- **Legal changes.** In 1998, Congress enacted new laws intended to prevent perceived abuses by IRS agents and auditors. These new protections also made it more difficult for the IRS to go after those who cheated on or evaded their taxes.

According to the IRS Oversight Board, the IRS lacks the resources to pursue the over $30 billion in taxes known to be incorrectly reported or not paid each year. In 2001, the nation's "tax gap"—the total inventory of taxes that are known and not paid—was estimated at between $312 billion and $353 billion.

Both the IRS and Congress are aware of the IRS's enforcement problems and have taken some steps to ameliorate them. The IRS has received moderate budget increases in the past few years and has placed a renewed emphasis on enforcement. Staff has been shifted from performing service functions like answering taxpayer questions to doing audits.

The precipitous decline in audit rates that began in the mid-1990s may have ended, but audit rates remain at low levels. However, the IRS Commissioner promises that audit rates will go up in the next few years, with the self-employed as one of the main targets. With huge federal budget deficits yawning as far as the eye can see, it seems likely that this is one government promise that will be kept.

You Are the IRS's Number One Target

Although the IRS is a troubled agency and the audit rate is at or near an all-time low, hundreds of thousands of people still get audited every year. Moreover, the unfortunate fact is that self-employed people are the IRS's number one target. This is shown by audit rate statistics: In 2006, the IRS audited 288,626 of the 9,533,326 tax returns filed by Schedule C filers—the category that includes the vast majority of the self-employed.

Every year, the IRS releases statistics about who got audited the previous year. Below are the most recent available audit statistics.

IRS Audit Rates		
	2005 Audit Rate	2006 Audit Rate
Sole Proprietors		
Income under $25,000	3.68%	3.78%
$25,000 – $100,000	2.21%	2.09%
$100,000 and over	3.65%	3.90%
Partnerships (includes most LLCs)	0.33%	0.40%
S Corporations	0.30%	0.40%
C Corporations		
Assets under $250,000	0.74%	0.70%
$250,000 – $1 million	0.96%	1.00%
$1 million – $5 million	1.02%	1.20%
$5 million – $10 million	2.67%	3.40%

This chart shows that sole proprietors have a much greater chance of being audited by the IRS than businesses operated through partnerships or corporations. In 2006, 3.0% of sole proprietors earning more than $100,000 from their business were audited. In contrast, only 0.40% of S corporations and 0.70% of C corporations with less than $250,000 in assets were audited. Thus, sole proprietors earning over $100,000 were five times more likely to be audited than most corporations! Only corporations with assets worth more than $10 million were audited more often than sole proprietors.

These statistics undoubtedly reflect the IRS's belief that sole proprietors habitually underreport their income, take deductions to which they are not entitled, or otherwise cheat on their taxes. The lesson these numbers teach is that you need to take the IRS seriously. This doesn't mean that you shouldn't take all the deductions you're legally entitled to take, but you should understand the rules and be able to back up the deductions you do take with proper records.

Audit Time Limit

As a general rule, the law allows the IRS to audit a tax return up to 36 months after it's filed. This means you normally don't have to worry about audits for tax returns you filed more than three years ago. The IRS calls the years during which it can audit you "open years."

Types of Audits

There are three types of audits: correspondence audits, office audits, and field audits.

- **Correspondence audits.** As the name indicates, correspondence audits are handled entirely by mail. These are the simplest and shortest type of IRS audit, usually involving a single issue. The IRS sends you written questions about a perceived problem and may request additional information and/or documentation. If you don't provide satisfactory answers or information, you'll be assessed additional taxes. Correspondence audits are often used to question a home business about unreported income—income the IRS knows the taxpayer received because an IRS Form 1099 listing the payment was filed by a client or customer of the taxpayer.

- **Office audits.** Office audits take place face-to-face with an IRS auditor at one of the 33 IRS district offices. These are more complex than correspondence audits, often involving more than one issue or more than one tax year. If you make less than $100,000 per year, this is the type of in-person audit you're likely to face.

- **Field audits.** The field audit is the most comprehensive IRS audit, conducted by an experienced revenue officer. In a field audit, the officer examines your finances, your business, your tax returns, and the records you used to create the returns. As the name implies, a field audit is normally conducted at the taxpayer's place of business; this allows the auditor to learn as much about your business as possible. Field audits are ordinarily reserved for taxpayers who earn a lot of money. You probably won't be subjected to one unless your business earns more than $100,000 per year.

What the Auditor Does

When auditing self-employed business owners, the IRS is most concerned about whether you have done any of the following things:

- **Underreported your income.** Unlike employees who have their taxes withheld for them by their employers, sole proprietors have no automatic withholdings and many opportunities to underreport how much they earned, particularly if they run a cash business.

- **Claimed tax deductions to which you were not entitled.** For example, you claimed that nondeductible personal expenses, such as a personal vacation, were deductible business expenses.

- **Properly documented the amount of your deductions.** If you don't have paperwork to back up the amount of a deduction, the IRS may reduce it, either entirely or in part. Lack of documentation is the main reason small business owners lose deductions when they get audited.

- **Taken business deductions for a hobby.** If you continually lose money or are involved in a fun activity such as art, photography, crafts, or writing that doesn't earn profits every year, the auditor may also question whether you are really in business. If the IRS claims you are engaged in a hobby, you could lose every single deduction for the activity. (See Chapter 9 for more on the hobby loss rule.)

An IRS auditor is entitled to examine the business records you used to prepare your tax returns, including your books, check registers, canceled checks, and receipts. The auditor can also ask to see records supporting your business tax deductions, such as a mileage record if you took a deduction for business use of your car. The auditor can also get copies of your bank records, either from you or your bank, and check them to see whether your deposits match the income you reported on your tax return. If you deposited a lot more money than you reported earning, the auditor will assume that you didn't report all of your income, unless you can show that the deposits you didn't include on your tax return were not income. For example, you might be able to show that they were loans, inheritances, or transfers from other accounts. This is why you need to keep good financial records.

Handling Audits

You have the legal right to take anyone along with you to help during an audit—a bookkeeper, tax pro, or even an attorney. If you've hired a tax pro to prepare your returns, it can be helpful for him or her to attend the audit to help explain your business receipts and records and how the returns were prepared. Some tax pros include free audit services as part of a tax preparation package.

However, if you prepared your tax returns yourself, you can probably deal with an office audit yourself. It could cost more to hire a tax pro to represent you in an office audit than the IRS is likely to seek from you. If you're worried that some serious irregularity will come to light—for example, you've taken a huge deduction and can't produce a receipt or canceled check to verify it—consult with a tax pro before the audit.

For a field audit, however, it usually makes sense to have a tax pro represent you no matter who prepared your tax returns. Field audits can result in substantial assessments.

RESOURCE

For a detailed discussion of IRS small business audits, see *Tax Savvy for Small Business*, by Frederick W. Daily (Nolo).

Ten Tips to Avoid an Audit

Here are ten things you can do to minimize your chances of getting audited.

Be Neat, Thorough, and Exact

If you file by mail, submit a tax return that looks professional. This will help you avoid unwanted attention from the IRS. Your return shouldn't contain erasures or be difficult to read. Your math should be correct. Avoid round numbers on your return (like $100 or $5,000). This looks like

you're making up the numbers instead of taking them from accurate records. You should include, and completely fill out, all necessary forms and schedules. Moreover, your state tax return should be consistent with your federal return. If you do your own taxes, using a tax-preparation computer program will help you produce an accurate return that looks professional.

Mail Your Return by Certified Mail or Delivery Service

Mail your tax return by certified mail, return receipt requested. If the IRS loses or misplaces your return, your receipt will prove that you submitted it. The IRS also accepts returns from four private delivery services: Airborne Express, DHL Worldwide Express, Federal Express, and United Parcel Service. Contact these companies for details on which of their service options qualify and how to get proof of timely filing.

Don't File Early

Unless you're owed a substantial refund, you shouldn't file your taxes early. The IRS generally has three years after April 15 to decide whether to audit your return. Filing early just gives the IRS more time to think about whether you should be audited. You can reduce your audit chances even more by getting an automatic extension to file until October 15. Note, however, that filing an extension does not extend the date by which you have to pay any taxes due for the prior year: These must still be paid by April 15.

Don't File Electronically

The IRS would like all taxpayers to file their returns electronically—that is, by email. There is a good reason for this: It saves the agency substantial time and money. Every year, the IRS must hire thousands of temporary workers to enter the numbers from millions of paper returns into its computer system. This is expensive, so the IRS has only about 40% of the data on paper returns transcribed. The paper returns are then sent to a warehouse where they are kept for six years and then destroyed. The IRS makes its audit decisions based on this transcribed data. By filing electronically, you give the IRS easy access to 100% of the data on your return instead of just 40%.

Form a Business Entity

The audit rate statistics above show that partnerships and small corporations are audited far less often than sole proprietors. Incorporating your business or forming a limited liability company will greatly reduce your audit risk. However, you must balance this against the time and expense involved in forming a corporation or LLC and having to complete more complex tax returns. Moreover, in some states—most notably California—corporations and LLCs have to pay additional state taxes. (See Chapter 2 for a detailed discussion of business entities.)

Explain Items the IRS May Question

If your return contains an item that the IRS may question or that could increase the likelihood of an audit, include an explanation and documentation to prove everything is on the up and up. For example, if your return contains a substantial bad debt deduction, explain the circumstances to show that the debt is a legitimate business expense. This won't necessarily avoid an audit, but it may reduce your chances. Here's why: If the IRS computer chooses your return as a candidate for an audit, an IRS classifier screens it to see whether it really warrants an audit. If your explanations look reasonable, the screener may decide you shouldn't be audited after all.

Avoid Ambiguous or General Expenses

Don't list expenses under vague categories such as "miscellaneous" or "general expenses": Be specific. IRS Schedule C lists specific categories for the most common small business expenses. If an expense doesn't fall within one of these classifications, create a specific name for it.

Report All of Your Income

The IRS is convinced that self-employed people, including many home business owners, don't report all of their income. Finding such hidden income is a high priority. As mentioned above, IRS computers compare 1099 forms with tax returns to determine whether there are any discrepancies.

Watch Your Income-to-Deduction Ratio

Back in the 1990s, a statistics professor named Amir D. Aczel got audited by the IRS. The experience proved so unpleasant that he decided to conduct a statistical study of how and why people get selected for IRS audits. He carefully examined more than 1,200 returns that were audited and reported his findings in a book (now out of print) called *How to Beat the IRS at Its Own Game* (Four Walls Eight Windows, 1994). He concluded that the key factor leading to an audit was the ratio of a taxpayer's expenses to his or her income.

According to Aczel, if your total business expenses amount to less than 52% of your gross business income, you are "not very likely" to be audited. If your business expenses are 52% to 63% of your business income, there is a "relatively high probability" that the IRS computer will tag you for an audit. Finally, if your expenses are more than 63% of your income, Aczel claims you are "certain to be computer tagged for audit." Of course, this doesn't necessarily mean that you *will* be audited.

Less than 10% of returns that are computer tagged for audit are actually audited. But being tagged considerably increases the odds that you'll be audited.

Whether Aczel's precise numbers are correct or not is anyone's guess. However, his basic conclusion—that your income-to-deduction ratio is an important factor in determining whether you'll be audited—is undoubtedly true. (A former IRS commissioner admitted as much in a CNN interview in 1995.)

Beware of Abnormally Large Deductions

It is not just the total amount of your deductions that is important: Very large individual deductions can also increase your audit chances. How much is too much? It depends in part on the nature of your business. A $50,000 deduction for equipment would likely look abnormal for a psychologist who works from home, but not for a construction contractor.

Reducing Your Income Taxes

If you're like the vast majority of self-employed people, you must pay personal federal income tax on the net profit you earn from your business activities. This is true whether you're legally organized as a sole proprietor, S corporation, partnership, or limited liability company. The only exception is if you've formed a C corporation.

The key phrase here is "net profit." You are entitled to deduct the total amount of your business-related expenses from your gross income—that is, all the money or the value of other items you receive from your clients or customers. You pay income tax on your resulting net profit, not your gross self-employment income.

EXAMPLE:

Karen, a sole proprietor, earned $50,000 this year from her consulting business. Fortunately, she doesn't have to pay income tax on the entire $50,000. She qualifies for several business-related tax deductions, including a $5,000 home office deduction and a $10,000 deduction for equipment expenses. She deducts these amounts from her $50,000 gross income to arrive at her net profit: $35,000. She pays income tax on only that amount.

This chapter provides an overview of the many business-related federal income tax deductions that are available to reduce your gross profits and, therefore, reduce the amount of income tax you have to pay. Although this chapter is a good introduction to the complex subject of tax deductions, you may need more detailed information.

 RESOURCE

For a more detailed treatment of income taxes, see:

- *Tax Savvy for Small Business*, by Frederick W. Daily (Nolo)
- *Deduct It: Lower Your Small Business Taxes*, by Stephen Fishman (Nolo)

- *Home Business Tax Deductions: Keep What You Earn*, by Stephen Fishman (Nolo), and
- *Tax Deductions for Professionals*, by Stephen Fishman (Nolo).

In addition, many IRS publications dealing with income tax issues are mentioned below. You can obtain a free copy of any IRS publication by calling 800-TAX-FORM, visiting your local IRS office, or downloading the publications from the IRS website at www.irs.gov.

CAUTION

Most states have income taxes, too. All states except Alaska, Florida, Nevada, South Dakota, Texas, Washington, and Wyoming also impose personal state income taxes on the self-employed. (New Hampshire and Tennessee impose state income taxes only on dividend and interest income.) If you're incorporated, your corporation will likely have to pay state income taxes as well. Contact your state tax department for income tax information and the appropriate forms.

Reporting Your Income

Employers deduct income taxes from their employees' paychecks, which they remit and report to the IRS. They give all their employees an IRS Form W-2, *Wage and Tax Statement*, showing wages and withholding for the year. Employees must file a copy of the W-2 with their income tax returns so that the IRS can compare the amount of income employees report with the amounts their employers claim they paid.

When you're self-employed, no income tax is withheld from your compensation and you don't receive a W-2 form. However, this does not mean that the IRS doesn't have at least some idea of how much money you've made. If a client pays you $600 or more over the course of a year, the client must complete and file IRS Form 1099-MISC to report the payments.

The client must complete and file a copy of Form 1099 with:

- the IRS
- your state tax office (if your state has income tax), and
- you.

To make sure you're not underreporting your income, IRS computers check the amounts listed on your 1099 forms against the amount of income you report on your tax return. If the amounts don't match, the IRS will likely send you a letter asking for an explanation.

When Form 1099 Is Not Required

Your clients need not file a 1099 form if you've incorporated your business and the client hires your corporation, not you personally. This is one reason clients often prefer to hire incorporated businesses. The IRS uses Form 1099 as an important audit lead. If a company files more 1099 forms than average for its type of business, the IRS often concludes that it must be misclassifying employees as independent contractors and may conduct an audit.

Although 1099 forms need not be filed for corporations generally, there are two exceptions to this rule. If you are an incorporated doctor or lawyer and perform more than $600 in services for a business during the year, the business must file a Form 1099 reporting the payments. Such a form need be filed only when your patient or client is a business—for example, where a company hires a doctor to examine an employee so the company can purchase "key man" life insurance, or where a lawyer defends a business in a lawsuit. A 1099 form need not be filed when the medical or legal services are not performed for a business—for example, when a patient sees a doctor to care for his or her personal medical needs or when an individual retains a lawyer to draft a personal will.

In addition, a 1099 form need not be filed to report payments to you solely for merchandise or inventory.

What to Do With Your 1099 Forms

You should receive all your 1099 forms for the previous year by January 31 of the current year. Check the amount of compensation your clients say they paid you in each Form 1099 against your own records, to make sure they are consistent. If there is a mistake, call the client immediately and request a corrected Form 1099. Insist that a corrected Form 1099 be filed with the IRS. You don't want the IRS to think you've been paid more than you really were.

You don't have to file your 1099 forms with your tax returns. Just keep them in your records.

1099s May Be Sent Electronically

Hiring firms may send Form 1099s to independent contractors electronically—that is, by email. But they may do this only if the independent contractor agrees to it. If not, the firm must deliver them by mail or in person. If you have an email account, there is no disadvantage to getting your forms electronically. You'll probably get your Form 1099s faster. Indeed, you may wish to ask your clients to send your forms by email yourself, and they will probably be glad to comply. Be sure to save your Form 1099s. If you get them by email, print them out and keep them in a file.

If You Don't Receive a Form 1099

It's not unusual for clients to fail to file required 1099 forms. This may be unintentional—for example, the client may not understand the rules or may just be negligent in filing them. On the other hand, some clients purposefully fail to file 1099 forms because they don't want the IRS to know they're hiring independent contractors.

If, by January 31, you don't receive a Form 1099 from a client who paid you more than $600 for business-related services the prior year, call the client and ask for it. If the client still does not produce the form, don't worry about it. It's not your duty to see that 1099 forms are filed. This is your client's responsibility. The IRS will not impose any fines or penalties on you if a client fails to file a Form 1099. It may, however, impose a $100 fine on the client—and exact far more severe penalties if an IRS audit reveals that the client should have classified you as an employee.

Whether or not you receive a Form 1099, it is your duty to report all the self-employment income you earn each year to the IRS. If you're audited by the IRS, it will, among other things, examine your bank records to make sure you haven't underreported your income. If you have underreported, you'll have to pay back taxes, fines, and penalties.

Your Reported Income Must Jibe With Your 1099 Forms

It's very important that the self-employment income you report on your tax return be at least equal to that reported to the IRS on the 1099 forms your clients send in. If a client reimbursed you for expenses such as travel, be sure to check and see if the Form 1099 the client provides you includes this amount. Some clients routinely include expense reimbursements on their 1099 forms, others do not.

If a Form 1099 includes expenses, you must report the entire amount as income on your tax return. You then deduct the amount of the expense reimbursement as your own business expense on your Schedule C. This way, your net self-employment income will come out right, without raising a red flag for the IRS.

Income Tax Deduction Basics

A deduction is an expense or the value of an item that you can subtract from your gross income to determine your taxable income—that is, the amount you earn that is subject to taxation. The more deductions you have, the lower your taxable income and the less income tax you pay. When people speak of taking a deduction or deducting an expense from their income taxes, they mean that they subtract it from their gross income.

Most of the work involved in doing your taxes will go into determining what deductions you can take, how much you can take, and when you can take them. You don't have to become an income tax expert. But even if you have a tax pro prepare your tax returns, you need to have a basic understanding of what expenses are deductible so that you can keep proper records. This takes some time, but it's worth it. There's no point in working hard to earn a good income only to miss deductions to which you are entitled and turn over more of your income to the government than required.

What You Can Deduct

Virtually any expense is deductible as long as it is:

- ordinary and necessary
- directly related to your business, and
- for a reasonable amount.

Ordinary and Necessary Expenses

An expense qualifies as ordinary and necessary if it is common, accepted, helpful, and appropriate for your business or profession. An expense doesn't have to be indispensable to be necessary; it need only help your business in some way, even in a minor way. It's usually fairly easy to tell if an expense passes this test.

EXAMPLE 1:

Bill, a freelance writer, hires a research assistant for a new book he's writing about ancient Athens and pays her $15 an hour. This is a deductible business expense. Hiring research assistants is a common and accepted practice among professional writers. The assistant's fee is an ordinary and necessary expense for Bill's writing business.

EXAMPLE 2:

Bill, the freelance writer, visits a masseuse every week to work on his bad back. Bill claims the cost as a business expense, reasoning that avoiding back pain helps him concentrate on his writing. This is not an ordinary or customary expense for a freelance writer, so the IRS would not likely allow it as a business expense.

Expense Must Be Related to Your Business

An expense must be related to your business to be deductible. That is, you must use the item you buy for your business in some way. For example, the cost of a personal computer is a deductible business expense if you use the computer to write business reports.

You cannot deduct purely personal expenses as business expenses. The cost of a personal computer is not deductible if you use it just to play computer games. If you buy something for both personal and business reasons, you may deduct the business portion of the expense. For example, if you buy a cellular phone and use it half the time for business calls and half the time for personal calls, you can deduct half the cost of the phone as a business expense.

However, the IRS requires you to keep records showing when the item was used for business and when for personal reasons. One acceptable form of record would be a diary or log with the dates, times, and reason the item was used. This kind of record keeping can be burdensome and may not be worth the trouble if the item isn't very valuable.

To avoid having to keep such records, try to use items either only for business or only for personal use. For example, if you can afford it, purchase two computers and use one solely for your business and one for playing games and other personal uses.

Deductions Must Be Reasonable

There is usually no limit on how much you can deduct as long as it's not more than you actually spend and the amount is reasonable. Certain areas are hot buttons for the IRS—especially entertainment, travel, and meal expenses. The IRS won't allow such expenses to the extent it considers them lavish.

Also, if the amount of your deductions is very large relative to your income, your chance of being audited goes up dramatically. One recent analysis of almost 1,300 tax returns found that those whose business deductions exceeded 63% of their revenues were at high risk for an audit. You're relatively safe so long as your deductions are less than 52% of your revenue. If you have extremely large deductions, make sure you can document them in case you're audited.

Common Deductions for the Self-Employed

Self-employed workers are typically entitled to take a number of income tax deductions. The most common include:

- advertising costs—for example, the cost of a Yellow Pages advertisement, brochure, or business website
- attorney and accounting fees for your business
- bank fees for your business bank account
- business start-up costs
- car and truck expenses
- costs of renting or leasing vehicles, machinery, equipment, and other property used in your business
- depreciation of business assets

- education expenses—for example, the cost of attending professional seminars or classes required to keep up a professional license
- expenses for the business use of your home
- fees you pay to other self-employed workers you hire to help your business—for example, the cost of paying a marketing consultant to advise you on how to get more clients
- health insurance for yourself and your family
- insurance for your business—for example, liability, workers' compensation, and business property insurance
- interest on business loans and debts—for example, interest you pay for a bank loan you use to expand your business
- license fees—for example, fees for a local business or occupational license
- office expenses, such as office supplies
- office utilities
- postage
- professional association dues
- professional or business books you need for your business
- repairs and maintenance for business equipment such as a photocopier or fax machine
- retirement plan contributions
- software you buy for your business
- subscriptions for professional or business publications
- business travel, meals, and entertainment, and
- wages and benefits you provide your employees.

If Your Client Reimburses You for Expenses

Many self-employed people, especially professionals such as attorneys and accountants, typically have all or some of the expenses they incur while working for a client reimbursed by their clients or customers. This is particularly common for local and long-distance travel expenses.

Obviously, if you incur a deductible expense while performing services for a client, and the client does not reimburse you, you may deduct the expense on your own return. Your client gets no deduction for the expense, because it didn't pay for it.

But if your client reimburses you for an expense, your client gets the deduction, not you. However, you need not include the reimbursement in your income if you provide an adequate accounting of the expenses to your client. If the reimbursement is for entertainment expenses, the client must keep your records documenting each element of the expense. The reimbursement should not be included in any 1099-MISC form the client files with the IRS reporting how much you were paid for the year.

EXAMPLE:

Jason, an attorney based in Chicago, is hired by Acme Corp. to handle a trial in Albuquerque, New Mexico. He incurs $5,000 in travel expenses, which he fully documents. Acme reimburses Jason for the $5,000 expense. Jason need not include this amount in his income for the year. Acme may deduct it as a business expense.

To adequately account for an expense, you must comply with all the documentation requirements for the expense and provide your expense records to the client in a timely manner. An accounting is timely if it is made within 60 days after an expense is incurred. You must also return any payments from a client that exceed your actual expenses within 120 days after they are made.

If you do not adequately account to your client for these expenses, the client still gets to deduct the expense, but *you must pay tax on the reimbursement.* Moreover, the client must include the amount of the reimbursement in any 1099-MISC it files with the IRS reporting how much it paid you for your services.

EXAMPLE:

Assume that Jason doesn't keep proper records of his travel expenses, but is still reimbursed $5,000 by Acme. Acme must include the $5,000 payment in the 1099-MISC form it files with the IRS reporting how much it paid Jason. Jason will have to pay tax on the $5,000.

For simplicity in bookkeeping, some self-employed people routinely deduct all expenses they incur, even those that were reimbursed by clients. But they also include the amount of all the reimbursements they receive from their clients in their income and pay tax on them. This is fine with the IRS. What you cannot do is deduct an expense and not report as income a reimbursement you received for it.

When to Deduct

Some expenses can be deducted all at once; others have to be deducted over a number of years.

Current Expenses

The cost of anything you buy for your business that has a useful life of less than one year must be fully deducted in the year it is purchased. This includes, for example, rent, telephone and utility bills, photocopying costs and postage, and other ordinary business operating costs. Such items are called "current expenses."

Capital Expenses

Certain types of costs are considered part of your investment in your business rather than operating costs. These are called "capital expenses." Subject to an important exception for a certain amount of personal property, discussed later in this chapter, you cannot deduct the full value of such expenses in the year you incur them. Instead, you must spread the cost over several years and deduct part each year.

There are two main categories of capital expenses. They include:

- the cost of any asset you will use in your business that has a useful life of more than one year—for example, equipment, vehicles, books, furniture, machinery, and patents, and

- business start-up costs, such as fees for market research or attorney and accounting services to set up your business.

Inventory

Special rules apply to when you may deduct the cost of inventory. Inventory consists of the goods and products that a business keeps on hand to sell to customers in the ordinary course of business. It includes almost any tangible personal property that a business offers for sale. It makes no difference if you make the goods yourself or buy them from others to resell.

If the sale of inventory is an "income-producing factor" for your business, you may currently deduct only the value of the inventory you sell during the year (the "cost of goods sold"). The value of unsold inventory at the year-end must be carried on your books as a business asset and may not be deducted until the year it is sold or becomes worthless. This is called "carrying an inventory." You deduct the cost of goods sold during the year from your business receipts to determine your gross profit from the business. You then deduct your business expenses from your gross profit to determine your net profit, which is taxed.

When do sales become an "income-producing factor"? There's no exact figure, but many tax experts believe that a business that derives 8% or less of its total gross revenue from the sale or production of merchandise need not maintain an inventory. A business that makes at least 15% of its money from selling or producing merchandise has to maintain an inventory, and a business that earns 9% to 14% of its money from merchandise is in a gray area.

Many self-employed people do not have to worry about inventories because they provide only personal services to their clients or customers. However, if you sell your clients goods as well as services, you'll have to follow the inventory rules if your income from the goods is substantial. For example, the IRS held that a veterinarian had to carry inventories because the sale of drugs, pet foods, and livestock antibiotic food additives constituted approximately 50% of his gross receipts each year. (TAM 9218008 (May 1, 1992).)

RESOURCE

For more information on inventories, refer to the "Cost of Goods Sold" section in Chapter 7 of IRS Publication 334, *Tax Guide for Small Business*, and IRS Publication 538, *Accounting Periods and Methods*.

Supplies

Supplies are materials and property consumed or used up during the production of merchandise or provision of services. Good examples are rubber gloves and disposable syringes used by doctors and nurses to provide medical services. These items do not physically become part of merchandise a business sells, so they are not included in inventory.

Subject to one important exception, the cost of supplies *must be deducted in the year in which they are used or consumed*, which is not necessarily the year you purchase them. This means that you must keep track of how much material you use each year.

TIP

The same item can constitute supplies for one business and inventory for another. It all depends on whether the item is furnished to the client or customer, or consumed in performing a service. For example, the paper and ink used to prepare blueprints are inventory in the hands of a paper and ink manufacturer, but supplies in the hands of an architect.

However, you may deduct the entire cost of supplies that are incidental to your business in the year when you purchase them. Supplies are incidental if:

- they are of minor or secondary importance to your business (but if you treat the cost of supplies on hand as an asset for financial reporting purposes, they are not incidental) (TAM 9209007 (Feb. 28, 1992))
- you do not keep a record of when you use the supplies
- you do not take a physical inventory of the supplies at the beginning and end of the tax year (TAM 8630003 (Apr. 17, 1986) and TAM 9209007), and
- deducting the cost of supplies in the year you purchase them does not distort your taxable income (Treas. Reg. § 1.162-3; TAM 9209007).

The incidental-supplies exception swallows the general rule for many self-employed people, because they don't keep careful track of their supplies and they are not worth enough to be treated as a business asset.

EXAMPLE:

Carol is a self-employed graphic designer who creates book covers for her clients. Carol keeps on hand in her home office various kinds of drawing paper, colored pencils, pens, inks, paints, and brushes. She doesn't keep track of when she uses these supplies or take a physical inventory of them. They don't cost enough to be treated as a business asset. Carol's supplies are incidental supplies. She may deduct their cost in the year she paid for them.

Businesses That Lose Money

If the money you spend on your business exceeds your business income for the year, your business incurs a loss. There is a bright side: You can use a business loss to offset other income you may have—for example, interest income or your spouse's income if you file jointly. You can even accumulate your losses and apply them to reduce your income taxes in future or past years.

> **RESOURCE**
>
> For detailed information on deducting business losses, see IRS Publication 536, *Net Operating Losses (NOLs) for Individuals, Estates, and Trusts.* You can obtain this and all other IRS publications by calling the IRS at 800-TAX-FORM, visiting your local IRS office, or downloading the publications from the IRS website at www.irs.gov.

Recurring Losses

If you keep incurring losses year after year, you need to be very concerned about running afoul of what is known as the "hobby loss rule." This rule could cost you a fortune in additional income taxes.

The IRS created the hobby loss rule to prevent taxpayers from entering into ventures primarily to incur expenses they could deduct from their other incomes. The rule allows you to take a business expense deduction only if your venture qualifies as a business. Ventures that don't qualify as businesses are called hobbies. If the IRS views what you do as a hobby, there will be severe limits on what expenses you can deduct.

A venture is a business if you engage in it to make a profit. It's not necessary that you earn a profit every year. All that is required is that your main reason for doing what you do is to make a profit. A hobby is any activity you engage in mainly for a reason other than making a profit—for example, to incur deductible expenses or just to have fun.

The IRS can't read your mind to determine whether you want to earn a profit. And it certainly isn't going to take your word for it. Instead, it looks to see whether you do actually earn a profit or behave as if you want to earn a profit. It uses two tests to make this determination: the profit test and the behavior test.

Profit Test

If your venture earns a profit in three out of five consecutive years, the IRS presumes that you have a profit motive. The IRS and courts look at your tax returns for each year you claim to be in business to see whether you turned a profit. Any legitimate profit—no matter how small—qualifies; you don't have to earn a particular amount or percentage. Careful year-end planning can help your business show a profit for the year. If clients owe you money, for example, you can press for payment before the end of the year. You can also put off paying expenses or buying new equipment until the next tax year.

Even if you meet the three-of-five years profit test, the IRS can still claim that your activity is a hobby, but it will have to prove that you don't have a profit motive. In practice, the IRS usually doesn't attack ventures that pass the profit test unless the numbers have clearly been manipulated just to meet the standard.

The presumption that you are in business applies to your third profitable year and extends to all later years within the five-year period beginning with your first profitable year.

EXAMPLE:

Tom began working at home as a self-employed graphic designer in 2003. Due to economic conditions and the difficulty of establishing a new business, his income varied dramatically from year to year. However, as the chart below shows, he managed to earn a profit in three of the first five years that he was in business.

Year	Losses	Profits
2003	$10,000	
2004		$5,500
2005		$9,000
2006	$6,000	
2007		$18,000

If the IRS audits Tom's taxes for 2007, it must presume that he was in business during that year. Tom earned a profit during three of the five consecutive years ending with 2007, so the presumption that Tom is in business extends through 2008, five years after his first profitable year (2004).

Behavior Test

If you keep incurring losses and can't satisfy the profit test, you by no means have to throw in the towel and treat your venture as a hobby. You can continue to treat it as a business and fully deduct your losses. However, you must take steps to convince the IRS that your business is not a hobby in case you're audited.

You must be able to convince the IRS that earning a profit—not having fun or accumulating tax deductions—is the primary motive for what you do. This can be particularly difficult if you're engaged in an activity that could objectively be considered fun—for example, creating artwork, photography, or writing—but it can still be done. People who have incurred losses for seven, eight, or nine years in a row have convinced the IRS that they were running a business.

You must show the IRS that your behavior is consistent with that of a person who really wants to make money. There are many ways to accomplish this.

First and foremost, you must show that you carry on your enterprise in a businesslike manner—for example, you:

- maintain a separate checking account for your business
- keep good business records
- make some effort to market your services—for example, have business cards and, if appropriate, a Yellow Pages or similar advertisement

Losing Golfer Scores Hole-in-One in Tax Court

Donald, a Chicago high-school gym teacher, decided to become a golf pro when he turned 40. He became a member of the Professional Golfers of America, which entitled him to compete in certain professional tournaments. Donald kept his teaching job and played in various professional tournaments during the summer. His expenses exceeded his income from golfing for five straight years.

Year	Golf Earnings	Golf Expenses	Losses
1978	$ 0	$2,538	$2,538
1979	148	1,332	1,184
1980	400	4,672	4,272
1981	904	4,167	3,263
1982	1,458	8,061	6,603

The IRS sought to disallow the losses for 1981 and 1982, claiming that golf was a hobby for Donald. Donald appealed to the Tax Court and won.

The court held that Donald played golf to make a profit, not just to have fun. He carefully detailed the expenses he incurred for each tournament he entered and recorded the prize money available. He attended a business course for golfers and assisted a professional golfer from whom he also took lessons. He practiced every day, up to 12 hours during the summer. He also traveled frequently to Florida during the winter to play. Although his costs increased over the years, his winnings steadily increased each year as well. The court concluded that, although Donald obviously enjoyed golfing, he honestly wanted to earn a profit from it. (*Kimbrough v. Commissioner*, 55 T.C.M. 730 (1988).)

- have business stationery and cards printed
- obtain a federal employer identification number
- secure all necessary business licenses and permits
- have a separate phone line for your business if you work at home
- join professional organizations and associations, and
- develop expertise in your field by attending educational seminars and similar activities.

You should also draw up a business plan with forecasts of revenue and expenses. This will also be helpful if you try to borrow money for your business.

RESOURCE
For detailed guidance on how to create a business plan, see *How to Write a Business Plan,* by Mike McKeever (Nolo).

The more time and effort you put into the activity, the more it will look like you want to make money. So try to devote as much time as possible to your business and keep a log showing the time you spend on it.

It's also helpful to consult with experts in your field and follow their advice about how to modify your operations to increase sales and cut costs. Be sure to document your efforts.

EXAMPLE:
Otto, a professional artist, has incurred losses from his business for the past three years. He consults with Cindy, a prominent art gallery owner, about how he can sell more of his work. He writes down her recommendations and then documents his efforts to follow them—for example, he visits art shows around the country and talks with a number of gallery owners about representing his work.

You'll have an easier time convincing the IRS that your venture is a business if you earn a profit in at least some years. It's also very helpful if you've earned profits from similar businesses in the past.

Tax Effect

If the IRS determines that your venture is a hobby, you'll lose valuable deductions and your income tax burden will increase. Unlike business expenses, expenses for a hobby are personal expenses that you can deduct only from income you earn from the hobby. They can't be applied to your other income, such as your or your spouse's salary or interest income.

EXAMPLE:
Bill holds a full-time job as a college geology teacher. He also paints part time and shows his work in art galleries. The IRS has decided that painting is a hobby for Bill, because he's never earned a profit from it. In one year, Bill spent $2,000 on the painting hobby, but earned only $500 from the sale of one painting. His expenses can be deducted only from the $500 income derived from painting. This wipes out the $500, but Bill cannot apply the remainder of the loss ($1,500) to his other income. Because of the hobby loss rule, Bill has lost $1,500 worth of tax deductions.

Tax Savings From Deductions

Because tax deductions are subtracted from income before the income is taxed and not from the taxes you owe, only part of any deduction will end up as an income tax saving. For example, a $5,000 tax deduction will not result in a $5,000 income tax savings—it will lower your taxable income by $5,000.

How much you'll save depends on your tax rate. The tax law assigns a percentage income tax rate to specified income levels. People with high incomes pay income tax at a higher rate than those with lower incomes. These percentage rates are called "tax brackets."

To determine how much income tax a deduction will save you, you need to know your "marginal tax bracket." This is the tax bracket in which the last dollar you earn falls. The income tax brackets are adjusted each year for inflation.

RESOURCE

For the current brackets, see IRS Publication 505, *Tax Withholding and Estimated Tax*. You can obtain this and all other IRS publications by calling the IRS at 800-TAX-FORM, visiting your local IRS office, or downloading the publications from the IRS website at www.irs.gov.

The table below shows the tax brackets for 2007. For example, if you are single and earn $50,000 in 2007, your marginal tax bracket is 25%—that is, you have to pay 25 cents in income tax for every additional dollar you earned.

To determine how much tax a deduction will save you, multiply the amount of the deduction by your marginal tax bracket. If your marginal tax bracket is 25%, you will save 25 cents in income taxes for every dollar you are able to claim as a deductible business expense.

EXAMPLE:

Barry, a single self-employed consultant, earns $50,000 in 2007 and is therefore in the 25% marginal tax bracket. He was able to take a $5,000 home office deduction. His actual income tax saving was 25% of the $5,000 deduction, or $1,250.

You can also deduct most business-related expenses from your income for self-employment tax purposes. (See Chapter 10.) The effective self-employment tax rate is about 12% on net self-employment income up to the Social Security tax cap ($97,500 in 2007). (See Chapter 10.)

In addition, you may deduct your business expenses from your state income taxes. State income tax rates vary, but they average about 6%. (However, Alaska, Florida, Nevada, South Dakota, Texas, Washington, and Wyoming don't have state income taxes.)

When you add all this together, you can see the true value of a business tax deduction. For example, if you're in the 25% federal income tax bracket, all the tax deductions you can obtain for business-related expenses add up to 43% of what you spend (25% + 12% + 6% = 43%). So you end up deducting about 43% of the cost of your business expenses from your state and federal

2007 Federal Personal Income Tax Brackets

Tax Rate	Income If Single	Income If Married Filing Jointly
10%	Up to $7,825	Up to $15,560
15%	From $7825 – $31,850	$15,561 – $63,700
25%	$31,851 – $77,100	$63,701 – $128,500
28%	$77,101 – $169,850	$128,501 – $195,850
33%	$169,851 – $349,700	$195,851 – $349,700
35%	All over $349,700	All over $349,700

taxes. If, for example, you buy a $1,000 computer for your business, you may end up deducting about $430 of the cost from your taxes. That's a whopping tax savings. In effect, the government is paying for almost half of your business expenses. This is why it's so important to take all the business deductions to which you're entitled.

Business Use of Your Home

Many self-employed people work from home, particularly when they're starting out. If you can meet some strict requirements, you're allowed to deduct your expenses for the business use of part of your home—what's known as the "home office deduction." For a detailed discussion of the home office deduction, see Chapter 4.

Cost of Business Assets

One of the nice things about being self-employed is that you can deduct the money you spend for things you use to help produce income for your business—for example, computers, calculators, and office furniture. You can take a full deduction whether you pay cash for an asset or buy on credit.

If you qualify for the Section 179 deduction discussed below, you can deduct the entire cost of these items in the year you pay for them. Otherwise, you have to deduct the cost over a period of years—a process called depreciation.

The rules for deducting business assets can be complex, but it's worth spending the time to understand them. After all, by allowing these deductions, the U.S. government is, in effect, offering to help you pay for your equipment and other business assets. All you have to do is take advantage of the offer.

Section 179 Deduction

If you learn only one section number in the tax code, it should be Section 179. This section provides one of the greatest tax boons for small business owners. Section 179 permits you to deduct a large amount of your business asset purchases in the year you make them, rather than having to depreciate them over several years. This is called "first year expensing" or "Section 179 expensing."

EXAMPLE:

Ginger buys an $8,000 photocopy machine for her business. She can use Section 179 to deduct the entire $8,000 expense from her income taxes for the year.

It's up to you to decide whether to use Section 179. It may not always be in your best interests to do so. If you do use it, you can not change your mind later and decide to use depreciation (discussed later in this chapter) instead.

Property You Can Deduct

You can use Section 179 to deduct the cost of any tangible personal property you use for your business that the IRS has determined will last more than one year—for example, computers, business equipment, and office furniture. (Special rules apply to cars.) You can't use Section 179 for land, buildings, or intangible personal property such as patents, copyrights, and trademarks.

You may use Section 179 expensing only for used or new property that you purchase—whether you pay with cash, credit card, borrowed funds, or buy on an installment plan. You may not use it for property you lease, inherit, or are given. Nor may you use it for property you buy from a relative or from a corporation or other organization you control.

If you use property both for business and personal purposes, you may deduct it under Section 179 only if you use it for business purposes more than half the time. You must reduce the amount of your deduction by the percentage of personal use. You'll need to keep records showing your business use of such property. If you use an item for business less than half the time, you must depreciate it, as explained in "Depreciation," below.

Deduction Limit

There is a limit on the total amount of business property expenses you can deduct each year using Section 179. The limit is $125,000 in 2008.

Starting in 2011, the Section 179 limit is scheduled to be reduced to $25,000. Congress may act to make the $125,000 limit permanent—but no one knows or can predict what Congress will do. So, if you're planning to buy more than $25,000 worth of property for your business in one year and you want to deduct the whole amount under Section 179, you should make your purchases before 2011.

This dollar limit applies to all of your businesses together, not to each business you own and run. You do not have to claim the full cost of the property. It's up to you to decide how much you want to deduct. But you won't lose out on the remainder; you can depreciate any cost you do not deduct under Section 179.

Year	Section 179 Deduction Limit	Property Value Limit
2006	$108,000	$430,000
2007	$125,000	$500,000
2008–2010	$125,000 + annual inflation adjustment	$500,000 + annual inflation adjustment
2011	$25,000	$200,000

Because the $108,000 Section 179 limit is so large, most smaller and even medium-sized businesses will be unable to exceed it each year. However, if you purchase enough business property in one year to exceed the limit, you can divide the deduction among the items you purchase in any

way you want, as long as the total deduction is not more than the Section 179 limit. It's usually best to apply Section 179 to property that has the longest useful life (and therefore the longest depreciation period). This reduces the total time you will have to wait to get your deductions.

EXAMPLE:

In 2008, Acme Printing, LLC, a printing company, buys a substantial amount of equipment, including two new printing presses for $40,000 each, two $15,000 copiers, and a $25,000 custom computer system. This adds up to $130,000 in business property purchases, $22,000 more than the Section 179 limit for 2008. Acme can divide its Section 179 deduction among these items any way it chooses. The copiers and computer system would have to be depreciated over five years, but the printing presses over seven years. Therefore, Acme should apply Section 179 to the printing presses first and then to the copiers or computer system. Any portion of the cost of the copier or presses that exceeds the Section 179 limit can be depreciated over five years. This way, Acme has to wait only five years (rather than seven) to get its full deduction for all of the year's purchases.

Limits on Section 179 Deductions

You can't use Section 179 to deduct more in one year than the total of your profit from all of your businesses and your salary, if you have a job in addition to your business. If you're married and file a joint tax return, you can include your spouse's salary and business income in this total as well. But you can't count investment income—for example, interest you earn on your savings.

You can't use Section 179 to reduce your taxable income below zero. But you can carry forward any amount you cannot use as a Section 179 deduction and possibly deduct it in the next tax year.

EXAMPLE:

In 2008, Amelia earned a $5,000 profit from her engineering consulting business and $10,000 from a part-time job. She spent $17,000 for computer equipment. She can use Section 179 to deduct $15,000 of this expense in 2008 and deduct the remaining $2,000 the next year.

In the unlikely event that you buy over $500,000 of Section 179 property in one year ($200,000 in 2011 and later), your deduction is reduced by one dollar for every dollar you spend over that amount. For example, if you buy $600,000 in Section 179 property in 2008, your Section 179 deduction would be limited to $25,000: $600,000 is $100,000 more than the $500,000 Section 179 limit, so the $100,000 excess must be subtracted from the normal $125,000 Section 179 limit, leaving only $25,000. This rule is intended to prevent large businesses that buy huge amounts of equipment from benefiting from the Section 179 deduction.

Minimum Period of Business Use

When you deduct an asset under Section 179, you must continue to use it for business at least 50% of the time for as many years as it would have been depreciated had you not used Section 179. For example, if you use Section 179 for a computer, you must use it for business at least 50% of the time for five years, because computers have a five-year depreciation period.

If you don't meet these rules, you'll have to report as income part of the deduction you took under Section 179 in the prior year. This is called "recapture."

RESOURCE

For more information, see IRS Publication 946, *How to Depreciate Property*. You can obtain this and all other IRS publications by calling the IRS at 800-TAX-FORM, visiting your local IRS office, or downloading the publications from the IRS website at www.irs.gov.

Depreciation

Because it provides a big tax deduction immediately, most small business owners look first to Section 179 to deduct asset costs.

However, you must use depreciation instead if:

- you use the item or property less than 51% of the time for business
- the item is personal property that you converted to business use
- the property is a structure, such as a building or building component
- you financed the purchase with a trade-in (the value of the trade-in must be depreciated)
- the item is an intangible asset, such as a patent, copyright, or trademark
- you bought the item from a relative
- you inherited or received the property as a gift, or
- the item is an air-conditioning or heating unit.

Depreciation involves deducting the cost of a business asset a little at a time over a period of years. This means it will take you much longer to get your full deduction than under Section 179. However, this isn't always a bad thing. Indeed, you may be better off in the long run using depreciation instead of Section 179 if you expect to earn more in future years than you will in the current year. Remember that the value of a deduction depends on your income tax bracket. If you're in the 15% bracket, a $1,000 deduction is worth only $150. If you're in the 28% bracket, it's worth $280. So spreading out a deduction until you're in a higher tax bracket can make sense.

EXAMPLE:

Marie, a self-employed consultant, buys a $5,000 photocopier for her business in 2008. She elects to depreciate the copier instead of using the Section 179 deduction. This way, she can deduct a portion of the cost from her gross income each year for the next six years. Marie is only in the 15% tax bracket in 2008 but expects to be in the 28% bracket in 2009.

You may also prefer to use depreciation rather than Section 179 if you want to puff up your business income for the year. This can help you get a bank loan or help your business show a profit instead of incurring a loss—and therefore, avoid running afoul of the hobby loss limitations.

What Must Be Depreciated

Whether you must depreciate an item depends on how long it can reasonably be expected to last—what the IRS calls its "useful life." Depreciation is used to deduct the cost of any asset you buy for your business that has a useful life of more than one year—for example, buildings, equipment, machinery, patents, trademarks, copyrights, and furniture. Land cannot be depreciated because it doesn't wear out. The IRS, not you, decides the useful life of your assets.

You can also depreciate the cost of major repairs that increase the value or extend the life of an asset—for example, the cost of a major upgrade to make your computer run faster. However, you have to deduct normal repairs or maintenance in the year they're incurred as a business expense.

Mixed Use Property

If you use property for both business and personal purposes, you can take depreciation only for the business use of the asset. Unlike the Section 179 deduction, however, you don't have to use an item more than half the time for business to depreciate it.

EXAMPLE:

Carl uses his photocopier 75% of the time for personal reasons and 25% for business. He can depreciate 25% of the cost of the copier.

Keep a diary or log with the dates, times, and reasons the property was used to distinguish business from personal use. (Recordkeeping is covered in Chapter 14.)

Depreciation Period

The depreciation period—called the "recovery period" by the IRS—begins when you start using the asset and lasts for the entire estimated useful life of the asset. The tax code has assigned an estimated useful life for all types of business assets, ranging from three to 39 years. Most of the assets you buy for your business will probably have an estimated useful life of five to seven years.

RESOURCE

If you need to know the depreciation period for an asset not included in the table "Asset Depreciation Periods" below, see IRS Publication 946, *How to Depreciate Property*. You can obtain this and all other IRS publications by calling the IRS at 800-TAX-FORM, visiting your local IRS office, or downloading the publications from the IRS website at www.irs.gov.

You are free to continue using property after its estimated useful life expires, but you can't deduct any more depreciation.

Calculating Depreciation

There are several different systems you can use to calculate depreciation. Most tangible property, however, is depreciated using the Modified Accelerated Cost Recovery System (MACRS). A slightly different system, the Alternative Depreciation System, or ADS, applies to depreciation of specified "listed property," property used outside the United States, and certain farm and imported property.

Under MACRS, there are three different methods you can use to calculate your depreciation deduction: the straight-line (SL) method or one of two accelerated-depreciation methods. Once you choose your method, you're stuck with it for the entire life of the asset.

In addition, you must use the same method for all property of the same kind purchased during the year. For example, if you use the straight-line method to depreciate a computer, you must use that method to depreciate all other computers you purchase for your business during that year.

The straight-line method requires you to deduct an equal amount each year over the useful life of an asset. However, you ordinarily deduct only a half-year's worth of depreciation in the first year. You make up for this by adding an extra year of depreciation at the end.

EXAMPLE 1:

Sally buys a $1,000 fax machine for her business in 2008. It has a useful life of five years. (See "Asset Depreciation Periods," below.) Using the straight-line method, she would depreciate the asset over six years. Her annual depreciation deductions are as follows:

2008	$100
2009	$200
2010	$200
2011	$200
2012	$200
2013	$100
TOTAL	$1,000

Most small businesses use one of two types of accelerated depreciation: the "double declining-balance" method or the "150% declining-balance" method. The advantage to these methods is that they provide larger depreciation deductions in the earlier years and smaller ones later on. The double declining-balance method starts out by giving you double the deduction you'd get for the first full year with the straight-line method. The 150% declining-balance method gives you one and one-half times the straight-line deduction.

EXAMPLE 2:

Sally decides to use the fastest accelerated-depreciation method to depreciate her $1,000 fax machine—the double declining-balance method. Her annual depreciation deductions are as follows:

2008	$200
2009	$320
2010	$192
2011	$115
2012	$115
2013	$ 58
TOTAL	$1,000

However, using accelerated depreciation is not necessarily a good idea if you expect your income to go up in future years, because as previously explained, the deduction is more valuable if you're in a higher tax bracket. There are also some restrictions on when you can use accelerated depreciation. For example, you can't use it for cars, computers, and certain other property that is used for business less than 50% of the time.

Determining which depreciation method is best for you and calculating how much depreciation you can deduct is a complex task. If you want to do it yourself, you should probably get and use a tax preparation computer program that can help you do the calculations. (See Chapter 8.)

Cars, Computers, and Cellular Phones

The IRS imposes special rules on certain items that can easily be used for personal as well as business purposes. These items, called "listed property," include:

- cars, boats, airplanes, and other vehicles (see the next section for rules on mileage and vehicle expenses)
- computers
- cellular phones, and

Asset Depreciation Periods	
Type of Property	**Recovery Period**
Computer software (software that comes with your computer is not separately depreciable unless you're separately billed for it)	3 years
Office machinery (computers and peripherals, calculators, copiers, typewriters)	5 years
Cars and light trucks	5 years
Construction and research equipment	5 years
Office furniture	7 years
Residential buildings	27.5 years
Nonresidential buildings purchased before 5/12/93	31.5 years
Nonresidential buildings purchased after 5/12/93	39 years

- any other property generally used for entertainment, recreation, or amusement—for example, VCRs, cameras, and camcorders.

The IRS fears that taxpayers might use listed property items for personal reasons but claim business deductions for them. For this reason, you're required to document your business use of listed property. You can satisfy this requirement by keeping a logbook showing when and how the property is used. (See Chapter 14.)

Exception to Record-Keeping Rule

You normally have to document your use of listed property even if you use it 100% for business. However, there is an exception to this rule: If you use a computer only for business and keep it at your business location, you need not comply with the record-keeping requirement. This includes a computer you keep at your home office if the office qualifies for the home office deduction.

EXAMPLE:

John, a freelance writer, works full time in his home office, which he uses exclusively for writing. The office is clearly his principal place of business and qualifies for the home office deduction. He buys a $4,000 computer for his office and uses it exclusively for his writing business. He does not have to keep records showing how he uses the computer.

Depreciating Listed Property

If you use listed property for business more than 50% of the time, you can depreciate it just like any other property. However, if you use it 50% or less of the time for business, you must use the straight-line depreciation method and an especially long recovery period. If you start out using accelerated depreciation and your business use drops to 50% or less, you have to switch to the straight-line method and pay taxes on the benefits of the prior years of accelerated depreciation.

Car Expenses

Most self-employed people do at least some driving related to business—for example, to visit clients or customers, to pick up or deliver work, to obtain business supplies, or to attend seminars. Of course, driving costs money—and you are allowed to deduct your driving expenses when you use your car, van, pickup, or panel truck for business.

There are two ways to calculate the car expense deduction. You can:

- use the standard mileage rate, which requires relatively little record keeping, or

- deduct your actual expenses, which requires much more record keeping.

You'll often get a larger deduction using the actual expense method. However, this isn't always the case. The standard mileage rate may give you a larger deduction if you drive many business miles each year, especially if you drive an inexpensive car. But even if the standard mileage rate does give you a lower deduction, the difference is often so small that it doesn't justify the extra record keeping you will have to do to use that method.

Either way, you'll need to keep records showing how many miles you drive your car for business during the year—also called "business miles." Keep a mileage logbook for this purpose.

CAUTION

Commuting expenses are not deductible. You usually cannot deduct commuting expenses—that is, the cost involved in getting to and from work. However, if your main office is at home, you may deduct the cost of driving to meet clients. This is one of the advantages of having a home office. (See Chapter 4.)

Standard Mileage Rate

The easiest way to deduct car expenses is to take the standard mileage rate. When you use this method, you need only keep track of how many business miles you drive, not the actual expenses for your car (such as gas or repairs).

You can use the standard mileage rate for a car that you own or lease. You must use the standard mileage rate in the first year you use a car for business or you are forever foreclosed from using that method for that car. If you use the standard mileage rate the first year, you can switch to the actual expense method a later year. For this reason, if you're not sure which method you want to use, it's a good idea to use the standard mileage rate the

first year you use the car for business. This leaves all your options open for later years. However, this rule does not apply to leased cars. If you lease your car, you must use the standard mileage rate for the entire lease period if you use it in the first year.

There are some restrictions on switching back to the standard mileage rate after you have used the actual expense method. You can't switch back to the standard mileage rate after using the actual expense method if you took accelerated depreciation, a Section 179 deduction, or bonus depreciation on the car. You can switch back to the standard mileage rate only if you used the straight line method of depreciation during the years you used the actual expense method. This depreciation method gives you equal depreciation deductions every year, rather than the larger deductions you get in the early years using accelerated depreciation methods.

Each year, the IRS sets the standard mileage rate: a specified amount of money you can deduct for each business mile you drive during the year. In 2008, the rate is 50.5¢ per mile. The rates are the same whether you own or lease your car.

To figure out your deduction, simply multiply your business miles by the standard mileage rate.

EXAMPLE:

Ed, a salesman, drove his car a total of 10,000 miles for business in 2007. His deduction is $4,850 (48.5¢ x 10,000 = $4,850).

If you choose to take the standard mileage rate, you cannot deduct actual operating expenses—for example, depreciation or Section 179 deduction, maintenance, repairs, gasoline and its taxes, oil, insurance, and vehicle registration fees. These costs are already factored into the standard mileage rate.

The only expenses you can deduct (because these costs aren't included in the standard mileage rate) are:

- interest on a car loan
- parking fees and tolls for business trips (but you can't deduct parking ticket fines or the cost of parking your car at your place of work), and
- personal property tax that you paid when you bought the vehicle based on its value (often included as part of your auto registration fee).

Auto loan interest is usually the largest of these expenses. Unfortunately, many people fail to deduct it because of confusion about the tax law. Taxpayers are not allowed to deduct interest on a loan for a car that is for personal use, so many people believe they also can't deduct interest on a business car. This is not the case. You may deduct interest on a loan for a car you use in your business.

If you use your car for both business and personal trips, you can deduct only the business use percentage of interest and taxes.

Actual Expenses

Instead of taking the standard mileage rate, you can elect to deduct the actual expenses of using your car for business. To do this, deduct the actual cost of depreciation for your car (subject to limitations), interest payments on a car loan, lease fees, rental fees, license fees, garage rent, repairs, gas, oil, tires, and insurance. The total deductible amount is based on the percentage of time you use your car for business. You can also deduct the full amount of any business-related parking fees and tolls.

Deducting all these items will take more time and effort than using the standard mileage rate because you'll need to keep records of all your expenses. However, it may provide you with a larger deduction than the standard rate.

EXAMPLE:

In January 2007, Vicky bought a $20,000 car. During the year, she drove it 10,000 miles for her consulting practice and 5,000 miles for

personal purposes. If she used the standard mileage rate, she would be entitled to a $4,850 deduction: 48.5¢ x 10,000 miles = $4,850. Instead, however, she takes the actual expense deduction. She keeps careful records of all of her costs for gas, oil, repairs, insurance, and depreciation. These amount to $6,200 for the year. She gets an extra $1,350 deduction by using the actual expense method.

Mixed Uses

If you use your car for both business and personal purposes, you must also divide your expenses between business and personal use.

EXAMPLE:

In one recent year Laura, a salesperson, drove her car 10,000 miles for her business and 10,000 miles for personal purposes. She can deduct 50% of the actual costs of operating her car.

If you own only one car, you normally can't claim to use it only for business. An IRS auditor is not likely to believe that you walk or take public transportation everywhere except when you're on business. You might convince the IRS to accept your deduction if you live in a place with developed transportation systems, such as Chicago, New York City, or San Francisco, and drive your car only when you go out of town on business.

Expense Records Required

When you deduct actual car expenses, you must keep records of the costs of operating your car. This includes not only the number of business miles and total miles you drive, but also gas, repair, parking, insurance, and similar costs. (See Chapter 14.) If this seems to be too much trouble, use the standard mileage rate. That way, you'll have to keep track only of how many business miles you drive, not what you spend for gas and similar expenses.

Limits on Depreciation Deductions

Passenger automobiles have a five-year recovery period (but, as explained, it takes six calendar years to depreciate a car). As a result, you'd think it would take at most six years to fully depreciate a car. Unfortunately, this is usually not the case. Depreciating a passenger automobile is unique in one very important way: The annual depreciation deduction for automobiles is limited to a set dollar amount each year. The annual limit applies to all passenger vehicles, no matter how much they cost. Because the limits are so low, it can take many years to fully depreciate a car, far longer than the six years it takes to depreciate other assets with a five-year recovery period.

Starting in 2003, the IRS established two different sets of deduction limits for passenger automobiles: limits for passenger automobiles other than trucks and vans, and slightly higher limits for trucks and vans that qualify as passenger automobiles (based on their weight) and are built on truck chassis. This includes any minivan or SUV built on a truck chassis, as long as it meets the weight limit. Passenger automobiles are those that have a gross loaded vehicle weight of 6,000 pounds or less.

The charts below show the maximum annual depreciation deduction allowed for passenger automobiles and trucks and vans placed in service in 2007. (You can triple these limits if you buy an electric car after May 6, 2003.) The second chart shows the limits for passenger automobiles that are trucks and vans as defined above. Both charts assume 100% business use of the vehicle. You can find all the deduction limits in IRS Publication 946, *How to Depreciate Property,* and Publication 463, *Travel, Entertainment, Gift, and Car Expenses.*

Depreciation Limits for Passenger Automobiles Placed in Service During 2007	
1st tax year	$3,060
2nd tax year	$4,900
3rd tax year	$2,850
each succeeding year	$1,775

Depreciation Limits for Trucks and Vans Placed in Service During 2007	
1st tax year	$3,260
2nd tax year	$5,200
3rd tax year	$3,050
each succeeding year	$1,875

The depreciation limits are not reduced if a car is in service for less than a full year. This means that the limit is not reduced when the automobile is either placed in service or disposed of during the year.

EXAMPLE 1:

Mario pays $50,000 for a new passenger automobile on June 1, 2007, and uses it 100% for his psychiatric practice. He may deduct a maximum of $3,060 in 2007; $4,900 in 2008; $2,850 in 2009; and $1,775 thereafter.

The deduction limits in the above charts are based on 100% business use of the automobile. If you don't use your car solely for business, the deduction limits are reduced based on your percentage of personal use.

EXAMPLE 2:

Assume that Mario uses his new car 50% for business. His first-year deduction is limited to $1,530 (50% x $3,060 = $1,530), his second-year deduction to $2,450, and so on.

Expensing SUVs and Other Weighty Vehicles

The depreciation limits discussed above apply only to passenger automobiles—that is, vehicles with a gross loaded weight of less than 6,000 pounds. Vehicles that weigh more than this are not subject to the limits. Until 2004, this created a great deduction opportunity for professionals who purchased SUVs they used more than 50% for business: They could deduct as much as $102,000 of the cost in one year using the Section 179 deduction.

However, allowing these huge deductions for Hummers and other SUVs bought for business purposes caused such an uproar that Congress limited the Section 179 deduction for SUVs to $25,000. The limit applies to any SUV placed in service after October 22, 2004.

For these purposes, an SUV is any four-wheeled vehicle primarily designed or used to carry passengers over public streets, roads, or highways, that has a gross vehicle weight of 6,000 to 14,000 pounds. However, the $25,000 limit does not apply to any vehicle that seats more than nine, has a cargo area of at least six feet, or has an enclosed driver's compartment with no rear seating. Thus, for example, the $25,000 limit does not apply to most pickups or vans that weigh more than 6,000 pounds. (It doesn't apply to any vehicle that weighs more than 14,000 pounds.)

Although the Section 179 deduction for SUVs weighing over 6,000 pounds is limited to $25,000, this is still a very good deal compared to the allowable deduction for passenger automobiles. For example, a person who buys a $50,000 SUV that weighs 6,000 pounds and is used 100% for business can deduct $35,000 of the cost the first year ($25,000 Section 179 deduction + $10,000 regular depreciation using the 200% declining-balance method and half-year convention). But a person who buys a $50,000 passenger automobile can deduct only $3,060 the first year. If the person used the SUV only 60% for business, he or she could still deduct $21,000 the first year (60% of the $35,000 amount for 100% business use), whereas the first-year deduction for a 60% business-use passenger automobile would be only $1,836. Note that an SUV must be used at least 51% of the time for business to take any Section 179 deduction.

Leasing a Car

If you lease a car that you use in your business, you can deduct the part of each lease payment that goes toward the business use of the car. However, you cannot deduct any part of a lease payment that is for commuting or personal use of the car.

Leasing companies typically require you to make an advance or down payment to lease a car. You must spread such payments over the entire lease period for purposes of deducting their cost. You cannot deduct any payments you make to buy a car, even if the payments are called lease payments.

> **CAUTION**
>
> **The deduction can be reduced for luxury cars.** If you lease what the IRS considers to be a luxury car for more than 30 days, your deduction may be reduced. A luxury car is currently defined as one with a fair market value of more than $15,500.
>
> The amount by which you must reduce your deduction—called the "inclusion amount"—is based on the fair market value of your car and the percentage of time that you use it for business. The IRS recalculates it each year. You can find the inclusion amount for the current year in the tables published in IRS Publication 463, *Travel, Entertainment, Gift, and Car Expenses.* For example, if you leased a $40,000 car in 2007 and used it solely for business, you would have to reduce your car expense deduction by $172 for the year. If you used the car only 50% for business, the reduction would be $86. The inclusion amount for the first year is prorated based on the month when you start using the car for business.

RESOURCE

For more information about the rules for claiming car expenses, see IRS Publication 463, *Travel, Entertainment, Gift, and Car Expenses*. You can obtain this and all other IRS publications by calling the IRS at 800-TAX-FORM, visiting your local IRS office, or downloading the publications from the IRS website at www.irs.gov.

Travel Expenses

If you travel for your business, you can deduct your airfare, hotel bills, and other expenses. If you plan your trip right, you can even mix business with pleasure and still get a deduction for your airfare. However, IRS auditors scrutinize these deductions closely. Many taxpayers claim them without complying with the copious rules the IRS imposes. To avoid unwanted attention, you need to understand the limitations on this deduction and keep proper records.

Travel Within the United States

Some businesspeople seem to think they have the right to deduct the cost of any trip they take. This is not the case. You can deduct a trip within the United States only if:

- it's primarily for business
- you travel outside your city limits, and
- you're away at least overnight or long enough to require a stop for sleep or rest.

Business Purpose of Trip

For your trip to be deductible, you must spend more than half of your time on activities that can reasonably be expected to help advance your business.

Acceptable activities include:

- visiting or working with clients or customers
- attending trade shows, or
- attending professional seminars or business conventions where the agenda is clearly connected to your business.

Business does not include sightseeing or recreation that you attend by yourself or with family or friends, nor does it include personal investment seminars or political events.

Use common sense before claiming that a trip is for business. The IRS will likely question any trip that doesn't have some logical connection to your business. For example, if you build houses in Alaska, an IRS auditor would probably be skeptical about a deduction for a trip you took to Florida to learn about new home air-conditioning techniques.

Again, if your trip within the United States is not primarily for business, none of your travel expenses are deductible. But you can still deduct expenses you incur on your trip that are directly related to your business—for example, the cost of making long-distance phone calls to your office or clients while on vacation.

Travel Outside City Limits

You don't have to travel any set distance to get a travel expense deduction. However, you can't take this deduction if you just spend the night in a motel across town. You must travel outside your city limits. If you don't live in a city, you must go outside the general area in which your business is located.

Sleep or Rest

Finally, you must stay away overnight or at least long enough to require a stop for sleep or rest. You cannot satisfy the rest requirement by merely napping in your car.

EXAMPLE 1:

Phyllis, a self-employed salesperson based in Los Angeles, flies to San Francisco to meet potential clients, spends the night in a hotel, and returns home the following day. Her trip is a deductible travel expense.

EXAMPLE 2:

Andre, a self-employed truck driver, leaves his workplace on a regularly scheduled roundtrip between San Francisco and Los Angeles and returns home 18 hours later. During the run, he has six hours off at a turnaround point where he eats two meals and rents a hotel room to get some sleep before starting the return trip. Andre can deduct his meal and hotel expenses as travel expenses.

Combining Business With Pleasure

Provided that your trip is primarily for business, you can tack on a vacation to the end of the trip, make a side trip purely for fun, or go to the theater and still deduct your entire airfare. What you spend while having fun is not deductible, but you can deduct your expenses while on business.

EXAMPLE:

Bill flies to Miami for a four-day business meeting. He then stays an extra three days in Miami swimming and enjoying the sights. Because Bill spent over half his time on business—four days out of seven—the cost of his flight is entirely deductible, as are his hotel and meal costs during the business meeting. He may not deduct his hotel, meal, or other expenses during his vacation days.

Foreign Travel

The rules differ if you travel outside the United States and are more lenient in some ways. However, you must have a legitimate business reason for your foreign trip. A sudden desire to investigate a foreign business won't qualify: You can't deduct business expenses for a business unless you're already involved in it.

Trips Lasting No More Than Seven Days

If you're away no more than seven days and you spend the majority of your time on business, you can deduct all of your travel costs.

However, even if your trip was primarily a vacation, you can deduct your airfare and other transportation costs as long as at least part of the trip was for business. You can also deduct your expenses while on business. For this reason, it's often best to limit business-related foreign travel to seven days.

EXAMPLE:

Jennifer flies to London for a two-day business meeting. She then spends five days sightseeing. She can deduct the entire cost of her airfare and the portion of her hotel and meals she spent while attending the meeting.

Trips Lasting More Than Seven Days

More stringent rules apply if your foreign trip lasts more than one week. To get a full deduction for your expenses, you must spend at least 75% of your time away on business.

If you spend less than 75% of your time on business, you must determine the percentage of your time spent on business by counting the number of business days and the number of personal days. You can deduct only the percentage of your travel costs that relates to business days. A business day is any day you have to spend at a particular place on business or in which you spend four or more hours on business matters. Days spent traveling to and from your destination also count as business days.

EXAMPLE:

Sam flies to London and stays 14 days. He spends seven days on business and seven days sightseeing. He therefore spent 50% of his time on business. He can deduct half of his travel costs.

Foreign Conventions

Different rules apply if you attend a convention outside North America. In such cases, a deduction is allowed only if:

- the meeting has a definite, clear connection to your business, and
- it's reasonable for the convention to be held outside North America—for example, if all those attending are plumbers from New York, it would be hard to justify a convention in Tahiti.

Travel on Cruise Ships

Forget about getting a tax deduction for a pleasure cruise. However, you may be able to deduct part of the cost of a cruise if you attend a business convention, seminar, or similar meeting directly related to your business while onboard. Personal investment or financial planning seminars don't qualify.

But there is a major restriction: You must travel on a U.S.-registered ship that stops only in ports in the United States or its possessions, such as Puerto Rico or the U.S. Virgin Islands. Not many cruise ships are registered in the United States, so you'll likely have trouble finding a cruise that qualifies. If a cruise sponsor promises you'll be able to deduct your trip, investigate carefully to make sure it meets these requirements.

If you go on a cruise that is deductible, you must file with your tax return a signed note from the meeting or seminar sponsor listing the business meetings scheduled each day aboard the ship and certifying how many hours you spent in attendance. Your annual deduction for cruising is limited to $2,000.

Taking Your Family With You

Generally, you cannot deduct the expense of taking your spouse, children, or others along with you on a business trip or to a business convention. The only deductions allowed are for expenses of a spouse or other person who is your employee and has a genuine business reason for going on a trip with you. Typing notes or assisting in entertaining customers are not enough to warrant a deduction; the work must be essential. For example, if you hire your adult child as a salesperson for your product or service and he or she calls on prospective customers during the trip, both of your expenses are deductible.

When you travel with your family, you deduct your business expenses as if you were traveling alone. However, the fact that your family is with you doesn't mean you have to reduce your deductions. For example, if you drive to your destination, you can deduct the entire cost of the drive, even if your family rides along with you. Similarly, you can deduct the full cost of a single hotel room even if you obtain a larger, more expensive room for your whole family.

Deductible Expenses

You can deduct virtually all of your expenses when you travel on business, including:

- airfare to and from your destination
- hotel or other lodging expenses
- taxi, public transportation, and car rental expenses
- telephone and fax expenses
- the cost of shipping your personal luggage or samples, displays, or other things you need for your business
- computer rental fees
- laundry and dry-cleaning expenses, and
- tips you pay on any of the other costs.

However, only 50% of the cost of meals is deductible. The IRS reasons that you would have eaten at home and spent less had you stayed home. You cannot deduct expenses for personal sightseeing or recreation.

You must keep good records of your expenses. (See Chapter 14.)

Entertainment and Meal Expenses

Depending on the nature of your business, you may find it helpful or even necessary to entertain clients, customers, suppliers, employees, other self-employed people, professional advisors, investors, and other business associates. It's often easier to do business in a nonbusiness setting. Entertainment includes, for example, going to restaurants, the theater, concerts, sporting events, or nightclubs; throwing parties; and boating, hunting, or fishing outings.

In the past, you could deduct entertainment expenses even if business was never discussed. For example, if you took a client to a restaurant, you could deduct the cost even if you spent the whole time drinking martinis and talking about sports. This is no longer the case. To deduct an entertainment expense, you must discuss business either before, during, or after the entertainment.

The IRS doesn't have spies lurking about in restaurants, theaters, or other places of entertainment, so it has no way of knowing whether you really discussed business with a client or other business associate. You're pretty much on the honor system here. However, be aware that the IRS closely scrutinizes this deduction because many taxpayers cheat when taking it. You'll have to comply with stringent record-keeping requirements. (See Chapter 14.)

Discussing Business During Entertainment

You're entitled to deduct part of the cost of entertaining a client or other business associate if you have an active business discussion during the entertainment aimed at obtaining income or other benefits. You don't have to spend the entire time talking business, but the main character of the meal or other event must be business.

EXAMPLE:
Ivan, a self-employed consultant, takes a prospective client to a restaurant where they discuss and finalize the terms of a contract for Ivan's consulting services. Ivan can deduct the cost of the meal as an entertainment expense.

The IRS will not believe you discussed business if the entertainment occurred in a place where it is difficult or impossible to talk business because of distractions—for example, at a nightclub, theater, or sporting event, or at an essentially social gathering such as a cocktail party.

On the other hand, the IRS will presume you discussed business if a meal or entertainment took place in a clear business setting—for example, a catered lunch at your office.

Discussing Business Before or After Entertainment

You are also entitled to deduct the full expense of an entertainment event if you have a substantial business discussion with a client or other business associate before or after it. This requires that you have a meeting, negotiation, or other business transaction designed to help you get income or some other specific business benefit.

Generally, the entertainment should occur on the same day as the business discussion. However, if your business guests are from out of town, the entertainment can occur the day before or the day after.

The entertainment doesn't have to be shorter than your business discussions, but you can't spend only a small fraction of your total time on business. You can deduct entertainment expenses at places such as nightclubs, sporting events, or theaters.

EXAMPLE:

Following lengthy contract negotiations at a prospective client's office, you take the client to a baseball game to unwind. The cost of the tickets is a deductible business expense.

50% Deduction Limit

You can deduct only entertainment expenses you paid. If a client picks up the tab, you obviously get no deduction. If you split the expense, you may deduct only what you paid.

Moreover, you're allowed to deduct only 50% of your expenses—for example, if you spend $50 for a meal in a restaurant, you can only deduct $25. However, you must keep track of all you spend and report the entire amount on your tax return. The cost of transportation to and from a business meal or other entertainment is not subject to the 50% limit.

You can deduct the cost of entertaining your spouse and the client's spouse only if it's impractical to entertain the client without his or her spouse and your spouse joins the party because the client's spouse is attending.

If you entertain a client or other business associate while away from home on business, you can deduct the cost either as a travel expense or an entertainment expense, but not as both.

RESOURCE

For additional information, see IRS Publication 463, *Travel, Entertainment, Gift, and Car Expenses*. You can obtain this and all other IRS publications by calling the IRS at 800-TAX-FORM, visiting your local IRS office, or downloading the publications from the IRS website at www.irs.gov.

Champagne and Caviar Might Not Be Deductible

Your entertainment expenses must be reasonable to be fully deductible. You can't deduct entertainment expenses that the IRS considers lavish or extravagant. There is no dollar limit on what is "reasonable," nor are you necessarily barred from entertaining at deluxe restaurants, hotels, nightclubs, or resorts.

Whether your expenses will be considered reasonable depends on the particular facts and circumstances. For example, a $250 expense for dinner with a client and two business associates at a fancy restaurant would likely be considered reasonable if you closed a substantial business deal during the meal. Because there are no concrete guidelines, use common sense.

Health Insurance

Self-employed people must pay for their own health insurance. If you don't make a lot of money, this can be tough. Fortunately, there are some specific tax deductions designed to help you.

Deducting Health Insurance Premiums

If you're a sole proprietor, partner in a partnership, owner of an S corporation, or member of a limited liability company, you may deduct 100% of the cost of health insurance covering you, your spouse, and your dependents. This is not a business deduction. It is a special personal deduction for the self-employed. The deduction applies to your federal, state, and local income taxes but not to self-employment taxes (Social Security and Medicare taxes). Moreover, this deduction can't exceed the net profit from your business.

EXAMPLE:

Kim is a sole proprietor who pays $10,000 each year for health insurance for herself, her husband, and her three children. Her business earned a $100,000 profit for the year. She may deduct her $10,000 annual health insurance expense from her gross income for federal and state income tax purposes. Her combined federal and state income tax rate is 35%, so she saves $3,500 in income taxes (35% x $10,000 = $3,500). She may not deduct her premiums from her income when she figures her self-employment taxes—in other words, she must pay the 15.3% self-employment tax on her full $90,000 business profit.

You get the deduction whether you purchase your health insurance policy as an individual or have your business obtain it. But, you can't take this deduction if you're an employee and are eligible for health insurance through your employer, or your spouse is employed and you're eligible for coverage through his or her employer.

If you form a C corporation, it may deduct the entire cost of health insurance it provides you and any other employees.

Health Savings Accounts

Starting in 2004, self-employed people were allowed to establish health savings accounts (HSAs). These are designed to be used in conjunction with high-deductible health insurance plans and provide important tax benefits. For detailed information on HSAs, see Chapter 6.

Start-Up Costs

The IRS refers to expenses you incur before you actually start your business as "business start-up costs." Such costs include, for example, license fees, fictitious business name registration fees, advertising costs, attorney and accounting fees, travel expenses, market research, and office supplies expenses. Business start-up costs are capital expenses because you incur them to acquire an asset (a business) that will benefit you for more than one year. Normally, you can't deduct these types of capital expenses until you sell or otherwise dispose of the business. However, a special tax rule allows you to deduct up to $5,000 in start-up expenses the first year you are in business and then deduct the remainder in equal amounts over the next 15 years. (I.R.C. § 195.) Without this special rule for business start-up costs, these expenses (capital expenses) would not be deductible until you sold or otherwise disposed of your business.

EXAMPLE:

Diana decides to start a freelance public relations business. Her office opens for business on July 1. Before that date, however, Diana incurs various expenses, including travel expenses to obtain office space, office rent and utilities, lease expenses for office furniture and computer equipment, and advertising expenses. She spent $10,000 of her life savings to get her business up and running. Because these are start-up expenses, she cannot deduct them all in her first year of business. But she can deduct up to $5,000 the first year she is in business and the remainder in equal amounts over the next 15 years. (I.R.C. § 195.)

If you have more than $50,000 in start-up expenses, however, you are not entitled to the full $5,000 deduction. You must reduce the $5,000 deduction by the amount that your start-up expenditures exceed $50,000. For example, if you have $53,000 in start-up expenses, you may deduct only $2,000 the first year, instead of $5,000. If you have $55,000 or more in start-up expenses, you get no current deduction for start-up expenses. Instead, the whole amount must be deducted over 180 months.

RESOURCE

For more information on business start-up costs, see IRS Publication 535, *Business Expenses*. You can obtain a free copy by calling the IRS at 800-TAX-FORM, visiting your local IRS office, or downloading it from the IRS website at www.irs.gov.

The Bane of Self-Employment Taxes

All Americans who work in the private sector are required to pay taxes to help support the Social Security and Medicare systems. Although these taxes are paid to the IRS, they are entirely separate from federal income taxes.

Employees have their Social Security and Medicare taxes directly deducted from their paychecks by their employers, who must make matching contributions. Such taxes are usually referred to as "FICA" taxes.

But if you're self-employed, your clients or customers will not pay or withhold your Social Security and Medicare taxes. You must pay them to the IRS yourself. When self-employed workers pay these taxes, they are called "self-employment" taxes or SE taxes. This chapter shows you how to determine how much you must pay in SE taxes.

SKIP AHEAD

If your net income from your business for the year is less than $400, you don't have to pay any self-employment taxes. You can skip this chapter.

Who Must Pay

Sole proprietors, partners in partnerships, and members of limited liability companies must all pay self-employment (SE) taxes if their net earnings from self-employment are $400 or more for the year.

Corporations do not pay SE taxes. However, if you're incorporated and work as an employee of your corporation, you will ordinarily be paid a salary on which you must pay FICA taxes, just like any other employee. You do not pay SE taxes. You corporation, however, must withhold half of your Social Security and Medicare taxes from your salary and pay the other half. (See Chapter 6.)

Self-Employment (SE) Tax Rates

The SE tax consists of a 12.4% Social Security tax and a 2.9% Medicare tax for a total tax of 15.3%. It is a flat tax—that is, the tax rate is the same no matter what your income level. However, there is an annually-adjusted income ceiling on the Social Security portion of the tax. You need not pay the 12.4% Social Security tax on your net self-employment earnings that exceed the ceiling amount. If the ceiling didn't exist, people with higher incomes would end up paying far more than they could ever get back as Social Security benefits. The Social Security tax ceiling is adjusted annually for inflation. The ceiling was $97,500 in 2007.

However, there is no similar limit for Medicare: You must pay the 2.9% Medicare tax on your entire net self-employment income, no matter how large. Congress enacted this rule a few years ago to save Medicare from bankruptcy.

EXAMPLE:

Mona, a self-employed consultant, earned $150,000 in net self-employment income in 2007. She must pay both Social Security and Medicare taxes on the first $97,500 of her income—a 15.3% tax. She must also pay the 2.9% Medicare tax on her remaining $52,500 in income.

Earnings Subject to SE Taxes

You pay self-employment taxes on your net self-employment income, not your entire income. To determine your net self-employment income, you must first figure out the net income you've earned from your business. Your net business income includes all income from your business, minus all business deductions allowed for income tax purposes. However, you can't deduct retirement contributions you make for yourself to a Keogh or SEP plan or the self-employed health insurance deduction. If you're a sole proprietor, as are most self-employed people, use IRS Schedule C, *Profit or Loss From Business*, to determine your net business income.

If you have more than one business, combine the net income or loss from them all. If you have a job in addition to your business, your employee income is not included in your self-employment income. Nor do you include investment income, such as interest you earn on your savings.

You then get one more valuable deduction before determining your net self-employment income: You're allowed to deduct 7.65% from your total net business income. This is intended to help ease the tax burden on the self-employed. To do this, multiply your net business income by 92.35%, or 0.9235.

EXAMPLE:

Billie, a self-employed consultant, earned $70,000 from her business and had $20,000 in business expenses, leaving a net business income of $50,000. She multiplies this amount by 0.9235 to determine her net self-employment income, which is $46,175. This is the amount on which Billie must pay SE and income tax.

Because of this extra deduction, the "real" self-employment tax rate is lower than the official rate of 15.3%.

The following chart shows the effective self-employment tax rates.

Income Tax Bracket	Effective Social Security Tax Rate
15%	13.07%
25%	12.36%
28%	12.15%
33%	11.80%

Deducting business expenses from your SE income makes these expenses doubly valuable: They will not only reduce your income taxes, but your SE taxes as well.

S Corporation Status: A Way Around the SE Tax Thicket

As a person in business for yourself, you may be able to take advantage of an important wrinkle in the SE tax rules: Distributions from S corporations to their owners are not subject to SE taxes. This is so even though such distributions are included in your income for income tax purposes.

If you incorporate your business and elect to become an S corporation, you may distribute part of your corporation's earnings to yourself without paying SE taxes on them. You can't distribute all your earnings to yourself this way, however, because your S corporation must pay you a reasonable salary on which FICA taxes must be paid.

Computing SE Taxes

It's easy to compute the amount of SE tax you will owe. First, determine your net self-employment income as described above. If your net self-employment income is below the Social Security tax income ceiling—$97,500 in 2007—multiply it by 15.3%, or 0.153, to determine your SE tax.

EXAMPLE:

Mark, a self-employed consultant, had $50,000 in net self-employment income in 2007. He must multiply this by 0.153 to determine the SE tax he owes, which is $7,650.

If your net self-employment income is more than the Social Security tax income ceiling, things are a bit more complicated. Multiply your income up to the ceiling by 12.4% and all of your income by the 2.9% Medicare tax; then add both amounts together to determine your total SE tax.

EXAMPLE:

Martha had $120,000 in net self-employment income in 2006. She multiplies the first $97,500 of this amount by the 12.4% Social Security tax, resulting in a tax of $12,090. She then multiplies her entire $120,000 income by the 2.9% Medicare tax, resulting in a $3,480 tax. She adds these amounts together to determine her total SE tax, which is $15,570.

In another effort to make the SE tax burden a little lighter for the self-employed, the IRS allows you to deduct half of the amount of your SE taxes from your business income for income tax purposes. For example, if you pay $10,000 in SE taxes, you can deduct $5,000 from your gross income when you determine your taxable income for your federal income taxes.

Paying and Reporting SE Taxes

Pay SE taxes directly to the IRS during the year as part of your estimated taxes. You have the option of either:

- paying the same amount in tax as you paid the previous year, or
- estimating what your income will be this year and basing your estimated tax payments on that. (See Chapter 11.)

When you file your annual tax return, you must include IRS Form SE, *Self-Employment Tax*, along with your income tax return. This form shows the IRS how much SE tax you were required to pay for the year. You file only one Form SE no matter how many unincorporated businesses you own. Add the SE tax to your income taxes on your personal income tax return (Form 1040) to determine your total tax.

Even if you do not owe any income tax, if you owe $400 or more in SE taxes, you must still complete Form 1040 and Schedule SE.

Outside Employment

If, in addition to being self-employed, you have an outside job in which you're classified as an employee for which Social Security and Medicare taxes are withheld from your wages, you must pay the Social Security tax on your wages (rather than your SE income) first. If your wages are at least equal to the Social Security tax income ceiling, you won't have to pay the 12.4% Social Security tax on your SE income. But no matter how much you earn from your job, you'll have to pay the 2.9% Medicare tax on all your SE income.

EXAMPLE:

Anne earned $100,000 in employee income and $10,000 from a part-time business in 2007. Her employer withheld Social Security and Medicare taxes from her salary and made its required matching contributions. Social Security taxes had to be paid on her salary only up to the Social Security income limit for the year ($97,500), but Medicare taxes had to be paid on her entire salary. Since her employee wages exceeded the $97,500 Social Security income limit for the year, Anne did not have to pay any Social Security taxes on her $10,000 self-employment income. She did, however, have to pay Medicare taxes on all her self-employment income.

However, if your employee wages are lower than the Social Security tax income ceiling, you'll have to pay Social Security taxes on your SE income until your wages and SE income combined exceed the ceiling amount.

EXAMPLE:

Bill earned $40,000 in employee wages and $80,000 in self-employment income in 2007. His employee wages were lower than the $97,500 Social Security tax income ceiling for the year. His employer withheld his portion of Social Security and Medicare taxes on all his wages. Bill also had to pay a 12.4% Social Security tax on $57,500 of his SE income. He stopped paying the Social Security tax after his wages and income combined equaled $97,500. This meant he didn't have to pay the Social Security tax on $22,500 of the $80,000 he earned as an IC. However, he had to pay the 2.9% Medicare tax on all $80,000 of his SE income. ●

Paying Estimated Taxes

What many self-employed people like best about their employment status is that it allows freedom to plan and handle their own finances. Unlike employees, they don't have taxes withheld from their compensation by their clients or customers. As a result, many self-employed people have higher take-home pay than employees earning similar amounts.

Unfortunately, however, self-employed workers do not have the luxury of waiting until April 15 to pay all their taxes for the previous year. The IRS wants to get its money a lot faster than that, so the self-employed are required to pay taxes on their estimated annual incomes in four payments spread out over each year. These are called "estimated taxes" and include both income taxes (see Chapter 9) and self-employment taxes (see Chapter 10).

Because the self-employed have to pay estimated taxes, self-employed people need to budget their money carefully. If you fail to set aside enough of your earnings to pay your estimated taxes, you could face a huge tax bill on April 15—and have a tough time coming up with the money to cover it.

CAUTION

Most states have estimated taxes, too. If your state has income taxes, it probably requires the self-employed to pay estimated taxes. The due dates are generally the same as for federal estimated taxes. Contact your state tax office for information and the required forms. You can find your state tax agency at www.taxadmin.org/fta/link.

Tax Withholding on Government Contracts Starting in 2011

Historically, the self-employed have not had any taxes withheld from their pay (unless they failed to provide the hiring firm a correct taxpayer identification number and became subject to back-up withholding). However, this is scheduled to change starting in 2011, when amounts paid out under government contracts will be subject to 3% income tax withholding. This will affect the self-employed who have contracts with the federal government, state governments, or any municipality that pays out $100 million or more on contracts a year. Interest and payments for real estate are exempt. Organizations representing the self-employed are strongly opposed to this change and are attempting to have it reversed by Congress.

Who Must Pay Estimated Taxes

You must pay estimated taxes if you are a sole proprietor, partner in a partnership, or member of a limited liability company and you expect to owe at least $1,000 in federal tax for the year. If you've formed a C corporation, the corporation may also have to pay estimated taxes.

However, if you paid no taxes last year—for example, because your business made no profit or you weren't working—you don't have to pay any estimated tax this year, no matter how much tax you expect to owe. But this is true only if you were a U.S. citizen or resident for the year and your tax return for the previous year covered the whole 12 months.

Sole Proprietors

A sole proprietor and his or her business are one and the same for tax purposes, so you simply pay your estimated taxes out of your own pocket. You, not your business, pay the taxes.

Partners and Limited Liability Companies

Partnerships and limited liability companies (LLCs) are similar to sole proprietorships. They don't pay any taxes; instead, all partnership and LLC income passes through to the partners or LLC members. The partners or LLC members must pay individual estimated tax on their shares of the partnership or LLC's income. This is so whether the income is actually paid to them or not. The partnership or LLC itself pays no tax. The only exception is if the owners of an LLC elect to be taxed as a C corporation, which is very unusual.

Corporations

A corporation is separate from you for tax purposes. Both you and your corporation might have to pay estimated taxes.

Ordinarily, you will be an employee of your corporation and receive a salary from it. The corporation must withhold income and employment taxes from your salary just as for any employee. (See Chapter 13.) You won't need to pay any estimated tax on your salary. But if you receive dividends or distributions from your corporation, you'll need to pay tax on them during the year—unless the total tax due on the amounts you received is less than $500. You can either pay estimated tax or increase the tax withheld from your salary; it doesn't make much practical difference which you choose.

If you've formed a C corporation, it must pay quarterly estimated taxes if it will owe $500 or more in corporate tax on its profits for the year. These taxes are deposited with a bank, not paid directly to the IRS. However, most small C corporations don't have to pay any income taxes or estimated taxes because all the profits are taken out of the corporation by the owners in the form of salaries, bonuses, and benefits. (See Chapter 2.)

Usually, S corporations don't have to pay estimated taxes because all profits are passed through to the shareholders, as in a partnership or LLC. (See Chapter 2.)

RESOURCE
For detailed guidance on estimated taxes for your C corporation, see IRS Publication 542, *Corporations.* You can obtain this and all other IRS publications by calling the IRS at 800-TAX-FORM, visiting your local IRS office, or downloading them from the IRS website at www.irs.gov.

How Much You Must Pay

You should determine how much estimated tax to pay after completing your tax return for the previous year. Most people want to pay as little estimated tax as possible during the year so they can earn interest on their money instead of handing it over to the IRS. However, the IRS imposes penalties if you don't pay enough estimated tax. There's no need to be overly concerned about these penalties: They aren't terribly large and it's easy to avoid them. All you have to do is pay at least the lesser of:

- 90% of your total tax due for the current year, or
- 100% of the tax you paid the previous year; 110% if you're a high-income taxpayer, as described in "High-Income Taxpayers," below.

Generally, you make four estimated tax payments each year. As described in this section, there are three different ways you can calculate your payments. You can use any one of the three methods without paying a penalty as long as you pay the minimum total the IRS requires, as explained above. One of the methods—basing your payments on last year's tax—is extremely easy to use. The other two are more complex to figure out but might permit you to make smaller payments.

Payments Based on Last Year's Taxes

The easiest and safest way to calculate your estimated tax is to pay 100% of the total federal taxes you paid last year. You can base your estimated tax on the amount you paid last year, even if you weren't in business that year, as long as your return covered a full 12-month period.

You should determine how much estimated tax to pay for the current year at the same time that you file your tax return for the previous year—no later than April 15. Take the total amount of tax you had to pay for the year and divide by four. If this comes out to an odd number, round up to get an even number. These are the amounts you'll have to pay in estimated tax. You'll make four equal payments throughout the year and the following year. (See the chart in "When to Pay," below, to learn when you must make your payments).

EXAMPLE:

Gary, a self-employed consultant, earned $50,000 last year. He figures his taxes for the prior year on April 1 of this year and determines he owes $9,989.32 in taxes for the year. To determine his estimated tax for the current year he divides this amount by four: $9,989.32 divided by four equals $2,497.33. He rounds this up to $2,500. He'll make four $2,500 estimated tax payments to the IRS throughout the current year. As long as he pays this much, Gary won't have to pay a penalty even if he ends up owing more than $10,000 in taxes for the current year (due to increased income or decreased deductions).

High-Income Taxpayers

To avoid penalties for paying too little estimated taxes, high-income taxpayers—those with adjusted gross incomes of more than $150,000 (or $75,000 for married couples filing separate returns)—must pay more than 100% of their prior year's tax. They must pay 110% of the prior year's income tax for returns filed in 2004 and after.

Your adjusted gross income, or AGI, is your total income minus deductions for:

- IRA, Keogh, solo 401(k), and SEP-IRA contributions
- health insurance
- one-half of your self-employment tax, and
- alimony, deductible moving expenses, and penalties you pay for early withdrawals from a savings account before maturity or early redemption of certificates of deposit.

To determine your AGI, look at line 37 on your last year's tax return, Form 1040.

EXAMPLE:

Mary, a self-employed consultant, earned $250,000 in gross income in 2007. Her adjusted gross income was $200,000 after subtracting the value of her Keogh Plan contributions, her health insurance deduction, and half of her self-employment taxes. Mary paid $50,000 in income and self-employment taxes in 2007. In 2008, Mary must pay 110% of the tax she paid in 2007—$55,000 in estimated tax. As long as she pays this amount she won't have to pay a penalty to the IRS even if she ends up owning more in taxes than she did in 2007.

Midcourse Correction

Your third estimated tax payment is due on September 15. By this time you should have a pretty good idea of what your income for the year will be. If you're reasonably sure that your income for the year will be at least 25% less than what you earned last year, you can forgo the last estimated tax payment due on January 15 of the next year. You have already paid enough estimated tax for the year.

If it looks as if your income will be greater than last year, you don't have to pay more estimated tax. The IRS cannot penalize you so long as you pay 100% of what you paid last year, or 110% if you're a high-income taxpayer.

You May Owe Tax on April 15

Basing your estimated tax on last year's income is generally the best method to use if you expect your income to be higher this year than last year. You'll be paying the minimum possible without incurring a penalty. Of course, if you do end up earning more than last year, you will have to make up the underpayment when you file your tax return for the year. To make sure you have enough money for this, it's a good idea to sock away a portion of your income in a separate bank account just for taxes.

Payments Based on Estimated Taxable Income

If you're absolutely certain your net income will be less this year than last year, you'll pay less estimated tax if you base your tax on your taxable income for the current year instead of basing it on last year's tax. This is not worth the time and trouble, however, unless you'll earn at least 30% less this year than last.

The problem with using this method is that you must estimate your total income and deductions for the year before they happen to figure out how much to pay. Obviously, this can be difficult or impossible to compute accurately. And there are no magic formulas to look to for guidance. The best way to proceed is to sit down with your tax return for the previous year.

Try to figure out whether your income this year will be less than last year. You'll find all your income for last year listed on lines 7 through 22 of your Form 1040. Also, determine whether your deductions will be greater than last year. You'll find these listed in the "Adjusted Gross Income" and "Tax and Credits" sections of your Form 1040, lines 23 through 57.

Pay special attention to your business income and expense figures in Parts I and II of your Schedule C, *Profit or Loss From Business*. Decide whether it's likely that you'll earn less business income this year

than last. You'll probably earn less, for example, if you plan to work fewer hours than last year, you've lost important clients, or business conditions are generally poor. Also, determine whether your deductible business expenses will be greater this year than last—for example, because you plan to purchase expensive business equipment and deduct the cost. (See Chapter 9.)

Take comfort in knowing that you need not make an exact estimate of your taxable income. You won't have to pay a penalty if you pay at least 90% of your tax due for the year.

EXAMPLE:

Larry, a self-employed consultant, earned $45,000 last year and paid $10,000 in income and self-employment taxes. Larry expects to earn much less this year because a key client has gone out of business. The lost client accounted for more than one-third of Larry's income last year, so Larry estimates he'll earn about $30,000 this year. The minimum estimated tax Larry must pay is 90% of the tax he will owe on his $30,000 income, which he estimates to be $6,000.

SEE AN EXPERT

IRS Form 1040-ES contains a worksheet to use to calculate your estimated tax. You can obtain the form by calling the IRS at 800-TAX-FORM, visiting your local IRS office, or downloading it from the IRS website at www.irs.gov.

A tax preparation computer program can also help you with the calculations.

If you have your taxes prepared by an accountant, he or she should determine what estimated tax to pay. If your income changes greatly during the year, ask your accountant to help you prepare a revised estimated tax payment schedule.

Payments Based on Quarterly Income

A much more complicated way to calculate your estimated taxes is to use the "annualized income installment method." It requires that you separately calculate your tax liability at four points during the year—March 31, May 31, August 31, and December 31—prorating your deductions and personal exemptions. You base your estimated tax payments on your actual tax liability for each quarter. (See the table "Estimated Tax Due," below.)

This method is often the best choice for people who receive income very unevenly throughout the year—for example, those who work in seasonal businesses. Using this method, they can pay little or no estimated tax for the quarters in which they earned little or no income.

EXAMPLE:

Ernie's income from his air-conditioning repair business is much higher in the summer than it is during the rest of the year. By using the annualized income installment method, he makes one large estimated tax payment on September 15, after the quarter in which he earns most of his income. His other three annual payments are quite small.

If you use this method, you must file IRS Form 2210 with your tax return to show your calculations.

SEE AN EXPERT

You'll need help with the math. You really need a good grasp of tax law and mathematics to use the annualized income installment method. The IRS worksheet used to calculate your payments using this method contains 43 separate steps. If you want to use this method, give yourself a break and hire an accountant or at least use a tax preparation computer program to help with the calculations.

RESOURCE

See IRS Publication 505, *Tax Withholding and Estimated Tax*, for a detailed explanation of the annualized income method. You can obtain the form by calling the IRS at 800-TAX-FORM, visiting your local IRS office, or downloading it from the IRS website at www.irs.gov.

When to Pay

You must ordinarily pay your estimated taxes in four installments, with the first one due on April 15. However, you don't have to start making payments until you actually earn income. If you don't receive any income by March 31, you can skip the April 15 payment. In this event, you'd ordinarily make three payments for the year, starting on June 15. If you don't receive any income by May 31, you can skip the June 15 payment as well and so on.

Estimated Tax Due	
Income received for the period	**Estimated tax due**
January 1 through March 31	April 15
April 1 through May 31	June 15
June 1 through August 31	September 15
September 1 through December 31	January 15 of the next year

Special Rule for Farmers and Fishermen

If at least two-thirds of your annual income comes from farming or fishing, you need make only one estimated tax payment on January 15. The first three payment periods in the chart above don't apply.

You can also skip the January 15 payment if you file your tax return and pay all taxes due for the previous year by January 31 of the current year. This is a little reward the IRS gives you for filing your tax return early. However, it's rarely advantageous to file early because you'll have to pay any tax due on January 15 instead of waiting until April 15—meaning you'll lose three months of interest on your hard-earned money.

> **CAUTION**
>
> **The year may not begin in January.** Don't get confused by the fact that the January 15 payment is the fourth estimated tax payment for the previous year, not the first payment for the current year. The April 15 payment is the first payment for the current year.

Your estimated tax payment must be postmarked by the dates noted above, but the IRS need not actually receive them then. If any of these days falls on a weekend or legal holiday, the due date is the next business day.

> **CAUTION**
>
> **Beware the ides of April.** April 15 can be a financial killer for the self-employed because you not only have to pay any income and self-employment taxes that are due for the previous year, you also have to make your first estimated tax payment for the current year. If you've underpaid your estimated taxes by a substantial amount, you could have a whopping tax bill.

Many self-employed people establish separate bank accounts to save up for taxes into which they deposit a portion of each payment they receive from clients. This way they have some assurance that they'll have enough money to pay their taxes. The amount you should deposit depends on your federal and state income tax brackets and the amount of your tax deductions. Depending on your income, you'll probably need to deposit 25% to 50% of your pay. If you deposit too much, of course, you can always spend the money later on other things.

EXAMPLE:

Wilma, a self-employed worker who lives in Massachusetts, is in the 25% federal income tax bracket and must pay a 6% state income tax. She must also pay a 15.3% self-employment tax. All these taxes amount to 46.3% of her pay. But she doesn't have to set aside this much because her deductions will reduce her actual tax liability. Using the amount of her deductions from last year as a guide, Wilma determines she needs to set aside 35% to 40% of her income for estimated taxes.

How to Pay

The IRS wants to make it easy for you to send in your money, so the mechanics of paying estimated taxes are very simple. You have four choices of how to pay:

- by mail
- electronically, using the government's EFTPS system
- by electronic withdrawal from your bank account, or
- by credit card.

Paying by Mail

To pay by mail, you file federal estimated taxes using IRS Form 1040-ES. This form contains instructions and four numbered payment vouchers for you to send in with your payments. You must provide your name, address, Social Security number (or EIN if you have one), and amount of the payment on each voucher. You file only one payment voucher with each payment, no matter how many unincorporated businesses you have. If you're married and file a joint return, the names on your estimated tax vouchers should be exactly the same as those on your income tax return even if your spouse isn't self-employed so that the money gets credited to the right account.

If you made estimated tax payments last year, you should receive a copy of the current year's Form 1040-ES in the mail. It will have payment vouchers preprinted with your name, address, and Social Security number. If you did not pay estimated taxes last year, get a copy of Form 1040-ES from the IRS by calling the IRS at 800-TAX-FORM, visiting your local IRS office, or downloading the form from the IRS website at www.irs.gov. After you make your first payment, the IRS should mail you a Form 1040-ES package with the preprinted vouchers.

Use the preaddressed return envelopes that come with your Form 1040-ES package. If you use your own envelopes, make sure you mail your payment vouchers to the address shown in the Form 1040-ES instructions for the region in which you live. Do not mail your estimated tax payments to the same place you sent your Form 1040.

Paying by EFTPS

The IRS has created the Electronic Federal Tax Payment System (EFTPS) to enable taxpayers to pay their taxes. The system allows taxpayers to use the phone, personal computer software, or the Internet to initiate tax payments to EFTPS directly. The system is free to use. The payments are debited from your bank account.

You must enroll with EFTPS before you can use it. You can enroll online at the EFTPS website. Within 15 calendar days your personal identification number (PIN) will be mailed to your IRS address of record. You will also receive confirmation materials including instructions on how to obtain your Internet password for secure use of EFTPS. For more information or details on how to enroll, visit www.EFTPS.gov or call EFTPS Customer Service at 800-555-4477.

Paying by Credit Card

The IRS accepts your credit cards—VISA, MasterCard, Discover Card, or American Express —but you must pay through one of two private companies that provides this service. You'll have to pay the company a fee based on the amount of your payment (the fee does not go to the IRS). You can arrange to make your payment by phone or through the Internet.

You may contact these companies at:
- LINK2GOV Corporation, 888-658-5465, www.PAY1040.com
- Official Payments Corporation, 800-272-9829, www.officialpayments.com

Paying by Electronic Funds Withdrawal

If you filed your tax return electronically, you may pay your estimated tax through an electronic funds withdrawal from your bank account. You make your first payment when you electronically file your Form 1040 for the previous year by authorizing an electronic funds withdrawal from your checking or savings account. Whether or not you have a balance due on your electronically filed tax return, you can schedule one estimated tax payment with an effective date of April 15, 2008; June 15, 2008; or September 15, 2008. Do not send in a Form 1040-ES payment voucher when you schedule an estimated tax payment by electronic funds withdrawal.

CAUTION

Keep your canceled checks. It's not unheard of for the IRS to make a bookkeeping error and claim you paid less estimated tax than you did or to apply your payment to the wrong year. If this happens and you paid by check, provide the IRS with a copy of the front and back of your canceled estimated tax checks. The agency encodes a series of tracking numbers on the endorsement side of any check that enable it to locate where payments were applied in its system.

Paying the Wrong Amount

If you pay too little estimated tax, the IRS will make you pay a penalty. If you pay too much, you can get the money refunded or apply it to the following year's estimated taxes.

Paying Too Little

The IRS imposes a monetary penalty if you underpay your estimated taxes. Fortunately, the penalty is not very onerous. You have to pay the taxes due plus a percentage penalty for each day your estimated tax payments were unpaid. The percentage is set by the IRS each year.

The penalty has ranged between 6% and 8% in recent years. This is the mildest of all IRS interest penalties. The penalty is comparable to the interest you'd pay on borrowed money.

RESOURCE
You can find out what the current penalty is in the most recent version of IRS Publication 505, *Tax Withholding and Estimated Tax*. You can obtain the form by calling the IRS at 800-TAX-FORM, visiting your local IRS office, or downloading it from the IRS website at www.irs.gov.

Many self-employed people decide to pay the penalty at the end of the tax year rather than take money out of their businesses during the year to pay estimated taxes. If you do this, though, make sure you pay all the taxes you owe for the year by April 15 of the following year. If you don't, the IRS will tack on additional interest and penalties. The IRS usually adds a penalty of 0.5% to 1% per month to a tax bill that's not paid when due.

To avoid these charges, you can pay your estimated taxes by credit card. But if you don't pay off your balance quickly, the interest you pay on your credit card balance may exceed the IRS penalty.

Because the penalty is figured separately for each payment period, you can't avoid having to pay it by increasing the amount of a later payment. For example, you can't avoid a penalty by doubling your June 15 payment to make up for failing to make your April 15 payment. If you miss a payment, the IRS suggests that you divide the amount equally among your remaining payments for the year. But this won't avoid a penalty on payments you missed or underpaid.

Because the penalty must be paid for each day your estimated taxes remain unpaid, you'll have to pay more if you miss a payment early in the tax year rather than later. For this reason, you should try to pay your first three estimated tax payments on time. You can let the fourth payment (due on January 15) go. The penalty you'll have to pay for missing this payment will likely be very small.

The IRS will assume you've underpaid your estimated taxes if you file a tax return showing that you owe $500 or more in additional tax, and the amount due is more than 10% of your total tax bill for the year.

If you have underpaid, you can determine the amount of the underpayment penalty by completing IRS Form 2210, *Underpayment of Estimated Tax by Individuals*, and pay the penalty when you send in your return. Tax preparation programs can also do this calculation for you. However, it is not necessary for you to compute the penalty you owe. You can leave it to the IRS to determine the penalty and send you a bill. If you receive a bill, you may wish to complete Form 2210 anyway to make sure you aren't overcharged.

Paying Too Much

If you pay too much estimated tax, you have two options: You may have the IRS refund the over-payment to you, or you can credit all or part of the overpayment to the following year's estimated taxes. Unfortunately, you can't get back the interest your overpayment earned while sitting in the IRS coffers; that belongs to the government.

To take the credit, write in the amount you want credited instead of refunded to you on line 68a of your Form 1040. The payment is considered to have been made on April 15. You can use all the credited amount toward your first estimated tax payment for the following year, or you can spread it out any way you choose among your payments. Be sure to take the amount you have credited into account when figuring your estimated tax payments.

It doesn't make much practical difference which option you choose. Most people take the credit so they don't have to wait for the IRS to send them a refund check.

Rules for Salespeople, Drivers, and Clothing Producers

This chapter covers statutory employee and statutory independent contractor rules—specific rules for people who work in certain industries.

SKIP AHEAD

Read this chapter only if you work as a:

- business-to-business salesperson
- full-time life insurance salesperson
- clothing or needlecraft producer who works at home
- driver who distributes food products, beverages, or laundry
- direct seller, or
- licensed real estate agent.

If you fall within the first four categories, you may be a statutory employee; read the next section. If you fall within the last two categories, you may be a statutory independent contractor (IC); skip directly to "Statutory Independent Contractors." If none of these apply to you, skip this chapter.

Statutory Employees

If you are a business-to-business or life insurance salesperson; clothing producer who works at home; or driver who distributes food products, beverages, or laundry; and if you also meet several other primary requirements described below, you are a "statutory employee." For certain purposes, Congress has passed statutes (laws) that govern your employment status.

Practically speaking, being a statutory employee has only two consequences for you, but neither of them is particularly good. The first and worst consequence of statutory employee status is that the hiring firms for which you work must pay half of your Social Security and Medicare taxes themselves and withhold the other half from your pay for the IRS, just as for any other employee. (See Chapter 13.) As a result, you'll receive less take-home pay. This is not only because 7.65%

of your earnings must be deducted from your paychecks but also because hiring firms will probably insist on paying you less compensation than they would if you were an IC to make up for the fact that they have to pay a 7.65% Social Security and Medicare tax for you. The upside is that you won't need to include these Social Security and Medicare taxes in your own estimated tax payments. (See Chapter 11.)

The second consequence of being a statutory employee is that you'll receive a Form W-2, *Wage and Tax Statement*, from the hiring firms for which you work instead of a Form 1099-MISC, the form used to report ICs' income to the IRS. (See Chapter 13.) The W-2 will show the Social Security and Medicare tax withheld from your pay and your Social Security and Medicare income. You'll have to file your W-2s with your tax returns, so the IRS will know exactly how much income you've earned as a statutory employee. The hiring firms will also file a copy with the Social Security Administration.

As a statutory employee, you report income and earnings on Schedule C, *Profit or Loss From Business*, the same form used by self-employed people who are sole proprietors. Unlike regular employees whose business deductions are strictly limited, you can deduct the full amount of your business expenses. (See Chapter 9.)

Fortunately, it's easy to avoid being classified as a statutory employee and to be an independent contractor (IC) instead. You are an IC for income tax purposes as long as you qualify under the regular IRS rules. (See Chapter 15.) If you qualify, no income tax need be withheld from your compensation, so you'll have higher take-home pay. But you will need to pay your income taxes four times during the year in the form of estimated taxes. (See Chapter 11.)

Most hiring firms would prefer that you be classified as an IC for employment tax purposes instead of as a statutory employee. That would allow them to avoid the burden of paying half of your FICA (Social Security and Medicare) taxes themselves and withholding your share from your pay. This chapter describes some simple ways you can avoid this status. Doing so may help you get work you might be denied as a statutory employee.

If You Have Multiple Businesses

If you have another business in which you are not classified as a statutory employee, you must file a separate Schedule C for that business. You aren't allowed to use expenses from your statutory employment to offset earnings from your self-employment.

EXAMPLE: Margaret works as a business-to-business salesperson in which she qualifies as a statutory employee. She also works part time as a self-employed marketing consultant. This year she had $5,000 in travel expenses from her selling job. She can't deduct any of this expense from her earnings as a consultant. She can deduct it only from her income as a salesperson. When Margaret does her taxes, she must file a separate Schedule C for each of her occupations.

Requirements for Statutory Employee Status

You're a statutory employee only if you satisfy all of these requirements:

- you perform services personally for the hiring firm
- you make no substantial investment in the equipment or facilities you use to work, and
- you have a continuing relationship with the hiring firm.

Personal Service

You're a statutory employee only if your oral or written agreement with the hiring firm requires you to do substantially all the work yourself. In other words, you can't hire helpers or subcontract the work out to others.

No Substantial Investment

Statutory employees must not have a substantial investment in equipment or premises used to perform their work—for example, office space, machinery, or office furniture. An investment is substantial if it is more than an employee would be expected to provide—for example, paying office rent or buying expensive computer equipment. Vehicles you use on the job do not count as substantial investments.

Avoiding Statutory Employee Status

Even if you do the type of work normally performed by a statutory employee, you can avoid being classified as one. To do this, set up your work relationship so that it does not satisfy one or more of the three requirements discussed above. For example, you can:

- Sign a written agreement with the person or firm that hires you stating that you have the right to subcontract or delegate the work out to others. This way, you make clear that you don't have to do the work personally.
- Avoid having a continuing relationship with any one hiring firm by working on single projects, not ongoing tasks.
- Invest in outside facilities, such as your own office.

However, even if you do these things, some hiring firms may want to classify you as a statutory employee because they don't understand the law. You may have to educate the people or firms you work for about these rules.

Continuing Relationship

A continuing relationship means you work for the hiring firm on a regular or recurring basis. A single job is not considered a continuing relationship. But regular part-time or seasonal employment qualifies.

Types of Statutory Employees

You won't be a statutory employee just because you satisfy the three threshold requirements explained above. You must also satisfy additional requirements for each type of statutory employee occupation. These rules present you with yet more ways to avoid statutory employee status. If the type of work you do and the way you do it don't fall squarely within the additional rules below, you won't be classified as a statutory employee.

Business-to-Business Salespeople

If you're a business-to-business salesperson (that is, you sell products or services on behalf of a business to other businesses, not consumers), you're a statutory employee only if you satisfy the three threshold requirements discussed above and you also:

- work at least 80% of the time for one person or company
- sell on behalf of, or turn your orders over to, the hiring firm
- sell merchandise for resale or supplies for use in the buyer's business operations, as opposed to goods purchased for personal consumption at home, and
- sell only to wholesalers, retailers, contractors, or those who operate hotels, restaurants, or similar establishments (but this does not include manufacturers, schools, hospitals, churches, municipalities, or state and federal governments).

EXAMPLE:
Linda sells books to retail bookstores for Scrivener & Sons Publishing Company. Her territory covers the entire Midwest. She works only for Scrivener and is paid a commission based on the amount of each sale. She turns her orders over to Scrivener's, which ships the books to each bookstore customer. Linda is a statutory employee of Scrivener's.

Life Insurance Salespeople

If your full-time occupation is soliciting life insurance applications or annuity contracts, you're a statutory employee only if you satisfy the threshold requirements explained above and:

- you work primarily for one life insurance company, and
- the company provides you with work necessities such as office space, secretarial help, forms, rate books, and advertising material.

EXAMPLE:
Walter works full time selling life insurance for the Old Reliable Life Insurance Company. He works out of Old Reliable's Omaha office, where he is provided with a desk, clerical help, rate books, and insurance applications. Walter is Old Reliable's statutory employee.

Clothing or Needlecraft Producers

If you make or sew buttons, quilts, gloves, bedspreads, clothing, needlecraft, or similar products, you're a statutory employee only if you satisfy the threshold requirements explained above and you:

- work away from the hiring firm's place of business—usually in your own home or workshop or in another person's home
- work only on goods or materials the hiring firm furnishes

- work according to the hiring firm's specifications (generally, such specifications are simple and consist of patterns or samples), and
- are required to return the processed material to the hiring firm or person designated by it.

If your work setup meets all these requirements, the hiring firm must pay the employer's share of FICA on your compensation and withhold your share of FICA taxes from your pay. However, no FICA tax is imposed if the hiring firm pays you less than $100 for a calendar year.

EXAMPLE:

Rosa works at home, sewing buttons on shirts and dresses. She does work for various companies, including Upscale Fashions, Inc. Upscale provides Rosa with all the clothing and the buttons she must sew. The only equipment Rosa provides is a needle. Upscale gives Rosa a sample of each outfit showing where to put the buttons. When Rosa finishes each batch of clothing, she returns it to Upscale. Rosa is a statutory employee.

Food, Beverage, and Laundry Distributors

You're also a statutory employee if you work as a driver and distribute meat or meat products, vegetables or vegetable products, fruits or fruit products, bakery products, beverages other than milk, or laundry or dry cleaning to customers designated by the hiring firm as well as those you solicit. It makes no difference whether you operate from your own truck or trucks that belong to the person or firm that hired you.

EXAMPLE:

Alder Laundry and Dry Cleaning enters into an agreement with Sharon to pick up and deliver clothing for its customers. Sharon is a statutory employee because she meets all three threshold requirements: Her agreement with

Alder acknowledges that she will do the work personally, she has no substantial investment in facilities (her truck doesn't count because it's used to deliver the product), and she has a continuing relationship with Alder.

Statutory Independent Contractors

If you're a direct seller or licensed real estate agent, you are automatically considered an independent contractor for Social Security, Medicare, and federal unemployment tax purposes, provided that:

- your pay is based on sales commissions, not on the number of hours you work, and
- you have a written contract with the hiring firm providing that you will not be treated as an employee for federal tax purposes.

Consider yourself lucky, and be thankful that your industry lobbyists were able to get these special rules adopted by Congress. Because your worker status is automatically determined by law, hiring firms need not worry about the IRS. This should make it very easy for you to get work as an independent contractor in your chosen field.

You undoubtedly know whether or not you're a licensed real estate agent whom the IRS will automatically classify as a statutory independent contractor.

You're a direct seller for IRS purposes if you sell consumer products to people in their homes or at a place other than an established retail store—for example, at swap meets. Consumer products include tangible personal property that is used for personal, family, or household purposes— for example, vacuum cleaners, cosmetics, encyclopedias, and gardening equipment. It also includes intangible products such as cable services and home study educational courses.

EXAMPLE:

Larry is a Mavon Guy, selling men's toiletries door to door. Mavon pays him a 20% commission on all his sales, and nothing else. He has a written contract with Mavon that provides that he will not be treated as an employee for federal tax purposes. Larry is a statutory nonemployee—that is, an independent contractor—for federal employment tax purposes.

If they also satisfy the requirements outlined above, people who sell or distribute newspapers or shopping news are also considered to be direct sellers. This is true whether they are paid based on the number of papers they deliver or whether they purchase newspapers, sell them, and keep the money they earn from the sales. ●

Taxes for Workers You Hire

If, like many self-employed people, you hire others to assist you, it's wise to learn a little about federal and state tax requirements that apply to you and your workers. This chapter covers these requirements.

SKIP AHEAD

If you do all the work in your unincorporated business yourself, you don't need to read this chapter.

Hiring People to Help You

Sooner or later, most self-employed people need to hire people to help them—for example:

- A freelance graphic designer might hire a part-time assistant to help meet a pressing deadline from the biggest client.
- An architect might hire a computer consultant to help choose and install a new computer system and explain how to use new design software.
- A seller of books from several publishers to bookstores might hire someone to cover a sales territory while the seller is on vacation.

Whenever you hire a helper, you need to be concerned about obeying federal and state tax laws.

Independent Contractors Versus Employees

The tax rules you have to follow when you hire helpers differ depending upon whether your helpers qualify as employees or as self-employed independent contractors (ICs) by the IRS and other government agencies.

If you hire an employee, you must withhold taxes from the person's pay, and you must pay other taxes for the employee yourself. You must also comply with complex and burdensome bookkeeping and reporting requirements.

If you hire an IC, you need not comply with these requirements. All you have to do is report the amount you pay the IC to the IRS and your state tax department.

However, hiring an IC is not necessarily cheaper than hiring an employee. Some ICs charge far more than what you'd pay an employee to do similar work. Nevertheless, many self-employed people still prefer to hire ICs instead of employees because of the smaller tax and bookkeeping burdens.

Determining Worker Status

Initially, it's up to you to determine whether any person you hire is an employee or an IC. If you decide that a worker is an employee, you must comply with the federal and state tax requirements discussed in the next section. If you decide the worker is an IC, you need only comply with simpler income reporting and tax identification number requirements, also discussed below.

However, your decision about how to classify a worker is subject to review by various government agencies, including:

- the IRS
- the Department of Labor
- your state's tax department
- your state's labor department
- your state's unemployment compensation insurance agency, and
- your state's workers' compensation insurance agency.

Any agency that determines that you misclassified an employee as an IC may impose back taxes, fines, and penalties.

Scrutinizing agencies use various tests to determine whether a worker is an IC or an employee. The determining factor is usually whether you have the right to control the worker. If you have the right to control the way a worker does his or her work—both as to the final results and the details of when, where, and how the work is done—then the worker is your employee. On the other hand, if your control over the worker's work is limited to accepting or rejecting the final results the worker achieves, he or she is an IC. (See Chapter 15 for a detailed discussion of how to determine whether a worker is an IC or an employee.)

Safe Harbor Makes It Easier to Win Audits

A part of the Tax Code known as the "Safe Harbor," or Section 530, enables firms that hire ICs to win IRS employment tax audits.

To qualify for Safe Harbor protection, you must satisfy three requirements. You must have:

- filed all required 1099 forms for the workers in question
- consistently treated the workers involved and others doing substantially similar work as ICs, and
- had a reasonable basis for treating the workers as ICs—for example, treating such workers as ICs is a common practice in your industry, or an attorney or accountant told you that the workers qualified as ICs.

If you're audited for employment tax purposes, the auditor must first determine whether you qualify for Safe Harbor protection. If you do, no assessments or penalties may be imposed. You may continue treating the workers involved as ICs for these purposes, and the IRS will not question their status.

This means you need not pay the employer's share of the workers' Social Security and Medicare taxes or withhold income or Social Security taxes from their pay. However, the workers could still be considered employees for other purposes, such as pension plan rules and state unemployment compensation taxes.

 CAUTION

Part-timers and temps can be employees. Don't think that a person you hire to work part time or for a short period must be an IC. People who work for you only temporarily or part time are your employees if you have the right to control the way they work.

 RESOURCE

For a detailed discussion of the practical and legal issues employers face when hiring ICs, see *Working With Independent Contractors*, by Stephen Fishman (Nolo).

Tax Concerns When Hiring Employees

Any time you hire an employee, you become an unpaid tax collector for the federal government. You are required to withhold and pay both federal and state taxes for the worker. These taxes are called "payroll taxes" or "employment taxes."

You must also satisfy these requirements if you incorporate your business and continue to actively work in it. In this event, you will be an employee of your corporation.

Federal Payroll Taxes

The IRS regulates federal payroll taxes, which include:

- Social Security and Medicare taxes—also known as FICA
- unemployment taxes—also known as FUTA, and
- income taxes—also known as FITW.

 CAUTION

Don't forget yourself. If you incorporate your business and work as an employee of your corporation, your corporation—not you personally—must pay these payroll taxes for you.

Pros and Cons of Hiring Employees Versus ICs

There are advantages and disadvantages to hiring both employees and ICs.

Hiring Employees

Pros	Cons
You don't need to worry about government auditors claiming you misclassified employees.	You must pay federal and state payroll taxes for employees.
You can closely supervise employees.	You must provide employees with office space and equipment.
You can give employees extensive training.	You are liable for your employees' actions.
Employees can't sue you for damages if they are injured on the job, provided you have workers' compensation insurance.	You must usually provide employees with workers' compensation coverage.
You automatically own any intellectual property employees create on the job.	You ordinarily provide employees benefits such as vacations and sick leave.
Employees can generally be fired at any time.	You can be sued for labor law violations.

Hiring ICs

Pros	Cons
You don't have to pay federal and state payroll taxes for ICs.	You risk exposure to audits by the IRS and other agencies.
You don't have to provide office space or equipment for ICs.	You can't closely supervise or train ICs.
You are generally not liable for ICs' actions.	You may lose copyright ownership if you don't obtain an assignment of rights.
You don't have to provide workers' compensation insurance for ICs.	ICs can sue you for damages if they are injured on the job.
You don't have to provide employee benefits to ICs.	ICs may usually work for your competitors as well as you.
Your exposure to lawsuits for labor law violations is reduced with ICs.	ICs usually can't be terminated unless they violate their contracts.

RESOURCE

IRS Publication 15 (Circular E), *Employer's Tax Guide,* provides detailed information on federal payroll taxes. It is an outstanding resource that you should have if you hire employees. You can get a free copy by calling the IRS at 800-TAX-FORM, visiting your local IRS office, or downloading it from the IRS website at www.irs.gov.

FICA

FICA is an acronym for Federal Income Contributions Act, the law requiring employers and employees to pay Social Security and Medicare taxes. The IRS imposes FICA taxes on both employers and employees. If you hire an employee, you must collect and remit his or her part of the taxes by withholding it from paycheck amounts and sending it to the IRS. You must also pay a matching amount yourself for each employee.

The IRS determines the amounts you must withhold and pay each year. For 2007, for example, employers and employees are each required to pay 7.65% on the first $97,500 of an employee's annual wages. The 7.65% figure is the sum of the 6.2% Social Security tax and the 1.45% Medicare tax.

There is no Social Security tax on the portion of an employee's annual wages that exceed the $97,500 income ceiling. However, there is no such limit on the Medicare tax: Both you and the employee must pay the 1.45% Medicare tax on any wages over $97,500. The ceiling for the Social Security tax changes annually. You can find the Social Security tax income ceiling as well as the Social Security and Medicare tax rates for the current year in IRS Publication 15 (Circular E), *Employer's Tax Guide*.

FUTA

FUTA is an acronym for the Federal Unemployment Tax Act—the law that establishes federal unemployment insurance taxes. Most employers must pay both state and federal unemployment taxes. But even if you're exempt from the state tax, you may still have to pay the federal tax. Employers alone are responsible for FUTA; you may not collect or deduct it from employees' wages.

You must pay FUTA taxes if:

- You pay $1,500 or more to employees during any calendar quarter—that is, any three-month period beginning with January, April, July, or October, or

- You had at least one employee for some part of a day in any 20 or more different weeks during the year. The weeks don't have to be consecutive, nor does it have to be the same employee each week.

Technically, the FUTA tax rate is 6.2%, but in practice, you rarely pay this much. You are given a credit of 5.4% if you pay the applicable state unemployment tax in full and on time. This means that the actual FUTA tax rate is usually 0.8%. In 2008, the FUTA tax is assessed on only the first $7,000 of an employee's annual wage—which means that the FUTA tax is usually $56 per year per employee.

FITW

FITW is an acronym for federal income tax withholding. When you hire an employee you're not only a tax collector for the government, but you are also a manager of your employee's income. The IRS fears that employees will not save enough from their wages to pay their tax bill on April 15. It also wants to speed up tax collections. So the IRS tells you, the employer, not to pay your employees their entire wages but to send the money to the IRS. This practice is the employee version of the estimated taxes that ICs must pay. (See Chapter 11.)

As an employer, you must calculate and withhold federal income taxes from all your employees' paychecks. You normally deposit the funds in a bank, which transmits the money to the IRS. Employees are solely responsible for paying federal income taxes; the employer's only responsibility is to withhold the funds and remit them to the government.

You must ask each employee you hire to fill out IRS Form W-4, *Employee's Withholding Allowance Certificate*. The information on this form determines how much tax you must withhold from the employee's pay. By January 31 of each year, you must give each employee you hired the previous year a copy of IRS Form W-2, *Wage and Tax Statement*, showing how much he or she was paid and how much tax was withheld for the year. You must also send copies to the Social Security Administration.

You can obtain copies of these forms by calling the IRS at 800-TAX-FORM, visiting your local IRS office, or downloading them from the IRS website at www.irs.gov.

RESOURCE

For detailed information on FITW, see IRS Publication 505, *Tax Withholding and Estimated Tax*. You can obtain a copy by calling the IRS at 800-TAX-FORM, visiting your local IRS office, or downloading it from the IRS website at www.irs.gov.

Paying Payroll Taxes

You pay FICA, FUTA, and FITW either electronically or by making federal tax deposits at specified banks. The IRS will tell you how often you must make your payroll tax deposits. The frequency depends on the total taxes you pay. If you pay by mail, you must submit an IRS Federal Tax Deposit coupon (Form 8109-B) with each payroll tax payment. If you have employees, you must also report these payments to the IRS on Form 941, *Employer's Quarterly Federal Tax Return*, after each calendar quarter in which you have employees. Form 941 shows how many employees you had, how much they were paid, and the amount of FICA and income tax withheld. Employers with total employment tax liability of $1,000 or less may file employment tax returns once a year instead of quarterly. Those employers can use Form 944, *Employer's Annual Federal Tax Return*.

Once each year, you must also file IRS Form 940, *Employer's Annual Federal Unemployment Tax Return* (or the simpler Form 940-EZ). This form shows the IRS how much federal unemployment tax you owe.

Instead of depositing payroll tax payments by check with specified banks, you may pay them directly to the IRS electronically using the IRS's Electronic Federal Tax Payment System (EFTPS). Using EFTPS, you can make deposits by phone or computer. If you pay more than $200,000 in payroll taxes each year, using EFTPS is mandatory. If you pay less than $200,000, using the electronic system is optional. For information on EFTPS or to get an enrollment form, call EFTPS Customer Service at 800-555-4477.

RESOURCE

Figuring out how much to withhold, doing the necessary record keeping, and filling out the required forms can be complicated. Accounting software programs such as *QuickBooks* can help with the calculations and can be used to print out your employees' checks and IRS forms.

If you don't want to use EFTPS yourself, you can hire a bookkeeper or payroll tax service to do the work. Payroll tax services are usually not expensive, especially if you have only one or two employees.

Penalties for Failing to Pay FICA and FITW

As far as the IRS is concerned, an employer's most important duty is to withhold and pay Social Security and income taxes. Employee FICA and FITW are also known as "trust fund taxes" because the employer is deemed to hold the withheld funds in trust for the U.S. government.

If you fail to pay trust fund taxes, you can get into the worst tax trouble there is. The IRS can—and often does—seize a business's assets and force it to close down if it owes back payroll taxes. Although very rare, you can also get thrown in jail.

At the very least, you'll have to pay all the taxes due plus interest. The IRS may also impose a penalty known as the trust fund recovery penalty if it determines that you willfully failed to pay the taxes. The agency can claim you willfully failed to pay taxes if you knew the taxes were due and didn't pay them. If you paid such taxes in the past and then stopped paying them, that constitutes pretty good evidence that you knew the taxes were due.

The trust fund recovery penalty is also known as the 100% penalty because the amount of the penalty is equal to 100% of the total amount of employee FICA and FITW taxes the employer failed to withhold and pay to the IRS. This can be a staggering sum. As a business owner, you'll be personally liable for the 100% penalty—that is, you will have to pay it out of your own pocket, even if you've incorporated your business.

Their Dogs Ate Their Homework

You are responsible for making sure that your FICA and FITW taxes are paid—even if you hire someone else to deal with it for you. For example, the IRS assessed a $40,000 penalty against two brothers in the floor covering business when their company failed to pay FITW and FICA for its employees for over two years. The brothers had the money to pay the taxes and had entrusted the task to an office manager. The manager failed to make the payments. The brothers pleaded ignorance, claiming that the manager intercepted and screened the mail and altered check descriptions and quarterly reports.

Both the IRS and the court were unmoved. Although the court stated that it was not unreasonable for the brothers to entrust the payments to their office manager, the brothers were still ultimately responsible to make sure the taxes were paid and were therefore liable for the penalty. (*Conklin Bros. v. United States*, 986 F.2d 315 (9th Cir. 1993).)

RESOURCE

For guidance on how to deal with the IRS if you are having trouble meeting your payroll tax obligations, see *Tax Savvy for Small Business*, by Fred Daily (Nolo).

Rules for Family Members

Self-employed people often hire family members. A tax rule helps promote this family togetherness: If you hire your child, spouse, or parent as an employee, you may not have to pay FICA and FUTA taxes.

Employing your child. You need not pay FUTA taxes for services performed by your child who is under 21 years old. You need not pay FICA taxes for your child who is under 18 and works in your trade or business or a partnership owned solely by you and your spouse.

EXAMPLE:

Lisa, a 16-year-old, makes deliveries for her mother's mail order business, which is operated as a sole proprietorship. Although Lisa is her mother's employee, her mother need not pay FUTA taxes until Lisa reaches 21 and need not pay FICA taxes until Lisa reaches 18.

However, these rules do not apply—and you must pay both FICA and FUTA—if you hire your child to work for:

- your corporation, or
- your partnership, unless all the partners are parents of the child.

EXAMPLE:

Ron, a 17-year-old, works in a computer repair business that is half owned by his mother and half owned by her partner, Ralph, who is no relation to the family. The business must pay FICA and FUTA taxes for Ron because he is working for a partnership and not all of the partners are his parents.

In addition, if your child has no unearned income (for example, interest or dividend income), you have to withhold income taxes from your child's pay only if it exceeds the standard deduction for the year. The standard deduction was $5,350 in 2007 and is adjusted every year for inflation. Children who are paid less than this amount need not pay any income taxes on their earnings. However, you must withhold income taxes if your child has more than $250 in unearned income for the year and his or her total income exceeds $750.

EXAMPLE 1:

Connie, a 15-year-old girl, is paid $4,000 a year to help out in her parent's home business. She has no income from interest or any other source. Her parents need not withhold income taxes from Connie's salary.

EXAMPLE 2:

Connie is paid $4,000 in salary and has $500 in interest income on a savings account. Her parents must withhold income taxes from her salary because she has more than $250 in unearned income (the interest) and her total income for the year was more than $750.

Employing your spouse. If you pay your spouse to work in your trade or business, the payments are subject to FICA taxes and federal income tax withholding, but not FUTA taxes.

EXAMPLE:

Kay's husband, Simon, is a sole proprietor computer programmer. Kay works as his assistant, for which she is paid $1,500 per month. Simon must pay the employer's share of FICA taxes for Kay and withhold employee FICA and federal income taxes from her pay. Simon need not pay FUTA taxes for Kay.

But this rule does not apply—and FUTA must be paid—if your spouse works for:

- a corporation, even if you control it, or
- a partnership, even if your spouse is a partner along with you.

EXAMPLE:

Laura's husband, Rob, works as a draftsperson in Laura's architectural consulting firm, a corporation of which she is the sole owner. The corporation must pay FICA, FUTA, and FITW for Rob.

Income Tax Break for Child-Employees

You must withhold income taxes from your child's pay only if it exceeds the standard deduction for the year. The standard deduction was $5,350 in 2007 and is adjusted every year for inflation. A child who is paid less than this amount need not pay any income taxes on his or her salary.

You might consider getting your child to do some work around the office instead of paying him or her an allowance for doing nothing. If your child's pay is below the standard deduction amount, it is not only tax-free, but you can also deduct the amount from your own taxes as a business expense if the child's work is business-related—for example, cleaning your office, answering the phone, or making deliveries. However, you can deduct your child's wages only if they are reasonable—that is, if they are about what you'd pay a stranger for the same work. Don't try paying your child $100 per hour for office cleaning so you can get a big tax deduction.

If you pay your child $600 or more during the year, you must file Form W-2 reporting the earnings to the IRS. No matter how much you pay your child, each year you should fill out and have your child sign IRS Form W-4, *Employee's Withholding Allowance Certificate.* If you pay your child less than $200 per week, keep the form in your records. If you pay your child more than $200 per week, keep a copy of the form for your records and file a copy of the form with the IRS.

Employing a parent. The wages of a parent you employ in your trade or business are subject to income tax withholding and FICA taxes, but not FUTA taxes.

EXAMPLE:

Don owns and operates a graphic design firm and employs Art, his father, as a part-time designer. Because the firm is a business, Don must pay the employer's share of FICA taxes for Art and withhold employee FICA and federal income taxes from his pay. Dan need not pay FUTA taxes for Art.

State Payroll Taxes

Employers in all states are required to pay and withhold state payroll taxes for employees. These taxes include:

- state unemployment compensation taxes in all states
- state income tax withholding in most states, and
- state disability taxes in a few states.

Unemployment Compensation

Federal law requires that all states provide most types of employees with unemployment compensation, also called UC or unemployment insurance. Employers are required to contribute to a state unemployment insurance fund. Employees make no contributions, except in Alaska, New Jersey, and Pennsylvania, where employers must withhold small employee contributions from employees' paychecks. Employees who are laid off or fired for reasons other than serious misconduct are entitled to receive unemployment benefits from the state fund. You need not provide unemployment for independent contractors.

If your payroll is very small—below $1,500 per calendar quarter—you probably won't have to pay UC taxes. In most states, you must pay state UC taxes for employees if you're paying FUTA taxes. However, some states have more strict requirements. Contact your state labor department for details on your state's law.

State Income Tax Withholding

All states except Alaska, Florida, Nevada, South Dakota, Texas, Washington, and Wyoming have state income taxation. New Hampshire and Tennessee impose state income taxes on dividend and interest income only. If you do business in a state that imposes state income taxes, you must withhold the applicable tax from your employees' paychecks and pay it to the state taxing authority. No state income tax withholding is required for workers who qualify as independent contractors.

It's easy to determine whether you need to withhold state income taxes for a worker: If your state has state income taxes and you are withholding federal income taxes for a worker, you must withhold state income taxes as well. Each state has its own income tax withholding forms and procedures. Contact your state tax department for information.

State Disability Insurance

Five states have state disability insurance that provides employees with coverage for injuries or illnesses that are not related to work. Injuries that are job-related are covered by workers' compensation. The states with disability insurance are: California, Hawaii, New Jersey, New York, and Rhode Island. Puerto Rico also has a disability insurance program.

In these states, employees contribute to disability insurance in amounts their employers withhold from their paychecks. Employers must also make contributions in Hawaii, New Jersey, New York, and Puerto Rico.

Except in New York, the disability insurance coverage requirements are the same as for UC insurance. If you pay UC for a worker, you must withhold and pay disability insurance premiums as well. You need not provide disability for independent contractors.

Employers in California Must Withhold for Paid Leave

In 2004, California became the first state in the nation to provide its workers with paid family and medical leave, including parental leave. The program is funded by employees, through an increase in the withholdings employers take from their paychecks and pay into the state's disability insurance (SDI) fund. To fund the paid leave program, California employers must withhold a slightly larger amount from their employees' paychecks for SDI; there is no separate line item withholding required specifically for the paid leave program. For more information on the program, go to www.edd.ca.gov/direp/pflind.asp and click on the links on the left side of the Web page.

Workers' Compensation Insurance

Subject to some important exceptions, employers in all states must provide their employees with workers' compensation insurance to cover work-related injuries or illnesses. Workers' compensation is not a payroll tax. You must purchase a workers' compensation policy from a private insurer or state workers' compensation fund. (See Chapter 6.)

Tax Concerns When Hiring Independent Contractors

If you hire an independent contractor, or IC, you don't have to worry about withholding and paying state or federal payroll taxes or filling out lots of government forms. This is one reason self-employed people generally prefer to hire other ICs rather than employees.

However, if you pay an unincorporated IC $600 or more during the year for business-related services, you must:

- file IRS Form 1099-MISC telling the IRS how much you paid the worker, and
- obtain the IC's taxpayer identification number (or Social Security number if he or she does not have one).

The IRS imposes these requirements because it is very concerned that many ICs don't report all the income they earn to avoid paying taxes. To help prevent this, the IRS wants to find out how much you pay any ICs you hire and make sure it has their correct taxpayer ID numbers.

The filing and ID requirements apply to all ICs you hire who are sole proprietors or partners in partnerships, which includes the vast majority of ICs. However, they don't apply to corporations, probably because large businesses have a strong legislative lobby. The IRS has attempted to change the law to include corporations, but so far it hasn't succeeded.

This means that if you hire an incorporated IC, you don't have to file anything with the IRS.

EXAMPLE:

Bob, a self-employed consultant, pays $5,000 to Yvonne, a CPA, to perform accounting services. Yvonne has formed her own one-person corporation called Yvonne's Accounting Services, Inc. Bob pays the corporation, not Yvonne personally. Because Bob is paying a corporation, he need not report the payment on Form 1099-MISC or obtain Yvonne's taxpayer ID number.

This is one of the main advantages of hiring incorporated ICs, because the IRS uses Form 1099 as a lead to find people and companies to audit.

However, it's wise to make sure you have the corporation's full legal name and federal employer identification number. Without this information, you may not be able to prove to the IRS that the payee was incorporated. An easy way to do this is to have the IC fill out IRS Form W-9, *Request for Taxpayer Identification Number and Certificate,* and keep it in your files. This simple form merely requires the corporation to provide its name, address, and EIN. (You can obtain this form by calling the IRS at 800-TAX-FORM, visiting your local IRS office, or downloading it from the IRS website at www.irs.gov.)

If you're not sure whether you must file a Form 1099-MISC for a worker, go ahead and file one anyway. You lose nothing by doing so and will save yourself the severe consequences of not filing if you were legally required to do so.

CAUTION

When in doubt, file a Form 1099. The IRS may impose a $100 fine if you fail to file a Form 1099 when required. But, far more serious, you'll be subject to severe penalties if the IRS later audits you and determines that you misclassified the worker.

RESOURCE

For a detailed discussion of the consequences of not filing a 1099 form, see *Working With Independent Contractors,* by Stephen Fishman (Nolo).

There is one exception to the rule that you don't have to file 1099 forms for payments to corporations. You must report all payments of $600 or more you make to a doctor or lawyer who is incorporated, where the payments are for your business. You need not report payments you make to incorporated doctors or lawyers for personal services—for example, if you hire a doctor to take care of a personal health problem or hire a lawyer to write your will.

Threshold for Income Reporting

You need to obtain an unincorporated IC's taxpayer ID number and file a 1099 form with the IRS only if you pay the IC $600 or more during

a year for business-related services. It makes no difference whether the sum was one payment for a single job or the total of many small payments for multiple jobs.

EXAMPLE:

Andre, a computer consultant, hires Thomas, a self-employed programmer, to help create a computer program. Andre classifies Thomas as an IC and pays him $2,000 during the year. Thomas is a sole proprietor. Because Andre paid Thomas more than $599 for business-related services, Andre must obtain Thomas's taxpayer ID number and file Form 1099 with the IRS to report the payment.

In calculating whether the payments made to an IC total $600 or more during a year, you must include payments for parts or materials the IC used in performing the services. For example, if you hire a painter to paint your home office, the cost of the paint would be included in the tally.

However, not all payments you make to ICs are counted toward the $600 threshold, as explained above.

Payments for Merchandise

You don't need to count payments solely for merchandise or inventory. This includes raw materials and supplies that will become a part of merchandise you intend to sell.

EXAMPLE:

Betty pays $5,000 to purchase 100 used widgets from Joe's Widgets, a sole proprietorship he owns. Betty intends to repair and resell the widgets. The payment need not be counted toward the $600 threshold because Betty is purchasing merchandise, not services, from Joe.

Payments for Personal Services

You need only count payments you make to ICs for services they perform in the course of your trade or business. A trade or business is an activity carried on for gain or profit. You don't count payments for services that are not related to your business, including payments you make to ICs for personal or household services or repairs—for example, payments to babysitters, gardeners, and housekeepers. Running your home is not a profit-making activity.

EXAMPLE:

Joe, a self-employed designer, pays Mary a total of $1,000 during the year for gardening services for his residence. None of the payments count toward the $600 threshold because they don't relate to Joe's design business. Joe need not obtain Mary's taxpayer ID number or file a 1099 form reporting the payments to the IRS.

Obtaining Taxpayer Identification Numbers

Some ICs work in the underground economy—that is, they're paid in cash and never pay any taxes or file tax returns. The IRS may not even know they exist. The IRS wants you to help it find these people by supplying the taxpayer ID numbers from all ICs who meet the requirements explained above.

If an IC won't give you his or her number or the IRS informs you that the number the IC gave you is incorrect, the IRS assumes the person isn't going to voluntarily pay taxes. So it requires you to withhold taxes from the compensation you pay the IC and remit them to the IRS. This is called "backup withholding." If you fail to backup withhold where required, the IRS will impose an assessment against you equal to 28% of what you paid the IC.

Avoiding Backup Withholding

Backup withholding can be a bookkeeping burden for you. Fortunately, it's very easy to avoid. Have the IC fill out and sign IRS Form W-9, *Request for Taxpayer Identification Number*, and retain it in your files. (You can obtain this form by calling the IRS at 800-TAX-FORM, visiting your local IRS office, or downloading it from the IRS website at www.irs.gov.) You don't have to file the W-9 with the IRS. This simple form merely requires the IC to list his or her name, address, and taxpayer ID number. Partnerships and sole proprietors with employees must have a federal employer identification number (EIN), which they obtain from the IRS. In the case of sole proprietors without employees, the taxpayer ID number is the IC's Social Security number.

If the IC doesn't already have an EIN but promises to obtain one, you don't have to backup withhold for 60 days after he or she applies for one. Have the IC fill out and sign the W-9 form, stating "Applied For" in the space where the ID number is supposed to be listed. If you don't receive the IC's ID number within 60 days, start backup withholding.

Backup Withholding Procedure

If you are unable to obtain an IC's taxpayer ID number or the IRS informs you that the number the IC gave you is incorrect, you'll have to begin backup withholding as soon as you pay an IC $600 or more during the year. You need not backup withhold on payments totaling less than $600.

To backup withhold, deposit with your bank 28% of the IC's compensation every quarter. You must make these deposits separately from the payroll tax deposits you make for employees. Report the amounts withheld on IRS Form 945, *Annual Return of Withheld Federal Income Tax*. This is an annual return you must file by January 31 of the following year. See the instructions to Form 945 for details. You can obtain a copy of the form by calling the IRS at 800-TAX-FORM, visiting your local IRS office, or downloading it from the IRS website at www.irs.gov.

Filling Out Your Form 1099

You must file a 1099-MISC form for each IC to whom you paid $600 or more during the year. Each 1099 form contains multiple copies as well as two parts that can be used for two different workers. All your 1099 forms must be submitted together along with one copy of Form 1096, which is a transmittal form—the IRS equivalent of a cover letter.

You must obtain original 1099 forms and Form 1096 from the IRS: You cannot submit downloaded or photocopied versions because the original forms are printed in a way that the IRS can scan during processing. Obtain these forms by calling the IRS at 800-TAX-FORM or visiting your local IRS office.

Filling out Form 1099-MISC is easy. Follow this step-by-step approach. (A sample form is provided on the next page for your information, but you must get original forms from the IRS.)

- List your name and address in the first box for "PAYER'S name."

- Enter your taxpayer identification number in the box for "PAYER'S federal identification number."

- The IC you have paid is called the "Recipient" on this form, meaning the person who received the money. You must provide the IC's taxpayer identification number, name, and address in the boxes indicated. For sole proprietors, you must list the individual's name first, then you may list a different business name, though this is not required. You may not enter only a business name for a sole proprietor.

- Enter the amount of your payments to the IC in Box 7, "Nonemployee compensation." Be sure to fill in the right box or the Form 1099-MISC will be deemed invalid by the IRS.

- If you've done backup withholding for an IC who has not provided you with a taxpayer ID number, enter the amount withheld in Box 4.

The Form 1099-MISC contains five copies. These must be filed as follows:

- Copy A, the top copy, must be filed with the IRS no later than February 28 of the year after payment was made to the IC. If you don't use the remaining two spaces for other ICs, leave those spaces blank. Don't cut the page.

- Copy 1 must be filed with your state tax authority if your state has a state income tax. The filing deadline is February 28 for most states, but check with your state tax department to make sure. Your state may also have a specific transmittal form or cover letter you must use.

- Copy B and Copy 2 must be given to the worker no later than January 31 of the year after payment was made.

- Copy C is for you to retain for your files.

All the IRS copies of each 1099 form are filed together with Form 1096, the simple transmittal form. You must add up all the payments reported on all the 1099 forms and list the total in the box indicated on Form 1096. File the forms with the IRS Service Center listed on the back of Form 1096.

IRS Forms 1009-MISC and 1096

9595 ☐ VOID ☐ CORRECTED

PAYER'S name, street address, city, state, ZIP code, and telephone no.	1 Rents $	OMB No. 1545-0115	Miscellaneous Income
	2 Royalties $	**2007** Form **1099-MISC**	
	3 Other income $	4 Federal income tax withheld $	Copy A
PAYER'S federal identification number	RECIPIENT'S identification number	5 Fishing boat proceeds $	6 Medical and health care payments $

For
Internal Revenue
Service Center

File with Form 1096.

RECIPIENT'S name	7 Nonemployee compensation $	8 Substitute payments in lieu of dividends or interest $
Street address (including apt. no.)	9 Payer made direct sales of $5,000 or more of consumer products to a buyer (recipient) for resale ▶ ☐	10 Crop insurance proceeds $
City, state, and ZIP code	11	12

For Privacy Act
and Paperwork
Reduction Act
Notice, see the
**2007 General
Instructions for
Forms 1099,
1098, 5498,
and W-2G.**

Account number (see instructions)	2nd TIN not. ☐	13 Excess golden parachute payments $	14 Gross proceeds paid to an attorney $
15a Section 409A deferrals $	15b Section 409A income $	16 State tax withheld $ $	17 State/Payer's state no.	18 State income $ $

Form **1099-MISC**   Cat. No. 14425J   Department of the Treasury - Internal Revenue Service

Do Not Cut or Separate Forms on This Page — Do Not Cut or Separate Forms on This Page

---

Do Not Staple **6969**

Form **1096**
Department of the Treasury
Internal Revenue Service

Annual Summary and Transmittal of U.S. Information Returns

OMB No. 1545-0108

2007

┌ FILER'S name

  Street address (including room or suite number)

  City, state, and ZIP code ┘

Name of person to contact	Telephone number ( )	**For Official Use Only**
Email address	Fax number ( )	☐ ☐ ☐ ☐ ☐ ☐ ☐ ☐ ☐

1 Employer identification number	2 Social security number	3 Total number of forms	4 Federal income tax withheld $	5 Total amount reported with this Form 1096 $

Enter an "X" in only one box below to indicate the type of form being filed.   If this is your **final return**, enter an "X" here . . . ▶ ☐

W-2G 32	1098 81	1098-C 78	1098-E 84	1098-T 83	1099-A 80	1099-B 79	1099-C 85	1099-CAP 73	1099-DIV 91	1099-G 86	1099-H 71	1099-INT 92	1099-LTC 93
☐	☐	☐	☐	☐	☐	☐	☐	☐	☐	☐	☐	☐	☐

1099-MISC 95	1099-OID 96	1099-PATR 97	1099-Q 31	1099-R 98	1099-S 75	1099-SA 94	5498 28	5498-ESA 72	5498-SA 27	
☐	☐	☐	☐	☐	☐	☐	☐	☐	☐	

Return this entire page to the Internal Revenue Service. Photocopies are not acceptable.

Filing 1099s Electronically

If you wish, you may file your 1099s with the IRS electronically instead of by mail. You must get permission from the IRS to do this by filing IRS Form 4419, *Application for Filing Information Returns Electronically*. If you file electronically, the deadline for filing 1099s with the IRS is extended to March 31. For more information, you can visit the IRS website at www.irs.gov (click on "IRS e-file") or call the IRS Information Reporting Program at 304-263-8700.

You may also send 1099 forms to your ICs electronically—that is, by email. But you may do this only if the contractor agrees. If he or she doesn't agree, you must deliver the 1099 by mail or in person.

State New Hire Reporting Requirements

Several states require businesses that hire independent contractors to file a report with a state agency providing the contractor's contact information and how much the contractor is paid. The purpose of this requirement is to aid in the enforcement of child support orders issued against independent contractors.

The following states impose reporting requirements for independent contractors: Alabama, Alaska, California (if paid $600 or more per year), Connecticut (if paid over $5,000 per year), Iowa, Maine (only where contractor works for state), Massachusetts (if paid over $600 per year), Minnesota (only where contractor works for state), Mississippi, Nevada, New Hampshire, New Jersey, Ohio, and Tennessee. Find the state agency to contact at: www.acf.hhs.gov/programs/cse/newhire/employer/contacts/nh_matrix.htm.

Record Keeping and Accounting Made Easy

Unless it is your chosen trade, you probably didn't become self-employed so you could be a bookkeeper or accountant. But even though it can be a pain, all self-employed people need to keep records of their income and expenses. Among other things, keeping good records will enable you to reap a rich harvest in tax deductions. Time spent on record keeping is usually time well spent.

Simple Bookkeeping

Except in a few cases, the IRS does not require that you keep any special kind of records. You may choose any system suited to your business that clearly shows your income and expenses. If you are in more than one business, keep a separate set of books for each business.

If, like most self-employed people, you run a one-person service business and are a sole proprietor, you don't need a fancy or complex set of books. You can get along very nicely with just a few items. They include:

- a business checking account
- income and expense journals
- files for supporting documents, such as receipts and canceled checks, and
- an asset log to support your depreciation deductions if you buy business equipment like computers or copiers.

 CAUTION

There are more records if you have employees. If you have employees, you must create and keep a number of records, including payroll tax records, with-

---

Benefits of Keeping Records

Keeping good records will help you to do all of the following things:

- **Monitor the progress of your business.** Without records, you'll never have an accurate idea of how your business is doing. You may think you're making money when you're really not. Records can show whether your business is improving or if you need to make changes to increase the likelihood of success.

- **Prepare financial statements.** You need good records to prepare accurate financial statements. These include income (profit and loss) statements and balance sheets. These statements can be essential in dealing with your bank or creditors.

- **Keep track of deductible expenses.** You may forget expenses when you prepare your tax return unless you record them when they occur. Every $100 in expenses you forget to deduct will cost you about

$43 in additional income and self-employment taxes if you earn a mid-level income (in the 25% marginal tax bracket).

- **Prepare your tax returns.** You need good records to prepare your tax return or to enable an accountant to prepare your return for you in a reasonable amount of time. These records should show the income, expenses, and credits you report on your tax returns. Generally, these can be the same records you use to monitor your business and prepare your financial statements.

- **Win IRS audits.** If you're audited by the IRS, it will be up to you to prove that you have accurately reported your income and expenses on your tax returns. An IRS auditor will not simply take your word that your return is accurate. You need accurate records and receipts to back up your returns.

holding records, and employment tax returns. You must keep these records for four years.

For detailed information, see IRS Publication 15 (Circular E), *Employer's Tax Guide.* You can get a free copy by calling the IRS at 800-TAX-FORM, visiting your local IRS office, or downloading it from the IRS website at www.irs.gov.

Also, contact your state tax agency for your state's requirements. You can find your state's tax agency at www.taxadmin.org/fta/link.

Business Checkbook

One of the first things you should do when you become self-employed is set up a separate checking account for your business. Your business checkbook will serve as your basic source of information for recording your business expenses and income. Deposit all your self-employment compensation, such as the checks you receive from clients, into the account and make all business-related payments by writing checks from the account. Don't use your business account for personal expenses or your personal account for business expenses.

Keeping a separate business account is not required by law if you're a sole proprietor, but it will provide many important benefits:

- It will be much easier for you to keep track of your business income and expenses.

- It will prove helpful if you're audited by the IRS.

- It will help convince the IRS that you are running a business and not engaged in a hobby. Hobbyists don't generally have separate bank accounts for their hobbies. (See Chapter 9.)

- It will help to establish that you're an independent contractor, not an employee. Employees don't have separate business accounts.

Setting Up Your Bank Account

At a minimum, you'll need to open a separate checking account in which you will deposit all your self-employment income and from which you will pay all your business expenses. There is no need to open your business checking account at the same bank where you have your personal checking account. Shop around and open your account with the bank that offers you the best services at the lowest price.

If you're doing business under your own name, consider opening up a second individual account in your name and using it solely for your business instead of opening a business account. You'll usually pay less for a personal account than for a business account.

If you do open a business account, make sure it is in your business name. If you're a sole proprietor, this can be your personal name. (If you're doing business under an assumed name, you'll likely have to give your bank a copy of your fictitious business name statement.) If you've formed a corporation or limited liability company, the account should be in your corporate or company name.

Use a Separate Credit Card for Business

Use a separate credit card for business expenses instead of using one card for both personal and business items. Credit card interest for business purchases is 100% deductible while interest for personal purchases is not. Using a separate card for business purchases will help you keep track of how much interest you've paid for business purchases. The card doesn't have to be in your business name; it can just be one of your personal credit cards.

If you've incorporated, call your bank and ask what documentation is required to open the account. You will probably need to show the bank a corporate resolution authorizing the opening of a bank account and showing the names of the people authorized to sign checks.

Typically, you will also have to fill out a separate bank account authorization form provided by your bank. You will also need to have a federal employer identification number. (See Chapter 5.) Similarly, if you've established a limited liability company (see Chapter 2), you'll likely have to show the bank a company resolution authorizing the account.

You may also want to establish interest-bearing accounts for your business, in which you can deposit cash you don't need immediately. For example, you may want to set up a business savings account or a money market mutual fund in your business name.

Paying Yourself

To pay yourself when you're a sole proprietor, write a business check to yourself and deposit the money in your personal account. This is known as a withdrawal or "personal draw." Use your personal account to pay your nonbusiness or personal expenses.

When You Write Checks

If you already keep an accurate, updated personal checkbook, simply do the same for your business checkbook. If, however, like many people, you tend to be lax in keeping up your checkbook, you're going to have to change your habits. Now that you're in business, you can't afford this kind of carelessness. Unless you write large numbers of business checks, maintaining your checkbook won't take much time.

When you write business checks, you may have to make some extra notations besides the date, number, amount of the check, and the name of the person or company to whom the check is written. If it's not clear from the name of the payee what the check is for, describe the business reason for the check—for example, the equipment or service you purchased.

You can use the register that comes with your checkbook and write in all this information manually, or you can use a computerized register.

> ! **CAUTION**
>
> **Don't write checks for cash.** Avoid writing checks payable to cash, because it's unclear what specific business purpose such checks have and might lead to questions from the IRS if you're audited. If you must write a check for cash to pay a business expense, be sure to include the receipt for the cash payment in your records.

Making Deposits

When you make deposits into your business checking account, record in your check register:

- the date and amount of the deposit, and
- a description of the source of the funds—for example, the client's name.

Income and Expense Records

In addition to a business checkbook, you should maintain income and expense records.

These records, which should be updated at least monthly, will show you how much you're spending and for what, and how much money you're making. They will also make it easier for you or a tax pro to prepare your tax returns. Instead of having to locate, categorize, and add up the amount of each bill or canceled check at tax time, you can simply use the figures in your records.

You can track your expenses by creating what accountants call a "chart of accounts"—a listing by category of all your expenses and income. It's very easy to do this. You can do it manually on ledger sheets (blank sheets are provided in Appendix 1) or you can set up a computer spreadsheet program, such as *Excel* or *Lotus*, to do it. Many inexpensive shareware spreadsheet programs are also available.

If you already have or would prefer to use a financial computer program such as *Quicken*, you can do that instead of using the method described in this section. See "Computer Programs to Track Income and Expenses," below, for more information about such programs.

Expense Journal

Your expense journal will show what you buy for your business. You can easily create it by using ledger sheets you can get from any stationery or office supply store. Get ledger sheets with at least 12 or 14 columns. Devote a separate column to each major category of expenses you have.

Alternatively, you can purchase accounting record books with the expense categories already printed on them. These cost more, however, and may not offer categories that meet your needs. See Appendix A for a sample of an expense journal that you can copy or adapt and use.

To decide what your expense categories should be, sit down with your first month's bills and receipts and divide them up into categorized piles. Some common expense categories many self-employed people have include:

- business meals and entertainment
- travel
- telephone
- supplies and postage
- office rent
- utilities for an outside office
- professional dues, publications, and books
- business insurance
- payments to other self-employed people
- advertising costs
- equipment, and
- license fees.

You should always include a final category called "Miscellaneous" for various expenses that are not easily categorized.

Depending on the nature of your business, you may not need all these categories—or you might need additional or different headings. For example, a graphic designer might have categories for printing and typesetting expenses or a writer might have a category for agent fees.

You can add or delete expense categories as you go along—for example, if you find your Miscellaneous category contains many items for a particular type of expense, add it as an expense category.

You don't need a category for automobile expenses, because these expenses require a different kind of documentation for tax purposes.

In separate columns, list the check number for each payment, the date, and the name of the person or company paid. If you pay by check, record its number in the check number column.

Once a month, go through your check register, credit card slips, receipts, and other expense records and record the required information for each transaction. Also, total the amounts for each category when you come to the end of the page so you can keep a running total of what you've spent for each category for the year to date.

The following example shows a portion of an expense journal.

Expense Journal

Date	Check No.	Transaction	Amount	Advertising	Outside Contractors	Utilities	Supplies	Rent	Travel	Equipment	Meals & Entertainment	Misc.
5/1	123	ABC Properties	500					500				
5/1	124	Office Warehouse	150				150					
5/10	VISA	Computer World	1,000							1,000		
5/15	VISA	Cafe Olé	50								50	
5/16	CASH	Sam's Stationery	50				50					
5/18	125	Electric Co.	50			50						
5/30	126	Bill Carter	500		500							
Total This Page			2,300	200	500	50	200	500		1,000	50	
Total Year to Date			7,900	200	2,000	250	400	2,500	300	1,500	250	500

Income Journal

The income journal shows you how much money you're earning and the source of each payment. At a minimum, your income ledger should have columns for the source of the funds—for example, the client's name—your invoice number if there is one, the amount of the payment, and the date you received it. If you have lots of different sources of income, you can create different categories for each source and devote separate columns to them in your journal. (See Appendix A for a sample of an income journal that you can copy or adapt and use.)

Automobile Mileage and Expense Records

If you use a car or other vehicle for business purposes other than just commuting to and from work, you're entitled to take a deduction for gas and other auto expenses. You can either deduct the actual cost of your gas and other expenses or take the standard rate deduction based on the number of business miles you drive. In 2008, the standard rate was 50.5¢ per mile

Either way, you must keep a record of the total miles you drive during the year. And if you use your car for both business and personal use, you must record your business and personal mileage. Obtain a mileage log book from a stationery or office supply store; you can get one for a few

Income Journal			
Source	Invoice	Amount	Date Received
Joe Smith	123	$2,500	5/5
Acme Inc.	124	$1,250	5/15
Sue Jones	Personal Loan	$2,000	5/20
Total	---	$5,750	---

Car Mileage and Expense Logbook						
Date	Destination	Business Purpose	Mileage at Beginning of Trip	Mileage at End of Trip	Business Miles	User's Name
5/1	Fresno	See Art Andrews– potential client	50,000	50,100	100	Jack S.
5/5	Stockton	Delivered documents to Bill James	50,500	50,550	50	Jack S.
5/15	Sacramento	Meeting at Acme Corp.	51,000	51,100	100	Jack S.
Total Business Miles					250	

dollars. Keep it in your car with a pen attached. Note your odometer reading in the logbook on the day you start using your car for business. Record your mileage every time you use your car for business and note the business purpose for the trip. Add up your business mileage when you get to the end of each page in the logbook. This way you'll only have to add the page totals at the end of the year instead of slogging through all the individual entries. Above is an example of a portion of a page from a mileage logbook.

If you think you may want to take the deduction for your actual auto expenses instead of the standard rate, keep receipts for all your auto-related expenses, including gasoline, oil, tires, repairs, and insurance. You don't need to include these expenses in your ledger sheets; just keep them in a folder or envelope. At tax time, add them up to determine how big a deduction you'll get using the actual expense method. Also add in the amount you're entitled to deduct for depreciation of your auto. (See "Car Expenses" in Chapter 9 for more information on depreciating your vehicle.) Your total deduction using your actual auto expenses may or may not be larger than the deduction you'll get using the standard rate.

! CAUTION

Use a credit card for gas. If you use the actual expense method for car expenses, use a credit card when you buy gas. It's best that this be a separate card—either a gas company card or a separate bank card. The monthly statements you receive will serve as your gas receipts. If you pay cash for gas, you must either get a receipt or make a note of the amount in your mileage logbook.

Costs for business-related parking (other than at your office) and for tolls are separately deductible, whether you use the standard rate or the actual expense method. Get and keep receipts for these expenses.

Computer Programs to Track Income and Expenses

There are a number of computer programs designed to help people keep track of their finances. The most popular are *Quicken* and *Microsoft Money*. These programs work differently than the manual or spreadsheet system described in the preceding section, but they do the job just as well, if not better.

Programs like *Quicken* work off a computerized check register. You enter your deposits (income) and withdrawals (expenses) from your business checking account into the register. You can also record cash and credit card expenses using separate accounts. You note the category of each income or expense item in the register. *Quicken* can then take this information and automatically create income and expense reports—that is, it will show you the amounts you've spent or earned for each category. It can also create profit-and-loss statements. You can even import these amounts into tax preparation software, such as *TurboTax*, when it's time to do your income taxes.

Quicken or *Microsoft Money* provide all the tools most self-employed people will need to keep their books. But far more sophisticated accounting programs are available. Programs such as *QuickBooks*, *Mind Your Own Business*, and *Peachtree Accounting* can accomplish more complex bookkeeping tasks, such as double entry bookkeeping. You may need one of these programs if you sell goods and maintain an inventory.

Supporting Documents

The IRS knows very well that you can claim anything in your books, because you create them yourself. For this reason, the IRS requires that you have documents to support the entries in your books and on your tax returns. You don't have to file any of these documents with your tax returns, but you must have them available to back up your returns if you're audited.

Income Documents

When the IRS audits a small business, it usually asks for both your business and your personal bank statements. If you don't have them, the IRS may subpoena them from your bank. If your bank deposits are greater than the income you report on your tax return, the IRS auditor will assume you've underreported your income and impose additional tax, interest, and penalties.

To avoid this, you need to be able to prove the source of all your income. Keep supporting documents showing the source and amounts of all the income you receive as an independent contractor. This includes bank deposit slips, invoices, and the 1099-MISC forms your clients give you. Keep your bank statements as well.

Expense Documents

You also need documents that support your business expenses. In the absence of a supporting document, an IRS auditor will likely conclude that an item you claim as a business expense is really a personal expense and refuse to allow the deduction. If you're in the mid-level income, 25% tax bracket, every $100 in disallowed deductions will cost you $25 in federal taxes, plus interest and penalties. And your income subject to Social Security tax for the year will go up, costing you about $12 for every $100 in disallowed deductions.

Some people believe the only documentation they need to prove that an expense was for their business is a sales receipt. This is not the case. A sales receipt only proves that somebody purchased the item listed in the receipt. It does not show who purchased it. You could write a note on the receipt stating that you bought the item, but you could easily lie. Indeed, for all the IRS knows, you could hang around stores picking up receipts people throw away to create tax deductions for yourself.

Likewise, a cancelled check is not adequate documentation for a business expense. All a canceled check proves is that you spent money for something. It does not show what you bought. Of course, you can write a note on your check stating what you purchased, but why should the IRS believe what you write on your checks yourself?

However, when you put a canceled check together with a sales receipt (or an invoice, a cash register tape, or a similar document), you have concrete proof that you purchased the item listed in the receipt. The check proves that you bought something, and the receipt proves what that something was.

Using a credit card is a great way to pay business expenses. The credit card slip will prove that you bought the item listed on the slip. You'll also have a monthly statement to back up your credit card slips. You should use a separate credit card for your business.

Save supporting documents to prove to the IRS that an expense was related to your business. Sometimes it will be clear from the face of a receipt, sales slip, or the payee's name on your canceled check that the item you purchased was for your business. But if it's not clear, note what the purchase was for on the document.

Entertainment, Meal, and Travel Expense Records

Deductions for business-related entertainment, meals, and travel are a hot-button item for the IRS because they have been greatly abused by many taxpayers. You need to have more records for these expenses than for almost any others, and they will be closely scrutinized if you're audited.

Whenever you incur an expense for business-related entertainment, meals, or travel, you must document:

- the date the expense was incurred
- the amount
- the place

Proving Payment With Bank Statements

...ou'll need to use a bank account ...to prove an expense. Some banks no longer ...anceled checks, or you may pay for something w...an ATM card or electronic funds transfer. More-over, you may not always have a credit card slip when you pay by credit card—for example, when you buy an item over the Internet. In these situations, the IRS will accept an account statement as proof that you purchased the item. The chart below shows what type of information you need to include on such an account statement.

If payment is made by:	The statement must show:
Check	• Check number • Amount • Payee's name • Date the check amount was posted to the account by the bank
Electronic funds transfer	• Amount transferred • Payee's name • Date the amount transferred was posted to the account by the bank
Credit card	• Amount charged • Payee's name • Transaction date

• the business purpose for the expense, and

• if entertainment or meals are involved, the business relationship of the people at the event—for example, their names and occupations and any other information needed to establish their business relationship to you.

All this record keeping is not as hard as it sounds. Your receipts will ordinarily indicate the date, amount, and place in which you incurred the expense. You just need to describe the business purpose and business relationship if entertainment or meals are involved. You can write this directly on your receipt.

EXAMPLE:

Mary, a freelance computer programmer, has lunch with Harold, president of Acme Technologies, Inc., to discuss programming work. Her restaurant receipt shows the date, the name and location of the restaurant, the number of people served, and the amount of the expense. Because Mary paid by credit card, the receipt even shows the amount of the tip. Mary just has to document the business purpose for the lunch. She writes on the receipt: "Lunch with Harold Lipshitz, President, Acme Technologies, Inc. Discussed signing contract for programming services."

You must keep supporting documents for expenses (other than lodging) that tally more than $75. Keep your receipts or credit card slips for such expenses. Canceled checks alone are not sufficient; you must also have the bill for the expense.

Filing Supporting Documents

If you don't have a lot of receipts and other documents to save, you can simply keep them all in a single folder, shoebox, or other safe place.

If you have a lot of supporting documents to save or are the type of person who likes to be extremely well organized, separate your documents by category—for example, income, travel expenses, equipment purchases, and so on. You can use a separate file folder for each category or get an accordion file with multiple pockets.

Asset Records

When you purchase property such as computers, office furniture, copiers, or cellular telephones to use in your business, you must keep records to verify:

- when and how you acquired the asset
- the purchase price
- the cost of any improvements—for example, a major upgrade for your computer
- the Section 179 deduction you took (see Chapter 9)
- the deductions you took for depreciation (see Chapter 9)
- how you used the asset
- when and how you disposed of the asset
- the selling price, and
- the expenses of the sale.

Use an Asset Log

Set up an asset log showing this information for each item you purchase.

You can purchase asset logs from stationery or office supply stores, or set one up yourself using ledger paper or a spreadsheet program. (See Appendix A for a sample log you can copy and use.)

You can also use a computer accounting program such as *Quicken Home & Business* instead. If you have an accountant prepare your tax returns, he or she can create an asset log for you.

Be sure to keep your receipts for each asset purchase, because they'll usually verify what you purchased, when you bought the asset, and how much you paid.

EXAMPLE:

Patty purchases a $3,200 computer for her business on January 3. She uses it exclusively for business and decides to deduct the entire purchase price in a single year using Section 179. She prepares the following asset log for the computer:

Asset Log									
Description of Property	Date Placed in Service	Cost or Other Basis	Business/ Investment Use %	Section 179 Deduction	Depreciation Prior Years	Basis for Depreciation	Method/ Convention	Rate or Table %	Depreciation Deduction
Computer	1/3	3,200	100%	3,200	0	0	N/A	N/A	0
Total				3,200					0

Listed Property

"Listed property" is a term the IRS uses to refer to a certain type of business asset that can easily be used for personal as well as business purposes. Listed property includes:

- cars, boats, airplanes, and other vehicles
- computers
- cellular phones, and
- any other property generally used for entertainment, recreation, or amusement—for example, VCRs, cameras, and camcorders.

The IRS imposes special record keeping requirements to depreciate or take a Section 179 deduction for listed property. However, there is one exception: You need not keep special records of the time you use a business computer if you use the computer 100% for business (not for personal use) and keep it at your business location (or home office, if you can take the home office deduction).

EXAMPLE:

Mary, a freelance writer, does all of her work in her home office, which is clearly her business location. She purchases a computer for her office that she uses 100% for writing. She doesn't need to keep a log of her business use.

If you use listed property for both business and personal uses, you must document your usage—both business and personal. Keep a log book, business diary, or calendar showing the dates, times, and reasons for which the property is used. (See Appendix A for a sample log you can copy and use.) You also can purchase log books at stationery or office supply stores.

EXAMPLE:

Bill, an accountant, purchases a computer he uses 50% for business and 50% for personal uses, such as to play games. He must keep a log showing his business use of the computer. Following is a sample from one week in his log:

Usage Log for Personal Computer			
Date	Time of Business Use	Reason for Business Use	Time of Personal Use
5/1	4.5 hours	Prepared client tax returns	1.5 hours
5/1			3 hours
5/3	2 hours	Prepared client tax returns	
5/4			2 hours

How Long to Keep Records

You need to keep copies of your tax returns and supporting documents available in case you are audited by the IRS or other tax agency. You might also need them for other purposes—for example, to get a loan, mortgage, or insurance.

You should keep your records for as long as the IRS has to audit you after you file your returns for the year. These statutes of limitation range from three years to forever and are listed in the table below.

IRS Statue of Limitations	
If:	The limitation period is:
You failed to pay all the tax due	3 years
You underreported your gross income for the year by more than 25%	6 years
You filed a fraudulent return	No limit
You did not file a return	No limit

To be on the safe side, you should keep your tax returns indefinitely. They usually don't take up much space, so this shouldn't be a big hardship. Your supporting documents probably take up more space. You should keep these for at least six years after you file your return. If you file a fraudulent return, keep your supporting documents indefinitely (if you have any). If you're audited, they will show that at least some of your deductions were legitimate.

Keep your long-term asset records for three years after the depreciable life of the asset ends. For example, keep records for five-year property (such as computers) for eight years. You should keep your ledger sheets for as long as you're in business, because a potential buyer of your business might want to see them.

If You Don't Have Proper Tax Records

Because you're human, you may not have kept all the records required to back up your tax deductions. Don't despair, all is not lost—you may be able to fall back on what is known as the "*Cohan* rule." This rule (named after the Broadway entertainer George M. Cohan, who was involved in a tax case in the 1930s) is the taxpayer's best friend. The *Cohan* rule recognizes that all businesspeople must spend at least some money to stay in business, so they must have had at least some deductible expenses, even if they don't have adequate records to back them up.

If you're audited and lack adequate records for a claimed deduction, the IRS can use the *Cohan* rule to make an estimate of how much you must have spent and allow you to deduct that amount. However, you must provide at least some credible evidence on which to base this estimate, such as receipts, canceled checks, notes in your appointment book, or other records. Moreover, the IRS will allow you to deduct only the smallest amount you must have spent, based on the records you provide. In addition, the *Cohan* rule cannot be used for travel, meal, entertainment, or gift expenses, or for listed property.

If an auditor claims you lack sufficient records to back up a deduction, you should always bring up the *Cohan* rule and argue that you should still get the deduction based on the records you do have. At best, you'll probably get only part of your claimed deductions. If the IRS auditor disallows your deductions entirely or doesn't give you as much as you think you deserve, you can appeal in court and bring the *Cohan* rule up again there; you might have more success making this argument to a judge. However, you can't compel an IRS auditor or a court to apply the *Cohan* rule in your favor. They have discretion to decide whether to apply the rule and how large a deduction to give you.

EXAMPLE:

Ajuba Gaylord had a part-time business as a home-based salesperson. One year, she took a $474 deduction for postage and over $1,100 for meals and entertainment. The IRS disallowed both deductions because she had no documentary evidence showing that the expenses were for her business. However, the tax court applied the *Cohan* rule and allowed her a $75 deduction for postage. It reasoned that this was the least that she must have spent, given the nature of her business. However, the court would not use the *Cohan* rule to grant her a deduction for meal and entertainment expenses. (*Gaylord v. Comm'r.*, T.C. Memo 2003-273.)

Reconstructing Tax Records

If you can show that you possessed adequate records at one time, but now lack them due to circumstances beyond your control, you may reconstruct your records for an IRS audit. Circumstances beyond your control include acts of nature such as floods, fires, earthquakes, or theft. (Treas. Reg. 1.275.5(c)(5).) Losing your tax records while moving does not constitute a circumstance beyond your control. Reconstructing records means you either create brand new records specifically for your audit or you obtain other evidence to corroborate your deductions—for example, statements from people or companies from whom you purchased items for your business.

Accounting Methods

An accounting method is a set of rules used to determine when and how your income and expenses are reported. Accounting methods might sound like a rather dry subject, but your choice about how to account for your business expenses and income will have a huge impact on your tax deductions. You don't have to become an expert on the subject, but you should understand the basics.

You choose an accounting method when you file your first tax return for your business. If you want to change your accounting method later, you must get IRS approval. If you operate two or more separate businesses, you can use a different accounting method for each—for example, a dentist who also operates a separate laboratory business may use separate accounting methods for each business. (A business is separate for tax purposes only if you keep a separate set of books and records for it.)

There are two basic methods of accounting: cash basis and accrual basis. Most professionals use the cash basis method.

Cash Method

The cash basis method is by far the simpler method of accounting. Individuals who are not in business use this method, as do most small businesses that provide services and don't maintain inventory or offer credit. However, if you sell merchandise and keep an inventory, you might have to use the accrual method. (See below.)

The cash method is based on the common-sense idea that you haven't earned income for tax purposes until you actually receive the money, and you haven't incurred an expense until you actually pay the money. Using the cash basis method, then, is like maintaining a checkbook. You record income only when the money is received and expenses only when they are actually paid. If you borrow money to pay business expenses, you incur an expense under the cash method only when you make payments on the loan.

EXAMPLE 1:

Helen, a marketing consultant, completes a market research report on September 1, 2008, but isn't paid by the client until February 1, 2009.

Using the cash method, Helen records the payment in February 2009—when it's received.

EXAMPLE 2:

On December 1, 2008, Helen goes to the Acme electronics store and buys a laser printer for her consulting business. She buys the item on credit from Acme—she's not required to make any payments until March 1, 2009. Helen does not record the expense until 2009, when she actually pays for the printer.

When Is an Expense Paid?

Although it's called the cash method, a business expense is paid when you pay for it by check, credit card, or electronic funds transfer, as well as by cash. If you pay by check, the amount is deemed paid during the year in which the check is drawn and mailed—for example, a check dated December 31, 2007 is considered paid during 2007 only if it has a December 31, 2007 postmark. If you're using a check to pay a substantial expense, you may wish to mail it by certified mail so you'll have proof of when it was mailed.

Constructive Receipt

Under the cash method, payments are "constructively received" when an amount is credited to your account or otherwise made available to you without restrictions. Constructive receipt is as good as actual receipt. If you authorize someone to be your agent and receive income for you, you are considered to have received it when your agent receives it.

EXAMPLE:

Interest is credited to your business bank account in December 2008, but you do not withdraw it or enter it into your passbook until 2009. You must include the amount in gross business income for 2008, not 2009.

No Postponing Income

You cannot hold checks or other payments from one tax year to another to avoid paying tax on the income. You must report the income in the year the payment is received or made available to you without restriction.

EXAMPLE:

On December 1, 2008, Helen receives a $5,000 check from a client. She holds the check and doesn't cash it until January 10, 2009. She must still report the $5,000 as income for 2008 because she constructively received it that year.

Prepayment of Expenses

The general rule is that you cannot prepay expenses when you use the cash method—you can't hurry up the payment of expenses by paying them in advance. An expense you pay in advance can be deducted only in the year to which it applies.

However, an important exception to the general rule, called the 12-month rule, went into effect in 2004. Under the 12-month rule, you may deduct a prepaid expense in the current year if the expense is for a right or benefit that extends no longer than the earlier of:

- 12 months, or
- until the end of the tax year after the tax year in which you made the payment.

EXAMPLE 1:

You are a calendar year taxpayer and you pay $10,000 on July 1, 2008, for a small business insurance policy that is effective for one year beginning July 1, 2008. The 12-month rule applies because the benefit you've paid for— a business insurance policy—extends only 12 months into the future. Therefore, the full $10,000 is deductible in 2008.

EXAMPLE 2:

You are a calendar year taxpayer and you pay $3,000 in 2008 for a business insurance policy that is effective for three years, beginning July 1, 2008. This payment does not qualify for the 12-month rule because the benefit extends more than 12 months. Therefore, you must use the general rule: $500 is deductible in 2008; $1,000 is deductible in 2009; $1,000 is deductible in 2010; and $500 is deductible in 2011.

To use the 12-month rule, you must apply it when you first start using the cash method for your business. If you haven't been using the rule and want to start doing so, you must get IRS approval. You must file IRS Form 3115, *Application for Change in Accounting Method*, but such IRS approval is granted automatically. (See "Obtaining IRS Permission to Change Your Accounting Method," below.)

Accrual Method

In the accrual basis method of accounting, you report income or expenses as they are earned or incurred, rather than when they are actually collected or paid. Many self-employed people do not favor the accrual method because it can be complicated to use and can require them to pay tax on income they haven't actually received.

When Income Is Received

With the accrual method, transactions are counted as income when a service is provided, an order is made, or an item is delivered, regardless of when the money for it (the receivable) is actually received or paid. As a result, you can end up owing taxes on income you haven't been paid. This is particularly bad news for self-employed people, who often have to wait a while before they are paid by their clients or customers.

EXAMPLE:

Andrea, an architect, uses the accrual method of accounting. She is hired by a client to design a house. She finishes the job on December 15, 2008, and bills the customer for $25,000 that same day. However, the client turned out to be a slow payer. By April 15, 2009, Andrea still hadn't received her fee. However, because she's an accrual basis taxpayer, she must include the $25,000 as income on her 2008 tax return and pay taxes on it. Under the accrual method, the $25,000 became taxable income the year Andrea earned the money by completing her architecture services. It's immaterial that Andrea has not actually been paid.

Obviously, if you have many clients who owe you money, you could end up having to pay substantial taxes on income you haven't received. If it turns out that a client will never pay you, you may deduct the amount you're owed as a bad debt, but this will just wipe out the income you've already paid tax on in a prior year.

When Expenses Are Incurred

Under the accrual method, you generally deduct a business expense when:

- you are legally obligated to pay the expense
- the amount you owe can be determined with reasonable accuracy, and
- you have received or used the property or services involved.

EXAMPLE:

Bill, the owner of a welding shop, borrows $10,000 from his bank to help pay his business operating expenses. He signs a promissory note on Dec. 15, 2008 and receives the money the same day but doesn't start making payments to the bank until January 2009. Bill can deduct the expense in 2008 because on Dec. 15, 2008 he became legally obligated to pay the expense by signing the note, the amount of the expense can be determined from the note, and he received the money that day.

Thus, when you use the accrual method, you can take a deduction for an expense you incur even if you don't actually pay for it until the following year. You can't do this under the cash basis method.

Businesses That Must Use the Accrual Method, and Exceptions

Businesses that sell, produce, or purchase merchandise and maintain an inventory are ordinarily required to use the accrual method. However, an important rule change took effect in 2001 that permits most self-employed people to use the cash method, even if they carry an inventory.

The rule change created two big exceptions to the requirement that businesses with inventories use the accrual method:

- **Exception #1: Businesses that earn less than $1 million.** Even if you deal in merchandise, you may use the cash method if your average annual gross receipts were $1 million or less for the three tax years ending with the prior tax year.

- **Exception #2: Some businesses that earn less than $10 million.** Even if your business earns more than $1 million per year, you may use the cash basis method if your average annual gross receipts were $10 million or less for the three tax years ending with the prior tax year, and your principal business is providing services. (Rev. Proc. 2001-10, 2001-2 I.R.B. 272; Rev. Proc. 2001-21, 2001-9 I.R.B. 742.)

So, as long as your business earns less than $10 million per year, you may be able to use the cash method even if you sell merchandise. However, you may deduct only the cost of inventory that you sell during the year.

Obtaining IRS Permission to Change Your Accounting Method

You choose your accounting method by checking a box on your tax form when you file your tax return for the first year you are in business. Once you choose a method, you cannot change it without getting permission from the IRS. Permission is granted automatically for many types of changes, including using the 12-month rule to deduct prepaid expenses. You must file IRS Form 3115, *Application for Change in Accounting Method*, with your tax return for the year you want to make the change (if the change is granted automatically).

Tax Year

You are required to pay taxes for a 12-month period, also known as the "tax year." Sole proprietors, partnerships, limited liability companies, S corporations, and personal service corporations (see Chapter 2) are required to use the calendar year as their tax years—that is, January 1 through December 31.

However, there are exceptions that permit some small businesses to use a tax year that does not end in December, also known as a "fiscal year." You need to get IRS permission to use a fiscal year. The IRS doesn't like businesses to use fiscal years, but it might grant you permission if you can show a good business reason for it.

One good reason to use a fiscal year is that your business is seasonal. For example, if you earn most of your income in the spring and incur most of your expenses in the fall, a tax year ending in July or August might be better than a calendar tax year ending in December, because the income and expenses on each tax return will be more closely related. To get permission, you must file IRS Form 8716, *Election to Have a Tax Year Other Than a Required Tax Year.*

Safeguarding Your Self-Employed Status

The IRS and other government agencies that rely on employee withholdings and taxes would prefer you to be an employee rather than a self-employed person. This chapter shows you how to avoid being viewed as an employee when you work for yourself.

The terms generally used to describe self-employed people for tax purposes are "independent contractor" or "IC." These terms are, therefore, used throughout this chapter.

Who Decides Your Work Status?

Initially, it's up to you and each hiring firm you deal with to decide whether you should be classified as an independent contractor or an employee. But the decision about how you should be classified is subject to review by various government agencies, including:

- the IRS
- your state's tax department
- your state's unemployment compensation insurance agency
- your state's workers' compensation insurance agency, and
- the U.S. Department of Labor and the National Labor Relations Board.

The IRS considers worker misclassification to be a serious problem that costs the U.S. government billions of dollars in taxes that would otherwise be paid if the workers were classified as employees and taxes were automatically withheld from their paychecks. Most state agencies live by the same theory.

The IRS or your state tax department might question your status in a routine audit of your tax returns. More commonly, however, you'll come to the government's attention if it investigates the classification practices of a firm that hired you. Government auditors may question you and examine your and your hiring firm's records. Because the rules for determining whether you're an independent contractor or employee are rather vague and subjective, it's often easy for the government to claim that you're an employee even though both you and the hiring firm sincerely believed you qualified as an independent contractor.

What Happens If the Government Reclassifies You?

If you're like most independent contractors, you probably think that a government agency determination that one or more of the firms that hire you should classify you as an employee is solely the hiring firm's problem. Unfortunately, this is not the case.

It is true that if the IRS or another government agency audits you or a hiring firm you've worked for and determines that you should have been classified as an employee instead of an independent contractor, it can and probably will impose assessments and penalties on the firm. Some companies have gone bankrupt because of such assessments.

Rest assured that the government will not penalize or fine *you* if you've been misclassified as an independent contractor. However, you can be affected adversely in other ways. For example, the hiring firm may end the working relationship because it doesn't want to pay the additional expenses involved in treating you as an employee. It is not unusual for IRS settlement agreements with hiring firms to require that the firms terminate contracts with independent contractors—with no input from the independent contractors themselves. Or the hiring firm may insist on reducing your compensation to make up for the extra employee expenses. And even if none of these things happen, you'll likely be treated differently on the job. For example, the hiring firm—now your employer—will probably expect you to follow its orders and may attempt to restrict you from working for other companies.

Worker Gets the Ax When the IRS Calls

Dave, a financial analyst, was hired by a large New York bank and classified as an independent contractor for IRS purposes. He signed an independent contractor agreement and submitted invoices to the bank's accounting department to be paid. The bank withheld no taxes from his pay, paid no Social Security or Medicare taxes for him, and provided him with no employee benefits.

Otherwise, however, Dave was treated largely as an employee. He worked on a team along with regular bank employees and shared their supervisor. He performed the same functions as the employees and worked the same core hours. Because the bank required him to work at its headquarters, he received an admittance card key, office equipment, and supplies from the bank.

Dave's happy worklife changed abruptly when the IRS notified the bank that it wanted to examine its employment records to determine whether the company was complying with tax laws. Fearing that it should have classified Dave as an employee instead of an independent contractor, the bank summarily fired him in the hope this would lessen potential problems with IRS auditors. It didn't work. The bank was required to reclassify Dave as an employee for the two years he had worked for the bank. Dave was entitled to a refund of half of his SE Social Security and Medicare taxes for those years, and he was able to collect unemployment benefits, but he was still out of a job.

Tax Consequences

An IRS determination that you should be classified as an employee can also have adverse tax consequences for you: You will have to file amended tax returns for the years involved. On the plus side, you'll be entitled to claim a refund for half the self-employment taxes you paid on the compensation you received as a misclassified independent contractor.

But you might lose valuable business deductions because business expenses, such as home offices and health insurance premiums, are either not deductible or limited for employees. You'll end up owing more taxes if the value of these lost deductions exceeds the amount of your self-employment tax refund. Your employer will also have to start withholding your income tax and Social Security tax from your pay.

From a tax perspective, however, by far the worst thing that can happen to you if you're reclassified as an employee by the IRS is that any Keogh retirement plan you have will lose its tax-qualified status. Generally, in a Keogh plan, your contributions are tax deductible, and you don't pay any tax on the interest your investment earns until you retire. (See Chapter 16.) But if your Keogh is disqualified, you'll have to pay tax on your contributions and on the interest you've earned from your investments. If you have a substantial amount invested in a Keogh plan, you could face a staggering tax bill.

Qualifying for Employee Benefits

One good thing that can happen if you're reclassified as an employee is that you may qualify for benefits your employer gives to its other employees, such as health insurance, pension benefits, and unemployment insurance.

If you've incurred out-of-pocket expenses for medical care, you may be entitled to reimbursement. However, these benefits may be short-lived if the hiring firm decides it can't afford to keep you on as an employee.

IRS Audit Silences Independent Contractor's Voice

John, a New Hampshire–based voice actor who narrated corporate videos and TV commercials, thought he was an independent contractor. He was characterized as one by hundreds of clients, for whom he usually worked for only a few hours or days.

However, when the IRS audited him, it determined that he was really his clients' temporary employee because he worked on the clients' premises and some of his clients paid his union dues. When John told his clients that they had to classify him as an employee, issue a W-2, and pay payroll taxes, some of them told him they couldn't afford to hire him anymore because of the added expense.

In addition, John had to refile his tax returns for the years in question and recharacterize the compensation he received as wages instead of self-employment income. John was entitled to a refund for half of the self-employment taxes he paid on this compensation. But he lost some substantial business deductions—for example, a $10,000 deduction he took in one year for mileage and auto expenses. The loss of these deductions more than outweighed the refund of self-employment taxes. As a result, John lost work for future years and had to pay more taxes for past years.

Determining Worker Status

Various government agencies and courts use slightly different tests to determine how workers should be classified. Unfortunately, these tests are confusing, subjective, and often don't lead to a conclusive answer about whether you're an independent contractor or employee. This is why some hiring firms are afraid to hire independent contractors.

This section provides an overview of the most important test for independent contractor status. However, it's practically impossible for anyone to learn and follow all the different tests various government agencies use to determine worker status. You'll be better off simply following the guidelines late in this chapter for preserving your independent contractor status.

Most, but not all, government agencies use the "right of control" test to determine whether you're an employee or independent contractor. You're an employee under this test if a hiring firm has the right to direct and control how you work—both as to the final results and as to the details of when, where, and how you perform the work.

The employer may not always exercise this right—for example, if you're experienced and well trained, your employer may not feel the need to closely supervise you. But if the employer has the right to do so, you're still considered an employee.

EXAMPLE 1:

Mary takes a job as a hamburger cook at the local AcmeBurger. AcmeBurger personnel carefully train her in how to make an AcmeBurger burger—including the type and amount of ingredients to use, the temperature at which the burger should be cooked, and so on.

Once Mary starts work, AcmeBurger managers closely supervise how she does her job. Virtually every aspect of Mary's behavior on the job is under AcmeBurger control—including what time she arrives at and leaves work, when she takes her lunch break, what she wears, and the sequence of the tasks she must perform. If Mary proves to be an able and conscientious worker, her supervisors may not look over her shoulder very often. But they have the right to do so at any time. Mary is AcmeBurger's employee.

In contrast, you're an independent contractor if the hiring firm does not have the right to control how you do the job. Because you're an independent businessperson not solely dependent on the firm for your livelihood, its control is limited to accepting or rejecting the final results you achieve. Or if a project is broken down into stages or phases, the firm's input is limited to approving the work you perform at each stage. Unlike an employee, you are not supervised daily.

EXAMPLE 2:

AcmeBurger develops a serious plumbing problem. AcmeBurger does not have any plumbers on its staff, so it hires Plumbing by Jake, an independent plumbing repair business owned by Jake. Jake looks at the problem and gives an estimate of how much it will cost to fix. The manager agrees to hire him, and Jake and his assistant commence work.

Because Jake is clearly running his own business, it's virtually certain that AcmeBurger does not have the right to control the way Jake performs his plumbing services. Its control is limited to accepting or rejecting the final result. If AcmeBurger doesn't like the work Jake has done, it can refuse to pay him. Jake is an independent contractor.

It can be difficult to figure out whether a hiring firm has the right to control you. Government auditors can't look into your mind to see if you are controlled by a hiring firm. They have to rely instead on indirect or circumstantial evidence indicating control or lack of it—for example, whether a hiring firm provides you with tools and equipment, where you do the work, how you're paid, and whether you can be fired.

The factors each agency relies upon to measure control vary. Some agencies look at 14 factors to see if you're an employee or independent contractor; some look at 11; some consider only three. Which of these factors is of the greatest or least importance is anyone's guess. This can make it very difficult to know whether you pass muster to be an independent contractor.

The IRS Approach to Worker Status

The IRS uses the right of control test to determine whether you're an independent contractor or employee for tax purposes. The agency developed a list of 20 factors its auditors were supposed to use to measure how much control a hiring firm had over you. This "20-factor test" became very well known—discussed in countless magazine and journal articles, posted all over the Internet, and practically memorized by many independent contractors. Many of your prospective clients will be aware of the test and may even ask you about it.

CAUTION

Special IRS rules apply to some workers. If you're a licensed real estate agent, direct seller, business-to-business salesperson, home worker who makes clothing items, full-time life insurance salesperson, or driver who distributes food products, beverages, or laundry, your status may be predetermined for IRS purposes under special rules. (See Chapter 12.)

It's important to understand, however, that the 20-factor test is only an analytical tool IRS auditors use to measure control. It is not the legal test the IRS uses for determining worker status. IRS auditors have never been restricted to considering only the 20 factors on the test, nor are they required to consider them all.

Unfortunately, the 20-factor test left much to be desired as an analytical tool. It proved to be so subjective and complex that trying to apply it was often a waste of time. Even the IRS found it difficult to apply the test consistently. People performing the same services have been found to be employees in some IRS districts and independent contractors in others. In one case, for example, a Methodist minister was found to be an employee of his church; a Pentecostal pastor was found to be an independent contractor of another the same year. (*Weber v. Commissioner*, 103 T.C. 378 (1994); *Shelley v. Commissioner*, T.C. Memo. 1994-432 (1994).)

Hiring firms, independent contractors, attorneys, and tax experts complained bitterly for years that it was impossible to know who was and was not an independent contractor under the 20-factor test and that aggressive IRS auditors took advantage of this confusion by classifying every worker as an employee. Legislation was introduced in Congress to clarify the issue by establishing a simple test for determining worker status—a test that would probably have led to far more workers qualifying as independent contractors than under current law.

In an obvious attempt to block such legislation and to set the rules itself, the IRS issued a training manual for its auditors in 1996, setting forth a somewhat simpler approach to measure control. It should be easier for you to qualify as an independent contractor for IRS purposes under this manual than under the 20-factor test. Although the manual doesn't have the force of law, IRS auditors are supposed to follow it.

The manual provides the best guidance the IRS has ever made public on how to classify workers. Even more important, it evinces a much kinder, gentler attitude by the IRS on worker classification issues. Declaring that classifying a worker as an independent contractor instead of an employee "can be a valid and appropriate business choice," the manual admonishes IRS auditors to "approach the issue of worker classification in a fair and impartial manner."

RESOURCE

You can download a free copy of the IRS manual, *Independent Contractor or Employee? Training Materials*, from the IRS website at www.irs.gov/pub/irs-utl/emporind.pdf. Or you can request a copy by calling the IRS at 800-TAX-FORM.

How the IRS Measures Control

IRS auditors look at three areas to determine whether a hiring firm has the right to control a worker. These are:

- your behavior on the job
- your finances, and
- your relationship with the hiring firm.

The chart on the following page shows the primary factors the IRS looks at in each area.

The IRS test is not a model of clarity. There is no guidance on how important each factor is and how many factors must weigh in favor of independent contractor status for you to be classified as an independent contractor. The IRS says there is no magic number of factors. Rather, the factors that show lack of control must outweigh those that indicate control. No one factor alone is enough to make you an employee or an independent contractor.

To make your life easier, this chapter offers a list of eight guidelines for you to follow when doing your work. If you do, it's likely that you will be viewed as an independent contractor by the IRS and any other government agency.

Payment by the Hour

If you want to be classified as an independent contractor, it's better not to be paid an hourly wage unless it's a common practice in your line of business. (The IRS recognizes that some independent contractors—lawyers, for example— are usually paid by the hour.) Instead, get paid by the job or project where feasible.

Expenses

Paying business expenses yourself rather than getting reimbursed by your client will help establish your IC status. It really makes no difference what

IRS Test for Worker Status		
Behavioral Control Factors showing whether a hiring firm has the right to control how you perform the specific tasks you've been hired to do	**You will more likely be considered self-employed if you:** • are not given instructions by the hiring firm • provide your own training	**You will more likely be considered an employee if you:** • receive instructions you must follow about how to do your work • receive training from the hiring firm
Financial Control Factors showing whether a firm has a right to control your financial life	**You will more likely be considered self-employed if you:** • have a significant investment in equipment and facilities • pay business or travel expenses yourself • make your services available to the public • are paid by the job • have opportunity for profit or loss	**You will more likely be considered an employee if you:** • have equipment and facilities provided by the hiring firm free of charge • have your business or traveling expenses reimbursed • make no effort to market your services to the public • are paid by the hour or other unit of time • have no opportunity for profit or loss—for example, because you're paid by the hour and have all expenses reimbursed
Relationship Between Worker and Hiring Firm Factors showing whether you and the hiring firm believe that you are self-employed or an employee	**You will more likely be considered self-employed if you:** • don't receive employee benefits such as health insurance • sign a client agreement with the hiring firm • can't quit or be fired at will • are performing services that are not a part of the hiring firm's regular business activities	**You will more likely be considered an employee if you:** • receive employee benefits • have no written client agreement • can quit at any time without incurring any liability to the hiring firm • can be fired at any time • are performing services that are part of the hiring firm's core business

the expense is, as long as it's for your business. It can be office rent, equipment, salaries, travel expenses, telephone bills, photocopying charges, or anything else.

Although not fatal, any expense that your client reimburses you for will not help establish your IC status—and it could actually impair your effort (and your client's efforts) to prove that you are not an employee of the client.

Advertising

Failure to offer your services to the public is a sign of employee status. In the past, the IRS usually considered only advertising in telephone books and newspapers as evidence that an independent contractor offered services to the public. Of course, many independent contractors don't get business this way; they rely primarily on word of mouth. The IRS now recognizes this fact of life and doesn't consider advertising essential for proving independent contractor status.

Form of Direction

The IRS makes a distinction between receiving instructions on how to work—a very strong indicator of employee status—and being given suggestions. A suggestion about how work is to be performed does not constitute the right to control. However, if you must comply with suggestions or suffer adverse consequences (such as being fired or not assigned more work), then the suggestions are, in fact, instructions.

Training

Periodic or ongoing training about how to do your work is strong evidence of an employment relationship. However, a client may provide you with a short orientation or information session about the company's policies, new product line, or new government regulations without jeopardizing your independent contractor status. Training programs that are voluntary and that you attend without receiving pay do not disqualify you from being classified as an independent contractor.

Investment

A significant investment in equipment and facilities is not necessary for independent contractor status. The manual notes that some types of work simply do not require expensive equipment—for example, writing and certain types of consulting. But even if expensive equipment is needed to do a particular type of work, an independent contractor can always rent it.

Performing Key Services

One of the most important factors IRS auditors look at is whether the services performed by a worker are key to the hiring firm's regular business. The IRS figures that if the services you perform are vital to a company's regular business, the company will be more likely to control how you perform them. For example, a law firm is less likely to supervise and control a painter it hires to paint its offices than a paralegal it hires to work on its regular legal business.

However, IRS auditors are required to examine all the facts and circumstances. For example, a paralegal hired by a law firm could very well be an independent contractor if he or she was a specialist hired to help with especially difficult or unusual legal work.

> **CAUTION**
>
> **Written agreements are more important than ever.** A written independent contractor agreement can never make you an independent contractor by itself. However, if the evidence is so evenly balanced that it is difficult or impossible for an IRS auditor to decide whether you're an independent contractor or employee, the existence of a written independent contractor agreement can tip the balance in favor of independent contractor status. This makes using written independent contractor agreements especially important. (See Chapter 18.)

Full-Time Work

Working full time for a single client should not by itself make you an employee in the eyes of the IRS. Nevertheless, it is never helpful to your IC status to work for just one client at a time. There may be many situations where it can't be avoided; for example, if you can't get any other work at the time or if the nature of the work you are doing for the client demands your full time and attention. Still, you should attempt to keep the period of exclusivity down to a minimum—no more than six months to a year. Performing the same services full time for the same client year after year inevitably makes you look like an employee of that client.

Long-Term Work for a Single Client

Performing services for the same client year after year used to be a sign that you were an employee. The IRS now recognizes that independent contractors may work for a client on a long-term basis, either because they sign long-term contracts or because their contracts are regularly renewed by the client because they do a good job, price their services reasonably, or no one else is readily available to do the work.

Time and Place of Work

It is not important to the IRS where or when you work. For example, the fact that you work at a client's offices during regular business hours is not considered evidence of employee status. On the other hand, the fact that you work at home at hours of your own choosing is not strong evidence that you're an independent contractor either, because many employees now work at home as well.

Rules for Technical Services Workers

If you're a computer programmer, systems analyst, engineer, or provide similar technical services and obtain work through brokers, special tax rules may make it very difficult for you to work as an independent contractor, even if you qualify under the IRS test.

Most hiring firms can rely on a defense, found in Section 530 of the Tax Code, if the IRS claims they misclassified workers. By using Section 530, an employer who misclassifies a worker as an independent contractor can avoid paying any fines or penalties for failing to pay employment taxes if it can show it had a reasonable basis for treating the worker as an independent contractor. Section 530 has made hiring firms' lives a little easier by giving them an additional defense against the IRS.

However, another part of the Tax Code, Section 1706, provides that the Section 530 defense may not be used by brokers that contract to provide their clients with:

- engineers
- designers
- drafters
- computer programmers
- systems analysts, or
- other skilled workers in similar technical occupations.

Section 1706 doesn't make anyone an employee. But it does make it harder for brokers to avoid paying assessments and penalties if the IRS claims they've misclassified a technical services worker as an independent contractor. Because of Section 1706, brokers who contract to provide companies with technical services workers usually classify the workers as their employees and issue them W-2s. One result of this is that you'll likely receive less pay from the broker than if you were classified as an independent contractor because it has to pay payroll taxes for you and provide workers' compensation.

Some brokers may make an exception and treat you as an independent contractor if you are clearly running an independent business—for example, you deal directly with many clients and are incorporated. For example, one Silicon Valley software tester occasionally obtains work through brokers and is never classified as an employee of the broker. Brokers feel safe treating her as an independent contractor because she has incorporated her business, has employees, and has many clients, including several Fortune 500 companies. The brokers sign a contract with the tester's corporation, not with her personally.

Section 1706 has no application at all if you contract directly with a client instead of going through a broker. But many high-tech firms are still wary of hiring independent contractors.

Tips for Preserving Your IC Status

If you consistently follow the guidelines discussed in this section, below, it's likely that any government agency or court would determine that you qualify as an independent contractor. However, there are no guarantees.

Some of these guidelines may be a bit stricter than those now followed by the IRS. This is because not all government agencies follow the IRS standards. Various state agencies, such as state tax departments and unemployment compensation and workers' compensation agencies, may have tougher classification standards than the IRS. This means you can't rely solely on the IRS rules.

EXAMPLE:

> Debbi, an independent-contractor accountant based in Rhode Island, clearly qualifies as an independent contractor under the IRS test. However, very restrictive Rhode Island employment laws require that she be classified as an employee for state purposes if she performs services for other accounting firms. This means they must withhold state income taxes from her pay, pay unemployment taxes, and provide her with workers' compensation insurance. In addition, if Debbi has employees of her own, they may become the firm's employees as well under Rhode Island law.

Some hiring firms are terrified of government audits and nervous about hiring independent contractors. Companies that have had problems with government audits in the past or are in industries that are targeted by government auditors are likely to be especially skittish. Recent targets include trucking firms, courier services, securities dealers, high technology firms, nurse registries, building contractors, and manufacturer representatives. Such hiring firms may be more willing to hire you as an independent contractor if you can show that you follow the guidelines. Document your efforts and be ready to show the documentation to nervous clients.

Many other companies don't give government audits a second thought and are more than happy to classify you as an independent contractor to save the money and effort involved in treating you as an employee. These companies may not worry about whether you qualify as an independent contractor, but you should. You could still end up getting fired, taking a pay cut, or having to pay extra taxes if some government bureaucrat decides you're really an employee. So even though your client may not appreciate your efforts, continue to follow the guidelines discussed here; both you and your client will be glad you did if the government comes calling.

Retain Control of Your Work

The most fundamental difference between employees and independent contractors is that employers have the right to tell their employees what to do. Never permit a hiring firm to supervise or control you as it does its employees. It's perfectly all right for the hiring firm to give you detailed guidelines or specifications for the results you're to achieve. But how you go about achieving those results should be entirely up to you.

A few guidelines will help emphasize that you are the one who is responsible:

- Do not ask for or accept instructions or orders from the hiring firm about how to do your job. For example, you should decide what equipment or tools to use, where to purchase supplies or services, who will perform what tasks, and what routines or work patterns must be used. It's fine for a hiring firm to give you suggestions about these things, but you must always preserve your right to accept or reject such suggestions.

- Do not ask for or receive training on how to do your work from a hiring firm. If you need additional training, seek it elsewhere.

- A hiring firm may give you a deadline for when your work should be completed, but you should generally establish your own working hours. For example, if you want, you could work 20 hours two days a week and take the rest of the week off. In some cases, however, it may be necessary to coordinate your working hours with the client's schedule—for example, where you must perform work on the client's premises or work with its employees.

- Decide on your own where to perform the work—that is, a client should not require you to work at a particular location. Of course, some services must be performed at a client's premises or other particular place.

- Decide whether to hire assistants to help you and, if you do, pay and supervise them yourself. Only you should have the right to hire and fire your assistants.

- Do not attend regular employee meetings or functions such as employee picnics.

- Avoid providing frequent formal reports about the progress of your work—for example, daily phone calls to the client. It is permissible, however, to give reports when you complete various stages of a project.

- Do not obtain, read, or pay any attention to a hiring firm's employee manuals or other rules for employees. The rules governing your relationship with the hiring firm are contained solely in your independent contractor agreement, whether written or oral. (See Chapter 18.)

If you work outside the client's premises, it's usually not difficult to avoid being controlled. Neither the client nor its employees will have much opportunity to try to supervise you. For example, Katherine, a freelance legal writer, never has any problems being controlled by a large legal publisher for whom she performs freelance assignments. She says anonymity on the job helps with this: "I get my freelance assignments by phone, do all the work at home and in the local law library, and then transmit my projects to the publisher via email. I've hardly ever been in the publisher's office."

On the other hand, you could have problems if you work in a client's workplace. The client's supervisors or managers may try to treat you like an employee. Before you start work, make clear to the client that you do not fall within its regular personnel hierarchy; you are an outsider. You might ask the client to designate one person with whom you will deal. If anyone in the company gives you a problem, you can explain that you deal only with your contact person and refer the problem person to your contact.

Note, however, that it's fine for a client to require you to comply with government regulations about how to perform your services. For example, a client may require a construction contractor to comply with municipal building codes that impose detailed rules on how a building is constructed. The IRS and other government agencies would not likely consider this to be an exercise of control over the contractor by the client.

Show Opportunities for Profit or Loss

Because they are in business for themselves, independent contractors have the opportunity to earn profits or suffer losses. If you have absolutely no risk of loss, you're probably not an independent contractor.

Business Expenses

The best way to show an opportunity to realize profit or loss is to have recurring business expenses. If receipts do not match expenses, you lose money and may go into debt. If receipts exceed expenses, you earn a profit.

Good examples of independent contractor expenses include:

- salaries for assistants
- travel and other similar expenses incurred in performing your services
- substantial investment in equipment and materials

- rent for an office or workplace
- training and educational expenses
- advertising
- licensing, certification, and professional dues
- insurance
- leasing of equipment
- supplies, and
- repairs and maintenance of business equipment.

Don't go out and buy things you don't really need. But if you've been thinking about buying equipment or supplies to use in your business, go ahead and take the plunge. You'll not only solidify your independent contractor status, you'll get a tax deduction as well. (See Chapter 9.)

In addition, it's best that you don't ask clients to reimburse you for expenses such as travel, photocopying, and postage. It's a better practice to bill clients enough for your services to pay for these items yourself. Setting your compensation at a level that covers your expenses also frees you from having to keep records of your expenses. Keeping track of the cost of every phone call or photocopy you make for a client can be a real chore and may be more trouble than it's worth.

Get Paid by the Project

Another excellent way to show opportunity for profit or loss is to be paid an agreed price for a specific project, rather than to bill by unit of time, such as by the hour. If the project price is higher than the expenses, you'll make money; if not, you'll lose money.

However, this form of billing may be too risky for many independent contractors. And some professions—for example, attorneys and accountants—are typically paid by the hour. If hourly payment is customary in your field, this factor should not affect your independent contractor status.

Look Like an Independent Business

Take steps to make yourself look like an independent businessperson. There are several things you can do to cultivate this image:

- Don't obtain employee-type benefits from your clients, such as health insurance, paid vacation, sick days, pension benefits, or life or disability insurance; instead, charge your clients enough to purchase these items yourself.

- Incorporate your business or form an LLC instead of operating as a sole proprietor. (See Chapter 2.)

- Obtain a fictitious business name instead of using your own name for your business. (See Chapter 3.)

- Obtain all necessary business licenses and permits. (See Chapter 5.)

- Obtain business insurance. (See Chapter 6.)

- Maintain a separate bank account for your business. (See Chapter 14.)

You may have an easier time getting work if you do these things. For example, a large corporation that regularly used the services of one independent contractor asked her to incorporate or at least obtain a business license because it was worried she might otherwise be viewed as the company's employee.

Work Outside Hiring Firms' Premises

The IRS no longer considers working at a hiring firm's place of business to be an important factor in determining whether a worker is an independent contractor or employee, but many state agencies still do. For example, in about half the states you may be considered an employee for unemployment compensation purposes if you work at the hiring firm's place of business or another place it designates.

Working at a location specified by a hiring firm implies that the firm has control, especially if the work could be done elsewhere. If you work at a hiring firm's place of business, you're physically within the firm's direction and supervision. If you can choose to work off the premises, the firm obviously has less control.

Unless the nature of the services you're performing requires it, don't work at the hiring firm's office or other business premises. An independent contractor hired to lay a carpet or paint an office must obviously work at the hiring firm's premises. But if your work can be done anywhere, do it outside the client's premises.

Working at a home office will not, alone, show that you're an independent contractor as far as the IRS is concerned because many employees are now doing so. Renting an office outside your home, however, will show independent contractor status. It shows that you're operating your own business and gives you a recurring business expense to help establish risk of loss.

Make Your Services Widely Available

Independent contractors normally offer their services to the general public, not just to one person or entity. The IRS recognizes that many independent contractors rely on word of mouth to get clients and don't do any active marketing. However, nervous clients and other government auditors will be impressed if you market your services to the public.

There are many relatively inexpensive ways you can do so—for example:

- obtain business cards and stationery
- set up a website for your business
- hang a shingle in front of your home or office, advertising your services
- maintain listings in business and telephone directories (both print and online)
- attend trade shows and similar events
- join professional organizations

- advertise in newspapers, trade journals, and magazines, and on the Web
- mail brochures or other promotional materials to prospective clients, and
- phone potential clients to drum up business.

Keep copies of advertisements, promotional materials, and similar items to show to prospective clients and government auditors.

Have Multiple Clients

IRS guidelines provide that you can work full time for a single client on a long-term basis and still be an independent contractor. Nevertheless, having multiple clients shows that you're running an independent business because you are not dependent on any one firm for your livelihood. Government auditors will rarely question the status of an independent contractor who works for three or four clients simultaneously.

However, the nature of your work may require that you work full time for one client at a time. In this event, at least try to work for more than one client over the course of a year—for example, work full time for one client for six months and full time for another client for the other six months.

Having multiple clients also increases your economic security. One independent contractor thinks of herself as an eight-legged spider, with each client a separate leg. If she loses one client, things are still economically stable because she has her other legs to stand on.

If you seem to be locked into having just one client, you may be able to drum up new business by offering special rates for small jobs that you would otherwise lose.

 CAUTION

Don't sign noncompetition agreements. Some clients may ask or require you to sign noncompetition agreements restricting your ability to work for the client's competitors while working for the client, afterwards, or both. You should avoid such restrictions. Not only will they make you look like an employee, they may also make it impossible for you to earn a living.

Use Written Agreements

Use written independent contractor agreements for all but the briefest, smallest projects. Among other things, the agreement should make clear that you are an independent contractor and the hiring firm does not have the right to control the way you work. A written agreement by itself won't make you an independent contractor but it is helpful—particularly if you draft it rather than the hiring firm.

Also, don't accept new projects after the original project is completed without signing a new independent contractor agreement. You can easily be converted from an independent contractor to an employee if you perform assignment after assignment for a client without negotiating new contracts. (See Chapters 18 and 19 for more about written agreements.)

Avoid Accepting Employee Status

Some clients will refuse to hire you as an independent contractor and insist on classifying you as an employee. Some companies may hire you themselves as an employee. Others may insist that you contract with a broker or employment agency who treats you as its employee. The firm then hires you through the broker.

It's best to avoid performing the exact same services while classified as both an independent contractor and employee for the following reasons.

- Being classified as both an independent contractor and an employee on your tax returns may make an IRS audit more likely and lead government auditors to conclude that you're an employee for all purposes.

- You'll generally be paid less as an employee than if you were an independent contractor because the hiring firm or broker will have to provide you with workers' compensation and unemployment insurance. (However, you may be able to collect unemployment when your services end.)

- You may not be able to deduct unreimbursed expenses incurred while you were an employee or the deductions may be limited. (See Chapter 9.)

- You can't apply your employee income to your independent contractor business to help it show a profit. If your business keeps showing losses, the IRS might conclude that it is a hobby and disallow your business deductions. (See Chapter 9.)

Retirement Options for the Self-Employed

When you're self-employed, you don't have an employer to provide you with a retirement or pension plan. It's up to you to establish and fund your own plan to supplement any Social Security benefits you'll receive when you retire. This chapter provides an overview of the main retirement options for the self-employed. It is not a guide about where to invest your money.

But before you can decide how to invest your retirement money, you must first decide what type of retirement account or accounts to establish. There are several types of accounts specifically designed for the self-employed that provide terrific tax benefits. These will help you save for retirement and may reduce your tax burden when you retire.

Choosing what type of account or accounts to establish is just as important as deciding what to invest in once you open your account, if not more so. Once you establish your account, you can always change your investments with little or no difficulty. But changing the type of accounts you have may prove difficult and costly.

RESOURCE

Three easy-to-understand guides on retirement investing are:

- *Get a Life: You Don't Need a Million to Retire Well,* by Ralph Warner (Nolo)
- *Work Less, Live More,* by Bob Clyatt (Nolo), and
- *Investing for Dummies,* by Eric Tyson (IDG Books).

For additional information on the tax aspects of retirement, see:

- IRS Publication 560, *Retirement Plans for the Small Business,* and
- IRS Publication 590, *Individual Retirement Arrangements.*

You can obtain these and all other IRS publications by calling the IRS at 800-TAX-FORM, visiting your local IRS office, or downloading the publications from the IRS website at www.irs.gov.

Reasons to Have a Retirement Plan (or Plans)

In all likelihood, you will receive Social Security benefits when you retire. However, Social Security will probably provide you with no more than half of your needs, possibly less, depending upon your lifestyle. You'll need to make up the shortfall with your own retirement investments.

Luckily, when it comes to saving for retirement, the self-employed are actually better off than most workers. This is because the federal government allows you to set up retirement accounts specifically designed for small business people that provide terrific income tax benefits. These include SIMPLE IRAs, SEP-IRAs, Keogh plans, and solo 401(k)s. You can establish such accounts through a bank, savings and loan, credit union, insurance company, brokerage house, mutual fund company, or other financial institution.

Retirement accounts are simply shells to set aside money and protect you from being taxed by the government. After deciding what type of account you want, you must then decide what to invest in. You can invest in almost anything—for example, stocks, bonds, mutual funds, money market funds, or certificates of deposit. You can transfer your money from one type of investment to another within your account as market conditions change.

These accounts provide you with two enormous tax benefits:

- you pay no taxes on the income your retirement investments earn until you withdraw the funds upon retirement, and
- you can deduct the amount you contribute to your retirement account from your income taxes for the year, subject to certain limits.

Tax Deferral

The money you earn on an investment is ordinarily taxed in the year you earn it. For example, you must pay taxes on the interest you earn on a savings account or certificate of deposit when that interest accrues. When you sell an investment at a profit, you must pay income tax on this amount as well— for example, you must pay tax on the profit you earn from selling stock.

But this is not the case when you invest in a tax-qualified retirement account such as an IRA, SEP-IRA, or Keogh plan. The money your investment earns is not taxable to you until you withdraw the funds when you retire—when you will usually be in a lower income tax bracket than you were during your working years.

You're not supposed to make withdrawals until you reach age 59½, subject to certain exceptions. If you make early withdrawals, you must ordinarily pay regular income tax on the amount you take out, plus a 10% federal tax penalty.

RESOURCE

For detailed information on the tax aspects of withdrawals from retirement accounts, see *IRAs, 401(k)s & Other Retirement Plans: Taking Your Money Out*, by Twila Slesnick and John Suttle (Nolo).

Tax Deduction

Avoiding income tax on your retirement investments until you retire is a good deal in and of itself. But there is an additional outstanding tax benefit to retirement accounts: If you satisfy the requirements discussed below, you can deduct the amount you contribute to a retirement account from your income taxes (except Roth IRAs and Roth 401(k)s). This can give you a substantial income tax savings.

EXAMPLE:

Art, a self-employed sole proprietor, establishes a retirement account at his local bank and contributes $10,000 this year. He can deduct the entire amount from his income taxes. Because Art is in the 25% tax bracket, he saves $2,500 in income taxes for the year (25% x $10,000) and has saved $10,000 toward his retirement.

How much you can contribute each year depends on what type of account you establish and how much money you earn. However, you usually won't be able to make any contributions if you have a loss from your business. You must have self-employment income to fund these retirement accounts.

The combination of tax deferral and a current tax deduction makes a huge difference in how much you'll save for retirement. The chart below shows the difference in growth between a tax-deferred and a taxable account over 30 years.

How Much Money Will You Need When You Retire

How much money you'll need when you retire depends on many factors, including your lifestyle. You could need anywhere from 50% to 100% of the amount you earned while employed. The average is about 70% to 80% of preretirement earnings. But this is only an average: Your own needs and habits will determine how much you should sock away.

Individual Retirement Accounts (IRAs)

The simplest type of tax-deferred retirement account is the individual retirement account, or IRA. If you can afford to invest no more than a few thousand dollars per year in a retirement plan, an IRA is a good choice. You can establish an IRA for yourself as an individual and also set up one or more of the other types of retirement plans discussed below, which are just for businesses. However, there are limitations on your deductions for, or contributions to, IRAs if you have other retirement plans and your income exceeds certain limits.

An IRA is a trust or custodial account set up for the benefit of an individual or his or her beneficiaries. The trustee or custodian administers the account. The trustee can be a bank, mutual fund, brokerage firm, or other financial institution, such as an insurance company, which has been approved by the IRS. The custodian must meet strict IRS requirements regarding the safekeeping of your account.

IRAs are extremely easy to set up and administer. You need not file any special tax forms with the IRS. The financial institution you use to set up your account will ordinarily request that you complete IRS Form 5305, *Traditional Individual Retirement Trust Account*, which serves as a preapproved IRA agreement. Keep the form in your records.

Most financial institutions offer an array of IRA accounts that provide for different types of investments. You can invest your IRA money in just about anything—stocks, bonds, mutual funds, Treasury bills and notes, and bank certificates of deposit. However, you can't invest in collectibles such as art, antiques, stamps, or other personal property.

Growth of a Taxable Vs. Tax-Deferred Account

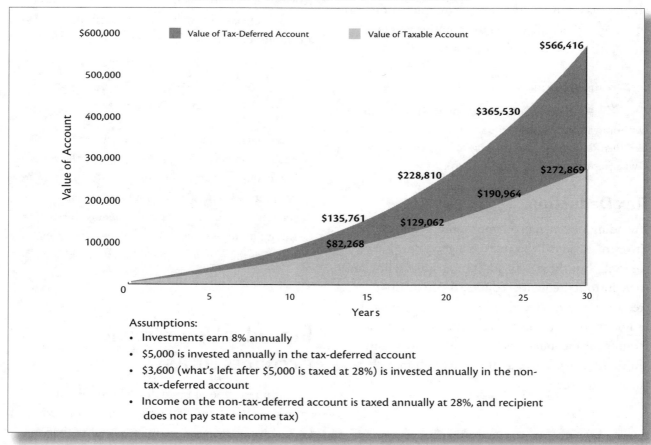

From *Get a Life: You Don't Need a Million to Retire Well,* by Ralph Warner (Nolo).

You have two different types of IRAs to choose from:

• traditional IRAs, and

• Roth IRAs.

You can have as many IRA accounts as you want. But there is a maximum amount you may contribute to all of your IRA accounts each year. This amount will increase over time as shown in the following chart:

Annual IRA Contribution Limits		
Tax Year	**Under Age 50**	**Age 50 and Over**
2007	$4,000	$5,000
2008 and later	$5,000	$6,000

After 2008, the limit will be adjusted for inflation in $500 increments each year.

In addition to these contribution limits, workers who are at least 50 years old at the end of the year may make increased annual contributions of $1,000 per year. This is intended to allow these older people to catch up with younger folks who will have many more years to make contributions at the higher levels.

These contribution limits may be doubled if you're married—for example, a married couple in 2008 could contribute up to $5,000 per spouse into their IRAs, for a total of $10,000, even if one spouse isn't working. But you must file a joint return, and the working spouse's earnings must be at least as much as the IRA contribution.

Traditional IRAs

Traditional IRAs have been around since 1974. The principal feature of these IRAs is that you can receive an income tax deduction for the amounts you contribute to your account each year, up to a set yearly limit. Thereafter, your earnings accumulate in the account tax-free until you withdraw them.

You can have both a traditional IRA and another retirement plan or plans. But if you or your spouse is covered by one of the other plans discussed in this chapter, your ability to deduct your contributions from your income taxes is limited.

The amount of contributions you may deduct also starts to phase out when your modified adjusted gross income exceeds certain levels. These limits are based on your and your spouse's annual modified adjusted gross income (MAGI for short). Your MAGI is your adjusted gross income before it is reduced by your IRA contributions and certain other more unusual items. These limits are set forth in the following chart.

Annual Income Limits for IRA Deductions				
Tax Year	**Married Filing Jointly**		**Single Taxpayer**	
	Full Deduction	**Partial Deduction**	**Full Deduction**	**Partial Deduction**
2007	Under $83,000	$83,000–$103,000	Under $52,000	$52,000–$62,000
2008	Under $80,000	$80,000–$100,000	Under $50,000	$50,000–$60,000

The money in a traditional IRA is not supposed to be withdrawn until you reach age 59½, unless you die or become disabled. The amounts you withdraw are then included in your regular income for income tax purposes. You must begin withdrawing your money from your IRA by April 1 of the year after you turn 70.

As a general rule, if you make early withdrawals, you must pay regular income tax on the amount you withdraw plus a 10% federal tax penalty. There are some exceptions to this early withdrawal penalty, including when you withdraw money to purchase a first home or pay educational expenses.

Roth IRAs

Like traditional IRAs, Roth IRAs allow your retirement savings to grow tax-free. The two main ways in which a Roth IRA is different from a contributory IRA are as follows:

- The contributions you make to a Roth IRA are not tax deductible: You pay regular income tax on the money you contribute.
- However, the distributions (money) you withdraw from a Roth account are tax-free in most circumstances.

In a traditional IRA, you do not pay income tax on the money you deposit, but do pay income tax when you withdraw distributions; the opposite is true for a Roth IRA.

Unlike a traditional IRA, you can establish a Roth IRA only if your income is below a certain level. If you are single, your ability to make a contribution starts to phase out when your income reaches $101,000 and ends completely when your income reaches $114,000. If you are married and filing a joint return with your spouse, your ability to make a contribution starts to phase out at $159,000 and ends at $166,000. These are the 2008 limits. The limits are adjusted for inflation each year. Roth IRAs have the same restrictions on early withdrawals as traditional IRAs. You are not, however, required to make withdrawals when you reach age 70½. Because Roth IRA withdrawals are tax free, the government doesn't care if you leave your money in your account indefinitely. However, your money will be tax-free on withdrawal only if you leave it in your Roth IRA for at least five years.

If the Roth IRA sounds attractive to you, and you already have a traditional IRA, you may convert it to a Roth IRA. This is called a "rollover."

Employer IRAs

The two IRAs described above—traditional IRAs and Roth IRAs—are retirement accounts that you can set up for yourself as an individual. In addition to those accounts, you can also set up something called an employer IRA.

You don't have to have employees to establish an employer IRA: You can establish this IRA as long as you're in business and earn a profit. It makes no difference how you organize your business, whether as a sole proprietor, partner in a partnership, member of a limited liability company, or owner of a regular or S corporation.

The great advantages of employer IRAs are that you can contribute more than the individual IRA contribution limits, and you can establish employer IRAs in addition to any individual IRA you may have. There are two kinds of employer IRAs: SEP-IRAs and SIMPLE IRAs, as described below

SEP-IRAs

SEP-IRAs, short for "simplified employee pension" IRAs, are specifically designed for the self-employed. Any person who receives any self-employment income from providing a service can establish a SEP-IRA. It doesn't matter whether you work full time or part time. You can even have a SEP-IRA if you are covered by a retirement plan as a full-time employee at another job.

A SEP-IRA is very similar to an IRA except that you can contribute much more money to it each year. If you are a sole proprietor, or your business is organized as a partnership, LLP, or LLC, you may contribute 20% of your net profit from self-employment up to the annual limit ($46,000 in 2008). If your business is incorporated and you work as its employee, you may invest up to 25% of your compensation every year, up to the annual limit. This limit also applies to employees who work for you. You don't have to make contributions every year, and your contributions can vary from year to year. As with IRAs, the range of investments available is nearly limitless.

You can deduct the contributions you make to your SEP-IRAs (up to the applicable limits) from your income taxes. The interest on your SEP-

IRA investments then accrues tax-free until you withdraw the money upon retirement.

Withdrawals from SEP-IRAs are subject to the same rules that apply to IRAs. This means that if you withdraw your money from your SEP-IRA before you reach age 59½, you'll have to pay a 10% tax penalty plus regular income taxes on your withdrawal, unless an exception applies.

SIMPLE IRAs

Self-employed people and companies with fewer than 100 employees can set up SIMPLE IRAs. If you establish a SIMPLE IRA, you are not allowed to have any other retirement plans for your business (although you may still have your own individual IRA). SIMPLE IRAs are easy to set up and administer, and you will be able to make larger annual contributions than you could to a SEP-IRA or Keogh plan if you earn less than $10,000 per year from your business.

SIMPLE IRAs may be established only by an employer on behalf of its employees. If you are a sole proprietor, you are deemed to employ yourself for purposes of this rule and you may establish a SIMPLE IRA in your own name as the employer. If you are a partner in a partnership, an LLC member, or the owner of an incorporated business, the SIMPLE IRA must be established by your business, not by you personally.

Contributions to SIMPLE IRAs are divided into two parts. You may contribute:

- up to 100% of your net income from your business up to an annual limit ($10,500 in 2008; $13,000 if you were born before 1955), which will be increased to reflect inflation in future years, and

- a matching contribution of up to 3% of your net business income, as long as this amount does not exceed your first contribution.

If you're an employee of your incorporated business, your first contribution—called a "salary reduction contribution"—comes out of your salary, and the matching contribution is paid by your business.

You can invest the money in a SIMPLE IRA like the money in any other IRA. Withdrawals from SIMPLE IRAs are subject to the same rules as traditional IRAs with one big exception: Early withdrawals from SIMPLE IRAs are subject to a 25% tax penalty if the withdrawal is made within two years after the date you first contributed to your account. Other early withdrawals are subject to a 10% penalty, as with traditional IRAs, unless an exception applies.

Keogh Plans

Keogh plans—named after the congressman who sponsored the legislation that created them—are just for self-employed people. Keoghs allow the self-employed to set aside more money for retirement than any other type of plan.

You can't have a Keogh if you incorporate your business. Keoghs require more paperwork to set up than employer IRAs, but they also offer more options: You can contribute more to them and still take an income tax deduction.

Types of Keogh Plans

There are two basic types of Keogh plans:

- defined contribution plans, in which benefits are based on the amount you contribute to and accumulate in the plan, and

- defined benefit plans, which provide for a set benefit upon retirement.

There are two types of defined contribution plans: profit-sharing plans and money purchase plans. These plans can be used separately or in conjunction with each other.

You can have as many defined contribution plans as you want, but annual contributions to all of them together cannot exceed the lesser of:

- 100% of the participant's annual compensation, or
- a certain amount adjusted each year for inflation—$46,000 in 2008.

Participants over 50 can contribute an additional $5,000 each year.

Profit-Sharing Plans

You may contribute up to 20% of your net self-employment income to a profit-sharing Keogh plan, up to a maximum of $45,000 for 2007. You can contribute any amount up to the limit each year, or not contribute at all.

Money Purchase Plans

In a money purchase plan, you contribute a fixed percentage of your net self-employment earnings every year. You decide how much to contribute each year. Make sure you will be able to afford the contributions each year because you can't skip them, even if your business earns no profit for the year. In return for giving up flexibility, you can contribute more to a money purchase plan—20% of your net self-employment earnings, up to a maximum of $46,000 for 2008.

Setting Up a Keogh Plan

You must establish your Keogh plan by the end of your tax year—but you can wait until your tax return is due the following year to make contributions. Ordinarily, your return is due by April 15, but you may file a request for an extension until August 15. By doing so, you'll have three extra months to contribute to your plan.

If you wish, you can deposit a small advance to set up your account and then wait until you file your tax return to make your full contribution for the year.

As with individual IRAs and employer IRAs, you can set up a Keogh plan at most banks, brokerage houses, mutual funds, other financial institutions,

and trade or professional organizations. Again, you have a huge array of investments from which to choose.

To set up your plan, you must adopt a written Keogh plan and set up a trust or custodial account with your plan provider to invest your funds. Your plan provider will ordinarily have an IRS-approved master or prototype Keogh plan for you to sign. You can also have a special plan drawn up for you, but this is expensive and unnecessary for most self-employed people.

Withdrawing Money From Your Keogh

You may begin to withdraw your money from your Keogh plan after you reach age 59½. If you have a profit-sharing plan, early withdrawals are permitted without penalty in cases of financial hardship, if you become disabled, or to pay health expenses in excess of 7.5% of your adjusted gross income. If you have a money purchase plan, early withdrawals are permitted if you become disabled, leave your business after age 55, or make child-support or alimony payments from the plan under a court order. Otherwise, early withdrawals from profit-sharing and money purchase Keogh plans are subject to a 10% penalty.

Solo 401(k) Plans

Most people have heard of 401(k) plans—retirement plans established by businesses for their employees. 401(k)s are a type of profit-sharing plan in which a business's employees make contributions from their salaries before they are taxed and the business usually (but not always) makes a matching contribution. These plans are complex to establish and administer and are generally used by larger businesses. Until recently, self-employed people and businesses without employees rarely used 401(k) plans, because they offered no benefit over other profit-sharing plans that are much easier to set up and run.

However, things have changed. Now, any business owner who has no employees (other than a spouse) can establish a solo self-employed 401(k) plan (also called a one-person or individual 401(k)). Solo 401(k) plans are designed specifically for business owners without employees and have several advantages over other retirement plans.

Like all 401(k)s, solo 401(k) contributions consist of two separate elements:

- a profit-sharing contribution of up to 20% of your net profit from self-employment, plus
- a salary deferral contribution of up to a certain limit—$15,500 in 2008.

The maximum total contribution per year is $46,000 in 2008 (the same maximum amount as for profit-sharing and money purchase plans discussed above). Business owners over 50 may make additional catch-up elective deferral contributions of up to $5,000 per year that are not counted toward this maximum.

For example, John, a 60-year-old self-employed consultant, earned $100,000 in net self-employment income in 2007. The maximum he can contribute to his solo 401(k) is $35,500. This consists of a:

- $20,000 profit sharing contribution (20% of John's net self-employment income), plus
- $15,500 salary deferral contribution, plus
- $5,000 catch-up contribution because he is over 50.

If your business is incorporated, you may contribute 25% of your employee compensation plus the elective deferral.

Also, you can borrow up to $50,000 from your solo 401(k) plan penalty-free, as long as you repay the loan within five years. You cannot borrow from a traditional IRA, Roth IRA, SEP-IRA, or SIMPLE IRA.

As with other plans, you must pay a 10% penalty tax on withdrawals you make before the age of 59½, but you may make penalty-free early withdrawals for reasons of personal hardship (defined as an "immediate financial need" that you can't meet any other way).

You can set up a solo 401(k) plan at most banks, brokerage houses, mutual funds, and other financial institutions, and you can invest the money in a variety of ways. You must adopt a written plan and set up a trust or custodial account with your plan provider to invest your funds. Financial institutions that offer solo 401(k) plans have preapproved plans that you can use.

Roth 401(k) Plans

In 2006, a brand new type of 401(k) plan became available—the Roth 401(k). Roth 401(k)s are much the same as regular 401(k)s with one big difference: The money you contribute to the plan is not tax deductible; in return, the withdrawals you make upon retirement are tax-free.

This is the same type of tax treatment you get with a Roth IRA. But one big advantage the Roth 401(k) has over the Roth IRA is that anyone can have one, no matter how high his or her income. In contrast, you can't contribute to a Roth IRA if your income exceeds $114,000 if you're single, or $166,000 if you're married and file a joint tax return.

Only the elective deferral portion of your annual 401(k) contribution receives the Roth treatment. This limits your contribution to $15,500 per year, or $20,500 if you're over 50. These are the 2007 limits. The limits are adjusted for inflation each year.

CAUTION

Beware of retirement account deadlines. If you want to establish any of the retirement accounts discussed in this chapter and take a tax deduction for the year, you must meet specific deadlines. The deadlines vary according to the type of account you set up, as shown in the following chart. Once you establish your account, you have until the due date of your tax return for the year (April 15 of the following year, plus any filing extensions) to contribute to your account and take a deduction.

Plan Type	Deadline for Establishing Plan
Traditional IRA	Due date of tax return (April 15 plus extensions)
Roth IRA	Due date of tax return (April 15 plus extensions)
SEP- IRA	Due date of tax return (April 15 plus extensions)
SIMPLE IRA	October 1
Keogh Profit-Sharing Plan	December 1
Keogh Money Purchase Plan	December 1
Keogh Defined Benefit Plan	December 1
Solo 401(k)	December 1
Roth 401(k)	December 1

Retirement Plans If You Have Employees

If you work for yourself and have no employees, you can probably choose, establish, and administer your own retirement plan with little or no assistance. The instant you add employees to the mix, however, virtually every aspect of your plan becomes more complex, due primarily to nondiscrimination rules. These rules are designed to ensure that your retirement plan benefits all employees and not just you. In general, the laws prohibit you from doing the following:

- making disproportionately large contributions for some plan participants (like yourself) and not for others
- unfairly excluding certain employees from participating in the plan, and
- unfairly withholding benefits from former employees or their beneficiaries.

If the IRS finds your plan to be discriminatory at any time (usually during an audit), the plan could be disqualified. If this happens, you and your employees could owe income tax and penalties.

Having employees also increases the plan's reporting requirements. You must provide employees with a summary of the terms of the plan, notification of any changes you make, and an annual report of contributions. And you must file an annual tax return.

Because of this complexity, any self-employed person who has employees should turn to professional consultants for help in choosing, establishing, and administering a retirement plan. ●

Copyrights, Patents, and Trade Secrets

Self-employed people are often hired to create or contribute to the creation of copyrights, patents, or trade secrets—for example, writings, photos, graphics, music, software programs, designs, or inventions. This chapter explains the legalities surrounding these creative works—who owns them and how those who create them can protect their rights.

Intellectual Property

Products of the human intellect that have economic value—that is, ideas or creations that are worth money—are tagged with the lofty name of "intellectual property." This includes works of which you are the author, such as writings, computer software, films, music, and inventions, as well as techniques, processes, or other information not generally known.

A body of federal and state law creates intellectual property ownership rights similar to those of tangible personal property, such as automobiles. Intellectual property may be owned, bought, and sold just like other property.

There are four separate bodies of law that protect intellectual property: copyrights and patents (which are governed solely by federal law) and trademarks and trade secrets (which are protected under both state and federal laws).

Copyrights

Federal copyright law (17 U.S.C. §§ 101 and following) protects all original works of authorship. A work of authorship is any work created by a person that other people can understand or perceive, either by themselves or with the help of a machine such as a computer or television. Authorship can include all kinds of written works, plays, music, artwork, graphics, photos, films and videos, computer software, architectural blueprints and designs, choreography, and pantomimes.

The owner of a copyright has a bundle of rights that enable him or her to control how the work may be used. These include the exclusive right to copy and distribute the protected work, to create works derived from it (updated editions of a book, for example), and to display and perform the work. These rights come into existence automatically the moment a work is created. The owner need not take any additional steps or file legal documents to secure a copyright.

Copyright owners typically profit from their works by selling or licensing all or some of these rights to others—publishers, for example. (See "Copyright Ownership," below, for more on establishing and transferring copyrights.)

RESOURCE

For a detailed discussion of copyrights and copyright law, see *The Copyright Handbook: What Every Writer Needs to Know,* by Stephen Fishman (Nolo).

Patents

Federal patent law (35 U.S.C. §§ 100 and following) protects inventions that are new, useful, and not obvious to someone versed in the relevant technology. To obtain a patent, an inventor must file an application with the U.S. Patent and Trademark Office (USPTO) in Washington, DC, and pay a fee. If the USPTO determines that the invention is sufficiently new, useful, and unobvious, it will issue the inventor a patent.

A patent gives an inventor a monopoly on the use and commercial exploitation of the invention. A patent lasts 20 years from the application date. Anyone who wants to use or sell a patented invention during a patent's term must obtain the patent owner's permission. A patent may protect articles—for example, machines, chemical manufactures, and biological creations—and processes—that is, methods of accomplishing things.

RESOURCE

For a detailed discussion of patents and patent law, see *Patent It Yourself,* by David Pressman (Nolo).

Trade Secrets

A trade secret is information that other people do not generally know and that provides its owner with a competitive advantage in the marketplace. The information can be an idea, writing, formula, process or procedure, technical design, customer list, marketing plan, or any other secret that gives the owner an economic advantage.

To establish a trade secret, you must take reasonable steps to keep the information or know-how a secret—for example, by not publishing it or otherwise making it freely available to the public. The laws of most states will protect the owner from disclosures of the secret by:

- the owner's employees
- people who agree not to disclose it, such as independent contractors the owner hires
- industrial spies, and
- competitors who wrongfully acquire the information.

In the course of your work, you may be exposed to your client's most valuable trade secrets—for example, highly confidential marketing plans, new products under development, manufacturing techniques, or customer lists. Understandably, your client doesn't want you blabbing its trade secrets to others, particularly its competitors.

To make sure you'll keep such information confidential, many clients will ask you to sign a nondisclosure agreement stating that you may not reveal the client's trade secrets to others without permission. A nondisclosure provision can be included in a client agreement or can be a separate document. Carefully review any nondisclosure provision a client asks you to sign.

On the other hand, you may have your own trade secrets you don't want others you deal with to disclose. In this event, you should ask them to sign your own nondisclosure agreement. (See "Using Nondisclosure Agreements," below, for a detailed discussion of nondisclosure agreements and a sample form.)

Trademarks

State and federal trademark laws protect the right to exclusively use a name, logo, or other device that identifies and distinguishes a product or service. In addition to names and logos, trademark law can be used to protect product packaging designs and the shape or design of a product—for example, a Coca-Cola bottle. If a competitor uses a protected trademark, the trademark holder can go to court to stop the use and obtain money damages.

RESOURCE

For additional information on trademarks, see *Trademark: Legal Care for Your Business & Product Name,* by Stephen Elias (Nolo).

Copyright Ownership

Any work of authorship you produce for a client is automatically protected by a copyright the moment it is created. At that same moment, somebody becomes the owner of the copyright. Who owns the copyright in a work you create is important because the owner alone has the right to copy, distribute, or otherwise commercially exploit the work—that is, to earn money from it. Unfortunately, self-employed people and hiring firms can get into disputes about who owns the copyright in the work the self-employed person creates.

To avoid disputes over ownership, you need to understand some of the basics of copyright law, which this section provides.

Types of Intellectual Property			
	What Is Protected?	**Examples**	**Length of Protection**
Trade Secret	Formula, method, device, machine, compilation of facts, or any information that is confidential and gives a business an advantage	Coca-Cola formula; special method for assembling a patented invention; new invention for which a patent application has not been filed	As long as information remains confidential and functions as a trade secret
Utility Patent	Machines, compositions, plants, processes, or articles of manufacture	Cellular telephone; the drug known as Vicodin; a hybrid daffodil; the Amazon one-click process; a rake	17 years from date of issue for patents filed before or on June 17, 1995; 20 years from date of filing for patent applications filed after June 17, 1995
Copyright	Books, photos, music, recordings, fine art, graphics, videos, film, architecture, or computer programs	*The Firm* (book and movie); Andy Warhol prints; Roy Orbison's Greatest Hits (music recording, compact disc, artwork, and video); architectural plans for design of apartment building; Macromedia Dreamweaver program	Life of the author plus 70 years for works created by a single author; 120 years from date of creation or 95 years from first publication for other works such as works made for hire
Trademark	Word, symbol, logo, design, slogan, trade dress, or product configuration	Nike name and distinctive swoosh logo; "What Do You Want To Do Today" slogan; Mr. Clean character; Absolut vodka bottle	As long as business continuously uses the trademark in connection with goods, but federal registrations must be renewed every 10 years

Works Created by Independent Contractors

Self-employed workers ordinarily qualify as independent contractors for copyright purposes. The fundamental rule is that independent contractors own the copyright in works of authorship they create for a client unless they sign a piece of paper transferring those rights to the client. Without your signature on such a document, the client—the person who paid you to create the work—may have no copyright rights at all or, at most, may share copyright ownership with you.

As the owner of the copyright, you have the right to resell your work to others or to copy, distribute, and create new works based on the work.

EXAMPLE:

Tom hires Jane, an independent-contractor computer programmer, to create a computer program. Tom and Jane have an oral work agreement. Jane creates the program. Because Jane never signed an agreement transferring any of her copyright rights to Tom, Jane still owns all the copyright rights in the program. Jane has the exclusive right to sell the program to others or permit them to use it. Even though Tom paid Jane to create the program, he doesn't own it and can't sell or license it to others.

In the real world, copyrights are rarely left to fate. Independent contractors are normally asked to sign written agreements transferring all or some of their copyright rights to the client who hires them. But

You Don't Need a C in a Circle to Have a Copyright

Many self-employed people don't know that a work need not contain a copyright notice—the familiar © symbol followed by the publication date and copyright owner's name—to be protected by copyright laws. Likewise, you are not required to register your copyright.

Giving others notice of the copyright and registering it are both optional. However, both are highly desirable if the work is published. They enable the copyright owner to receive the maximum money damages possible if someone copies and uses the work without permission and the owner files and wins a copyright-infringement suit.

You can register your copyright by filling out a short registration form and sending it to the U.S. Copyright Office in Washington, DC, along with one or two copies of the work and a fee.

For more information on copyrights, see *The Copyright Handbook: What Every Writer Needs to Know,* by Stephen Fishman (Nolo).

if you find yourself working with an inexperienced client who doesn't understand the ownership rules, be sure to take the initiative and set forth in writing who will own the copyright in your work.

Copyright transfers can take one of three forms, which we'll discuss further below. You can:

- transfer some of your rights
- transfer all of your rights, or
- sign a work-for-hire agreement, which transfers all of your copyright rights and then some.

Which rights you transfer to clients and which you keep for yourself is a matter for negotiation. If you give up your copyright, you may be able to negotiate a higher fee for your services, but you may lose future income on the copyright. (See "Dividing Up Your Copyright Bundle," below.)

After you and the client reach an agreement on copyright ownership, one of you must write a copyright transfer agreement, and you both must sign it to make it legally valid. You may include the understanding as a clause in a client agreement or negotiate it as a separate freestanding agreement.

! CAUTION

Beware of conflicting copyright transfers. If you're performing similar work for two or more clients simultaneously and agree to assign the intellectual property rights in your work to both clients, you could end up transferring the same rights twice. Before you agree to sell a client anything you create, review your existing agreements to make sure you haven't already sold it.

Transferring Some Rights

You are not legally required to give a client all your copyright rights. You can transfer some rights and retain others. When you do this, you may sell the rights you retain to people other than the client.

As discussed above, a copyright is really a bundle of rights, including the exclusive rights to copy, distribute, perform, and display a work and create derivative works (such as adaptations or new editions) from a work. Each of these rights can be transferred together or separately. They can also be divided and subdivided by media, geography, time, market segment, or any other way you and a client can think up. You can often make more money by dividing up your copyright rights and selling them piecemeal to several different purchasers than you could selling them all to a single client.

Exactly how you can most profitably divide your copyright rights depends on the nature of the work and the market for it. For example, the copyright in a computer program is often divided by geography or type of computer system.

Photographer Wins Pyrrhic Victory Against Magazine

Resolving copyright ownership disputes can take a great deal of time, angst, and money if you have to go to court. Even if you eventually win your case, you may feel like a loser. Consider the case of Marco, a professional photographer who took photographs for several issues of *Accent Magazine,* a trade journal for the jewelry industry, over a six-month period. Marco had an oral agreement with the magazine and was paid a fee of about $150 per photograph. *Accent,* claiming it owned the copyright in the photos, wanted to reuse them without paying Marco an additional fee. Marco claimed that he owned the photos and that *Accent* had to pay him for permission to use them again. Marco and the magazine were never able to resolve the issue of who owned the photos.

When the magazine tried to use the photos without Marco's permission, he asked a court to block publication. The court refused, and Marco filed an appeal with the federal appeals court in Philadelphia. After about two years, Marco won his appeal. But he probably ended up spending far more on attorneys' fees than the photos were worth. (*Marco v. Accent Publishing Co., Inc.,* 969 F.2d 1547 (3d Cir. 1992).)

EXAMPLE:

Bill, a famous freelance video game designer, is hired by Fun & Sun Gameware to create a new video game. He signs an agreement transferring to Gameware the right to distribute the game for the Nintendo video game system in the United States only. Bill retains all his other copyright rights. He sells the right to publish the game in Japan to Nippon Games and sells the right to create a film based on the game to Repulsive Pictures.

The copyright in a magazine article may be divided by priority of publication—that is, a writer may grant a magazine the right to publish an article for the first time and then retain the rights to sell it to others later. Freelance writers often earn substantial income by selling reprint rights to their work. Similarly, graphic artists often grant a client the right to use an image or design only in a certain publishing category and keep the right to resell their work for use in other categories.

EXAMPLE:

Sally, a self-employed graphic designer, creates and sells 25 spot illustrations for use in a school textbook. She grants the textbook publisher the exclusive right to use the images in textbooks but retains the right to sell them to others to use for different purposes—for example, in magazine articles.

When you divide up your copyright rights this way, the transfer is often called a "license." Licenses fall into two broad categories: exclusive and nonexclusive.

Exclusive Licenses

When a copyright owner grants someone an exclusive license, he or she gives that person, called the "licensee," the exclusive right to one or more, but not all, of the copyright rights. An exclusive license is a transfer of copyright ownership. It must be in writing to be valid.

EXAMPLE:

Jane writes an article on economics and grants *The Economist's Journal* the exclusive right to publish it for the first time in the United States and Canada. Jane has granted the *Journal* an exclusive license. Only the *Journal* may publish the article for the first time in the United States and Canada; the magazine owns this right. But Jane retains all her other copyright rights.

This means that she has the right to republish her article after it appears in the *Journal* and to include it in a book. She also retains the right to create derivative works from it—for example, to expand it into a book-length work.

Nonexclusive Licenses

In contrast, a nonexclusive license gives a person the right to exercise one or more of a copyright owner's rights but does not prevent the copyright owner from giving other people permission to exercise the same right or rights at the same time. A nonexclusive license is the most limited form of copyright transfer you can grant to a client.

As with exclusive licenses, nonexclusive licenses may be limited as to time, geography, media, or in any other way. They can be granted orally or in writing. The much better practice, however, is to put it in writing; this can avoid possible misunderstandings.

EXAMPLE:

Lawrence, a freelance computer programmer, agrees to create an accounting program for AcmePool, a swimming pool company. Lawrence thinks that other swimming pool companies might be interested in buying the program as well, so he grants AcmePool only a nonexclusive right to use the program. This means he can sell it to others, not just Acme-Pool. AcmePool has no right to sell the program. AcmePool agreed to the deal because Lawrence charged much less than he would have charged had AcmePool acquired ownership of the program.

Transferring All Rights

When people transfer all the copyright rights they own in a work of authorship, the transaction is called an "assignment" or an "all rights transfer." When such a transaction is completed, the original copyright owner no longer has any ownership rights at all. The new owner—the "assignee"—has all the copyright rights the transferor formerly held. The new owner is then free to sell licenses or to assign the copyright to someone else.

An assignment can be made either before or after a work is created, but it must be in writing to be valid. An assignment can be a separate document or it can be included in a client agreement.

EXAMPLE:

Tom hires Jane, a self-employed programmer, to create a computer program. Before Jane starts work, Tom has her sign an independent contractor agreement providing, among other things, that she transfers all her copyright rights in the program to Tom. Jane completes her work and delivers the program, and Tom pays her. Tom owns all the copyright rights in the program.

Works Made for Hire

When employees create works of authorship as part of their jobs, their employers automatically own all the copyright rights in the work. Works created on the job are called "works made for hire." Certain types of works created by independent contractors can also qualify as works made for hire. When a work is made for hire, the person who ordered or commissioned it and paid for it is considered to be the author for copyright purposes, not the person who created it. This commissioning party—not the actual creator—automatically owns all the copyright rights.

Types of Works Made for Hire

Nine categories of works created by independent contractors can be works made for hire:

- a contribution to a collective work (for example, a work created by more than one author, such as a newspaper magazine, anthology, or encyclopedia)
- a part of an audiovisual work (for example, a motion picture screenplay)
- a translation
- supplementary works (for example, forewords, afterwords, supplemental pictorial illustrations, maps, charts, editorial notes, bibliographies, appendixes, and indexes)
- a compilation (for example, an electronic database)

Assignments Can Be Revoked—Eventually

There are many sad stories about authors and artists who were paid a pittance when they were young or unknown, only to have their work become extremely valuable later in their lives or after their deaths. For example, the creators of Superman sold all their copyright rights in Superman to a comic book company for a mere $10,000 when they were in their early twenties. They lived to see the company earn millions from their creation, but they shared in none of this money.

To protect copyright owners and their families from unfair exploitation, the Copyright Act gives authors or their heirs the right to get back full copyright rights 35 years after they were assigned. Authors don't have to pay anything to reclaim their rights: They simply need to file the appropriate documentation with the Copyright Office and the copyright owner to whom they assigned their rights.

EXAMPLE: Art, a teenage video game enthusiast, is hired as an independent contractor in 1980 to create a new computer arcade game by Fun & Sun Gameware. He assigns all his copyright rights in the game to Fun & Sun Gameware for $1,500. The game becomes a best seller and earns Fun & Sun Gameware millions. Art is entitled to none of this money, but he or his heirs can terminate the transfer of copyright rights to Fun & Gameware in the year 2015 and get back all rights in the game without paying Fun & Gameware anything.

This termination right may be exercised only by individual authors or their heirs, and only as to copyright transfers made after 1977. This means that the earliest any assignment can be revoked is the year 2013 (for works created in 1978). However, the creator of a work made for hire has no such termination rights.

- an instructional text
- a test
- answer material for a test, and
- an atlas.

Written Agreement Requirement

It's not enough that your work falls into one of these categories. You and the client must sign a written agreement stating that the work you create shall be a work made for hire. The agreement must be signed before you begin work to be effective. The client cannot wait until after your work is completed and delivered and then decide that it should be a work made for hire.

Think of a work-for-hire agreement as the hydrogen bomb of copyright transfers: When you sign such an agreement, you not only give up all your ownership rights in the work until the end of time, you're not even considered the work's author. You won't be legally entitled to any credit for your work, such as having your name attached if the work is published, unless your agreement with the client requires it.

EXAMPLE:

The editor of *The Egoist Magazine* asks Gloria, a freelance writer, if she would be interested in writing an article for the magazine on nightlife in Palm Beach. Gloria agrees, and the editor sends her a letter agreement setting forth such terms as compensation, article length, and due date. The letter also specifies that the article "shall be a work made for hire."

Gloria signs the agreement, writes the article, and is paid by the magazine. Because the article qualifies as a work made for hire, the magazine is the initial owner of all the copyright rights in the article. The magazine is free to sell reprint rights in the article, film and TV rights, translation rights, and any other rights anyone wants to buy. Gloria is not entitled to license or sell any rights in the article because she doesn't own any.

Many writer and artist organizations strongly advise their members to refuse to sign work-for-hire agreements. However, an increasing number of clients insist on such agreements. In some cases, signing a work-for-hire agreement is a take-it-or-leave-it proposition: If you don't agree to sign, the client will find someone else who will. For example, the *New York Times* now requires freelance contributors to sign work-for-hire agreements; the paper will simply refuse to publish a freelance article unless the author signs on the dotted line.

On the other hand, you can often get a client to agree to something less than a work-for-hire agreement if you ask. If the client refuses, you can still sign the work-for-hire agreement, but you lose nothing by asking.

Sharing Ownership With Clients

If a client does not obtain a copyright transfer from you, you will own the work you create for the client. However, a client who qualifies as a coauthor might be considered a joint owner of the work along with you. For this to occur, the client must actually help you create the work. Giving suggestions or supervision is not enough.

A client who qualifies as a coauthor will jointly share copyright ownership in the work with you. As coauthors, you're each entitled to use or let other people use the work without obtaining approval of the other coauthor. But any profits you make must be shared with the other coauthors. This could cause problems—for example, if coauthors sold the same work to competing publishers, the value of the work could be diluted. It's usually in coauthors' interests to work together to avoid this.

EXAMPLE:

Marlon, a legendary actor, hires Tom, a freelance writer, to ghostwrite his autobiography. Tom is an independent contractor, not Marlon's employee. Marlon fails to have Tom sign a written agreement transferring to Marlon his copyright rights in the work. However, Marlon worked closely with Tom in writing the autobiography, contributing not only ideas but also writing portions of the book.

As a result, Marlon and Tom would probably be considered coauthors and joint owners of the autobiography. Both would have the right to sell the autobiography to a publisher, serialize it in magazines, sell it to movie producers, or otherwise commercially exploit the work. However, Marlon and Tom would have to share any profits earned.

If a client doesn't qualify as a coauthor, at most it will have a nonexclusive right to use the work. But it wouldn't be allowed to sell or license any copyright rights in the work because it wouldn't own any. The independent contractor would own all the rights and be able to sell or license them without the client's permission—and without sharing the profits with the client.

EXAMPLE:

Mark pays Sally, a freelance photographer, to take some pictures of toxic waste dumps to supplement his treatise on toxic waste management. Sally didn't sign an agreement transferring her copyright rights in the photos to Mark. Mark does not qualify as a coauthor of the photos because he didn't help take them. As a result, Sally owns the copyright in the photos. Mark has a nonexclusive license to use the photos in his treatise, but this doesn't prevent Sally from selling the photos to others or otherwise exploiting her copyright rights.

Patent Ownership

Patent rights initially belong to the person who develops an invention. However, patent rights can be assigned—that is, transferred—to others just as copyrights can. Firms that hire independent contractors to help create new technology or anything else that might qualify for a patent normally have the independent contractors assign to them in advance all patent rights in the work. Such an assignment may be included in an independent contractor agreement or in a separate document.

If you have no signed assignment, it's far from clear who will own inventions you develop. Unlike copyrights, where silence indicates independent contractor ownership, there is no such presumption in the world of patents. The law regarding ownership of inventions by employees is very clear—an employer owns any inventions an employee was hired to create. But courts have just begun to address who owns inventions made by independent contractors in the absence of a written ownership agreement.

You can assert ownership over your invention or other work, but be prepared for a costly legal dispute if you do. The client could claim you had a duty to assign your patent rights to it even though there was no written assignment agreement. You would probably have a good chance of winning such a case, but it would not be a sure thing. It's best to avoid such disputes in advance by clearly defining in writing who will own the work.

Trade Secret Ownership

Trade secret ownership rules are similar to those for patents. You are the initial owner of any trade secrets you develop while working for a client. But ownership rights in trade secrets can be assigned to others just as patents can be. Hiring firms typically require independent contractors to sign written agreements assigning their trade secret ownership rights to the client in advance.

In the absence of such an agreement, you probably own your trade secrets and can sell them to others, including the client's competitors. However, if you used the client's resources to develop the trade secret information, the client might have a nonexclusive license to use it without your permission. This is called a "shop right."

Using Nondisclosure Agreements

It is relatively simple to protect tangible valuables, like jewelry, computers, and luxury cars that you can lock up in vaults, drawers, or garages. But it is not so easy to protect knowledge and ideas, even though such intellectual property may be the key to building your creative dream. Many self-employed entrepreneurs are fearful of sharing their intellectual property with others, which they almost always have to do to gain financial backing on other essential deals or partnerships. Fortunately, the informed and consistent use of well-drafted nondisclosure agreements can help you protect these assets if you have to disclose them to potential backers, partners, clients, and others.

What Is a Nondisclosure Agreement?

Nondisclosure agreements—also known as NDAs or confidentiality agreements—are frequently used in the business world before confidential information is disclosed. Nondisclosure agreements have just one purpose: to protect your trade secrets. Trade secrets include any information that is not generally known that has economic value or gives you a competitive edge. It includes—but is not limited to—such things as:

- unpublished computer code
- product development (and other related) agreements

- business plans
- financial projections
- marketing plans
- sales data
- cost and pricing information
- customer lists, and
- patent pending applications.

By using a nondisclosure agreement, you agree to share such information only after the other party agrees, in writing, to keep the information secret.

Using a nondisclosure agreement accomplishes several basic purposes:

- It conclusively establishes that the person to whom you disclose the information has a legal duty not to disclose your trade secrets without your permission.
- It makes clear to the person who receives a trade secret that it must be kept in confidence. This will impress upon him or her that you are serious about maintaining your trade secrets.
- If you ever file a lawsuit, a signed nondisclosure agreement will help you prove that you treated the information you disclosed as a trade secret and that the person to whom you disclosed the information knew that he or she should keep it confidential.

When to Use a Nondisclosure Agreement

Before you give any person access to information that gives you a competitive advantage, you should have him or her sign a nondisclosure agreement. You may need to ask any or all of the following people to sign:

- clients and potential clients
- employees and potential employees
- consultants or independent contractors
- business partners and investors
- licensees or customers, and
- suppliers.

Clients

It will often be necessary for you to disclose your trade secrets to people and companies for whom you perform your services or sell your ideas. For example, a self-employed computer programmer may have to make trade secret computer code available to a client, or an inventor may have to disclose the idea for a new invention to a manufacturer. Always try to have the client sign a nondisclosure agreement before you disclose such information. (Some clients may refuse to do so—see "Nondisclosure Agreements Can Be a Touchy Issue," below.)

Employees

It is advisable to have all employees who may come into contact with your trade secrets sign nondisclosure agreements. Employees should sign such agreements before they begin work or on their very first day of work. If you have employees who have not signed nondisclosure agreements, you should ask them to do so before they are given access to any trade secrets.

If your business is a partnership, all partners should sign a partnership agreement containing a nondisclosure provision.

Consultants or Independent Contractors

The consultant you hire today may end up working for a competitor tomorrow. Never expose a consultant to trade secrets without having a signed nondisclosure agreement on file. It's best to include such an agreement within an overall consulting or independent contractor agreement that covers all aspects of the parties' relationship, including the services to be performed, who will own the consultant's or independent contractor's work product, and payment. Several consultant and independent contractor agreements are included in *Working With Independent Contractors*, by Stephen Fishman (Nolo).

Nondisclosure Agreements Can Be a Touchy Issue

In high-tech industries, nondisclosure agreements are as common as relatives at weddings. However, many people refuse to sign them. Often, venture capitalists, securities analysts, and top consultants refuse to sign NDAs because they review lots of ideas, many of which are similar. They think that signing NDAs will make it impossible for them to do business—and may expose them to the potential for expensive lawsuits. Instead, such people follow the honor system.

Refusal to sign nondisclosure agreements is also common in the publishing industry and in Hollywood, where editors and executives review large numbers of ideas for books and scripts that are often similar in content or focus. Occasionally, companies outside the United States, where business is sometimes less legalistic, may also balk at signing NDAs.

Possibly the best way to deal with this problem is to take the time to develop a relationship of trust with the people with whom you are considering working before telling them all your best ideas. This might involve dealing with lower-level information and ideas to see how they are treated before revealing your most important information.

However, some people and companies will never sign an NDA. In that event, you must decide whether to go ahead and disclose the information or walk away. If the person or company has an impeccable reputation for integrity, you may conclude that it is worthwhile to go ahead and make the disclosure anyway.

Keep in mind that you may be able to successfully sue such people for trade secret violations even if they haven't signed an NDA. You'll need to consult with a lawyer if you find yourself in this situation.

Business Partners and Investors

Trade secrets must frequently be disclosed during negotiations with prospective business partners, investors, licensees, suppliers, or customers. It's advisable to have the other party sign a non-disclosure agreement before you disclose any trade secrets. This way, you will be protected if the negotiations do not result in a final agreement.

Other Means of Protecting Trade Secrets

Using nondisclosure agreements is the single most important thing you can do to protect your trade secrets. But it's not your only strategy. You don't have to turn your office into an armed camp to protect your trade secrets, but you must take reasonable precautions to keep them confidential.

Such precautions may include:

- marking documents containing trade secrets "Confidential"
- locking away trade secret materials after business hours
- maintaining computer security
- limiting the number of people who know about your confidential information, and
- destroying documents containing trade secrets as soon as the documents are no longer needed.

Drafting a Nondisclosure Agreement

This section describes a sample nondisclosure agreement that you can use with any outside individual or company to whom you grant access to your trade secrets. The full agreement is included as a tear-out form in Appendix B.

Introductory Paragraph

Fill in the date the agreement will take effect. This can be the date it is signed or a date in the future. Next, fill in the name you use for your business. You are referred to as the "Discloser" throughout the rest of the agreement. Finally, fill in the name of the individual or company you are granting access to your trade secrets, referred to as the "Recipient."

Suggested Language:

This is an agreement, effective _____ , between _____ (the "Discloser") and _____ (the "Recipient"), in which Discloser agrees to disclose, and Recipient agrees to receive, certain trade secrets of Discloser on the following terms and conditions:

Trade Secrets

Select either alternative clause by checking the appropriate box. Here's how to choose:

Alternative 1. It's best to specifically identify the trade secrets covered by the agreement, so use this clause if you can individually list the material you are providing. However, be careful that your description is not so narrowly worded that it may leave out important information you wish to have covered by the agreement. If you later discover that you want to disclose confidential information not included in the agreement, you and the other person or company can complete and sign an addendum identifying the additional protected information. Alternatively, you could complete a whole new NDA.

Suggested Language:

Recipient understands and acknowledges that the following information constitutes trade secrets belonging to Discloser: _____

_____

Alternative 2. Use this clause if it's not possible to specifically identify the trade secrets you are providing—for example, if the information you will disclose does not exist when you sign the agreement, if you're not sure what you will be disclosing, or if it's simply too much trouble to identify everything that you could disclose. This clause contains a general description of the types of information covered. It includes virtually everything that could be a trade secret.

> **Suggested Language:**
>
> Recipient understands and acknowledges that Discloser's trade secrets consist of information and materials that are valuable and not generally known by Discloser's competitors. Discloser's trade secrets include:
>
> (a) Any and all information concerning Discloser's current, future, or proposed products, including, but not limited to, formulas, designs, devices, computer code, drawings, specifications, notebook entries, technical notes and graphs, computer printouts, technical memoranda and correspondence, product development agreements, and related agreements.
>
> (b) Information and materials relating to Discloser's purchasing, accounting, and marketing, including, but not limited to, marketing plans, sales data, business methods, unpublished promotional material, cost and pricing information, and customer lists.
>
> (c) Information of the type described above that Discloser obtained from another party and that Discloser treats as confidential, whether or not owned or developed by Discloser.
>
> (d) Other: _____
>
> _____

Purpose of Disclosure

Describe the reason for disclosing trade secrets. For example, this may be for you to perform consulting services for the recipient or to further the parties' business relationship.

> **Suggested Language:**
>
> Recipient shall make use of Discloser's trade secrets only for the purpose of: _____
>
> _____

Nondisclosure

This provision is the heart of the agreement. The Recipient promises to treat the Discloser's trade secrets with a reasonable degree of care and not to disclose them to third parties without the Discloser's consent. Recipient also promises not to make commercial use of the information without Discloser's permission.

Finally, the Recipient may not disclose the information to its employees or consultants unless they have signed confidentiality agreements protecting the trade secret rights of third parties, such as the Discloser. If an employee or consultant has signed such an agreement, it's not necessary for him or her to sign a separate agreement promising to keep the Discloser's information confidential.

If the Recipient breaks these promises, the Discloser can sue in court to obtain monetary damages and possibly a court order to prevent the Recipient from using the information.

Suggested Language:

In consideration of Discloser's disclosure of its trade secrets to Recipient, Recipient agrees that it will treat Discloser's trade secrets with the same degree of care and safeguards that it takes with its own trade secrets, but in no event less than a reasonable degree of care. Recipient agrees that, without Discloser's prior written consent, Recipient will not:

(a) disclose Discloser's trade secrets to any third party;

(b) make or permit to be made copies or other reproductions of Discloser's trade secrets; or

(c) make any commercial use of the trade secrets.

Recipient represents that it has, and agrees to maintain, an appropriate agreement with each of its employees and independent contractors who may have access to any of Discloser's trade secrets sufficient to enable Recipient to comply with all the terms of this Agreement.

Return of Materials

In this clause, the Recipient promises to return original materials you've provided, as well as copies, notes, and documents pertaining to the trade secrets. This agreement gives Recipient 30 days to return the materials, but you can change this time period if you wish.

Suggested Language:

Upon Discloser's request, Recipient shall promptly (within 30 days) return all original materials provided by Discloser and any copies, notes, or other documents in Recipient's possession pertaining to Discloser's trade secrets.

Exclusions

This provision describes all the types of information that are not covered by the agreement. These exclusions are based on court decisions and state trade secret laws that say these types of information do not qualify for trade secret protection.

Suggested Language:

This agreement does not apply to any information that:

(a) was in Recipient's possession or was known to Recipient, without an obligation to keep it confidential, before such information was disclosed to Recipient by Discloser;

(b) is or becomes public knowledge through a source other than Recipient and through no fault of Recipient;

(c) is or becomes lawfully available to Recipient from a source other than Discloser; or

(d) is disclosed by Recipient with Discloser's prior written approval.

Term of Agreement

There are two alternative provisions dealing with the agreement's "term," which is the length of time the agreement remains in effect. Select the clause that best suits your needs by checking the appropriate box.

Alternative 1. This provision has no definite time limit—in other words, the Recipient's obligation of confidentiality lasts until the trade secret information ceases to be a trade secret. This may occur when the information becomes generally known, is disclosed to the public by the Discloser, or ceases being a trade secret for some other reason. This gives the Discloser the broadest protection possible. Disclosers ordinarily prefer to use this provision.

Suggested Language:

This Agreement and Recipient's duty to hold Discloser's trade secrets in confidence shall remain in effect until the above-described trade secrets are no longer trade secrets or until Discloser sends Recipient written notice releasing Recipient from this Agreement, whichever occurs first.

Alternative 2. Some recipients don't want to be subject to open-ended confidentiality obligations. Use this clause if the Recipient requires that the agreement state a definite date by which the agreement—and the Recipient's confidentiality obligations—expires. Five years is a common time period, but the time limit can be much shorter, even as little as six months. In Internet and technology businesses, the time period may need to be shorter because of the fast pace of innovation. But the Discloser should attempt to make sure the time period lasts as long as the confidential information is likely to remain valuable.

Suggested Language:

This Agreement and Recipient's duty to hold Discloser's trade secrets in confidence shall remain in effect until _____ or until whichever of the following occurs first:

- Discloser sends Recipient written notice releasing Recipient from this Agreement, or
- the above-described trade secrets are no longer trade secrets.

No Rights Granted

This provision makes clear that the Recipient is acquiring absolutely no ownership rights in or to the information. This means the Recipient cannot sell or license the information to others.

Suggested Language:

Recipient understands and agrees that this Agreement does not constitute a grant or an intention or commitment to grant any right, title, or interest in Discloser's trade secrets to Recipient.

Warranty

A warranty is a promise. In this provision, the Discloser promises to the Recipient that it has the right to disclose the information. This is intended to assure the Recipient that it won't be sued by some third party who claims the trade secrets belonged to it and that the Discloser had no right to reveal them to the Recipient.

Suggested Language:

Discloser warrants that it has the right to make the disclosures under this Agreement.

Injunctive Relief

If the Recipient violates a nondisclosure agreement, one of the most important legal remedies a trade secret owner can obtain is an "injunction"—a court order preventing the violator from using or profiting from the Discloser's trade secrets.

This provision is intended to make such a court order easier for the Discloser to obtain. Some Recipients may object to including this provision because they want to make it as hard as possible for the Discloser to obtain an injunction.

> **Suggested Language:**
>
> Recipient acknowledges and agrees that in the event of a breach or threatened breach of this Agreement, money damages would be an inadequate remedy and extremely difficult to measure. Recipient agrees, therefore, that Discloser shall be entitled to an injunction to restrain Recipient from such breach or threatened breach. Nothing in this Agreement shall be construed as preventing Discloser from pursuing any remedy at law or in equity for any breach or threatened breach.

Attorneys' Fees

This agreement says that if a lawsuit is brought to enforce the agreement, the loser pays the winner's attorneys' fees. Without such a provision, attorneys' fees are usually not recoverable.

> **Suggested Language:**
>
> If any legal action arises relating to this Agreement, the prevailing party shall be entitled to recover all court costs, expenses, and reasonable attorneys' fees.

Modifications

This provision requires that any changes to the agreement be made in writing and signed by both parties to be legally effective. This means, for example, that a change agreed to over the telephone won't be legally enforceable. To be enforceable, one of the parties must write down the change and both parties must sign it.

> **Suggested Language:**
>
> This Agreement represents the entire agreement between the parties regarding the subject matter and supersedes all prior agreements or understandings between them. All additions or modifications to this Agreement must be made in writing and signed by both parties to be effective.

No Agency

This clause is intended to make clear to both parties that the nondisclosure agreement does not make the two parties partners or allow either party to act as an agent for the other. This prevents either party from entering into contracts or incurring debts on behalf of the other party.

> **Suggested Language:**
>
> This Agreement does not create any agency or partnership relationship between the parties.

Applicable Law

Every state has its own laws regarding contract interpretation. These laws differ from state to state. The parties can choose any state's laws to govern the agreement, regardless of where they are located or where the agreement is signed. It's usually advantageous to have the law of your home state govern the agreement, because this is the law both you and your attorney are probably most familiar with. However, state laws on trade secrecy don't differ enough to make this a make-or-break issue.

> **Suggested Language:**
>
> This Agreement is made under, and shall be construed according to, the laws of the State of _____
> _____.

Signatures

The parties don't have to be in the same room when they sign the agreement. It's even fine if the dates are a few days apart. But the NDA is not valid until both parties have signed it. So don't start revealing your secrets until then. Each party should sign at least two copies, and keep at least one. This way, both parties have an original signed agreement. (See "Putting Your Agreement Together," in Chapter 18, for detailed information on how to sign a legal agreement.)

Using Written Client Agreements

A contract—also called an agreement—is a legally binding promise. Whenever you agree to perform services for a client, you enter into a contract: You promise to do work, and the client promises to pay you for it.

The word "contract" often intimidates people who conjure up visions of voluminous legal documents laden with legalese. However, a contract need not be long or complex. Many contracts consist of only a few simple paragraphs. Indeed, most contracts don't even have to be in writing. Even so, it's never a good idea to rely on an oral agreement with a client.

Client Agreements Don't Have to Be Intimidating

Some self-employed workers shy away from using written agreements. You might be afraid of intimidating your clients or making them think you don't trust them. This could happen if you're not careful. For example, a prospective client might think twice about hiring you if you present a 20-page contract for a simple one-day project. The client might conclude that you're either paranoid, hard to deal with, or both.

You can avoid this problem, however, if you calibrate your agreements to your assignments. Use simple contracts or short letter agreements for simple projects and save the longer, more complex agreements for bigger jobs.

Reasons to Use Written Agreements

Most contracts don't have to be in writing to be legally binding. For example, you and a client can enter into a contract over the phone or during a lunch meeting at a restaurant; no magic words need be spoken. You just have to agree to perform services for the client in exchange for something of value—usually money. Theoretically, an oral agreement is as valid as a 50-page contract drafted by a high-powered law firm.

EXAMPLE:

Gary, a freelance translator, receives a phone call from a vice president of Acme Oil Co. The VP asks Gary to translate some Russian oil industry documents for $2,000. Gary says he'll do the work for the price. Gary and Acme have a valid oral contract.

Some Agreements Must Be in Writing

Some types of agreements must be in writing to be legally enforceable. Each state has a law, usually called the "Statute of Frauds," listing the types of contracts that must be in writing to be valid.

A typical list includes:

- Any contract that cannot possibly be performed in less than one year—for example: John agrees to perform consulting services for Acme Corp. for the next two years for $2,000 per month. Because the agreement cannot be performed in less than one year, it must be in writing to be legally enforceable.

- Contracts for the sales of goods—that is, tangible personal property such as a computer or car—worth $500 or more.

- A promise to pay someone else's debt—for example: The president of a corporation personally guarantees to pay for the services you sell to the corporation. The guarantee must be in writing to be legally enforceable.

- Contracts involving the sale of real estate or real estate leases lasting more than one year.

Any transfer of copyright ownership must also be in writing to be valid.

In the real world, however, using oral agreements is like driving without a seatbelt. Things will work out fine as long as you don't have an accident; but if you do have an accident, you'll wish you had buckled up. An oral agreement can work if you and your client agree completely about its terms and both obey them. Unfortunately, things don't always work this way.

Below are some of the most important reasons why you should always sign a written agreement with a client before starting work.

Avoiding Misunderstandings

Courts are crowded with lawsuits filed by people who enter into oral agreements with one another and later disagree over what was said. Costly misunderstandings can develop if you perform services for a client without a writing clearly stating what you're supposed to do. Such misunderstandings may be innocent—for example, you and the client may have simply misinterpreted one another. Or they may be purposeful: Without a writing to contradict him or her, a client can claim that you orally agreed to anything.

Consider a good written client agreement to be your legal lifeline. If disputes develop, the agreement will provide ways to solve them. If you and the client end up in court, a written agreement will establish your legal duties to each other.

For these same reasons, your clients should be happy to sign a well-drafted contract. Be wary of any client who refuses to put your agreement in writing. Such a client might be a bad credit risk. If a prospective client balks at signing an agreement, you may wish to obtain a credit report on the client or talk with others who have worked for that client to see if they had any problems. If you think the client might pose a problem when it comes to paying you, ask for a substantial down payment up front and for periodic payments if the project is lengthy.

Written Agreements Preempt Talk

When you put your agreement in writing, it is usually treated as the final word on the areas it covers. That is, it takes precedence over anything that you and the client said to each other but did not include in your written agreement.

However, if you and the client end up in court or arbitration because you disagree over the terms or meaning of your contract, the things you and the client said to each other during the negotiating process but didn't write down can be used to explain unclear terms in the written contract or to prove additional terms where the writing is incomplete. Because you and the client may disagree about what was said during negotiations, it's best to make the written contract as clear and complete as possible.

Assuring That You Get Paid

A written agreement clearly setting out your fees will help ward off disputes about how much the client agreed to pay you. If a client fails to pay and you have to negotiate or eventually even sue for your money, the written agreement will be proof of how much you're owed. Relying on an oral agreement with a client can make it very difficult for you to get paid in full—or at all.

Oral Agreement Costs IC $600

One self-employed worker learned the hard way that an oral agreement isn't worth the paper on which it's not printed. Jane, a commercial illustrator who worked as a freelancer, orally agreed to do a series of drawings for a dress designer. Jane did the drawings and submitted her bill for $2,000. The designer refused to pay, alternately claiming that payment was conditional on the drawings being published in a fashion magazine and that Jane was charging too much.

Jane filed a lawsuit against the designer in small claims court to collect her $2,000. The judge had no trouble finding that Jane had an enforceable oral contract with the designer, who admitted that he had asked Jane to do the work. However, the judge awarded Jane only $1,400 because she could not document her claim that she was to be paid $100 per hour, and the designer made a convincing presentation that illustrators usually charge no more than $70 per hour.

Defining Projects

The process of deciding what to include in an agreement helps both you and the client. It forces you both to think carefully, perhaps for the first time, about exactly what you're supposed to do. Hazy and ill-defined ideas get reduced to a concrete contract specification or description of the work that you will perform. This gives you and the client a yardstick by which to measure your performance, the best way to avoid later disputes that you haven't performed adequately.

Establishing Independent Contractor Status

A well-drafted client agreement will also help establish that you are an independent contractor, not the client's employee. You can suffer severe consequences if the IRS or another government agency decides you're an employee instead of an independent contractor. (See Chapter 15.)

Reviewing a Client's Agreement

Many clients have their own agreements they'll ask you to sign. This may be a copy of an agreement they've used in the past with other people they've hired, a standard agreement prepared by an attorney, or a letter summarizing the terms to which you've agreed. You'll almost always be better off using your own agreement, not one provided by your client, because it gives you the greatest control over the contract terms. Take the initiative and send the client an agreement to sign immediately after you accept an assignment: Do not wait for the client to provide you with an agreement of its own.

If a client insists on using its own agreement, read that document carefully. It may contain provisions that are unfair to you—for example, provisions requiring you to repay the client if an IRS auditor determines that you're an employee and imposes fines and penalties against the client. Pay special attention to noncompetition provisions that restrict your right to work for other companies and nondisclosure provisions that prevent you from using information you learn while working for the client.

Remember that any contract can be rewritten, even if the client claims it's a standard agreement that all outside workers sign. This is a matter for negotiation. Seek to delete or rewrite unfair provisions. There may also be provisions you want to add. (See "Provisions to Consider Adding" in Chapter 20.)

RESOURCE

For practical guidance on how to conduct contract negotiations, see:

- *Getting to Yes: Negotiating Agreement Without Giving In*, by Roger Fisher, et al. (Penguin Books)
- *Negotiating Rationally*, by Max H. Bazerman and Margaret A. Neale (Free Press), and
- *Win-Win Negotiating: Turning Conflict Into Agreement*, by Fred E. Jandt (Wiley).

Creating Your Own Client Agreement

You don't need to hire a lawyer to draft an independent contractor agreement. All you need is a brain and a little common sense. This book contains a number of sample forms you can use and guidance on how to tailor them to fit your particular needs. This may take a little work, but when you're done, you'll have an agreement you can use over and over again with minor alterations.

Types of Agreements

There are two main types of client agreements. Use the type of agreement that best suits your needs and the needs of your clients.

Letter Agreements

A letter agreement is usually a short contract written in the form of a letter. After you and the client reach a tentative agreement—over the phone, in a meeting, by fax, or by email—you set forth the contract terms in a letter written on your stationery, sign two copies, and send them to the client. If the client agrees to the terms in the letter, he or she signs both copies at the bottom and returns one signed copy to you. At that point, you and the client have a fully enforceable, valid contract. Many self-employed people use letter agreements because they seem less intimidating to clients than more formal-looking contracts. Others use them because of business custom.

Standard Contracts

A standard contract usually contains a number of paragraphs and captions. It is usually longer and more comprehensive than a letter agreement. It's a good idea to use a standard contract if:

- the project is long and complex or involves a substantial amount of money, or
- you're dealing with a client you don't trust, either because the client is new or because your past dealings indicate the client is untrustworthy.

Proposals Are Not Client Agreements

Clients often choose the outside workers they hire through a competitive bidding process. They ask a number of people to submit written proposals describing how they'll perform the work and the price they'll charge. The client chooses the IC who submits the best proposal.

Some self-employed people write quite lengthy and detailed proposals and depend on them instead of standard contracts. This is a mistake. Proposals do not normally address many important issues that should be covered in a contract, such as the term (length) of the agreement, how it can be terminated, and how disputes will be resolved. If a problem arises that is not covered by the proposal, you and the client will have to negotiate a solution in the middle of the project. If you can't reach a solution, either you or the client may end up taking the other to court to resolve the matter.

The best course is to have a signed contract in hand before starting work. If you submit a proposal to a client, it should state that if the client agrees to proceed, you will forward a contract for signature within a specified number of days.

The Drafting Process

Draft contract forms you can use over again with various clients. You can use the forms as the basis for your agreement and make alterations you need to suit the particular situation. If you perform the same type of work for every client, you might need just one or two form agreements. This might include a brief letter agreement for small jobs and a longer standard contract for larger projects. However, if your work varies, you may need several different agreements. If you hire self-employed people to work for you, you'll need an agreement for them as well. (See Chapter 19.)

EXAMPLE:

Ellen, a freelance publicist, usually uses a letter agreement with her clients. However, when she is hired to do a particularly long project, she prefers to use a longer standard contract because it affords her added protection if something goes wrong. She also occasionally hires other freelance publicists to work for her as ICs when she gets very busy. Ellen uses a lengthy subcontractor agreement with them because it helps to establish that they're ICs instead of her employees and makes their duties as clear as possible.

Ellen uses the forms in this book to draft three different IC agreements she keeps on her computer and uses over and over again: a letter agreement, a standard IC agreement, and a subcontractor agreement.

Using the Forms in This Book

Appendix B contains a sample client agreement that almost any self-employed person who sells services can adapt to meet his or her needs. Each of the clauses in the agreement is discussed in detail in Chapter 19. A sample brief letter agreement is also provided and discussed in Chapter 19.

There are two ways to use these clauses. You can retype the language suggested in this book to assemble your own final agreement. This will allow you to tailor your document to your specific needs. Alternatively, you can complete and use the tear-out sample agreement in Appendix B. This is easier than creating your own agreement but gives you less flexibility regarding the content of your agreement.

CAUTION

Retype this form. Your IC agreement will make the best impression on IRS and other government auditors if it looks like a custom-made agreement you've drafted specifically for the client, not a standard form you've torn out of a book. And making a good impression is important if you want to keep your self-employed status and not be viewed as an employee of the client. For this reason, it is advisable to retype the form provided here—whether on a computer or typewriter—and use that instead of the preprinted form in Appendix B.

Putting Your Agreement Together

Whether you use a simple letter agreement or formal standard contract, make sure it's properly signed and put together. This is not difficult if you know what to do.

Signatures

It's best for both you and the client to sign the agreement in ink. You need not be together when you sign, nor do you have to sign at the same time. There's no legal requirement that the signatures be located in any specific place in a business contract, but they are customarily placed at the end of the agreement; that helps signify that you both have read and agreed to the entire document.

It's very important that both you and the client sign the agreement properly. Failure to do so can have drastic consequences. How to sign depends on the legal form of your business and the client's business.

Sole Proprietors

If you or the client are sole proprietors, you can simply sign your own names because a sole proprietorship is not a separate legal entity.

However, if you use a fictitious business name (see Chapter 2), it's best for you to sign on behalf of your business. This will help show that you're an IC, not an employee.

EXAMPLE:

Chris Kraft is a sole proprietor who runs a marketing research business. Instead of using his own name for the business, he calls it AAA Marketing Research. He should sign his contracts like this:

AAA Marketing Research

By: _____

Chris Kraft

Partnerships

If either you or the client is a partnership, a general partner should sign on the partnership's behalf. Only one partner needs to sign. The signature block for the partnership should state the partnership's name and the name and title of the person signing on the partnership's behalf. If a partner signs only his or her name without mentioning the partnership, the partnership is not bound by the agreement.

EXAMPLE:

Chris, a self-employed marketing consultant, contracts to perform marketing research for a Michigan partnership called The Argus Partnership. Randy Argus is one of the general partners. He signs the contract on the partnership's behalf like this:

The Argus Partnership
A Michigan Partnership

By: _____

Randy Argus, a General Partner

If the client is a partnership and the person who signs the agreement is not a partner, the signature should be accompanied by a partnership resolution stating that the person signing the agreement has the authority to do so. A partnership resolution is a document signed by one or more of the general partners stating that the person named has the authority to sign contracts on the partnership's behalf.

Corporations

If either you or the client is a corporation, the agreement must be signed by someone who has authority to sign contracts on the corporation's behalf. The corporation's president or chief executive officer (CEO) is presumed to have this authority.

If someone other than the president of an incorporated client signs—for example, the vice president, treasurer, or other corporate officer— ask to see a board of directors resolution or corporate bylaws authorizing him or her to sign. If the person signing doesn't have authority, the corporation won't be legally bound by the contract.

Keep in mind that if you sign personally instead of on your corporation's behalf, you'll be personally liable for the contract.

The signature block for a corporation should state the name of the corporation and indicate by name and title the person signing on the corporation's behalf.

EXAMPLE:

Chris, a self-employed marketing consultant, contracts to perform marketing research with a corporation called Kiddie Krafts, Inc. The contract is signed by Susan Ericson. Because she is the president of the corporation, Chris doesn't need a corporate resolution showing she has authority to bind the corporation. The signature block should appear in the contract like this:

> Kiddie Krafts, Inc.
>
> A California Partnership
>
> By: _____
>   Susan Ericson, President

Limited Liability Companies

The owners of a limited liability company (LLC) are called "members." Members may hire others to run their LLC for them. These people are called "managers." If either you or your client is an LLC, the agreement should be signed by a member or manager on the LLC's behalf.

EXAMPLE:

Amy Smart, a California-based self-employed graphic artist, has formed an LLC to run her business called Great Graphics, LLC. She should sign all her agreements like this:

> Great Graphics, LLC
>
> A California Limited Liability Company
>
> By: _____
>   Amy Smart, Member

Dates

When you sign an agreement, include the date and make sure the client does, too. You can simply put a date line next to the place where each person signs—for example:

Date: _____ , 20xx

You and the client don't have to sign on the same day. Indeed, you can sign weeks apart.

Attachments or Exhibits

An easy way to keep a letter agreement or standard contract as short as possible is to use attachments, also called "exhibits." You can use them to list lengthy details such as performance specifications. This makes the main body of the agreement shorter and easier to read.

If you have more than one attachment or exhibit, they should be numbered or lettered—for example, "Attachment 1" or "Exhibit A." Be sure that the main body of the agreement mentions that the attachments or exhibits are included as part of the contract.

Altering the Contract

Sometimes it's necessary to make last-minute changes to a contract just before it's signed. If you use a computer to prepare the agreement, it's usually easy to make the changes and print out a new agreement.

However, it's not necessary to prepare a new contract. Instead, the changes may be handwritten or typed onto all existing copies of the agreement. If you use this approach, be sure that all those signing the agreement also sign their initials as close as possible to the place where the change is made. If both people who sign don't initial each change, questions might arise as to whether the change was part of the agreement.

Copies of the Contract

Prepare at least two copies of your letter agreement or standard contract. Make sure that each copy contains all the needed exhibits and attachments. Both you and the client should sign both copies—and you should each keep one copy of the complete agreement signed by both parties.

Faxing the Contract

It has become very common for self-employed people and their clients to communicate by email or fax. People often send drafts of their proposed agreement back and forth to each other by fax or email. When the parties reach a final agreement, one signs a copy of the contract and faxes it to the other, who signs it and faxes it back.

A faxed signature is probably legally sufficient if neither you nor the client dispute that it is a fax of an original signature. However, if a client claims that a faxed signature was forged, it could be difficult or impossible to prove it's genuine, because it is very easy to forge a faxed signature with modern computer technology. Forgery claims are rare, however, so this is usually not a problem. Even so, it's a good practice for you and the client to follow up the fax with signed originals exchanged by mail or delivery service.

Changing the Agreement After It's Signed

No contract is engraved in stone. You and the client can always modify or amend your contract if circumstances change. You can even agree to call the whole thing off and cancel your agreement.

EXAMPLE:

Barbara, a self-employed well digger, agrees to dig a 50-foot-deep well on property owned by Kate for $2,000. After digging ten feet, Barbara hits solid rock that no one knew was there. To complete the well, she'll have to lease expensive heavy equipment. To defray the added expense, she asks Kate to pay her $4,000 instead of $2,000 for the work. Kate agrees. Barbara and Kate have amended their original agreement.

Neither you nor the client is ever obligated to accept a proposed modification to your contract. Either of you can always say no and accept the consequences. At its most dire, this may mean a court battle over breaking the original contract. However, you're usually better off reaching some

sort of agreement with the client, unless he or she is totally unreasonable.

Unless your contract is one that must be in writing to be legally valid—for example, an agreement that can't be performed in less than one year—it can usually be modified by an oral agreement. In other words, you need not write down the changes.

EXAMPLE:

Art signs a contract with Zeno to build an addition to his house. Halfway through the project, Art decides that he wants Zeno to do some extra work not covered by their original agreement. Art and Zeno have a telephone conversation in which Zeno agrees to do the extra work for extra money. Although nothing is put in writing, their change to their original agreement is legally enforceable.

Many self-employed workers and their clients change their contracts often and never write down the changes. The flexibility afforded by such an informal approach to contract amendments might be just what you want. However, misunderstandings and disputes can arise from this approach. It's always best to have some sort of writing showing what you've agreed to do. You can do this informally. For example, you can simply send a confirming letter following a telephone call with the client summarizing the changes you both agreed to make. Be sure to keep a copy for your files.

However, if the amendment involves a contract provision that is very important—your payment, for example—insist on a written amendment and insist that you and the client sign it. The amendment should set forth all the changes and state that the amendment takes precedence over the original contract. Appendix B includes a contract amendment form you can use for this purpose. ●

Drafting Your Own Client Agreement

This chapter guides you in creating a client agreement that you can use for almost any type of service you provide your clients. This is a full-blown formal contract. It covers nearly all concerns you would want covered in an agreement. A tear-out version you can use is included in Appendix B.

Some self-employed people prefer not to use formal contracts because they're afraid they will intimidate clients. If you prefer something a little less formal, this book also provides a short, simple letter agreement that will meet your needs. (See "Using Letter Agreements," below.)

However, it's a good idea to use a more comprehensive formal contract if:

- you are hired to do a project that is long and complex or involves a substantial amount of money, or
- you're dealing with a new client or a client who has been untrustworthy in the past.

RESOURCE

The agreement provided here can be modified for use by almost any self-employed person. If you prefer a ready-made contract, you can find client agreements tailored to specific occupations in *Consultant & Independent Contractor Agreements*, by Stephen Fishman (Nolo), including agreements for use by consultants, household service providers, salespeople, accountants and bookkeepers, artists, writers, and construction contractors. The agreements in that book are included in both tear-out versions and on CD-ROM.

Essential Provisions

There are a number of provisions that should be included in most client agreements. All of these sample clauses are included in the sample agreement provided here. Later in the chapter we'll also show you how an entire agreement might look when assembled.

The provisions here may be all you need for a basic agreement. Or you may need to combine them with some of your own clauses or one or more of the optional clauses discussed in "Optional Provisions," below.

Title of agreement. You don't need a title for a client agreement, but if you want one, call it "Independent Contractor Agreement," "Client Agreement," "Agreement for Professional Services," or "Consulting Agreement." Consulting Agreement may sound a little more high-toned than Independent Contractor Agreement; it is most often used by highly skilled professionals. Because you are not your client's employee, do not use "Employment Agreement" as a title.

Suggested Language:

INDEPENDENT CONTRACTOR AGREEMENT

Names of parties. Here at the beginning of your contract, it's best to refer to yourself by your full business name. Later on in the contract, you can use an obvious abbreviation.

If you're a sole proprietor, use the full name you use for your business. This can be your own name or a fictitious business name or assumed name you use to identify your business. (See Chapter 2.) For example, if consultant Al Brodsky calls his one-person marketing research business "ABC Marketing Research," he would use that name on the contract. Using a fictitious business name helps show that you're a business, not an employee.

If your business is incorporated, use your corporate name, not your own name—for example: "John Smith, Incorporated" instead of "John Smith." Similarly, if you've formed a limited liability company (see Chapter 2), use the name of the LLC, not your personal name—for example, use "Jane Brown, a Limited Liability Corporation" instead of "Jane Brown."

For the sake of brevity, identify yourself and the client by shorter names in the rest of the agreement. You can use an abbreviated version of your full name—for example, "ABC" for ABC Marketing Research. Or you can refer to yourself simply as "Contractor" or "Consultant." Refer to the client initially by its company name and subsequently by a short version of the name or as "Client" or "Firm." Do not refer to yourself as an employee or to the client as an employer.

Include the addresses of the principal place of business of both the client and yourself. If you or the client have more than one office or workplace, the principal place of business is the main office or workplace.

Suggested Language:

This Agreement is made between [*Client's name*] (Client) with a principal place of business at [*Client's business address*] and [*Your name*] (Contractor), with a principal place of business at [*Your business address*].

Services to Be Performed

The agreement should describe in as much detail as possible what you are expected to accomplish. Word the description carefully to emphasize the results you're expected to achieve. Don't describe the method by which you will achieve the results. As an independent contractor, it should be up to you to decide how to do the work. The client's control should be limited to accepting or rejecting your final results. The more control the client exercises over how you work, the more you'll look like an employee. (See Chapter 15.)

EXAMPLE:

Jack hires Jill to prepare an index for his multivolume history of ancient Sparta. Jill should describe the results she is expected to achieve as: "Contractor agrees to prepare an index of Client's *History of Sparta* of at least 100 single-spaced pages. Contractor will provide Client with a printout of the finished index and a 3.5-inch computer disk version in ASCII format."

The agreement should *not* tell Jill how to create the index—for example: "Contractor will prepare an alphabetical three-level index of Client's *History of Sparta*. Contractor will first prepare 3-by-5 inch index cards listing every index entry beginning with Chapter One. After each chapter is completed, Contractor will deliver the index cards to Client for Client's approval. When index cards have been created for all 50 chapters, Contractor will create a computer version of the index using Complex Software Version 7.6. Contractor will then print out and edit the index and deliver it to Client for approval."

It's perfectly okay for the agreement to establish very detailed specifications for your finished work product. But the specs should describe only the end results you must achieve, not how to obtain those results. You can include the description in the main body of the agreement. Or if it's a lengthy explanation, put it on a separate document and attach it to the agreement.

Suggested Language—Alternative A—If Services Listed:

Contractor agrees to perform the following services: [*Describe services you will perform.*]

Suggested Language—Alternative B—If Exhibit Attached:

Contractor agrees to perform the services described in Exhibit A, which is attached to and made part of this Agreement.

Payment

Self-employed people who provide services to others can be paid in many different ways. The two most common payment methods are:

- a fixed fee, or
- payment by unit of time.

Fixed Fee

In a fixed-fee agreement, you charge an agreed amount for the entire project.

Suggested Language—Alternative A—Fixed Fee:

In consideration for the services to be performed by Contractor, Client agrees to pay Contractor $ _____ [*Amount*].

Unit of Time

Many self-employed people—for example, lawyers, accountants, and plumbers—customarily charge by the hour, day, or other unit of time. Charging by the hour does not support your independent contractor status, but you can get away with it if it's a common practice in the field in which you work.

Suggested Language—Alternative B—Unit of Time:

In consideration for the services to be performed by Contractor, Client agrees to pay Contractor at the rate of $ _____ [*Amount*] per _____ [*hour, day, week, or other unit of time*].

Capping Your Payment

Clients often wish to place a cap on the total amount they'll spend on the project when you're paid by the hour because they're afraid you might work slowly to earn a larger fee. If the client insists on a cap, make sure it allows you to work enough hours to get the project done.

Optional Language—Cap on Payment

[OPTIONAL: Contractor's total compensation shall not exceed $_____ [*Amount*] without Client's written consent.]

Terms of Payment

Terms of payment means how you will bill the client and be paid. Generally, you will have to submit an invoice to the client setting out the amount due before you can get paid. An invoice doesn't have to be fancy or filled with legalese. It should include an invoice number, the dates covered by the invoice, the hours expended if you're being paid by the hour, and a summary of the work performed. (See Chapter 7 for a detailed discussion and sample invoice form. A tear-out version of an invoice you can use is included in Appendix A.)

Payment Upon Completing Work

The following provision requires you to send an invoice after you complete work. The client is required to pay your fixed or hourly fee within a set number of days after you send the invoice. The time period of 30 days is a typical payment term, but it can be shorter or longer if you wish. Note that the time for payment starts to run as soon as you send your invoice, not when the client receives it. This will help you get paid more quickly.

Suggested Language—Alternative A— Payment on Completion:

Upon completing Contractor's services under this Agreement, Contractor shall submit an invoice. Client shall pay Contractor within _____ [*10, 15, 30, 45, 60*] days from the date of Contractor's invoice.

Divided Payments

You can also opt to be paid part of your fee when the agreement is signed and the remainder when the work is finished. The amount of the up-front payment is subject to negotiation. Many self-employed people like to receive at least one-third to one-half of a fee before they start work. If the client is new or might have problems paying you, it's wise to get as much money in advance as you can.

The following provision requires that you be paid a specific amount when the client signs the agreement and the rest when the work is finished.

Suggested Language—Alternative B—Divided Payments:

Contractor shall be paid $ _____ [*Amount*] upon signing this Agreement and the remaining amount due when Contractor completes the services and submits an invoice. Client shall pay Contractor within _____ [*10, 15, 30, 45, 60*] days from the date of Contractor's invoice.

Fixed Fee Installment Payments

If the project is long and complex, you may prefer to be paid in installments rather than waiting until the project is finished to receive the bulk of your payment. One way to do this is to break the job into phases or milestones and be paid a fixed fee when each phase is completed. Clients often like this pay-as-you-go arrangement too.

To do this, draw up a schedule of installment payments, tying each payment to your completion of specific services. It's usually easier to set forth the schedule in a separate document and attach it to the agreement as an exhibit. The main body of the agreement should simply refer to the attached payment schedule.

Suggested Language—Alternative C—Installment Payments:

Contractor shall be paid according to the Schedule of Payments set forth in Exhibit ___ [*A or B*] attached to and made part of this agreement.

The following is a form of a schedule of payments you can complete and attach to your agreement. This schedule requires four payments: a down payment when the contract is signed and three installment payments. However, you and your client can schedule as many payments as you like.

Suggested Language— Payment Schedule Exhibit— Schedule of Payments:

Client shall pay Contractor according to the following schedule of payments:

1) $ _____ [*Sum*] when this Agreement is signed.

2) $ _____ [*Sum*] when an invoice is submitted and the following services are completed:

[Describe first stage of services]

3) $ _____ [*Sum*] when an invoice is submitted and the following services are completed:

[Describe second stage of services]

4) $ _____ [*Sum*] when an invoice is submitted and the following services are completed:

[*Describe third stage of services*]

[*ADD ANY ADDITIONAL PAYMENTS*]

All payments shall be due within _____ [*10, 15, 30, 45, 60*] days from the date of Contractor's invoice.

Hourly Payment for Lengthy Projects

Use the following clause if you're being paid by the hour or other unit of time and the project will last more than one month. Under this provision, you submit an invoice to the client each month setting forth how many hours you've worked, and the client is required to pay you within a specific number of days from the date of each invoice.

Suggested Language—Alternative D— Payments After Invoice:

Contractor shall send Client an invoice monthly. Client shall pay Contractor within _____ [*10, 15, 30, 45, 60*] days from the date of each invoice.

Expenses

Expenses are the costs you incur that you can attribute directly to your work for a client. They include, for example, the cost of phone calls or traveling done on the client's behalf. Expenses do not include your normal fixed overhead costs, such as your office rent or the cost of commuting to and from your office; nor do they include materials the client provides you to do your work.

In the past, the IRS viewed the payment of a worker's expenses by a client as a sign of employee status. However, the agency now views this factor as less important. IRS auditors will focus instead on whether a worker has any expenses that were not reimbursed, particularly fixed ongoing costs such as office rent or employee salaries. (See Chapter 15.)

Even though the IRS has changed its stance, other government agencies may consider payment of a worker's business or travel expenses to be a strong indication of an employment relationship. For this reason, it is usually best that your compensation be high enough to cover your expenses; you should not be reimbursed separately for them.

Setting your compensation at a level high enough to cover your expenses has another advantage: It frees you from having to keep records of your expenses. Keeping track of the cost of every phone call or photocopy you make for a client can be a real chore and may be more trouble than it's worth.

However, if a project will require expensive travel, you may wish to bill the client separately for these costs. The following provision contains an optional clause that covers this.

**Suggested Language—Alternative A—
If IC Responsible for Expenses:**

Contractor shall be responsible for all expenses incurred while performing services under this Agreement.

[OPTIONAL: However, Client shall reimburse Contractor for all reasonable travel and living expenses necessarily incurred by Contractor while away from Contractor's regular place of business to perform services under this Agreement. Contractor shall submit an itemized statement of such expenses. Client shall pay Contractor within 30 days from the date of each statement.]

In some professions, however, clients customarily pay for the professionals' expenses. For example, attorneys, accountants, and many self-employed consultants typically charge their clients separately for photocopying charges, deposition fees, and travel. Where there is an otherwise clear independent contractor relationship and payment of expenses is customary in your trade or business, you can probably get away with doing it.

**Suggested Language—Alternative A—
If Client Responsible for Expenses:**

Client shall reimburse Contractor for the following expenses that are directly attributable to work performed under this Agreement:
- travel expenses other than normal commuting, including airfares, rental vehicles, and highway mileage in company or personal vehicles at $ _____ [Amount] per mile
- telephone, facsimile (fax), online, and telegraph charges
- postage and courier services
- printing and reproduction
- computer services, and
- other expenses resulting from the work performed under this Agreement.

Contractor shall submit an itemized statement of Contractor's expenses. Client shall pay Contractor within 30 days from the date of each statement.

Materials

Generally, you should provide all the materials and equipment necessary to complete a project. However, this might not always be possible. For example:

- a computer consultant may have to perform work on the client's computers
- a marketing consultant may need research materials from the client, or
- a freelance copywriter may need copies of the client's old sales literature.

Specify any materials you need from the client in your agreement.

You Provide All Materials

If you furnish all the materials and equipment, use the following clause.

> **Suggested Language—Alternative A—**
> **If IC Provides Materials:**
>
> Contractor will furnish all materials and equipment used to provide the services required by this Agreement.

Client Provides Materials or Equipment

List the materials or equipment the client will provide. If you need these items by a specific date, specify the deadline as well.

> **Suggested Language—Alternative B—**
> **If Client Provides Materials:**
>
> Client shall make available to Contractor, at Client's expense, the following materials, facilities, and equipment: _____
> _____ [List].
>
> These items will be provided to Contractor by _____ [Date].

Term of Agreement

The term of the agreement refers to when the agreement begins and ends. Unless the agreement provides a specific starting date, it begins on the date it is signed. If you and the client sign on different dates, the agreement begins on the date the last person signs. Normally, you shouldn't begin work until the client signs the agreement, so it's best not to provide a specific start date that might be before the client signs.

The agreement should have a definite ending date. Ordinarily, this date marks the final deadline

for you to complete your services. However, even if the project is lengthy, the end date should not be too far in the future. A good outside time limit is 12 months: A longer term makes the agreement look like an employment agreement, not an independent contractor agreement. If you have not completed the work at the end of 12 months, you can negotiate and sign a new agreement.

> **Suggested Language:**
>
> This Agreement will become effective when signed by both parties and will end no later than _____, 20xx.

Terminating the Agreement

Signing a contract doesn't make you bound by it permanently: You and the client can agree to call off your agreement at any time. In addition, contracts typically contain provisions that allow either person to terminate the agreement under certain circumstances. Termination means either party can end the contract without the other side's agreement.

When a contract is terminated, both you and the client stop performing—that is, you discontinue your work, and the client has no obligation to pay you for any work you may do after the effective date of termination. However, the client is legally obligated to pay you for any work you did prior to the termination date.

EXAMPLE:

Murray, a self-employed programmer, agrees to design a website for Mary. They sign a client agreement. About halfway through the project, Murray decides to terminate the agreement because Mary refuses to pay him the advance required by the contract. When the termination becomes effective, Murray has no obligation to do any further work for Mary, but he is still entitled to be compensated for the work he already did.

On the down side, however, you remain liable to the client for any damages it may have suffered due to your failure to perform as agreed before the termination date.

EXAMPLE:

Jill, a self-employed graphic artist, contracts with Aaron to design the cover for a book Aaron plans to publish. Aaron terminates the agreement when Jill fails to deliver the cover by the contract deadline. Jill has no duty to create the cover, and Aaron is not required to pay Jill even if she does produce a cover. However, Jill is liable for any damages Aaron suffered by her failure to live up to the agreement. The delay in providing a cover cost Aaron an extra $1,000 in printing bills. Jill is liable for this amount.

It's important to clearly define the circumstances under which you or the client may end the agreement.

In the past, the IRS viewed a termination provision giving either you, the client, or both of you the right to terminate the agreement at any time to be strong evidence of an employment relationship. However, the agency no longer considers this to be such an important factor. Even so, it's wise to place some limits on the client's right to terminate the contract. It's usually not in your best interest to give a client the right to terminate you for any reason or no reason at all, because the client may abuse that right.

Instead, both you and the client should be able to terminate the agreement without legal repercussions only if there is reasonable cause to do so; or, at the very least, only by giving written notice to the other.

Termination With Reasonable Cause

Termination with reasonable cause means either you or the client must have a good reason to end the agreement. A serious violation of the agreement is reasonable cause to terminate the agreement— but what is considered serious depends on the particular facts and circumstances.

A minor or technical contract violation is not serious enough to justify ending the contract for cause. For example, if a client promises to let you use its office space a few hours a week but fails to do so, this would be a minor transgression and wouldn't justify terminating the agreement. However, if a self-employed programmer agrees to perform programming services for an especially low price because the client promises to let her use its mainframe computer, and the client then reneges and tells the programmer to lease her own mainframe, the programmer would likely be justified in terminating the agreement.

Unless your contract provides otherwise, a client's failure to pay you on time may not necessarily constitute reasonable cause for you to terminate the agreement. You may, however, add a clause to your contract providing that late payments are always reasonable cause for terminating the contract.

The following suggested clause provides that you may terminate the agreement if the client doesn't pay you what you're owed within 20 days after you make a written demand for payment. For example, if you send a client an invoice due within 30 days and the client fails to pay within that time, you may terminate the agreement 20 days after you send the client a written demand to be paid what you're owed. This may give clients an incentive to pay you.

The suggested clause also makes clear that the client must pay you for the services you performed before the contract was terminated.

Suggested Language—Alternative A—Reasonable Cause:

With reasonable cause, either party may terminate this Agreement effective immediately by giving written notice of termination for cause. Reasonable cause includes:

- a material violation of this agreement, or
- nonpayment of Contractor's compensation 20 days after written demand for payment.

Contractor shall be entitled to full payment for services performed prior to the effective date of termination.

Termination Without Cause

Sometimes you or the client do not want to agree to a limited right to terminate. Instead, you want to be able to get out of the agreement at any time without incurring liability. For example, a client's business plans may change so that it no longer needs your services. Or you may have too much work and need to lighten your load.

If you want a broader right to end the work relationship, add a provision to the contract that gives either of you the right to terminate the agreement for any reason upon written notice. You need to provide at least a few days' notice—being able to terminate without notice tends to make you look like an employee. A period of 30 days is a common notice period, but shorter notice may be appropriate if the project is of short duration.

Suggested Language—Alternative A—Without Cause:

Either party may terminate this Agreement at any time by giving _____ [5, 10, 15, 30, 45, 60] days written notice of termination. Contractor shall be entitled to full payment for services performed prior to the date of termination.

Independent Contractor Status

One of the most important functions of an independent contractor agreement is to help establish that you are an independent contractor, not your client's employee. The key to doing this is to make clear that you, not the client, have the right to control how the work will be performed.

You will need to emphasize the factors the IRS and other agencies consider in determining whether a client controls how the work is done. Of course, if you merely recite what you think the IRS wants to hear but fail to adhere to these understandings, agency auditors won't be fooled. Think of this clause as a reminder to you and your client about how to conduct your business relationship. (See Chapter 15.)

Suggested Language:

Contractor is an independent contractor, not Client's employee. Contractor's employees or subcontractors are not Client's employees. Contractor and Client agree to the following rights consistent with an independent contractor relationship:

- Contractor has the right to perform services for others during the term of this Agreement.
- Contractor has the sole right to control and direct the means, manner, and method by which the services required by this Agreement will be performed.
- Contractor has the right to hire assistants as subcontractors or to use employees to provide the services required by this Agreement.
- Contractor or Contractor's employees or subcontractors shall perform the services required by this Agreement; Client shall not hire, supervise, or pay any assistants to help Contractor.
- Neither Contractor nor Contractor's employees or subcontractors shall receive any training from Client in the skills necessary to perform the services required by this Agreement.
- Client shall not require Contractor or Contractor's employees or subcontractors to devote full time to performing the services required by this Agreement.
- Neither Contractor nor Contractor's employees or subcontractors are eligible to participate in any employee pension, health, vacation pay, sick pay, or other fringe benefit plan of Client.

Local, State, and Federal Taxes

The agreement should address federal and state income taxes, Social Security taxes, and sales taxes.

Income Taxes

Your client should not pay or withhold any income or Social Security taxes on your behalf: Doing so is a very strong indicator that you are an employee, not an independent contractor. Indeed, some courts have classified workers as employees based upon this factor alone. Keep in mind that one of the best things about being self-employed is that you don't have taxes withheld from your paychecks. (See Chapter 8.)

Include a straightforward provision, such as the one suggested below, to help make sure the client understands that you'll pay all applicable taxes due on your compensation so the client should not withhold taxes from your payments.

> **Suggested Language:**
>
> Contractor shall pay all income taxes and FICA (Social Security and Medicare taxes) incurred while performing services under this Agreement. Client will not:
> - withhold FICA from Contractor's payments or make FICA payments on Contractor's behalf
> - make state or federal unemployment compensation contributions on Contractor's behalf, or
> - withhold state or federal income tax from Contractor's payments.

Sales Taxes

A few states require self-employed people to pay sales taxes, even if they only provide their clients with services. These states include Hawaii, New Mexico, and South Dakota. Other states require you to pay sales taxes on specified services.

Whether or not you're required to collect sales taxes, include the following provision in your agreement to make it clear that the client will have to pay these and similar taxes. States change sales tax laws frequently, and more are beginning to view services as a good source of sales tax revenue. This provision could come in handy in the future even if you don't need it now.

> **Suggested Language:**
>
> The charges included here do not include taxes. If Contractor is required to pay any federal, state, or local sales, use, property, or value-added taxes based on the services provided under this Agreement, the taxes shall be separately billed to Client. Contractor shall not pay any interest or penalties incurred due to late payment or nonpayment of any taxes by Client.

Notices

When you want to do something important regarding the agreement, you must tell the client about it. This is called giving notice. For example, you need to give the client notice if you want to modify or terminate the agreement.

The following suggested provision gives you several options for providing the client with notice—by personal delivery, mail, fax, or email followed by a confirming letter.

If you give notice by mail, it is not effective until three days after you send it. For example, if you want to end the agreement on 30 days' notice and you mail your notice of termination to the client, the agreement will not end until 33 days after you mail the notice.

Suggested Language:

All notices and other communications in connection with this Agreement shall be in writing and shall be considered given as follows:

- when delivered personally to the recipient's address as stated on this Agreement
- three days after being deposited in the United States mail, with postage prepaid to the recipient's address as stated on this Agreement, or
- when sent by fax or email to the last fax number or email address of the recipient known to the person giving notice. Notice is effective upon receipt, provided that a duplicate copy of the notice is promptly given by first-class mail or the recipient delivers a written confirmation of receipt.

No Partnership

You want to make sure that the client and you are considered separate legal entities, not partners. If a client is viewed as your partner, you'll be liable for its debts, and the client will have the power to make contracts that obligate you to others without your consent.

Suggested Language:

This Agreement does not create a partnership relationship. Neither party has authority to enter into contracts on the other's behalf.

Applicable Law

It's a good idea for your agreement to indicate which state's law will govern if you have a dispute with the client. This is particularly helpful if you and the client are in different states. There is some advantage to having the law of your own state control, because local attorneys will likely be more familiar with that law.

Suggested Language:

This Agreement will be governed by the laws of the state of _____ [*State in which you have your main office*].

Exclusive Agreement

When you put your agreement in writing, it is treated as the last word on the areas it covers, if you and the client intend it to be the final and complete expression of your agreement. The written agreement takes precedence over any written or oral agreements or promises made previously. This means that neither you nor the client can rely on letters or oral statements either of you may have made or other material not covered by the contract.

Business contracts normally contain a provision stating that the written agreement is the complete and exclusive agreement between those involved. This is to help make it clear to a court or a mediator or arbitrator that the parties intended the contract to be their final agreement. Such a clause helps avoid claims that promises not contained in the written contract were made and broken.

Make sure that all documents containing any of the client's representations upon which you are relying are attached to the agreement as exhibits. If they aren't attached, they likely won't be considered to be part of the agreement.

Suggested Language:

This is the entire Agreement between Contractor and Client.

Signatures

The end of the main body of the agreement should contain spaces for you to sign, write in your title, and date. Make sure the person signing the agreement has the authority to do so. (See "Putting Your Agreement Together" in Chapter 18.)

Suggested Language:

Client: _____[NAME OF CLIENT]_____

By: _____
(Signature)

_____
(Typed or Printed Name)

Title: _____

Date: _____

Contractor: ____[NAME OF CONTRACTOR]____

By: _____
(Signature)

_____
(Typed or Printed Name)

Title: _____

Taxpayer ID Number: _____

Date: _____

Signing by fax. It is common to use faxed signatures to finalize contracts. If you use faxed signatures, include a specific provision authorizing them at the end of the agreement.

Optional Language—Signatures by Fax:

[OPTIONAL: Contractor and Client agree that this Agreement will be considered signed when the signature of a party is delivered by facsimile transmission. Signatures transmitted by facsimile shall have the same effect as original signatures.]

Optional Provisions

There are several optional provisions you may wish to include in your agreement. They are not necessary for every client agreement, but they can be extremely helpful. You should carefully consider including them in your contracts. Pay especially close attention to the provisions regarding:

- resolving disputes
- contract changes, and
- attorneys' fees.

It's usually to your advantage to include all of these provisions in your agreement.

Resolving Disputes

As you probably know, court litigation can be very expensive. To avoid this cost, people have developed alternative forms of dispute resolution that don't involve going to court, including mediation and arbitration.

The suggested clause below requires the client and you to take advantage of these alternate forms of dispute resolution. You're first required to submit the dispute to mediation, described further in Chapter 21. You agree on a neutral third person to serve as a mediator to try to help you settle your dispute. The mediator has no power to impose a decision, only to try to help you arrive at one.

If mediation doesn't work, the clause provides that you must submit the dispute to binding arbitration. Arbitration is like an informal court trial without a jury, in which an arbitrator makes the decisions instead of a judge. It is usually much faster and cheaper than a lawsuit. You may, but are not required to, be represented by a lawyer.

You should indicate where the mediation or arbitration would occur. You'll usually want this to be in the city or county where your office is located. You don't want to have to travel a long distance to attend a mediation or arbitration.

However, every state has an alternative to mediation or arbitration that can be even cheaper and quicker than either of these approaches: small claims court. Small claims courts are designed to help resolve disputes involving a relatively small amount of money. The amount ranges from about $2,000 to $15,000, depending on the state in which you live. If your dispute involves more money than the small claims limit, you can waive the excess (that is, give up your right to sue for anything over the limit) and still bring a small claims suit. You don't need a lawyer to sue in small claims court; indeed, lawyers are barred from small claims court in several states. Small claims court is particularly useful when a client owes you a relatively small amount of money. (See Chapter 7.)

The following clause also provides that you or the client can elect to skip mediation and arbitration—and take your dispute to small claims court.

Suggested Language:

If a dispute arises under this Agreement, the parties agree to first try to resolve the dispute with the help of a mutually agreed-upon mediator in _____ [*City or county where mediation will occur*]. Any costs and fees other than attorneys' fees associated with the mediation shall be shared equally by the parties.

If it proves impossible to arrive at a mutually satisfactory solution through mediation, the parties agree to submit the dispute to binding arbitration in _____ [*City or county where arbitration will occur*] under the rules of the American Arbitration Association. Judgment upon the award rendered by the arbitrator may be entered in any court having jurisdiction to do so.

However, the complaining party may refuse to submit the dispute to mediation or arbitration and instead bring an action in an appropriate small claims court.

Modifying the Agreement

It's very common for both you and your client to want to change the terms of an agreement after you have started work. For example, the client might want to make a change in the contract specifications that could require you to do more work. Or you might discover that you underestimated how much time the project will take and need to charge more to complete it.

When you modify your agreement in this way, you should write down the changes on a separate document, have both parties sign it, and attach it to your original agreement. (See Appendix B for a tear-out form you can use to do this—a contract amendment.)

The following provision recognizes that the original agreement you enter into with the client may have to be changed. This provision states that you and the client must write down your changes and both sign the writing. Such a contract provision may be overkill—that is, both you and the client can still make changes without writing them down. However, making this requirement explicit stresses the importance of documenting changes in writing.

Neither you nor the client must accept a proposed change to a contract. Because you are obligated to deal with each other fairly and in good faith, however, you cannot simply refuse all modifications without attempting to reach a resolution.

! **CAUTION**

Resolve disputes over modification with alternative dispute resolution (ADR). If you use this clause, check to be sure you have also included the optional provision on resolving disputes. That way, if you and the client can't agree on the changes, the agreement will require that you submit your dispute to mediation; and, if that doesn't work, to binding arbitration. This avoids expensive lawsuits in court.

> **Suggested Language:**
>
> Client and Contractor recognize that:
> - Contractor's original cost and time estimates may be too low due to unforeseen events or to factors unknown to Contractor when this Agreement was made.
> - Client may desire a mid-project change in Contractor's services that would add time and cost to the project and possibly inconvenience Contractor.
> - Other provisions of this Agreement may be difficult to carry out due to unforeseen circumstances.
>
> If any intended changes or any other events beyond the parties' control require adjustments to this Agreement, the parties shall make a good faith effort to agree on all necessary particulars. Such agreements shall be put in writing, signed by the parties, and added to this Agreement.

Attorneys' Fees

Under the following provision, if either person has to sue the other in court to enforce the agreement and wins—that is, becomes the prevailing party—the loser is required to pay the other person's attorneys' fees and expenses.

If you have to sue the client in court to enforce the agreement and you win, this provision can make filing a lawsuit economically feasible—for example, it might help you to convince a lawyer to file a case against your client without you having to provide an up-front cash retainer. It will also give the client a strong incentive to negotiate with you if you have a good case.

Sometimes, however, an attorneys' fees provision can work against you. It may help your client find an attorney to sue you and make you more eager to settle. And it can make litigation more stressful for you, because if you lose—for example, because you don't have enough evidence to support your case—you could be stuck with a very big bill. Particularly if you think you're more likely to violate the

agreement than your client is, an attorneys' fees provision is probably not a good idea.

> **Suggested Language:**
>
> If any legal action is necessary to enforce this Agreement, the prevailing party shall be entitled to reasonable attorneys' fees, costs, and expenses in addition to any other relief to which he or she may be entitled.

Late Fees

Many self-employed people charge a late fee if the client doesn't pay within the time specified in the IC agreement or invoice. Charging late fees for overdue payments can get clients to pay on time. The late fee is normally expressed as a monthly interest charge.

If you wish to charge a late fee, make sure it's mentioned in your agreement. You should also clearly state your late fee on all your invoices.

CAUTION

Some states restrict late fees. Your state might restrict how much you can charge as a late fee. You'll have to investigate your state laws to find out. Check the index to the annotated statutes for your state—sometimes called a code—available in any law library. (See Chapter 21.) Look under the terms "interest," "usury," or "finance charges." Also, a professional or trade organization may have helpful information on late-fee restrictions.

You can safely charge as a late fee at least as much as banks charge businesses to borrow money. Find out the current bank interest rate by calling your bank or looking in the business section of your local newspaper.

The math requires two steps. First, divide the annual interest rate by 12 to determine your monthly interest rate.

EXAMPLE 1:

Sam, a self-employed consultant, decides to start charging clients a late fee for overdue payments. He knows banks are charging 12% interest per year on borrowed money and decides to charge the same. He divides this rate by 12 to determine his monthly interest rate: 1%.

Then, multiply the monthly rate by the amount due to determine the amount of the monthly late fee.

EXAMPLE 2:

Acme Corp. is 30 days late paying Sam a $10,000 fee. Sam multiples this amount by his 1% finance charge to determine his late fee: $100 (0.01 x $10,000). He adds this amount to Acme's account balance. He does this every month for which the payment is late.

Suggested Language:

Late payments by Client shall be subject to late penalty fees of _____% per month from the date due until the amount is paid.

Liability to the Client

If something goes wrong with your work, you might end up getting sued by the client and having to pay damages.

EXAMPLE:

Julie, a self-employed computer programmer, designs an inventory accounting program for a cosmetics company. A bug in the program causes the program to crash, and the company is unable to conduct normal business for several days, losing tens of thousands of dollars. The company sues Julie, claiming that her program design was deficient.

Such lawsuits could easily cost more than you were paid for your work and could even bankrupt you. To avoid this, many self-employed people include provisions in their agreements limiting their liability. This is particularly wise if problems with your work or services could cause the client substantial injuries or economic losses.

Liability Cap

The following optional clause limits your total liability for any damages to the client to a set dollar amount or to no more than you were paid, whichever is less. It also relieves you of liability for lost profits or other special damages to the client.

Such damages are also called "incidental" or "consequential" damages. These are damages that can far exceed the amount the client actually paid you for your work. They arise out of circumstances you knew about or should have foreseen when the contract was made. This type of damages often involves lost profits that logically result from your failure to live up to your agreement. For example, if you knew that your failure to deliver your work on time could cost the client a valuable business opportunity, you could be required to make up the lost profits the client would have earned had you delivered the work on time. The optional clause below states that you will not be responsible for these types of damages.

Suggested Language—Alternative A—Cap on Liability:

Contractor's total liability to Client under this Agreement for damages, costs, and expenses, regardless of cause, shall not exceed $_____ or the compensation received by Contractor under this Agreement, whichever is less. Contractor shall not be liable for Client's lost profits, or special, incidental, or consequential damages.

No Liability to Client

The following provision limits your liability to the client to the maximum extent possible. It provides that you are not liable to the client for any losses or damages arising from your work.

Suggested Language—Alternative B—No Liability:

Contractor shall not be liable to Client for any loss, damages, or expenses resulting from Contractor's services under this Agreement.

Liability to Others

The work that you do can affect people other than the client. Such people are called third parties. You need to be particularly concerned about your liability to third parties if you're engaged in a hazardous or risky project that could result in injuries to others if something goes wrong.

Third parties typically enter the picture when they are directly or indirectly injured by the work you've performed for a client. The injuries can be physical, economic, or both. For example, if an elevator crashes due to faulty software a self-employed programmer designed for the elevator manufacturer, the injured elevator passengers would be third parties to the programmer. Even though the programmer never met or contracted with them, the programmer might be legally responsible for their injuries.

If third parties are damaged as a result of the work you perform for a client, they'll likely sue everyone involved—including you. Both you and the client may be liable for the full amount of such claims. Legal clauses called "indemnification provisions" require one party to pay the other's attorneys' fees and damages arising from such claims. Such provisions don't affect third parties who sue you, nor do they absolve you from liability to third parties for your actions. An indemnification clause requires only one party (for example, your client) to pay any amounts due from the other (for example, you) as a result of such liability.

EXAMPLE:

Bart, a self-employed software engineer, creates an experimental software program designed to automate a chemical factory for BigCorp. The program fails, which results in a chemical spill, damaging nearby property.

The property owners affected by the chemical spill could sue not only BigCorp but Bart as well, claiming that he negligently designed the software. Bart could be forced to defend himself against the lawsuit filed by total strangers to him.

You may wish to include the following provision in your agreement requiring the client to indemnify you against third-party claims. This means the client will be responsible for defending any lawsuits and for all damages and injuries that third parties suffer if something goes wrong with your work.

To accomplish this, the provision uses a standard legal phrase that is a bit convoluted. It states that the client shall "indemnify, defend, and hold harmless" the contractor against third-party claims. This means the client is required to assume responsibility for dealing with third-party claims and must repay you if they end up costing you anything.

Many clients will balk at including an indemnification provision in your agreement. Moreover, as a practical matter, such a provision is useless if the client doesn't have the money or insurance to pay the amount due. You may be better off charging the client enough to obtain your own liability insurance protecting you against third-party claims. (See Chapter 6.)

Suggested Language:

Client will indemnify, defend, and hold harmless Contractor against all liabilities, damages, and expenses, including reasonable attorneys' fees, resulting from any third-party claim or lawsuit arising from Contractor's performance under this Agreement.

CAUTION

Don't agree to indemnify the client. Some clients will not only refuse to indemnify you against third party claims, they'll want you to indemnify them. In that case, you'll have to repay the client if a third party sues. For obvious reasons, you should say no to such provisions. (See Chapter 20.)

Intellectual Property Ownership

If you're hired to create or contribute to the creation of intellectual property—for example, important business documents, marketing plans, software programs, graphics, designs, photos, music, inventions, or trademarks—the agreement should specify who owns your work.

There are many options regarding ownership of intellectual property that self-employed people create, explained in detail in Chapter 17. Typically, your client will want to own all the intellectual property rights in your work, but this doesn't have to be the case. For example, you could retain sole ownership and grant the client a license to use your work. The only limit on how you deal with ownership of your work is your imagination—and the agreement of your client.

You Retain Ownership

Under the following clause, you keep ownership of your work and merely give the client a nonexclusive license to use it. This means that the client may use your work but does not own it and may not sell

it to others. The license is royalty-free—meaning that the sole payment you receive for it is the sum the client paid you for your services. The client will make no additional payments for the license.

Suggested Language—Alternative A— Nonexclusive Transfer:

Contractor grants to Client a royalty-free nonexclusive license to use anything created or developed by Contractor for Client under this Agreement ("Contract Property"). The license shall have a perpetual term, and the Client may not transfer it. Contractor shall retain all copyrights, patent rights, and other intellectual property rights to the Contract Property.

You Transfer Ownership to Client

Under the following clause you transfer all your ownership rights to the client. But you must first receive all your compensation from the client.

You also agree to help prepare any documents necessary to help the client obtain any copyright, patent, or other intellectual property rights at no charge to the client. This would probably amount to no more than signing a patent or copyright registration application. However, the client is required to reimburse you for the expense of getting and assigning the rights.

Suggested Language—Alternative B—Transfer All Rights:

Contractor assigns to Client all patent, copyright, and trade secret rights in anything created or developed by Contractor for Client under this Agreement. This assignment is conditioned upon full payment of the compensation due Contractor under this Agreement.

Contractor shall help prepare any documents Client considers necessary to secure any copyright, patent, or other intellectual property rights at no charge to Client. However, Client shall reimburse Contractor for reasonable out-of-pocket expenses.

Reusable Materials

Many self-employed people who create intellectual property for clients have certain materials they use over and over again for different clients. For example, computer programmers may have certain utilities or program tools they incorporate into the software they create for many different clients.

You may lose the legal right to reuse such materials if you transfer all your ownership rights in your work to the client. To avoid this, include a provision like the one below in your agreement. It provides that you retain ownership of such materials and only gives the client a nonexclusive license to use them. The license is royalty-free, which means that the sole payment you receive for it is the sum the client paid you for your services. The client will make no additional payments for the license. The license also has a perpetual term, meaning it will last as long as your copyright, patent, or other intellectual property rights do.

If you know what such materials consist of in advance, it's a good idea to list them in an exhibit attached to the agreement. This isn't required, however.

Optional Language—Right to Refuse:

Contractor owns or holds a license to use and sublicense various materials in existence before the start date of this Agreement (Contractor's Materials).

[OPTIONAL: Contractor's Materials include, but are not limited to, those items identified in Exhibit __ , attached to and made part of this Agreement.]

Contractor may, at its option, include Contractor's Materials in the work performed under this Agreement. Contractor retains all right, title, and interest, including all copyrights, patent rights, and trade secret rights in Contractor's Materials. Contractor grants Client a royalty-free nonexclusive license to use any Contractor's Materials incorporated into the work performed by Contractor under this Agreement. The license shall have a perpetual term and may not be transferred by Client.

Assignment and Delegation

An assignment is the process by which rights or benefits under a contract are transferred to someone else. For example, a client might assign the right to receive the benefit of your services to someone else. Such a person is called an assignee. When this occurs, the assignee steps into the original client's shoes. You must now work for the assignee, not the client with whom you contracted. If you fail to perform, the assignee may sue you for breach of contract.

EXAMPLE 1:

Terri, a self-employed designer, agrees to design a cover and chapter headings for several books published by Scrivener & Sons. Scrivener assigns this right to Pop's Books. This means that Terri must perform the work for Pop's instead of Scrivener. If Terri fails to do so, Pop's can sue her for breach of contract.

You may also assign the benefits you receive under an IC agreement to someone else.

EXAMPLE 2:

Jimmy agrees to provide Fastsoft 20 hours of computer programming services in exchange for being able to use its computer for 100 hours. Jimmy assigns, or transfers, the right to the computer time to his friend Kate. This means Fastsoft must let Kate use its computer.

Delegation is the flipside of assignment. Instead of transferring benefits under a contract, you transfer the duties. As long as the new person does the job correctly, all will be well. However, the person delegating duties under a contract usually remains responsible if the person to whom the delegation was made fails to perform competently.

EXAMPLE 3:

Jimmy delegates to Mindy his duty to perform 20 hours of programming services for Fastsoft. This means that Mindy, not Jimmy, will now do the work. But Jimmy remains liable if Mindy doesn't perform adequately.

Legal Restrictions

Unless a contract provides otherwise, you can ordinarily assign and delegate freely, subject to some important legal limitations. For example, a client can't assign the benefit of your services to someone else without your consent if it would increase the work you must do or otherwise magnify your burden under the contract. Similarly, you can't delegate your duties without the client's consent if it would decrease the benefits the client would receive.

One of the most important limitations for self-employed people is that contracts for personal services are ordinarily not assignable or delegable without the client's consent. This type of contract involves services that are personal in nature. Examples include contracts for the services of lawyers, physicians, architects, writers, and artists. In such cases, courts consider it unfair for either a client or a self-employed person to change horses midstream.

EXAMPLE:

Arthur contracts with Betty, a freelance artist, to paint his portrait. She later attempts to delegate her duties to her friend Carla—that is, require Carla to paint Arthur's portrait instead of her. Arthur does not have to agree to this change because Betty's contract with Arthur was a contract for personal services.

Contract Restrictions

Your contract may also place limits on assignment and delegation. Contractual limits on your right to delegate your duties to others are not supportive of your independent contractor status because they allow the client to control who will do the work. Moreover, it is often advantageous for you to have the right to delegate your contractual obligations to others. This gives you flexibility, for example, to hire someone else to do the work if you don't have time to do it.

However, some clients may balk at allowing you to delegate your contractual duties without the client's consent. This is usually where the client has hired you because of your special expertise, reputation for performance, or financial stability, and the client doesn't want some other person performing the services. Also, there may be cases in which you do not want the client to have the right to assign the benefit of your services to someone else, who may turn out to be incompetent.

In this event, you may include the following provision in your agreement. It bars both you and the client from assigning your rights or delegating your duties without the other party's consent.

> **Suggested Language:**
>
> Neither party may assign any rights or delegate any duties under this Agreement without the other party's prior written approval.

Sample Client Agreement

The following sample agreement is a fixed-fee agreement calling for mediation and arbitration of disputes and payment of attorneys' fees. If you don't understand any of the provisions, refer back to the relevant discussion in this chapter.

Sample General IC Agreement

Independent Contractor Agreement

This Agreement is made between Acme Widget Co. (Client), with a principal place of business at 123 Main Street, Marred Vista, CA 90000, and ABC Consulting, Inc. (Contractor), with a principal place of business at 456 Grub Street, Santa Longo, CA 90001.

Services to Be Performed

Contractor agrees to perform the following services: Install and test Client's DX9-105 widget manufacturing press so that it performs according to the manufacturer's specifications.

Payment

In consideration for the services to be performed by Contractor, Client agrees to pay Contractor $20,000.

Terms of Payment

Upon completing Contractor's services under this Agreement, Contractor shall submit an invoice. Client shall pay Contractor within 30 days from the date of Contractor's invoice.

Expenses

Contractor shall be responsible for all expenses incurred while performing services under this Agreement.

Materials

Contractor will furnish all materials and equipment used to provide the services required by this Agreement.

Term of Agreement

This Agreement will become effective when signed by both parties and will end no later than May 1, 20xx.

Terminating the Agreement

With reasonable cause, either party may terminate this Agreement effective immediately by giving written notice of termination for cause. Reasonable cause includes:

- a material violation of this agreement, or
- nonpayment of Contractor's compensation 20 days after written demand for payment.

Contractor shall be entitled to full payment for services performed prior to the effective date of termination.

Independent Contractor Status

Contractor is an independent contractor, not Client's employee. Contractor's employees or subcontractors are not Client's employees. Contractor and Client agree to the following rights consistent with an independent contractor relationship:

- Contractor has the right to perform services for others during the term of this Agreement.
- Contractor has the sole right to control and direct the means, manner, and method by which the services required by this Agreement will be performed.
- Contractor has the right to hire assistants as subcontractors, or to use employees to provide the services required by this Agreement.
- Contractor or Contractor's employees or subcontractors shall perform the services required by this Agreement; Client shall not hire, supervise, or pay any assistants to help Contractor.

Sample General IC Agreement (continued)

- Neither Contractor nor Contractor's employees or subcontractors shall receive any training from Client in the skills necessary to perform the services required by this Agreement.
- Client shall not require Contractor or Contractor's employees or subcontractors to devote full time to performing the services required by this Agreement.
- Neither Contractor nor Contractor's employees or subcontractors are eligible to participate in any employee pension, health, vacation pay, sick pay, or other fringe benefit plan of Client.

Local, State, and Federal Taxes

Contractor shall pay all income taxes and FICA (Social Security and Medicare taxes) incurred while performing services under this Agreement. Client will not:

- withhold FICA from Contractor's payments or make FICA payments on Contractor's behalf
- make state or federal unemployment compensation contributions on Contractor's behalf, or
- withhold state or federal income tax from Contractor's payments.

Sales Taxes

The charges included here do not include taxes. If Contractor is required to pay any federal, state, or local sales, use, property, or value-added taxes based on the services provided under this Agreement, the taxes shall be separately billed to Client. Contractor shall not pay any interest or penalties incurred due to late payment or nonpayment of any taxes by Client.

Notices

All notices and other communications in connection with this Agreement shall be in writing and shall be considered given as follows:

- when delivered personally to the recipient's address as stated on this Agreement
- three days after being deposited in the United States mail, with postage prepaid to the recipient's address as stated on this Agreement, or
- when sent by fax or email to the last fax number or email address of the recipient known to the person giving notice. Notice is effective upon receipt provided that a duplicate copy of the notice is promptly given by first-class mail, or the recipient delivers a written confirmation of receipt.

No Partnership

This Agreement does not create a partnership relationship. Neither party has authority to enter into contracts on the other's behalf.

Applicable Law

This Agreement will be governed by the laws of the state of California.

Exclusive Agreement

This is the entire Agreement between Contractor and Client.

Resolving Disputes

If a dispute arises under this Agreement, the parties agree to first try to resolve the dispute with the help of a mutually agreed-upon mediator in Mariposa County. Any costs and fees other than attorneys' fees associated with the mediation shall be shared equally by the parties.

Sample General IC Agreement (continued)

If it proves impossible to arrive at a mutually satisfactory solution through mediation, the parties agree to submit the dispute to binding arbitration in Mariposa County under the rules of the American Arbitration Association. Judgment upon the award rendered by the arbitrator may be entered in any court having jurisdiction to do so.

However, the complaining party may refuse to submit the dispute to mediation or arbitration and instead bring an action in an appropriate small claims court.

Modifying the Agreement

Client and Contractor recognize that:

- Contractor's original cost and time estimates may be too low due to unforeseen events or to factors unknown to Contractor when this Agreement was made.

- Client may desire a mid-project change in Contractor's services that would add time and cost to the project and possibly inconvenience Contractor.

- Other provisions of this Agreement may be difficult to carry out due to unforeseen circumstances.

If any intended changes or any other events beyond the parties' control require adjustments to this Agreement, the parties shall make a good faith effort to agree on all necessary particulars. Such agreements shall be put in writing, signed by the parties, and added to this Agreement.

Attorneys' Fees

If any legal action is necessary to enforce this Agreement, the prevailing party shall be entitled to reasonable attorneys' fees, costs, and expenses in addition to any other relief to which he or she may be entitled.

Signatures

Client: _____ Acme Widget Co. _____

By: _____ *Basilio Chew* _____
(Signature)

BASILIO CHEW
(Typed or Printed Name)

Title: _____ President _____

Date: _____ April 30, 20xx _____

Contractor: _____ ABC Consulting, Inc. _____

By: _____ *George Bailey* _____
(Signature)

GEORGE BAILEY
(Typed or Printed Name)

Title: _____ President _____

Taxpayer ID Number: _____ 123-45-6789 _____

Date: _____ April 30, 20xx _____

Using Letter Agreements

Many self-employed people and their clients use letter agreements instead of more formal standard contracts. A letter agreement is usually a short contract written in the form of a letter. Although letter agreements may lack the appearance of gravitas of standard agreements, they are perfectly valid, binding contracts.

Typically, when you use a letter agreement, you and a client will first reach a tentative agreement in a meeting, over the phone, by fax or email, or through some combination of these. Then, one of you drafts a letter documenting the important terms, signs it, and sends it to the other person to sign.

Some clients have their own form letter agreements they use with all self-employed people they hire and will insist on using them. Review the letter carefully to make sure it meshes with the client's and your own oral statements and does not contain unfair provisions. (See Chapter 20.)

However, many clients will be happy for you to take on the work of drafting the agreement. You'll almost always be better off if you draft the agreement yourself because you can:

- avoid including any terms that are unduly favorable to the client, and
- make sure the agreement is completed and sent out quickly.

Take the initiative and offer to draw up the letter agreement. Explain that this is part of your service and that using an agreement you've drafted helps establish that you're not the client's employee.

Use the information in this chapter to draft one or more appropriate form letters you can use over and over again with minor alterations. This will be particularly easy to do if you use a computer and keep the forms on your hard drive or a disk.

> **CAUTION**
>
> **Don't begin work until the client signs on the bottom line.** No matter who drafts a letter agreement, don't begin work until you have a copy signed by the client. You don't want to begin work only to discover that the client wants to cancel the project or make major changes in your agreement.

Pros and Cons of Letter Agreements

Letter agreements are usually shorter and easier to draft than regular contracts. They are also less formal looking. As a result, they often seem less intimidating to clients. Many clients who are fearful of signing a formal contract without having a lawyer review it will sign a letter agreement with no hesitation.

In some fields, using letter agreements is the commonly accepted practice for doing business. For example, letter agreements are commonly used when freelance writers accept short assignments from magazines or other publications. If this is the case in your field of work, you may have to use letter agreements as a matter of course.

Because letter agreements are usually much shorter than standard client agreements, they are particularly useful for brief projects where relatively little money is involved. A potential client could well think you're crazy if you insist on a lengthy formal contract for a simple one-day project.

However, in the interests of brevity, letter agreements typically make no mention of many provisions contained in longer standard agreements that could prove useful if a problem arises—for example, provisions concerning dispute resolution, how the agreement may be terminated, or cementing your status as an independent contractor.

Both your client and you may be better off using a standard client agreement if:

- the project is a large and complex one that involves a substantial amount of money
- you're dealing with a new client you're not sure you can trust, or
- you are otherwise worried that problems or disputes may occur.

What to Include

A letter agreement can be as short as one-half page. At a minimum, however, it should contain:

- a description of the services you will perform
- the deadline by which you must complete your services
- the fees you will charge, and
- when you will be paid.

Your agreement doesn't have to end here, however. Depending on the nature of your services and the client, you may want to include any of several other provisions.

Services to Be Performed

The single most important part of the agreement is the description of the services you'll perform for the client. This description will set out the specifics of the work you're required to do and will serve as the yardstick to measure whether your performance was satisfactory.

Describe the work you're expected to accomplish in as much detail as possible. However, word the description carefully to emphasize the results you're expected to achieve. Don't describe the method by which you will achieve the results. It should be up to you to decide how to do the work. The client's control should be limited to accepting or rejecting your final results.

It's fine for the agreement to establish detailed specifications for your finished work product—but it should describe only the end results you must achieve, not how to obtain those results.

You can include the description in the main body of the agreement. Or, if it's a lengthy explanation, you can put it on a separate document and attach it to the letter agreement.

Suggested Language—Alternative A— Description in Agreement:

I will perform the following services on your behalf: [*Describe services you will perform.*]

Suggested Language—Alternative B—Description Attached:

I will perform the services described in the Exhibit attached to this Agreement.

Deadlines

The agreement should also make clear when your work will be completed and delivered to the client. Make sure you give yourself enough time to complete the job. It's better to err on the side of caution and give yourself more time than you think you'll need.

Suggested Language:

I agree to complete these services on or before _____ [*Date*].

Payment

Self-employed people can be paid in many different ways. The two most common payment methods are:

- a fixed fee, and
- payment by unit of time.

Fixed fee

In a fixed-fee agreement, you charge an agreed amount for the entire project.

Suggested Language—Alternative A—Fixed Fee

In consideration of my performance of these services, you agree to pay me $ _____ [*Amount*].

Unit of Time

Many self-employed people charge by the hour, day, or other unit of time—for example, lawyers, accountants, and plumbers. Charging by the hour does not necessarily support the idea that you're an independent contractor, but you can get away with it if it's a common practice in your field.

Suggested Language—Alternative B—United of Time:

In consideration of my performance of these services, you agree to pay me at the rate of $ _____ [*Amount*] per _____ [*Hour, day, week, or other unit of time*].

Clients often wish to place a cap on the total amount they'll spend on the project when you're paid by the hour because they're afraid you might work slowly just to earn a larger fee. If the client insists on a cap, make sure it allows you to work enough hours to get the project done.

Optional Language—Cap on Payment

[OPTIONAL: My total compensation shall not exceed $_____ [*Amount*] without your written consent.]

Terms of Payment

Terms of payment means how you will bill the client and be paid. The client will not likely pay you for your work until you submit an invoice setting out the amount due. An invoice doesn't have to be fancy. It should include an invoice number, the dates covered by the invoice, the hours expended if you're being paid by the hour, and a summary of the work performed. (See "Getting Paid" in Chapter 7 for a detailed discussion and sample invoice form. A tear-out version of an invoice you can use is included in Appendix A.)

Full Payment Upon Completing Work

The following provision requires you to send an invoice after you complete work. The client is required to pay your fixed or hourly fee within a set number of days after you send the invoice. Thirty days is a typical payment term, but it can be shorter or longer if you wish. Note that the time for payment starts to run as soon as you send your invoice, not when the client receives it. This will help you get paid more quickly.

Suggested Language—Alternative A— Payment on Completion:

I will submit an invoice after my services are completed. You shall pay me within ____ [*10, 15, 30, 45, 60*] days from the date of the invoice.

Divided Payments

You can also opt to be paid part of your fee when the agreement is signed and the remainder when the work is finished. When you're paid by the hour, such an up-front payment is often called a retainer. The amount of the up-front payment is subject to negotiation. Many self-employed people like to receive at least one-third to one-half of their fees before they start work. If the client is new or might have problems paying you, it's wise to get as much money in advance as you can.

The following provision requires that you be paid a specific amount when the client signs the agreement and the rest when the work is finished.

Suggested Language—Alternative B—Divided Payments:

I will be paid in two installments. The first installment shall be $ _____ [*Amount*] and is payable by [*due date*]. The remaining $_____ [*Amount*] will be due within _____ [*10, 15, 30, 45, 60*] days after I complete my services and submit an invoice.

Optional Provisions

There are a number of other provisions you can add to a letter agreement. These aren't necessary, but they can be helpful to you. They are all discussed in detail in the first part of this chapter. They include provisions that:

- require the client to reimburse you for expenses you incur in performing the work
- require the client to provide you with materials, equipment, or facilities
- require mediation and arbitration of disputes
- allow you to obtain attorneys' fees if you sue the client and win
- require the client to pay a fee for late payments
- limit your liability to the client if something goes wrong, and
- restrict the client's ability to assign its benefits or delegate its duties under the agreement.

In addition, if your work involves the creation of intellectual property—for example, any type of work of authorship, such as an article or other written work—you should include a provision in your agreement that states who will own your work.

Putting the Agreement Together

There are two ways to handle a letter agreement. The old-fashioned way is to prepare and sign two copies and mail or deliver them to the client to sign. The client signs both copies, then returns one signed copy to you by mail or messenger and retains one copy for its records. Both copies are original, binding contracts.

Today, however, it's very common for an IC to draft a letter agreement, sign it, and then fax a copy to the client. The client signs the letter and faxes a copy back to you. This has the advantage of speed, but you don't have the client's original signature on the letter, only a copy.

A faxed signature is probably legally sufficient if you and the client don't dispute that it is a fax of an original signature. However, if a client claims that a faxed signature was forged, it could be difficult or impossible to prove it's genuine because it is very easy to forge a faxed signature with modern computer technology. Forgery claims are rare, however, so this is usually not a problem. Even so, it's a good practice for you and the client to follow up the fax with signed originals exchanged by mail or delivery service.

Sample Letter Agreement

The following is a sample letter agreement between a self-employed public relations consultant and an oil company. The consultant agrees to create a marketing plan for the company's new oil additive called Zotz. The consultant will perform the work for a fixed fee paid in two installments.

Sample Letter Agreement

MALONEY & ASSOCIATES
1000 GRUB STREET
MARRED VISTA, CA 90000

February 1, 20xx

Jerry Wellhead
Vice President
Acme Oil Co.
1000 Greasy Way
Tulsa, OK 10000

Dear Jerry:

I am pleased to have the opportunity to provide my services. This letter will serve as our agreement.

I will perform the following services on your behalf: I will create a marketing plan for the rollout of Acme's new oil additive called Zotz. The plan will include guidelines for magazine, radio, and television advertising.

I agree to complete these services on or before March 1, 20xx.

In consideration of my performance of these services, you agree to pay me $5,000.

I will be paid in two installments. The first installment shall be $2,500 and is payable by February 5, 20xx. The remaining $2,500 will be paid within 30 days after I complete my services and submit an invoice.

If this Agreement meets with your approval, please sign below to make this a binding contract between us. Please sign both copies and return one to me. Keep one signed copy for your records.

Sincerely,

Susan Maloney

Susan Maloney

Agreed to: Acme Oil Co.

By: _____
   (Signature)

   Jerry Wellhead

   Title: Vice President

   Date: _____

Reviewing a Client's Agreement

Many clients have their own agreement forms they will want to use. This is particularly likely if you work for firms that often use third parties to perform services or for large companies that have their own legal departments. A client may present you with a lengthy, complex agreement, hand you a pen, and tell you to sign. You may be told that the agreement is only a standard form that all nonemployees who work for the client sign.

However, signing a client agreement is never a mere technical formality. A client agreement is not simply a bunch of words on a piece of paper. It's a binding, legal document that will have important consequences for you in the real world.

Because client-drafted agreements are usually written with the client's best interests in mind, not yours, you'll almost always be better off if you use your own agreement. A client will be more willing to do this if you:

- provide a well-drafted agreement of your own (see Chapter 19), and
- point out that if the client is audited, an IRS or other government auditor will be far more impressed by an agreement you drafted than a standard form prepared by the client: Using your agreement helps establish that you're an independent contractor, not the client's employee, and may help the client avoid assessments and penalties in the event of an audit.

If the client insists on using its own agreement, be sure to review the document before you accept the project. Read the agreement carefully, and make sure you understand and are comfortable with it before signing. If there are any provisions you don't understand, ask the client to explain them to you and rewrite them so that you do understand them.

No matter what the client may say, no agreement is engraved in stone, even if it's a "standard" agreement the client claims everybody signs.

You can always request that an unfair or unduly burdensome provision be deleted or changed. If the client refuses, you have the option of turning down the project or going ahead anyway, but you lose nothing by asking.

When you review a client's agreement, you'll want to make sure it:

- jibes with the client's statement and your own oral statement
- contains all necessary provisions, and
- does not contain unfair provisions.

There may also be provisions you want to add.

Careless Doctor Done In by Unread Agreement

One emergency room physician learned the hard way that it's always necessary to carefully read and understand an agreement before signing it. The doctor, who worked on the East Coast, received an offer to work as an independent contractor for a hospital in Hawaii. The doctor agreed to take the job and signed a lengthy independent contractor agreement prepared by the hospital without reading it carefully. The agreement provided a two-year term. She thought this meant she had guaranteed work for two years and this would justify the expense of moving to Hawaii.

The doctor moved to Hawaii and started work. But within three months, she had serious disagreements with hospital officials over various clinical and administrative issues. The hospital notified her that she was being terminated. She protested, pointing out that her contract was for two years. When she took a closer look, however, she discovered that the agreement included a provision allowing the hospital to terminate her if it concluded it was necessary to do so to operate efficiently.

Make Sure the Agreement Is Consistent With the Client's Promises

Unfortunately, some clients are in the habit of telling people they hire one thing to get them to accept the project, then writing something very different in the agreements they prepare. If a client says one thing to you in person and the agreement says something else, the agreement ordinarily will control. For example, if the client tells you that your work must be completed in two months, but the agreement imposes a one-month deadline, the work will have to be done in one month.

For this reason, make absolutely sure the agreement meshes with what the client has told you and what you have told the client. If there are differences, point them out. And if they're important differences, change the document to reflect your true agreement.

How to Change an Agreement

If you want to delete all or part of a provision, you can simply cross it out. Minor wording changes can be written in by hand or typed. Both you and the client should write your initials as near the deletions or additions as possible to indicate your consent.

If you wish to add an extensive amount of new wording, it's best to redo the entire agreement to prevent it from becoming illegible or downright confusing. It's easy to revise if you wrote and saved the agreement on a computer or disk.

Another approach is to write the changes on a separate piece of paper, called an "attachment," that you and the client sign. If you use an attachment, state that if there is a conflict between the attachment and the main contract, the attachment will prevail. (See "Attachments or Exhibits" in Chapter 18.)

Make Sure the Contract Covers at Least the Basics

You should also make sure that the agreement contains all necessary provisions. At a bare minimum, it should include:

- your name and address
- the client's name and address
- the dates the contract begins and ends
- a description of the services you'll perform
- how much you'll be paid, and
- how you'll be paid.

These and other standard provisions are normally included in client agreements. If the client's agreement lacks any of these provisions, you should add them. (See "Essential Provisions" in Chapter 19.)

If you're creating or helping to create intellectual property—for example, writings, photos, graphics, music, software programs, designs, or inventions—the agreement should also contain a clause making it clear who will own your work. (See "Intellectual Property Ownership" in Chapter 19.)

Provisions to Avoid

Clients' agreements sometimes contain provisions that are patently unfair to you. You should seek to delete these entirely or at least replace them with provisions that are more equitable. Examine the agreement carefully for provisions such as the following.

Indemnifying the Client

"Indemnification" is a legal word that means a promise to repay someone for their losses or damages if a specified event occurs. Some contracts may contain indemnification provisions that require you to repay the client if various problems occur—for example, if a problem with your work injures a third party who sues the client. In effect, these provisions require you to act as the client's insurer.

When it comes to indemnifying the client, your rule should be to just say "no." Examine the client's agreement carefully to see if it contains such a provision. If you find one, try to delete it. Indemnification clauses can be hard to spot and even harder to understand. They'll usually contain the words "indemnification" or "hold harmless," but not always. Any provision that requires you to defend or repay the client is an indemnification provision.

Problems With the IRS and Other Agencies

If the IRS or another government agency determines that the client has misclassified you as an independent contractor, the client may have to pay back taxes, fines, and penalties. (See Chapter 15.) Some hiring firms try to shift the risk of IRS or other penalties to the independent contractor's shoulders by including an indemnification clause in their agreements. Such provisions typically require you to repay the hiring firm for any losses suffered if you are reclassified as an employee. The following is an example of such a provision:

> If Contractor is determined to be Client's employee, Contractor shall indemnify and hold Client harmless from any and all liabilities, costs, and expenses Client may incur, including attorneys' fees and penalties.

Do not sign an agreement that contains such a provision. The cost of fighting an IRS or other government audit and paying the possible penalties for worker misclassification can be enormous. This provision makes you responsible for paying all of these costs. If you are presented with an agreement containing such a provision, strike it out or refuse to sign the contract.

Injuries and Damages Arising From Your Services

Your work or services on the client's behalf may damage or injure third parties—that is, people other than you and the client. For example, a passerby might be injured by a dropped hammer while walking by a construction project undertaken by a self-employed building contractor. Or a software program written by an outside programmer designed to run an elevator might fail and cause injuries. It's likely that the people injured in these situations—the passerby and the elevator passengers—would sue the hiring firm to pay for the costs of their medical care and other expenses related to their injuries.

Hiring firms often include indemnification provisions in their contracts, making the people they hire responsible for all damages and injuries that other people suffer if something goes wrong with their work. Many of these provisions are so broadly written they require you to indemnify the client even if the claim is frivolous, mainly the client's fault, or already covered by the client's insurance.

EXAMPLE:

Art, a self-employed engineer, designs and installs a new type of widget in BigCorp's factory. Art signed an agreement prepared by BigCorp's lawyers that contains the following indemnification provision:

> Contractor shall indemnify and hold Client harmless from any and all claims, losses, actions, damages, interest, penalties, and reasonable attorneys' fees and costs arising by reason of Contractor's performance under this Agreement.

One of BigCorp's employees alters the widget's setting without Art's permission. As a result, the widget explodes and injures a visitor at the factory, who sues BigCorp. Art has to pay all of BigCorp's costs of defending the lawsuit and any damages the injured person recovers, even though the explosion wasn't his fault. This is because the indemnification clause requires Art to repay BigCorp for any claim brought that could be said to "arise" from Art's services for BigCorp.

Most indemnification clauses are even more convoluted and harder to read than the one in the example above. The wisest course is to strike any such provision from the client's agreement.

If the client insists on keeping such a provision, you should seek to add a provision to the agreement limiting your total liability to the client to a specified dollar amount or no more than the client pays you. This will prevent you from losing everything you own or going bankrupt. Also, make sure you have enough liability insurance to cover any potential claims. Feel free to charge the client more to cover your increased insurance costs. (See Chapter 7.)

Intellectual Property Infringement

If you create or help create intellectual property for a client, the client may seek to have you indemnify it for the costs involved if other people claim that your work infringes their copyright, patent, trade secret, or other intellectual property rights.

EXAMPLE:

Jennifer, a self-employed computer programmer, creates a program for Acme Corp. A few months later, BigCorp, Jennifer's former employer, claims that she stole substantial portions of the program from software it owned, and sues Jennifer and Acme for copyright infringement. Because Jennifer's contract with Acme contained an indemnification provision, she is legally obligated to pay Acme's attorneys' fees for defending the lawsuit and any money Acme may have to pay BigCorp as damages or to settle the claim.

Intellectual property indemnity clauses are routinely included in publishing contracts, software consulting agreements, and almost any other type of agreement involving the creation of intellectual property. You'd be better off without such a clause —that is, less of your own money will be at risk on the job—but it's often hard to get clients to remove them. After all, the clauses are mainly aimed at ensuring proper behavior. You shouldn't commit intellectual property infringement, and clients do not to want to pay any damages if you do.

Instead of deleting the clause, your best approach may be to add a provision limiting your total liability to the client to a specified dollar amount or to no more than the client pays you.

Insurance Requirements

Look carefully to see if the client's agreement contains a provision that requires you to maintain insurance coverage. Many clients want all self-employed people they hire to have extensive insurance coverage because it helps eliminate an injured person's motivation to attempt to recover from the client for fear you won't be able to pay. It's not unreasonable for a client to require you to have liability insurance.

However, some clients go overboard and require you to obtain an excessive amount of insurance or obtain unusual and expensive policies. For example, one self-employed courier recently contracted with a courier firm to make document deliveries using his own car. The contract included an insurance clause requiring him to obtain cargo insurance. His insurance agent told him this type of coverage was usually obtained only by trucking firms and would cost several thousand dollars per year. It was ridiculous for a document courier to be required to obtain such coverage, because it provided far more coverage than the client needed and cost far more than the courier could afford to pay. The courier simply ignored the contract and never obtained the cargo insurance.

The better practice is to delete provisions requiring excessive insurance from your contract or demand substantially more compensation to pay for the extra insurance. Make it clear to the client that you have to charge more than you usually do because it's requiring you to carry so much insurance coverage.

The following is a very reasonable provision requiring you to carry liability insurance you can add to a client's agreement in place of an unreasonable insurance clause:

Suggested Language:

Client shall not provide any insurance coverage for Contractor or Contractor's employees or contract personnel. Contractor agrees to maintain an insurance policy to cover any negligent acts committed by Contractor or Contractor's employees or agents while performing services under this Agreement.

Noncompetition Restrictions

Businesses that hire self-employed people sometimes want to restrict them from performing similar services for their competitors. To do this, they include a noncompetition clause in a client agreement barring them from working for competitors. Try to eliminate such provisions because they limit your ability to earn a living.

At most, you might agree to the following provision barring you from performing the same services for named competitors of the client while you're performing them for the client.

Suggested Language:

Contractor agrees that, while performing services required by this Agreement, Contractor will not perform the exact same services for the following competitors of Client: _____
[List competitors].

Confidentiality Provisions

Many clients routinely include confidentiality provisions in their agreements. These provisions bar you from disclosing to others the client's trade secrets—for example, marketing plans, information on products under development, manufacturing techniques, or customer lists. It's not unreasonable for a client to want you to keep its secrets away from the eyes and ears of its competitors.

Unfortunately, however, many of these provisions are worded so broadly that they can make it difficult for you to work for other clients without fear of violating your duty of confidentiality. If, like most self-employed people, you make your living by performing similar services for many firms in the same industry, insist on a confidentiality provision that is reasonable in scope and defines precisely what information you must keep confidential. Such a provision should last for only a limited time—five years at the most, but preferably one or two.

Unreasonable Provision

A general provision barring you from making any unauthorized disclosure or using any technical, financial, or business information you obtain directly or indirectly from the client is unreasonable. Such broad restrictions can make it very difficult for you to do similar work for other clients without violating the confidentiality clause. The following is an example of an overbroad provision:

Contractor may be given access to Client's proprietary or confidential information while working for Client. Contractor agrees not to use or disclose such information except as directed by Client.

Such a provision doesn't make clear what information is and is not the client's confidential trade secret, so you never know for sure what information you must keep confidential and what you can disclose when working for others.

Also, because this provision bars you from later using any of the client's confidential information to which you have access, it could prevent you from using information you already knew before working with the client. It could also bar you from using information that becomes available to the public. You would then be in the absurd position of not being allowed to use information that the whole world knows about. Always attempt to delete or rewrite such an overbroad provision.

Specifically, do not sign a contract requiring you to keep confidential any information:

- you knew about before working with the client
- you learn from a third person who has no duty to keep it confidential
- you develop independently even though the client later provides you with similar or identical information, or
- that becomes publicly known through no fault of your own—for example, you wouldn't have to keep a client's manufacturing technique confidential after it is disclosed to the public in a trade journal article written by someone other than you.

Reasonable Provision

A reasonable nondisclosure provision makes clear that, while you may not use confidential information the client provides, you have the right to freely use information you obtain from other sources or that the public learns later.

The following nondisclosure provision enables you to know for sure what material is, and is not, confidential by requiring the client to mark "confidential" any document you get in the course of that work. A client who tells you confidential information must later write it down and deliver it to you within 15 days.

Suggested Language:

During the term of this Agreement and for ____ [*6 months to 5 years*] afterward, Contractor will use reasonable care to prevent the unauthorized use or dissemination of Client's confidential information. "Reasonable care" means at least the same degree of care Contractor uses to protect its own confidential information from unauthorized disclosure.

Confidential information is limited to information clearly marked as confidential or disclosed orally and summarized and identified as confidential in a writing delivered to Contractor within 15 days of disclosure.

Confidential information does not include information that:

- Contractor knew before Client disclosed it
- is or becomes public knowledge through no fault of Contractor
- Contractor obtains from sources other than Client who owe no duty of confidentiality to Client, or
- Contractor develops independently.

Unfair Termination Provisions

Your agreement can always be terminated if you or the client breaches one of its major terms—for example, you seriously fail to satisfy the project specifications. Ordinarily, however, neither you nor the client can terminate the agreement just because you feel like it. Some clients add termination provisions to their contracts allowing them to terminate the agreements at will—that is, for any reason or no reason at all. For example, the agreement may provide that the client has the right to terminate the agreement on ten days' written notice.

If you sign an agreement with such a provision, you lose the security of knowing the client must allow you to complete your assignment and pay you for it provided you live up to the terms of your agreement. Instead, you can be fired at any time, just like an employee.

If the client insists on such a provision, fairness dictates that it be mutual—that is, you should have the same termination rights as the client. The client should also be required to give you reasonable notice of the termination. How long the notice should be depends on the length of the project. For lengthy projects, 30 days' notice may be appropriate. For short projects, it may make sense to require just a few days' notice. Finally, the agreement should make clear that the client must pay you for all the work you performed prior to termination.

"Time Is of the Essence" Clause

Examine the client's agreement carefully to see if it contains the phrase "time is of the essence." You'll often find such clauses in the portion of the contract dealing with the project deadlines.

These simple words can have a big legal impact. Ordinarily, a delay in performance of your contractual obligations is not considered important enough to constitute a material breach of the agreement. This means the client can sue you for any damages sustained due to your lateness but is not entitled to terminate the contract.

EXAMPLE 1:

Barney, a construction contractor, contracts to build a new wing on the AAA Motel. The contract provides that the wing is to be completed by April 1. Barney completes the new wing four weeks late. AAA may sue him for any damages caused by the delay. But because the contract does not include a "time is of the essence" clause, it may not terminate the contract and is legally obligated to pay Barney the contract price.

However, if the contract includes a "time is of the essence" provision, most courts hold that even a slight delay in performance will constitute a material breach. The client cannot only sue you for damages

but can terminate the contract. This means the client need not perform its contractual obligations—for example, the client need not pay you.

EXAMPLE 2:

Assume that Barney's contract in the above example did include a "time is of the essence" clause. This would mean that the AAA Motel was legally entitled to terminate the contract and sue Barney for breach of contract when Barney missed the completion deadline.

If you want to be able to have flexibility in your deadlines, delete any "time is of the essence" clause from the client's agreement.

Provisions to Consider Adding

There are a number of provisions that benefit you that you may wish to add to the client's agreement. These provisions are discussed in detail in "Optional Provisions" in Chapter 19 and include:

- requiring mediation and arbitration of disputes
- recognizing that the contract may have to be modified in the future and providing a mechanism to do so
- allowing you to obtain attorneys' fees if you sue the client and win
- requiring the client to pay a late fee for late payments
- limiting your liability to the client if something goes wrong, and
- restricting the client's ability to assign its benefits or delegate its duties under the agreement.

Client Purchase Orders

Not all clients use standard contracts. Instead, you may be handed a preprinted form that looks very different from the contracts in this book.

Such a form is usually called a "purchase order." Some clients use purchase orders instead of, or in addition to, standard contracts.

A purchase order is an internal form developed by a client authorizing you to perform work and bill for it. Typically, purchase orders are used by larger companies that have separate accounting departments. Accounting departments often don't want to have to deal with lengthy or confusing client agreements.

Purchase orders are designed to provide the minimum information a company needs to document the services you'll perform and how much you'll be paid. They typically contain much of the same information as a letter agreement: a description of the services you'll perform, payment terms, and deadlines. (See Chapter 18.) The order should be signed by the client. You should include the purchase order number on your invoices and all correspondence with the client.

Some companies use purchase orders in conjunction with standard contracts or letter agreements. That is, either you or the client will prepare a contract or letter agreement, and the client will also prepare a purchase order. In this event, make sure the terms of the purchase order are consistent with your client agreement.

Other companies use purchase orders alone for small projects because they don't want to go to the trouble of drafting a client agreement. Some companies' accounting departments will not pay you unless you have a signed purchase order, even if you have a signed letter agreement or standard client agreement.

Before you start work for a client, find out if it uses purchase orders. If it does, insist on being provided a signed order before you start work. Make certain the purchase order is filled out properly. This should include an accurate description of the services you'll perform, the due date, and the terms of payment.

Below is an example of a typical purchase order for services.

Purchase Order

Acme, Inc.

P.O. #: 123

Vendor: Gerard & Associates
123 Solano Avenue
Berkeley, CA 99999
510-555-5555

Date: 8/1/20xx

Delivery Date: 9/1/20xx

Terms: 18¢ per word translated. Total price not to exceed $6,084.

Description of Services: Contractor will translate Acme instruction manual from the English language into idiomatic Russian using the Cyrillic alphabet. The translated material will be provided in WordPerfect format. Contractor will provide one disk copy and one printed copy of all translated material.

Authorized by: _____
                        Joe Jones

Help Beyond This Book

If a client claims that your work doesn't meet the contract specifications, insists that you've missed a deadline, or fails to pay you for any reason, you've got a potential legal dispute on your hands. The best way to handle these disputes is usually through informal negotiations. Call or meet with the client and talk out your differences. If you reach a settlement, write it down promptly and have all parties involved sign it.

EXAMPLE:

Gene, a self-employed computer programmer, is hired by Acme Corp. to create a custom software program for $10,000. Gene delivers the program on time. However, Acme refuses to pay Gene because it claims the program doesn't fully live up to the contract specifications. Gene meets with Acme's president and admits that the program doesn't do everything it's supposed to do.

However, Gene demonstrates that the program fulfills at least 80% of Acme's requirements. Gene offers, therefore, to accept $8,000 as full payment instead of the $10,000 stated as full payment in the original contract. Acme's president agrees. Gene drafts a short agreement stating that Acme will pay him $8,000 in full settlement of their dispute.

Help Resolving Disputes

If informal negotiations don't work, and provided your contract doesn't dictate what to do, you have a number of options:

- alternative dispute resolution, which includes mediation and arbitration, and
- filing a lawsuit in court.

This chapter discusses these options in detail. It also provides guidance on how to find and use more specific legal resources, including lawyers and other knowledgeable experts. And, finally, it explains the basics of doing your own legal research.

Mediation and Arbitration

Mediation and arbitration—often lumped together under the term "alternative dispute resolution," or ADR—are two methods for settling disputes without resorting to expensive lawsuits. People often confuse the two, but they are in fact very different. Mediation is never binding on the participants, whereas arbitration usually is binding and often takes the place of a court action.

Mediation

If you've ever had a dispute with a friend or relative that another friend or relative helped resolve by meeting with you both and helping you talk things over, you've already been through a process very much like mediation. In mediation, a neutral third person called a "mediator" meets with the people involved in the dispute and makes suggestions as to how to resolve their controversy. Typically, the mediator either sits both sides down together and tries to provide an objective view of their dispute or shuttles between them as a hopefully cool conduit for what may be hot opinions.

When the underlying problem is actually a personality conflict or simple lack of communication, a good mediator can often help those involved in the dispute find their own compromise settlement. When the argument is more serious, a mediator may at least be able to lead them to a mutually satisfactory ending of both the dispute and their relationship that will obviate time-consuming and expensive litigation.

Mediation is nonbinding, which means that if either person involved in the dispute doesn't like the outcome of the mediation, he or she does not have to agree and can ask for binding arbitration or go to court.

Arbitration

If those involved in a dispute cannot resolve it by mediation, they often submit it to arbitration. The arbitrator—again, a neutral third person—is either selected directly by those involved in the dispute or is designated by an arbitration agency.

An arbitrator's role is very different from that of a mediator. Unlike a mediator, who seeks to help the parties resolve their dispute themselves, an arbitrator decides on and imposes a solution him or herself.

The arbitrator normally hears both sides at an informal hearing. You can be represented by a lawyer at the hearing, but it's not required. The arbitrator acts as both judge and jury: After the hearing, he or she issues a decision called an "award." The arbitrator follows the same legal rules a judge or jury would follow in deciding whether you or the other side has a valid legal claim and should be awarded money, but can usually hear more evidence than a court would allow.

Arbitration can be either binding or nonbinding. If arbitration is nonbinding, either person named in the award can take the matter to court if he or she doesn't like the outcome. Binding arbitration is usually final. You cannot go to court and try the dispute again if you don't like the arbitrator's decision—except in unusual cases where you can show the arbitrator was guilty of fraud, misconduct, or bias. In effect, binding arbitration takes the place of a court trial.

If the losing party to a binding arbitration doesn't pay the money required by an arbitration award, the winner can easily convert the award into a court judgment that can be enforced just like any other court judgment. In other words, a binding arbitration award is just as good as a judgment you could get from a court.

Finding a Mediator or Arbitrator

It is usually up to you and the hiring firm to decide who should serve as a mediator or arbitrator. You can normally choose anyone you want unless your contract restricts your choice.

You can choose a professional mediator or arbitrator, or just someone you both respect. A professional organization may be able to refer you to a good mediator or arbitrator. Businesses often use private dispute resolution services that maintain a roster of mediators and arbitrators— often retired judges, attorneys, or businesspeople with expertise in a particular field. The best known of these services is the American Arbitration Association. This is the oldest and largest private dispute resolution service, with offices in most major cities. It handles both mediations and arbitrations. The main office is in New York City, reachable by phone at 800-778-7879. The American Arbitration Association also has a very informative website at www.adr.org.

Agreeing to Mediation and Arbitration

No one can be forced into arbitration or mediation; you must agree to it, either in the contract or later when a dispute arises. Business contracts today commonly include an arbitration provision, and many also require mediation. This is primarily because of two factors: speed and cost.

Mediation and arbitration are usually much faster than lawsuits in court. Most arbitrations and mediations are concluded in less than six months. Court litigation often takes years.

No one can tell you exactly how much a court case will cost, but it's usually a lot. Lawyers who represent small businesses typically charge from $200 to $300 per hour. Unless the amount of money involved is small and the case can be tried in small claims court, arbitration and mediation are usually far cheaper than a lawsuit. A private dispute resolution company will typically charge about $500 to $1,000 for a half-day of arbitration or mediation.

RESOURCE

For detailed guidance on mediation, see *Mediate, Don't Litigate: Strategies for Successful Mediation*, by Peter Lovenheim and Lisa Guerin (Nolo) (available as an eBook only at www.nolo.com).

Filing a Lawsuit

If your attempts to settle the dispute through informal negotiations or mediation fail and the client won't agree to binding arbitration, your remaining alternative is to sue the client in court. Or you or the client may choose to skip informal negotiations or arbitration altogether and immediately go to court.

Most legal disputes between self-employed people and their clients involve a breach of contract. A person who fails to live up to the terms of a contract is said to have "breached" it. In a typical breach of contract case, the person who sues—called the "plaintiff"—asks the judge to issue a judgment against the person being sued—called the "defendant." Usually, the plaintiff wants money, also known as "damages."

What You Need to Prove

Proving a breach of contract case is not compli-cated. You must first show that the contract existed. If it is written, the document itself should be presented to the court. If the contract is oral, you'll have to testify as to its terms. You must also show that you did everything you were required to do under the contract.

You must then make clear how the client breached the contract and show the amount of damages you have suffered as a result. In many situations, this amounts to no more than showing that the client committed itself to buy certain

services from you, that you provided those services, and that the client has not paid a legitimate bill for a stated number of dollars. If you have documents to back up your story, you should take them.

EXAMPLE:

Ted, a self-employed graphic designer, contracted with the Acme Sandblasting Company to redesign its logo and newsletter. Ted completed the work, but Acme refused to pay him. After informal negotiations failed, Ted sued Acme in court. To win his case, Ted should produce the written contract with Acme, a decent-looking sample of the redesigned newsletter, and a letter from someone with expertise in the field stating that the work met or exceeded industry standards. Ted would also be wise to try to rebut the likely points the client might make. For example, if the design work was a few weeks late, Ted would want to present a good excuse, such as the fact that Acme asked for time-consuming changes.

What You Can Sue For

If you sue a client for breach of contract, forget about collecting the huge awards you hear about people getting when they're injured in accidents and sue for personal injuries. Damages for breach of contract are strictly limited by law. As a general rule, you'll get just enough to compensate you for your direct economic loss—that is, the amount of money you lost because the client failed to live up to its promises. For example, if a client promised to pay you $1,000 for your services but failed to pay after you performed them, you'd be entitled to $1,000 in damages.

You can't get punitive damages—special damages designed to punish wrongdoers—or damages to compensate you for your emotional pain or suffering, even though clients who breach their contracts can really be a pain. On the bright side, however, if a client sues you for breach of contract, damages are limited in the same way.

Small Claims Court

Most business contract suits are filed in state court. All states have a special court especially designed to handle disputes where only a small amount of money is involved, called "small claims courts." The amount for which you can sue in small claims court varies from state to state but usually ranges from $2,500 to $15,000.

Small claims court has the same advantages as arbitration: It's usually fast and inexpensive. You don't need a lawyer to go to small claims court. Indeed, some states don't allow lawyers to represent people in small claims court. Also, small claims courts are less formal than regular courts.

Small claims court is particularly well suited to help you collect against clients who fail to pay you, provided the amount is relatively small.

RESOURCE

For detailed guidance on how to represent yourself in small claims court, see *Everybody's Guide to Small Claims Court* (National and California editions), by Ralph Warner (Nolo).

Suing in Other Courts

If your claim exceeds the small claims court limit for your state, you'll need to file your lawsuit in another court. Most business lawsuits are handled in state courts. Every state has its own trial court system with one or more courts that deal with legal disputes between people and businesses. These courts are more formal than small claims courts and the process usually takes longer. You may be represented by a lawyer, but you don't have to be. Many people have successfully handled their own cases in state trial courts.

RESOURCE

For detailed guidance on how to represent yourself, see *Represent Yourself in Court: How to Prepare & Try a Winning Case,* by Paul Bergman and Sara J. Berman-Barrett (Nolo). This book explains how to handle a civil case yourself, without a lawyer, from start to finish.

Finding and Using a Lawyer

An experienced attorney may help answer your questions and allay your fears about setting up and running your business. Many different areas of law may be involved when you're self-employed, including:

- federal tax law
- state tax law
- contract law, and
- general business law.

Fortunately, there are attorneys who specialize in advising small businesses. These lawyers are a bit like general practitioner doctors: They know a little about a lot of different areas of law. A lawyer with plenty of experience working with businesses like yours should be able to answer your questions.

Such a lawyer can help you:

- start your business—for example, review incorporation documents
- analyze zoning ordinances, land use regulations, and private title documents that may restrict your ability to work at home
- review client agreements
- coach or represent you in lawsuits or arbitrations where the stakes are high or the legal issues are complex
- deal with intellectual property issues—such as copyrights, trademarks, patents, trade secrets, and business names, or
- look over a proposed office lease.

Finding a Lawyer

When you begin looking for a lawyer, try to find someone with experience representing businesses similar to yours. The best way to locate a lawyer is through referrals from other self-employed people in your community. Industry associations and trade groups are also excellent sources of referrals. If you already have or know a lawyer, he or she might also be able to refer you to an experienced person who has the qualifications you need. Other people, such as your banker, accountant, or insurance agent, may know of good business lawyers.

It's usually not wise to start your search by consulting phone books or advertisements. Lawyer referral services operated by bar associations are usually equally unhelpful. Often, they simply supply the names of lawyers who have signed onto the service, accepting the lawyer's own word for what types of skills he or she has.

RESOURCE

Check out Nolo's Lawyer Directory. Unlike other general directories, Nolo offers a directory that provides a detailed profile for each attorney with information to help you select the right lawyer. The profiles describe the lawyer's experience, education, and fees, and also tell you something about the lawyer's general approach to practicing law. (For example, each lawyer states whether he or she is willing to review documents or coach clients who are doing their own legal work.) Nolo has confirmed that every listed attorney has a valid license and is in good standing with their bar association. Currently, the directory covers only a handful of states, but new lawyers are being added regularly. Visit www.lawyers.nolo.com to see if your local area is included.

Paying a Lawyer

Most business lawyers charge by the hour. Hourly rates vary, but in most parts of the United States you can get competent services for your business for $200 to $300 an hour. Comparison shopping among lawyers will help you avoid overpaying. But the cheapest hourly rate isn't necessarily the best. A novice who charges only $80 an hour may take three hours to review a consulting contract while a more experienced lawyer who charges $300 an hour may do the same job in half an hour

and make better suggestions. If a lawyer will be delegating some of the work on your case to a less experienced associate, paralegal, or secretary, that work should be billed at a lower hourly rate. Be sure to get this information recorded in your initial written fee agreement.

Sometimes, a lawyer may quote you a flat fee for a specific job. For example, a lawyer may offer to incorporate your business for a flat fee of $2,000. You pay the same amount regardless of how much time the lawyer spends. This can be cheaper than paying an hourly fee, but not always.

Alternatively, some self-employed people hire lawyers on "retainer"—that is, they pay a flat annual fee in return for the lawyer handling all their routine legal business. However, few small businesses can afford to keep a lawyer on retainer.

Whenever you hire a lawyer, insist upon a written explanation of how the fees and costs will be paid.

Using a Lawyer as a Legal Coach

One way to keep your legal costs down is to do as much work as possible yourself and simply use the lawyer as your coach. For example, you can draft your own agreements, giving your lawyer the relatively quick and inexpensive task of reviewing them.

But get a clear understanding about who's going to do what. You don't want to do the work yourself and then get billed for it because the lawyer duplicated your efforts. And you certainly don't want any crucial elements to fall through the cracks because you each thought the other person was attending to the work.

Help From Other Experts

Lawyers aren't the only ones who can help you deal with the legal issues involved in being self-employed. Tax professionals, members of trade groups, and the Small Business Administration can also be very helpful.

Tax Professionals

Tax professionals include tax attorneys, certified public accountants, and enrolled agents. Tax pros can answer your tax questions and help you with tax planning, preparing your tax returns, and dealing with IRS audits.

Industry and Trade Associations

Business or industry trade associations or similar organizations can be useful sources of information and services. Many such groups track federal and state laws, lobby Congress and state legislatures, and even help members deal with the IRS and other federal and state agencies. Many also offer their members insurance or other benefits and have useful publications.

There are hundreds of such organizations representing every conceivable occupation—for example, the American Society of Home Inspectors, the Association of Independent Video and Filmmakers, and the Graphic Artists Guild. There are also national membership organizations that allow all types of self-employed people to join—for example, the National Association of the Self-Employed.

If you don't know the name and address of an organization you may be eligible to join, ask other self-employed people. Also, most of these organizations have websites, so you should be able to find the one you want by doing an Internet search.

Small Business Administration

The U.S. Small Business Administration, or SBA, is an independent federal agency that helps small businesses. The SBA is best known for providing loan guarantees to bolster small businesses that want to start or expand, but it provides several other useful services for small businesses, including:

- **SBA Answer Desk.** The Answer Desk is a nationwide, toll-free information center that helps callers with questions and problems about starting and running businesses. Service is provided through a computerized telephone message system augmented by staff counselors. It is available 24 hours a day, seven days a week, with counselors available Monday through Friday, 9 a.m. to 5 p.m. Eastern time. You can reach the Answer Desk at 800-U-ASK-SBA (800-827-5722). Questions may also be emailed to the Answer Desk at answerdesk@sba.gov.

- **Publications.** The SBA also produces and maintains a library of publications, videos, and computer programs. Many SBA publications can be downloaded from its website at www.sba.gov. These are also available by mail to SBA customers for a nominal fee. SBA field offices also offer free publications that describe SBA programs and services.

- **SBA website.** You can download SBA publications from the SBA website and obtain information about SBA programs and services, points of contact, and calendars of local events. The Web address is www.sba.gov.

- **SCORE program.** The Service Corps of Retired Executives, or SCORE, is a group of retired business people who volunteer to help others in business. To find a SCORE chapter in your area, visit the SCORE website at www.score.org or call the national SCORE office at 800-634-0245.

The SBA has offices in all major cities. Look in the phone book under "U.S. Government" for the office nearest you.

Doing Your Own Legal Research

If you decide to investigate the law on your own, your first step should be to obtain a good guide to help you understand legal citations, use the law library, and understand what you find there. There are a number of sources that provide a good introduction to legal research, including *Legal Research: How to Find & Understand the Law*, by Stephen Elias and Susan Levinkind (Nolo). This book explains in a simple way how to use all major legal research tools and helps you frame your research questions.

Next, you need to find a law library that's open to the public. Your county should have a public law library, often at the county courthouse. Public law schools often contain especially good collections and generally permit the public to use them. Some private law schools grant access to their libraries—at times for a modest fee. The reference department of a major public or university library may have a fairly decent legal research collection. And don't overlook the law library in your own lawyer's office. Many lawyers will agree to share their books with their clients.

Researching Federal Tax Law

Many resources are available to augment and explain the tax information in this book. Some are free and others are reasonably priced. Tax publications for professionals are expensive but are often available at public libraries or law libraries.

IRS Website

The IRS has perhaps the most useful and colorful Internet site of any government agency. It contains virtually every IRS publication and tax form. This site is located at www.irs.gov.

IRS Booklets

The IRS also publishes more than 350 free booklets explaining the Tax Code, many of which are clearly written and useful. These IRS publications range from several pages to several hundred pages in length. Many of the most useful IRS publications are cited in the tax chapters in this book.

The following IRS publications cover basic tax information that every self-employed person should know about:

- Publication 334, *Tax Guide for Small Business*
- Publication 505, *Tax Withholding and Estimated Tax,* and
- Publication 15 (Circular E), *Employer's Tax Guide.*

IRS publications are available in IRS offices, by calling 800-TAX-FORM, or by sending in an order form. They can also be downloaded from the IRS's website at www.irs.gov.

> **CAUTION**
>
> **Don't rely exclusively on the IRS.** IRS publications are useful to obtain information on IRS procedures and to get the agency's view of the tax law. But keep in mind that these publications present only the IRS's interpretation of the law, which may be very one-sided and even contrary to court rulings. Don't rely exclusively on IRS publications for information.

IRS Telephone Information

The IRS also offers a series of prerecorded informational messages on various tax topics on a toll-free telephone service called TELETAX at 800-829-4477. See IRS Publication 910, *IRS Guide to Free Tax Services,* for a list of topics.

You can talk to an IRS representative at 800-829-1040, but expect difficulty getting through from January through May. Double-check anything an IRS representative tells you over the phone; the IRS is notorious for giving misleading or outright wrong answers to taxpayers' questions over the telephone. And the IRS does not stand behind oral advice that turns out to be incorrect.

Directories of IRS Rulings

The IRS has issued thousands of rulings on how workers in every conceivable occupation should be classified for tax purposes. Tax experts have collected and categorized these rulings by occupation. By using these publications, you can find citations to IRS rulings involving workers similar to you. Several such publications are available as follows:

- *Employment Status—Employee v. Independent Contractor,* 391 3rd T.M., by Helen Marmoll, summarizes and provides citations to IRS rulings on classification of workers in 374 different occupations—everything from accountants to yacht sales agents. You can find this summary at www.bndtax.com.

- An online database of hundreds of cases involving ICs categorized by occupation can be found at the website www.workerstatus .com. Unfortunately, you must pay a membership fee to access the database.

- Many state chambers of commerce publish guides that list IRS rulings for various occupations. Call your state chamber of commerce—which usually has an office in your state capital—to see if it publishes such a guide for your state.

An industry trade group or association may also be aware, or even have copies, of helpful IRS rulings and court decisions.

Tax Guides

Dozens of privately published self-help tax guides are available, which you can find in many public libraries. Among the most detailed and authoritative of these are:

- *U.S. Master Tax Guide* (Commerce Clearing House (CCH))
- *RIA Federal Tax Handbook* (Research Institute of America), and

- *Prentice Hall's Federal Taxation 2008: Comprehensive* (Prentice Hall).

Researching Other Areas of Law

Many fields of law other than federal tax law are involved when you're self-employed. For example, your state laws may control how you form a sole proprietorship or corporation, protect trade names, form contracts, and resolve disputes.

If you have questions about your state workers' compensation, tax, or employment laws, first contact the appropriate state agency for more information. Many of these agencies publish informative pamphlets.

In-depth research into your state law will require you to review:

- legislation—also called statutes, codes, or laws—passed by your state legislature
- administrative rules and regulations issued by state administrative agencies—such as your state tax department and unemployment compensation agency, and
- published decisions of your state courts.

Many states, particularly larger ones, have legal encyclopedias or treatises that organize summaries of state case law and some statutes alphabetically by subject. Through citation footnotes, you can locate the full text of the cases and statutes. These works are a good starting point for in-depth state law research.

It's also helpful if you can find a treatise on the subject you're researching. A "treatise" is a book that covers a specific area of law. The West Publishing Company publishes a series of short paperback treatises called the Nutshell Series. If you are facing a possible contract dispute, you may want to look at *Contracts in a Nutshell,* by Claude D. Rohwer and Anthony M. Skroki, or *The Law of Corporations in a Nutshell,* by Robert W. Hamilton.

A relatively unknown resource for quickly locating state business laws is the *United States*

How to Read a Case Citation

To locate a published court decision, you must understand how to read a case citation. A citation provides the names of the people or companies involved on each side of the case, the volume of the legal publication—called a reporter—in which the case can be found, the page number on which it begins, and the year in which the case was decided. Here is an example of what a legal citation looks like: *Smith v. Jones Int'l*, 123 F.3d 456 (1995). Smith and Jones Int'l are the names of the people having the legal dispute. The case is reported in volume 123 of the Federal Reporter, Third Series, beginning on page 456; the court issued the decision in 1995.

Federal court decisions. There are several different federal courts, and the decisions of each are published in a different reporter. Opinions by the federal district courts are in a series called the Federal Supplement, or F.Supp.

Any case decided by a federal court of appeals is found in a series of books called the Federal Reporter. Older cases are contained in the first series of the Federal Reporter, or F. More recent cases are contained in the second or third series of the Federal Reporter, F.2d or F.3d.

Cases decided by the U.S. Supreme Court are found in three publications: United States Reports (identified as U.S.), the Supreme Court Reporter (identified as S.Ct.), and the Supreme Court Reports, Lawyer's Edition (identified as L.Ed.). Supreme Court case citations often refer to all three publications.

There are also federal courts that specialize in handling tax disputes, including the United States Tax Court and United States Claims Court—formerly Court of Claims. Published decisions of the United States Tax Court can be found in the Tax Court Reports, or TC, published by the U.S. Government Printing Office. Tax Court decisions can also be found in a reporter called Tax Court Memorandum Decisions, or TCM, published by Commerce Clearing House, Inc. (CCH).

Decisions from all federal courts involving taxation can be found in a reporter called U.S. Tax Cases, or USTC, published by Commerce Clearing House, Inc. (CCH).

State court decisions. Most states publish their own official state reports. All published state courts' decisions are also included in the West Reporter System. West has divided the country into seven regions—and publishes all the decisions of the supreme and appellate state courts in the region together. These reporters are:

A. and A.2d. Atlantic Reporter (First and Second Series), which includes decisions from Connecticut, Delaware, the District of Columbia, Maine, Maryland, New Hampshire, New Jersey, Pennsylvania, Rhode Island, and Vermont.

N.E. and N.E.2d. Northeastern Reporter (First and Second Series), which includes decisions from New York, Illinois, Indiana, Massachusetts, and Ohio.

N.W. and N.W.2d. Northwestern Reporter (First and Second Series), which includes decisions from Iowa, Michigan, Minnesota, Nebraska, North Dakota, South Dakota, and Wisconsin.

P. and P.2d. Pacific Reporter (First and Second Series), which includes decisions from Alaska, Arizona, California, Colorado, Hawaii, Idaho, Kansas, Montana, Nevada, New Mexico, Oklahoma, Oregon, Utah, Washington, and Wyoming.

S.E. and S.E.2d. Southeastern Reporter (First and Second Series), which includes decisions from Georgia, North Carolina, South Carolina, Virginia, and West Virginia.

How to Read a Case Citation (continued)

So. and So.2d. Southern Reporter (First and Second Series), which includes decisions from Alabama, Florida, Louisiana, and Mississippi.

S.W. and S.W.2d. Southwestern Reporter (First and Second Series), which includes decisions from Arkansas, Kentucky, Missouri, Tennessee, and Texas.

All California appellate decisions are published in a separate volume, the California Reporter (Cal. Rptr.) and all decisions from New York appellate courts are published in a separate volume, New York Supplement (N.Y.S.).

Law Digest volume of the *Martindale-Hubbell Law Directory.* It contains a handy summary of laws for each state. Dozens of business law topics are covered, including corporations, insurance, leases, statute of frauds, and trademarks, trade names, and service marks. The *Martindale-Hubbell Law Directory* is in most public libraries. A free online version can also be found at www.lawyers.com.

Online Resources

The online world includes the Internet, commercial online services such as America Online and CompuServe, and specialized computer databases such as Westlaw and Lexis. All contain useful information for the computer-savvy self-employed.

Internet Resources

A vast array of information for small business owners is available on the Internet. To get access to the Internet, you need a computer and Internet connection, appropriate software, and an account with an Internet access provider. You can get Internet access free in many university and public libraries.

There are hundreds of websites dealing with small business issues, such as starting a small business, marketing, and business opportunities. Beware, however, that no one checks these sites for accuracy. A good way to find these sites is through an Internet directory such as Yahoo!,

which you can access at www.yahoo.com. Click on "Directory" (above the search box), type "small business information," and click to search.

A few particularly useful websites for self-employed people include:

- the CCH Business Owner's Toolkit at www.toolkit.cch.com
- the *Quicken* small business website at www.quicken.com/small_business
- the Yahoo! Small Business Center at http://smallbusiness.yahoo.com, and
- the Small Business Taxes & Management website at www.smbiz.com.

A growing number of court decisions are also available on the Internet for free or at nominal cost. You can find a comprehensive set of links to free caselaw websites at www.findlaw.com. You can also obtain legal decisions from the subscription websites www.westlaw.com and www.lexis.com.

Nolo Website

Nolo maintains a website that is useful for the self-employed. The site contains helpful articles, information about new legislation, book excerpts, and the Nolo catalog. The site also includes numerous articles with specific information for people who are self-employed, as well as a legal research center you can use to find state and federal statutes. The Internet address is www.nolo.com.

Yet another resource on the Internet are Usenet newsgroups. These are collections of electronic-mail messages, called "postings," on specific topics that can be read by anybody with access to the Internet. Most newsgroups are completely open—meaning anybody can just jump into the discussion by posting anything they want—although users are usually encouraged to keep to the topic of the newsgroup. Other newsgroups are moderated, meaning that there is a moderator who reviews postings before allowing them to appear in that newsgroup. Moderated newsgroups almost always contain more focused discussion, as the moderators want to keep the conversation on track.

You can use newsgroups to network with other self-employed people, ask specific questions, and even find work. Some of the many newsgroups of interest to the self-employed include:

- misc.taxes.moderated
- misc.jobs.contract
- misc.entrepreneurs
- misc.business.consulting
- alt.computer.consultants, and
- alt.computer.consultants.moderated.

You can access these and other newsgroups through the Google Groups website at http://groups.google.com. ●

Forms and Documents

Asset Log

Expense Journal

Income Journal

Invoice

Asset Log

Description of Property	Date Placed in Service	Cost or Other Basis	Business/ Investment Use %	Section 179 Deduction	Bonus Depreciation	Depreciation Prior Years	Basis for Depreciation	Method/ Convention	Rate or Table %	Depreciation on Deduction

Asset Log

NOLO
www.nolo.com

EXPENSE JOURNAL

Expense Journal

Date	Check No.	Transaction	Amount	1 Advertising	2 Supplies, Postage, Etc.	3 Outside Contractors
Total This Page						
Total Year to Date						

4 Travel	5 Equipment	6 Rent	7 Utilities	8 Meals and Entertainment	9	10	11 Miscellaneous

NOLO
www.nolo.com

Income Journal

Source	Invoice	Date	Amount
		Total	

NOLO
www.nolo.com

Invoice

Date: _____

Invoice Number: _____

Your Order Number: _____

Terms: _____

Time Period: _____

To: _____

_____

_____

_____

Services: _____

_____

_____

Material Costs: _____

Expenses: _____

TOTAL AMOUNT OF THIS INVOICE: _____

Signed by: _____

Sample Agreements

General Independent Contractor Agreement

Contract Amendment

Nondisclosure Agreement

Independent Contractor Agreement

This Agreement is made between _____ (Client),
with a principal place of business at _____ , and
_____ (Contractor), with a principal place of
business at _____ .

Services to Be Performed

(Check and complete applicable provision.)

☐ Contractor agrees to perform the following services:

_____

_____

OR

☐ Contractor agrees to perform the services described in Exhibit A, which is attached to and made part of this Agreement.

Payment

(Check and complete applicable provision.)

☐ In consideration for the services to be performed by Contractor, Client agrees to pay Contractor $_____
[*Amount*].

OR

☐ In consideration for the services to be performed by Contractor, Client agrees to pay Contractor at the rate of
$_____ [*Amount*] per _____ [*Hours, day, week, or other unit of time*].

(Check if applicable.)

☐ Contractor's total compensation shall not exceed $_____ [*Amount*] without Client's written consent.

Terms of Payment

(Check and complete applicable provision.)

☐ Upon completing Contractor's services under this Agreement, Contractor shall submit an invoice. Client shall pay
Contractor within _____ [*10, 15, 30, 45, 60*] days from the date of Contractor's invoice.

OR

☐ Contractor shall be paid $_____ [*Amount*] upon signing this Agreement, and the remaining amount
shall be due when Contractor completes the services and submits an invoice. Client shall pay Contractor within
_____ [*10, 15, 30, 45, 60*] days from the date of Contractor's invoice.

OR

☐ Contractor shall be paid according to the Schedule of Payments set forth in Exhibit _____ [*A or B*] attached to and
made part of this Agreement.

OR

☐ Contractor shall send Client an invoice monthly. Client shall pay Contractor within _____ [*10, 15, 30, 45, 60*] days
from the date of each invoice.

Late Fees

(Check and complete if applicable.)

☐ Late payments by Client shall be subject to late penalty fees of _____% per month from the date due until the amount is paid.

Expenses

(Check applicable provision.)

☐ Contractor shall be responsible for all expenses incurred while performing services under this Agreement.

(Check if applicable.)

☐ However, Client shall reimburse Contractor for all reasonable travel and living expenses necessarily incurred by Contractor while away from Contractor's regular place of business to perform services under this Agreement. Contractor shall submit an itemized statement of such expenses. Client shall pay Contractor within 30 days from the date of each statement.

OR

☐ Client shall reimburse Contractor for the following expenses that are directly attributable to work performed under this Agreement:

- travel expenses other than normal commuting, including airfares, rental vehicles, and highway mileage in company or personal vehicles at _____ cents per mile

- telephone, facsimile (fax), online, and telegraph charges

- postage and courier services

- printing and reproduction

- computer services, and

- other expenses resulting from the work performed under this Agreement.

Contractor shall submit an itemized statement of Contractor's expenses. Client shall pay Contractor within 30 days from the date of each statement.

Materials

(Check and complete applicable provision.)

☐ Contractor will furnish all materials and equipment used to provide the services required by this Agreement.

☐ Client shall make available to Contractor, at Client's expense, the following materials, facilities, and equipment:
_____ [List]. These items will be provided to Contractor by _____ [Date].

Term of Agreement

This Agreement will become effective when signed by both parties and will end no later than _____ , 20___ .

Terminating the Agreement

(Check applicable provision.)

☐ With reasonable cause, either party may terminate this Agreement effective immediately by giving written notice of termination for cause. Reasonable cause includes:

- a material violation of this agreement, or

- nonpayment of Contractor's compensation 20 days after written demand for payment.

Contractor shall be entitled to full payment for services performed prior to the effective date of termination.

☐ Either party may terminate this Agreement at any time by giving _____ [5, 10, 15, 30, 45, 60] days' written notice of termination. Contractor shall be entitled to full payment for services performed prior to the effective date of termination.

Independent Contractor Status

Contractor is an independent contractor, not Client's employee. Contractor's employees or subcontractors are not Client's employees. Contractor and Client agree to the following rights consistent with an independent contractor relationship:

- Contractor has the right to perform services for others during the term of this Agreement.
- Contractor has the sole right to control and direct the means, manner, and method by which the services required by this Agreement will be performed.
- Contractor has the right to hire assistants as subcontractors or to use employees to provide the services required by this Agreement.
- Contractor or Contractor's employees or subcontractors shall perform the services required by this Agreement; Client shall not hire, supervise, or pay any assistants to help Contractor.
- Neither Contractor nor Contractor's employees or subcontractors shall receive any training from Client in the skills necessary to perform the services required by this Agreement.
- Client shall not require Contractor or Contractor's employees or subcontractors to devote full time to performing the services required by this Agreement.
- Neither Contractor nor Contractor's employees or subcontractors are eligible to participate in any employee pension, health, vacation pay, sick pay, or other fringe benefit plan of Client.

Local, State, and Federal Taxes

Contractor shall pay all income taxes and FICA (Social Security and Medicare taxes) incurred while performing services under this Agreement. Client will not:

- withhold FICA from Contractor's payments or make FICA payments on Contractor's behalf
- make state or federal unemployment compensation contributions on Contractor's behalf, or
- withhold state or federal income tax from Contractor's payments.

The charges included here do not include taxes. If Contractor is required to pay any federal, state, or local sales, use, property, or value-added taxes based on the services provided under this Agreement, the taxes shall be billed to Client separately. Contractor shall not pay any interest or penalties incurred due to late payment or nonpayment of such taxes by Client.

Notices

All notices and other communications in connection with this Agreement shall be in writing and shall be considered given as follows:

- when delivered personally to the recipient's address as stated in this Agreement
- three days after being deposited in the United States mail, with postage prepaid to the recipient's address as stated in this Agreement, or
- when sent by fax or email to the last fax number or email address of the recipient known to the person giving notice. Notice is effective upon receipt, provided that a duplicate copy of the notice is promptly given by first-class mail, or the recipient delivers a written confirmation of receipt.

No Partnership

This Agreement does not create a partnership relationship. Neither party has authority to enter into contracts on the other's behalf.

Applicable Law

This Agreement will be governed by the laws of the state of _____ .

Exclusive Agreement

This is the entire Agreement between Contractor and Client.

Dispute Resolution

(Check if applicable.)

☐ If a dispute arises under this Agreement, the parties agree to first try to resolve the dispute with the help of a mutually agreed-upon mediator in _____ [*City or county where mediation will occur*]. Any costs and fees other than attorneys' fees associated with the mediation shall be shared equally by the parties.

If it proves impossible to arrive at a mutually satisfactory solution through mediation, the parties agree to submit the dispute to binding arbitration in _____ [*City or county where arbitration will occur*] under the rules of the American Arbitration Association. Judgment upon the award rendered by the arbitrator may be entered in any court having jurisdiction to do so.

However, the complaining party may refuse to submit the dispute to mediation or arbitration and instead bring an action in an appropriate small claims court.

Contract Changes

(Check if applicable.)

☐ Client and Contractor recognize that:

- Contractor's original cost and time estimates may be too low due to unforeseen events or to factors unknown to Contractor when this Agreement was made,
- Client may desire a mid-project change in Contractor's services that would add time and cost to the project and possibly inconvenience Contractor, and
- other provisions of this Agreement may be difficult to carry out due to unforeseen circumstances.

If any intended changes or any other events beyond the parties' control require adjustments to this Agreement, the parties shall make a good faith effort to agree on all necessary particulars. Such agreements shall be put in writing, signed by the parties, and added to this Agreement.

Attorneys' Fees

If any legal action is necessary to enforce this Agreement, the prevailing party shall be entitled to reasonable attorneys' fees, costs, and expenses in addition to any other relief to which he or she may be entitled.

Signatures

Client: _____
(Name of Client)

By: _____
(Signature)

_____
(Typed or Printed Name)

Title: _____

Date: _____

Contractor: _____
(Name of Contractor)

By: _____
(Signature)

_____
(Typed or Printed Name)

Title: _____

Taxpayer ID Number: _____

Date: _____

If Agreement Is Faxed

Contractor and Client agree that this Agreement will be considered signed when the signature of a party is delivered by facsimile transmission. Signatures transmitted by facsimile shall have the same effect as original signatures.

Contract Amendment

This Amendment is made between _____ and

_____ to amend the Original Agreement titled

_____ signed by them on

_____ .

The Original Agreement is amended as follows:

_____

_____

_____

_____

All provisions of the Original Agreement, except as modified by this Amendment, remain in full force and effect and are reaffirmed. If there is any conflict between this Amendment and any provision of the Original Agreement, the provisions of this Amendment shall control.

Client: _____
(Name of Client)

By: _____
(Signature)

_____
(Typed or Printed Name)

Title: _____

Date: _____

Contractor: _____
(Name of Contractor)

By: _____
(Signature)

_____
(Typed or Printed Name)

Title: _____

Date: _____

NOLO
www.nolo.com

Nondisclosure Agreement

1. Introduction

This is an agreement, effective _____ , between _____ (the "Discloser") and _____ (the "Recipient"), in which Discloser agrees to disclose, and Recipient agrees to receive, certain trade secrets of Discloser on the following terms and conditions:

2. Trade Secrets

(Check and complete applicable provision.)

☐ Recipient understands and acknowledges that the following information constitutes trade secrets belonging to Discloser: _____

☐ Recipient understands and acknowledges that Discloser's trade secrets consist of information and materials that are valuable and not generally known by Discloser's competitors. Discloser's trade secrets include:

(a) Any and all information concerning Discloser's current, future, or proposed products, including, but not limited to, formulas, designs, devices, computer code, drawings, specifications, notebook entries, technical notes and graphs, computer printouts, technical memoranda and correspondence, product development agreements, and related agreements.

(b) Information and materials relating to Discloser's purchasing, accounting, and marketing, including, but not limited to, marketing plans, sales data, business methods, unpublished promotional material, cost and pricing information, and customer lists.

(c) Information of the type described above that Discloser obtained from another party and that Discloser treats as confidential, whether or not owned or developed by Discloser.

(d) Other: _____

3. Purpose of Disclosure

Recipient shall make use of Discloser's trade secrets only for the purpose of:

_____

4. Nondisclosure

In consideration of Discloser's disclosure of its trade secrets to Recipient, Recipient agrees that it will treat Discloser's trade secrets with the same degree of care and safeguards that it takes with its own trade secrets, but in no event less than a reasonable degree of care. Recipient agrees that, without Discloser's prior written consent, Recipient will not:

(a) disclose Discloser's trade secrets to any third party;

(b) make or permit to be made copies or other reproductions of Discloser's trade secrets; or

(c) make any commercial use of the trade secrets.

Recipient represents that it has, and agrees to maintain, an appropriate agreement with each of its employees and independent contractors who may have access to any of Discloser's trade secrets sufficient to enable Recipient to comply with all the terms of this Agreement.

5. Return of Materials

Upon Discloser's request, Recipient shall promptly (within 30 days) return all original materials provided by Discloser and any copies, notes, or other documents in Recipient's possession pertaining to Discloser's trade secrets.

6. Exclusions

This agreement does not apply to any information that:

(a) was in Recipient's possession or was known to Recipient, without an obligation to keep it confidential, before such information was disclosed to Recipient by Discloser;

(b) is or becomes public knowledge through a source other than Recipient and through no fault of Recipient;

(c) is or becomes lawfully available to Recipient from a source other than Discloser; or

(d) is disclosed by Recipient with Discloser's prior written approval.

7. Term

(Check and complete applicable provision.)

☐ This Agreement and Recipient's duty to hold Discloser's trade secrets in confidence shall remain in effect until the above-described trade secrets are no longer trade secrets or until Discloser sends Recipient written notice releasing Recipient from this Agreement, whichever occurs first.

☐ This Agreement and Recipient's duty to hold Discloser's trade secrets in confidence shall remain in effect until _____ or until whichever of the following occurs first:

• Discloser sends Recipient written notice releasing Recipient from this Agreement, or

• the above-described trade secrets are no longer trade secrets.

8. No Rights Granted

Recipient understands and agrees that this Agreement does not constitute a grant or an intention or commitment to grant any right, title, or interest in Discloser's trade secrets to Recipient.

9. Warranty

Discloser warrants that it has the right to make the disclosures under this Agreement.

10. Injunctive Relief

Recipient acknowledges and agrees that in the event of a breach or threatened breach of this Agreement, money damages would be an inadequate remedy and extremely difficult to measure. Recipient agrees, therefore, that Discloser shall be entitled to an injunction to restrain Recipient from such breach or threatened breach. Nothing in this Agreement shall be construed as preventing Discloser from pursuing any remedy at law or in equity for any breach or threatened breach.

11. Attorneys' Fees

If any legal action arises relating to this Agreement, the prevailing party shall be entitled to recover all court costs, expenses, and reasonable attorneys' fees.

12. Modifications

This Agreement represents the entire agreement between the parties regarding the subject matter and supersedes all prior agreements or understandings between them. All additions or modifications to this Agreement must be made in writing and signed by both parties to be effective.

13. No Agency

This Agreement does not create any agency or partnership relationship between the parties.

14. Applicable Law

This Agreement is made under, and shall be construed according to, the laws of the state of _____ .

15. Signatures

Discloser: _____

By: _____
(Signature)

_____
(Typed or Printed Name)

Title: _____

Date: _____

Recipient: _____

By: _____
(Signature)

_____
(Typed or Printed Name)

Title: _____

Date: _____

Index

Electronic tax filing
  caution against, 134–135
  EFTPS, 180, 194
  Form 1099, 140, 203
Employee benefits
  from clients, 234
  COBRA protections, 84, 86–87
  for corporate employees, 16, 22
  HSAs, 85
  for independent contractors reclassified as employees, 225–226
  as overhead, 103, 106
  retirement plans, 246
  See also Health insurance; Retirement plans
Employees
  corporate employee-owners, 15–16, 168
  of home-based businesses, 51
  independent contractors reclassified as, 13, 15, 16–17, 224–226, 306
  nondisclosure agreements for, 258
  part-time, 191
  pros and cons of hiring, 190, 192
  recordkeeping requirements, 206–207
  of sole proprietorships, 71
  statuary, 184–187
  temporary, 191
  works made for hire by, 254–255
  See also Employment taxes; Worker classification
Employer Identification Numbers (EINs), 71–72, 179, 200–201, 208
Employer IRAs, 242–243
Employer liability lawsuits, 13
Employment law, researching, 321–323
Employment status. *See* Independent contractor status; Worker classification
Employment taxes, 190–203
  for C corporation shareholders, 28
  double rates for self-employed, 7
  employers' tax-reporting obligations, 139, 190, 193
  family members as employees, 195–197
  federal, 191–197
  FITW, 191, 193–195
  FUTA, 191, 193, 195–197
  help in preparing, 129
  hiring firms and, 4–5, 106
  how to pay, 194
  income splitting and, 20
  nonpayment penalties, 190, 194–195, 224–225, 231
  overview, 125, 190, 191
  for PSCs, 21
  recordkeeping and, 206–207
  Safe Harbor protection, 191
  for S corporation employees, 26
  for self-employed with outside jobs, 170–171
  software for calculating, 194
  state, 125, 197
  for statutory employees, 184, 187
  See also FICA taxes; Self-employment taxes; Withholding taxes

Engineers
  benefits of incorporating, 16
  business license requirements, 70
  PSCs for, 21, 29–30
  worker classification rules, 231
Enrolled agents (EAs), 130, 131, 319. *See also* Tax professionals
Entertainment and meal expenses, 103, 142, 163–164, 213–214
Equipment. *See* Business property
Equipment leases, by corporations, 18
Errors and omissions (E&O) insurance, 29, 91–92
Estimated taxes, 174–188
  help in calculating, 128
  how much to pay, 175–178
  how to pay, 179–181
  overpaying, 182
  overview, 5, 124, 125
  saving for, 177, 179
  underpayment penalties, 175, 177, 181–182
  when to pay, 127, 178–179
  who must pay, 174–175
  withholding on government contracts, 174
Evictions, from commercial spaces, 64
Exclusive agreement, agreement clauses, 285
Exclusive copyright licenses, 252–253
Exclusive use requirement, home office deduction, 56
Expense journals, 142, 209–210, 330–331
Expenses. *See* Business expenses

F

Family and medical leave, 6, 198
Family members
  business travel with, 162
  as employees, 195–197
Farmers, estimated taxes, 178
Faxed agreements and signatures, 272–273, 286, 300
Federal laws
  researching, 320–321, 322
  trademark protections, 42
Federal licenses and permits, 70
Federal Motor Carrier and Safety Administration, 70
Federal taxes
  help in preparing, 128
  overview, 124
  returns consistent with state returns, 134
  tax withholding on government contracts, 174
  See also IRS *entries*; Tax *entries*
Fee caps, 101, 278, 299
Fees
  homeowners' associations, 59
  for tax professionals, 131
  See also Attorneys' fees and costs
FICA (Medicare and Social Security) taxes
  as business form selection criterion, 33
  for corporate shareholders, 16, 26
  double rates for self-employed, 7
  for family members, 195–197

Vehicle expenses
actual expense method for calculating, 156, 157–160
car insurance, 92–93, 97, 212
commuting costs, 5, 48–49, 156
deductions for, 155–160
depreciation, 154–155, 156, 158
overview, 144, 155–156
recordkeeping, 156, 157, 209, 211–212
Section 179 deduction, 150–152
standard mileage rate for calculating, 156–157
Vehicles
leased, 156, 159
personal creditors' claims on, 12
Veterinarians, PSCs for, 29–30
Voting, time off for, 6

W

Websites. *See* Domain names; Internet resources
Withholding taxes
backup withholding procedure, 200–201
for employees, 5, 124
for family members, 195–197
paid leave programs and, 198
professional help, 129
for shareholder employees, 16
See also Employment taxes; Estimated taxes; Self-employment
(SE) taxes
Worker classification
agencies that determine, 190, 224, 226, 232
determining worker status before hiring, 190–191
IRS audits, 15–17, 63, 93, 140, 190–191, 224–231, 268, 306,
336
right of control test, 226–227, 228, 229, 277
Safe Harbor protection, 191
technical services workers, 16, 231
20-factor test, 227–228
See also Independent contractor status

Workers' compensation insurance
cost of coverage, 94
as deductible expense, 97
for independent contractors reclassified as employees, 336
obtaining coverage, 94
overview, 93–94, 198
researching questions about, 321
self-employed and, 6
worker classification review, 93, 190, 224
Work-for-hire agreements, 255
Work of authorship, defined, 248
Workplaces, outside
deductions for, 65–68
independent contractor status and, 234–335
leasing, 18, 48, 63–68, 90
pros and cons of, 63
provided by self-employed, 6
See also Leases, commercial
Works made for hire, 254–255
Written agreements. *See* Agreements (contracts); Client agreement
entries

Y

Yahoo! Insurance Center, 97
Yahoo! Small Business Center, 323

Z

Zoning restrictions on home-based businesses, 48, 51–54, 64, 71,
317

Get the Latest in the Law

① **Nolo's Legal Updater**
We'll send you an email whenever a new edition of your book is published!
Sign up at **www.nolo.com/legalupdater**.

② **Updates at Nolo.com**
Check **www.nolo.com/update** to find recent changes in the law that
affect the current edition of your book.

③ **Nolo Customer Service**
To make sure that this edition of the book is the most recent one, call us at
800-728-3555 and ask one of our friendly customer service representatives
(7:00 am to 6:00 pm PST, weekdays only). Or find out at **www.nolo.com**.

④ **Complete the Registration & Comment Card ...**
... and we'll do the work for you! Just indicate your preferences below:

- -

Registration & Comment Card

NAME _____ DATE _____

ADDRESS _____

CITY _____ STATE _____ ZIP _____

PHONE _____ EMAIL _____

COMMENTS _____

WAS THIS BOOK EASY TO USE?   (VERY EASY)   5   4   3   2   1   (VERY DIFFICULT)

☐ Yes, you can quote me in future Nolo promotional materials. *Please include phone number above.*

☐ Yes, send me **Nolo's Legal Updater** via email when a new edition of this book is available.

Yes, I want to sign up for the following email newsletters:

    ☐ **NoloBriefs** (monthly)
    ☐ **Nolo's Special Offer** (monthly)
    ☐ **Nolo's BizBriefs** (monthly)
    ☐ **Every Landlord's Quarterly** (four times a year)

☐ Yes, you can give my contact info to carefully selected
partners whose products may be of interest to me.

NOLO

WAGE7

Nolo
950 Parker Street
Berkeley, CA 94710-9867
www.nolo.com

YOUR LEGAL COMPANION

MEET YOUR NEW ATTORNEY

"Loves walking in the rain and drawing up prenuptial agreements."

"Enjoys fine wine and creating living trusts."

"Spends time gardening and doing trademark searches."

Brent
San Francisco

Juliana
Phoenix

Ron
Seattle

Start a great relationship
(you can skip the walks on the beach)

You don't need just any attorney. You need that "special someone" – someone whose personality puts you at ease, whose qualifications match your needs, whose experience can make everything better.

With Nolo's Lawyer Directory, meeting your new attorney is just a click away. Lawyers have created extensive profiles that feature their work histories, credentials, philosophies, fees – and much more.

Check out Nolo's Lawyer Directory to find your attorney – you'll feel as if you've already met, before you ever meet.

Visit us and get a free eBook!
http://lawyers.nolo.com/book

Meet your new attorney **NOLO'S LAWYER DIRECTORY**